This third edition was researched and updated by **ANNA UDAGAWA** (above, centre), **WILLIAM ALLBERRY** (right) and **ISABEL HEYCOCK** (left). Between them in the UK they have walked Hadrian's Wall Path, The Ridgeway, Coast to Coast, Dales Way, West Highland Way and St Cuthbert's Way, as well as sections of the South Downs Way,

North Downs Way, Offa's Dyke and much of the South-West Coast Path. Elsewhere they have walked Dingle Way and Tour du Mont Blanc and climbed Kilimanjaro.

Anna is the co-author of *Japan by Rail* and has worked in travel publishing for many years, William is a retired vicar and Isabel a retired teacher. They all live in or near London.

JOEL NEWTON discovered a passion for walking national trails in 2007 when he tackled the 630-mile South-West Coast Path. Despite ill-fitting shoes that caused blisters and a bag that was far too heavy, that journey was the inspiration for many more on the long-distance paths of Britain. He has since completed Offa's Dyke Path, West Highland Way, Great Glen Way, Hadrian's Wall Path, Cotswold Way and sections of the Pennine Way. He is co-author of Trailblazer's *South West Coast Path* series and this is his fourth book.

Authors

The Thames Path First edition 2015; this third edition 2022

Publisher: Trailblazer Publications
The Old Manse, Tower Rd, Hindhead, Surrey, GU26 6SU, UK
trailblazer-guides.com

British Library Cataloguing in Publication Data
A catalogue record for this book is available from the British Library

ISBN 978-1-912716-27-2

© **Trailblazer** 2015, 2018, 2022; Text and maps

Editor: Anna Jacomb-Hood; **Layout & Index**: Anna Jacomb-Hood
Proofreading: Henry Stedman; **Cartography**: Nick Hill
Photographs (flora and fauna): © Bryn Thomas (unless otherwise indicated)
Cover and main photographs: © AU = Anna Udagawa, © WA = William Allberry,
© IH= Isabel Heycock, © HS = Henry Stedman, © JN = Joel Newton

The maps in this guide were prepared from out-of-Crown-
copyright Ordnance Survey maps amended and updated by Trailblazer.

Acknowledgements

FROM ANNA, WILLIAM and **ISABEL**: Firstly, thank you to Joel for writing the first edition of
this guide and Henry for updating the second edition. We are also very grateful to Steven
Tebbitt (National Trail Officer till Sep 2021), Wendy Tobitt (Thames Path National Trail
volunteer), Ruth Hutton (Hammersmith & Fulham), Alex Hatt (Tower Hamlets), Ian Bull,
Roderick Leslie, Nick Hill and Peter Gorecki for all their help as well as Joan Scriven, Tom
Heycock, Kazuo Udagawa and Caroline Gray for their company on the path.

At Trailblazer, thanks to Henry Stedman for proofreading, Nick Hill for a wonderful
job updating the maps and to Bryn Thomas for agreeing to let us all update this book.

Last but not least, thank you to all our readers who contacted us with tips and recom-
mendations for this latest edition, including Stuart Blackburne, Paul Chapman, Phil
Robinson, David Schache and Janine Watson.

A request

The authors and publisher have tried to ensure that this guide is as accurate and up to date
as possible. However, things change even on these well-worn routes. If you notice any
changes or omissions that should be included in the next edition of this guide, please email
or write to Trailblazer (address above). You can also contact us via the Trailblazer website
(🖳 trailblazer-guides.com). Those persons making a significant contribution will be
rewarded with a free copy of the next edition.

Warning – walking beside water can be dangerous

Please read the notes on when to go (pp11-15) and health and safety (pp73-6). Every effort
has been made by the authors and publisher to ensure that the information contained here-
in is as accurate and up to date as possible. However, they are unable to accept responsibility for any inconvenience, loss or injury sustained by anyone as a result of the advice and
information given in this guide.

Updated information will shortly be available on: 🖳 **trailblazer-guides.com**

Photos – Front cover & this page: London's iconic crossing point: Tower Bridge (©AU)
Previous page: Following the river path beside Wallingford Castle Meadows (©WA)
Overleaf: On a quiet stretch of the Thames Path between Sunbury and Shepperton (©IH)

Printed in China; print production by D'Print (☎ +65-6581 3832), Singapore

Thames Path

PLANNING – PLACES TO STAY – PLACES TO EAT
89 large-scale walking maps (1:20,000) and
99 guides to villages, towns and London districts

THAMES HEAD – WOOLWICH – THAMES HEAD

JOEL NEWTON

THIRD EDITION UPDATED BY
ANNA UDAGAWA,
WILLIAM ALLBERRY & ISABEL HEYCOCK

TRAILBLAZER PUBLICATIONS

INTRODUCTION

PART 1: PLANNING YOUR WALK

PART 2: THE ENVIRONMENT & NATURE

PART 3: MINIMUM IMPACT & SAFETY

PART 4: ROUTE GUIDE AND MAPS

Contents

PART 4: ROUTE GUIDE AND MAPS *(cont'd)*

APPENDICES

Contents

Above: Father Thames mural by the US embassy, Nine Elms, Vauxhall (©AU)

This guidebook contains all the information you need to walk the Thames Path. When you're all packed and ready to go, there's detailed information to get you to and from the Thames Path and, in the route guide, detailed maps (1:20,000) and town plans to help you find your way along it. The guide also includes:

● All types of accommodation with reviews of campsites, hostels, B&Bs, pubs/inns, guesthouses and hotels
● Walking companies if you'd like an organised tour and details of luggage-transfer services if you just want your luggage carried
● Suggested itineraries in both directions for all types of walkers
● Answers to all your questions: when to go, degree of difficulty, what to pack and the approximate cost of the whole walking holiday
● Walking times in both directions on route maps; GPS waypoints
● Details of cafés, pubs, teashops, takeaways and restaurants as well as shops and supermarkets for supplies
● Rail, bus and taxi information for towns and villages near the path
● Street maps of the main towns on or near the path
● Historical, cultural and geographical background information

---

❏ THIS GUIDE AND COVID

This edition was researched during 2021-22 when England was emerging from some pretty tight restrictions. As a result, many of the hotels, cafés, pubs, restaurants, offices and tourist attractions were operating at reduced hours and were uncertain if and when they would get back to a pre-Covid level.

As restrictions continue to ease, it's reasonable to assume that places will open on additional days and hours and, what's more, other businesses will reopen though sadly it is possible some will have closed.

In this book we have noted the opening times as they were at the time of research, or as the owners of the various establishments predicted they would be by the time this was published. It will be more important than usual for walkers to check opening hours though this is less of an issue in London as there are so many options. For this reason, for places out of London, we have noted businesses that have a Facebook page, as other than calling or searching on Google, that is generally the best place to check operating days/hours.

Booking was essential for many of the tourist attractions, and some restaurants, at the time of research so this also needs to be checked.

INTRODUCTION

This book follows the Thames Path National Trail between the river's source in Gloucestershire and Woolwich Foot Tunnel in London. When the path was created, the eastern end of the trail was the Thames Barrier but in January 2022 it was officially extended by a mile to Woolwich Foot Tunnel to link with the 47-mile TPECP route (see p248).

Officially, the Thames Path is now 185.2 miles (298km) in length based on following the southern riverbank route in London. The actual distance you walk depends on which of the alternative paths you take.

The path begins, as the river does, in a meadow in the Cotswolds

The path meanders, accompanied by its watery muse, through pristine and tranquil countryside, past historic sites and buildings, via pub, lock, weir and the occasional scattering of waterfowl to a city, once the fulcrum of an empire and now the heart of modern-day England. The river, responsible for the metropolis's very existence, inspires artists and authors, provides a home for swans, geese, and water voles, reflects the silhouettes of red kites and kingfishers, provides employment, entices adventurers

One of the many brightly painted narrowboats that cruise up and down the Thames; this one moored near Kelmscott (©HS).

Above: Lyd Well (see p80) is the first (or last) time you see water on this path. The start of your walk and the actual source of the Thames is about a mile NW of here at a spot marked by an inscribed stone (©WA).

and allows time for carefree pilgrims to meditate and think. And walking alongside it is a grand way to go for a ramble!

The path begins, as the river does, in a meadow in the Cotswolds. These early stages are lonely and wild, with the meadows and banks the domain of waterfowl and willow, while the riverbanks themselves are a collage of flowers, fishermen and farmers. As the waters deepen and spread, the settlements alongside begin to grow in both size and grandeur until, reaching Oxford, the solitude of the river slowly subsides and the trail becomes less about nature and more about history. There are venerable towns such as Lechlade, Abingdon, Wallingford and Henley as well as numerous ancient churches, abbeys and castles. Going through the ancient Goring Gap, dominated by the Chiltern Hills, you continue to Eton and Windsor, where the constant rumble of the planes overhead hint at the ominous size of the city to come, and then pass Runnymede – the site of the signing of the Magna Carta over 800 years ago.

The history continues as you pass Hampton Court and eventually reach Kingston upon Thames and the start of London. Walking in London is not as blighted by sound, fury and concrete as many may imagine, as the river – and

especially the route along the southern bank – remains relatively verdant, at least as far as Putney. From here as you continue eastwards the views of the Houses of Parliament and Tower Bridge are as fine as any along the Thames's green and scenic upper reaches. After central London the regenerated dockland areas of East London lure you to your journey's end and the conclusion of a most enjoyable and varied riparian ramble, quite unlike any other in Britain.

HISTORY OF THE PATH

The Thames Path is one of the 15 National Trails of England and Wales, though when the England Coast Path is completed – possibly in 2022 – there will be 16. Much of the trail follows the original towpaths along the river. Where there wasn't a towpath (because, for example, that portion of the riverbank was privately owned), either access has been negotiated with local landowners to allow you to continue along the banks, or bridges have been built to connect the trail with the opposite bank, so walkers can continue following the river wherever possible. Occasionally, where neither of these is feasible, there are diversions leading the trail temporarily away from the Thames. Indeed, the path owes its very existence to some protracted negotiations and long, hard campaigning by the River Thames Society, Ramblers Association (now Ramblers) and Countryside Commission (now Natural England).

The story began in 1984 when the then Countryside Commission published a study proving that the concept of a long-distance trail along the river was viable. This led to the official declaration of the Thames Path as a National Trail in 1987 though there was still much to do before it was officially opened – complete with the iconic National Trail acorns – in 1996. In 2021, the 25th anniversary of the path, the legal process of extending it officially to Woolwich Foot

Below: Sunset view from Woolwich, now the eastern end of the Thames Path (©AU).

Even near the start of the Thames, where the river is not much more than a trickle, you'll start to see swans. (©WA).

Tunnel was underway and this was completed in January 2022. At the foot tunnel the Thames Path extension path has become part of the 'Thames Path England Coast Path' to the Isle of Grain.

Responsible for the preservation of the Thames Path (amongst others) are Natural England, the Environment Agency, and the 22 highway authorities through whose territory the river runs. Much of the maintenance work, however, is carried out by National Trail staff and volunteers.

HOW DIFFICULT IS THE PATH?

Of all the great walks you could choose to do in the UK the Thames Path is perhaps the easiest. Indeed, the only aspect which makes it any sort of challenge at all is its sheer length. Investing a decent amount of time in the organisation of your trip and accepting that your body may need a day's rest occasionally will make the thought of trekking 185 miles far less daunting: indeed, you'll be surprised how quickly your mile-count adds up. With no need

Of all the great walks you could choose to do in the UK the Thames Path is perhaps the easiest.

for any climbing equipment (there is only one gradient of note) all you will need is some suitable clothing, a bit of money and a rucksack packed with determination. With the path well signposted and the river as your guide you're unlikely to get lost, either.

As with any walk, you can minimise what risks there are by preparing properly. Your greatest danger on the walk is likely to be from the weather – which can be so unpredictable in England – so it is vital that you dress for inclement conditions and always carry a set of dry clothes with you.

HOW LONG DO YOU NEED?

The Thames Path can be walked with relative ease in 16-17 days. We advise you not to do so, however, for whilst walking long distances across successive days is a great accomplishment, doing it so quickly allows little time to relax and

Although the Thames Path can be walked with relative ease in 16-17 days it's best to allow 18-21 days in total.

fully appreciate many of the magnificent sights along the path. Instead, it's better to plan for a couple of rest days (Oxford and Windsor being two spots where you may consider relaxing for a day). Adding

a day's travel to get to the start of the trail and another to get home again, 18-21 days in total should see you complete the trail. Yes, you'll be weary but

you'll also have a soul that's been soothed by the flowing waters of the river and a body far fitter (and lighter) than when you left home. There's nothing wrong with attempting to complete the path as quickly as possible, of course, if that's what you prefer – but what you mustn't do is try to push yourself too fast, or too far. That road leads only to exhaustion, injury or, at the absolute least, an unpleasant time.

When considering how long to allow, those planning to camp and carry their own luggage shouldn't underestimate just how much a heavy pack can slow them down.

If you have only a few days or one week don't try and walk too far; concentrate on one section such as the stretch between the source and Oxford or the approach to London. The river, after all, will still be there for you when you return and complete your adventure.

There are numerous old pubs to delay you on this walk, such as the Blacksmiths Arms in Rotherhithe (**above** ©AU) and the George Hotel, a 15th century coaching inn in Dorchester-on-Thames (**below**, ©WA).

When to go

SEASONS

Britain is a notoriously wet country and any Thames-side adventure is unlikely to do anything to alter this reputation in your mind. Few walkers manage to complete the walk without suffering at least one downpour; two or three per walk are more likely, even in summer. That said, it's equally unlikely that you'll spend a week in the area and not see any sun at all and even the most cynical of trekkers will have to admit that, during the summer walking season at least, there are more sunny days than showery ones. The unofficial season, by the way, starts at Easter and builds to a crescendo in August before steadily tailing off in October. Few people attempt the entire path after the end of October and the opening hours of many places will be more limited in winter – though there are still plenty of people using the path on day walks.

There is one further point to consider when planning your trip. Most people set off on the trail at a weekend. This means that you'll find the trail quieter during the week and so you may find it easier to book accommodation then.

Spring

A dry patch in springtime (around the end of March to mid June) means you're in for a treat. The wild flowers are coming into bloom, lambs are skipping in the meadows and the grass is green and lush. Of course, the chances of avoiding rain completely are low but occasionally it happens and you have lovely sunny days.

Another advantage with walking earlier in the year is that there will be fewer walkers and finding accommodation is relatively easy, though do check that the hostels/B&Bs/campsites have opened. Easter – the first major holiday in the year – is the exception, for it can be very busy at this time too.

Summer

Summer, on the other hand, can be a bit *too* busy, at least in the towns and tourist centres, and over a weekend in August can be both suffocating and insufferable. Still, the chances of a prolonged period of sunshine are of course higher at this time of year than any other, the days are much longer, and all the facilities are operating. If you're flexible and want to avoid seeing too many people on the trail, avoid the school holidays, which basically means ruling out the tail end of July, all of August and the first few days of September. Alternatively, if you crave the company of other walkers, summer will provide you with the opportunity of meeting plenty, though do remember that you must book your

accommodation in advance at this time, especially if staying in B&Bs or similar accommodation. Despite the higher than average chance of sunshine, take clothes for any eventuality – it will probably still rain at some point.

Autumn

September is a wonderful time to walk; many tourists have returned home and the path is clear. The weather is usually reliably sunny too, at least at the beginning of September. The first signs of win-

Queen Victoria looks down upon the tourist hordes outside Windsor Castle (see p183, ©JN).

ter will be felt in October but there's nothing really to deter the walker. In fact there's still much to entice you, such as the fine, unimpeded views of the river (that are otherwise hidden by the foliage in summer) and the arrival of flotillas of migrating waterfowl on their way to warmer climes further south. By the end of October, however, the weather will begin to get a little wilder and the nights will start to draw in. The walking season is almost at an end and most campsites and some B&Bs may close.

Winter

November can bring crisp clear days which are ideal for walking, although you'll definitely feel the chill when you stop for a break. Winter temperatures rarely fall below freezing but the incidence of gales and storms increases. You need to be fairly hardy to walk in December and January and you may have to alter your plans because of the weather. By February the daffodils and primroses are already appearing but even into March it can still be decidedly chilly if the sun is not out.

While winter is definitely the low season, this can be more of an advantage than a disadvantage. Very few people walk at this time of year, giving you long stretches of the trail to yourself. If and when you do stumble across other walkers they will probably be as happy as you to stop and chat. Finding B&B accommodation is easier as you will rarely have to book more than a night ahead (though it is still worth checking in advance as some B&Bs close out of season). Remember, however, if you are planning to camp, or are on a small budget, you will find the choice of places to stay much more limited.

WEATHER

Before departing, tell yourself this: at some point on the walk it is going to rain. That's not to say it will, but at least if it does you will have come prepared. Besides, walking in the rain can be fun (especially if it isn't cold), at least for a while: the gentle drumming of rain on hood can be quite relaxing, the path is

Left: A tranquil stretch of the river between Lechlade and Newbridge (©HS).

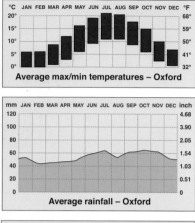

Average max/min temperatures – Oxford

Average rainfall – Oxford

Hours of daylight – Oxford

usually quiet and if it really does chuck it down at least it provides an excuse to linger in tearooms longer and have that extra scone. As long as you dress accordingly and take note of the safety advice given on pp73-5, walking in moderate rain is no more dangerous than walking at any other time; though do be careful, particularly on exposed sections, if the path becomes slippery or the wind picks up.

DAYLIGHT HOURS

If walking in winter, autumn or even early spring, you must take account of how far you can walk in the available light; it won't be possible to cover as many miles as you would in summer. Conversely, in the summer months there is enough available light until at least 9pm. Remember, too, that you will get a further 30-45 minutes of usable light before sunrise and after sunset depending on the weather.

THE BEST DAY AND WEEKEND WALKS

There's nothing quite like the satisfaction of having walked an entire long distance footpath from beginning to end. However, some people just don't have the time so the following offers you a 'smörgåsbord' of the best walks along the Thames, each with good public transport (see pp56-61) at the start and finish.

Day walks
● **Newbridge to Oxford** As lonely as the Thames Path gets, this is 14 miles (22.5km) of sheer solitude, passing isolated locks and friendly riverside pubs as the Thames weaves its way to historic and magnificent Oxford; see pp104-21.
● **Abingdon to Wallingford** Laid out between two of the most attractive Thames-side towns, this 13½-mile (21.7km) stretch visits a number of other places of note including ancient Dorchester (quarter of a mile off the trail), picturesque Clifton Hampden and several locks; see pp130-41.
● **Bourne End to Windsor** This easy 11-mile (17.7km) stroll allows time to admire Cookham village as well as peer up at Windsor Castle; see pp173-85.

❏ FESTIVALS AND EVENTS

You may wish to consider either avoiding or participating in the following events whilst planning your walk. Note that, as well as those mentioned, many other major events occur in or near to places on the Thames Path and these may push up the price of accommodation and also mean it gets fully booked. A useful website for information about major events in and around London is: 🖳 visitlondon.com/things-to-do/whats-on. For events along the tidal part of the river between Teddington and the Estuary see: 🖳 pla.co.uk/Events/Annual-Events-Calendar.

January-April
● **Blessing of the River Thames** (🖳 cathedral.southwark.anglican.org) On the first Sunday after January 6th clergy processs from both Southwark Cathedral and St Magnus the Martyr church and meet on London Bridge for the blessing ceremony.
● **The Boat Race** (🖳 theboatrace.org; see the box on p211) Also known as the Oxford and Cambridge Boat Race; this is held on a Saturday near Easter. The men's and women's races are on The Thames between Putney and Mortlake.

May
● **Lechlade Music Festival** (🖳 lechladefestival.co.uk) Three days of family friendly music; held over the Bank Holiday weekend at the end of May.
● **Cookham Festival** (🖳 cookhamfestival.co.uk) Ten days of music, poetry, drama and art; held early in May in alternate years, the next in 2022).
● **RHS Chelsea Flower Show** (🖳 www.rhs.org.uk/shows-events) England's premier flower show, a 5-day event in mid to late May in the grounds of Royal Hospital Chelsea.

June-July
● **Marlow Town Regatta and Festival** (🖳 marlowtownregatta.org) Includes canoe and dragon-boat races over a weekend in mid June.
● **GAP Festival** (🖳 goringandstreatleyfestival.org) Ten days of music, art, dance, theatre, comedy, poetry and workshops held in the villages of the Goring Gap (ie Goring & Streatley) in late June/early July on alternate years, the next in 2022.
● **Henley Royal Regatta** (🖳 hrr.co.uk) Held early July; see the box on p164.
● **Henley Festival** (🖳 henley-festival.co.uk) Hosts some of the biggest names in music and comedy, many of them performing on their floating stage. Held over five days in early to mid July. There is a strict black-tie dress code.
● **RHS Hampton Court Palace Flower Show** (🖳 rhs.org.uk/shows-events) Six days of floral displays and plants for all gardening fans, usually held early July.
● **Swan Upping** (🖳 www.royalswan.co.uk) An annual event in the third week of July during which the unmarked mute swans on the Thames are counted and also checked. These unmarked swans are owned by the Queen. The Royal Swan Uppers wear a scarlet uniform and travel in a rowing skiff between Sunbury and Abingdon.

August-September
● **Reading Festival** (🖳 readingfestival.com) Three days of music over the Bank Holiday weekend at the end of August at Little John's Farm (Map 33).
● **BunkFest**, Wallingford (🖳 bunkfest.co.uk) Free family festival also held over three days over the August Bank Holiday weekend or early September.
● **Greenwich & Docklands International Festival** (🖳 festival.org/gdif) Free 9-day long festival of outdoor performing arts in late August/early September.
● **Windsor Festival** (🖳 windsorfestival.com/autumn-festival) Fortnight-long music and arts festival.
● **Totally Thames Festival** (🖳 thamesfestivaltrust.org) Arts and cultural events along the 42-mile stretch of the Thames in London throughout September.

● **Windsor to Staines** An 8½-mile (13.7km) amble from the base of the Queen's favoured retreat at Windsor Castle via historic Runnymede and the impressive Bell Weir Lock to Staines; see pp185-92.

● **Putney Bridge to Tower Bridge** Follow the southern or northern bank (9¼-10 miles/14.9-16.1km) all the way – or maybe a mixture such as the southern to Westminster Bridge and then the northern bank – through the heart of London where historic sites (and tourists!) abound; see pp222-35.

Weekend walks: 2-4 days

● **Thames Head to Oxford** The perfect introduction to the river. You'll need four days to complete this 54-mile (86.9km) stretch of splendid isolation but you'll find yourself relishing every step. Frequent train services to and from both Kemble and Oxford make it easily accessible; see pp81-121.

● **Wallingford to Henley-on-Thames** This thoroughly enjoyable 27-mile (43.5km) hike can be accomplished easily over two days. Incorporating the oft-

photographed Goring Gap, a flirtation with the Chiltern Hills and the magical village of Sonning, both Wallingford and Henley-on-Thames can be reached with relative ease via public transport; see pp142-63.

● **Bourne End to Kingston upon Thames** This 3-day, 34¼-mile (55.1km) stretch of the river mixes the historic (Runnymede) and majestic (Windsor Castle, Hampton Court Palace) with the ever-scenic river as the Thames eddies and flows into London; see pp173-204.

Christchurch Bridge (**above**), for pedestrians and cyclists only, links Caversham with Reading. The Thames Path runs underneath the city's main bridge (**below**; ©WA).

Opposite – Top: Hampton Court Palace (©IH). **Bottom left**: The Bridge of Sighs, Oxford, connects two parts of a building (Hertford College) not the banks of the Thames (©AU). **Bottom right**: The Round House, Inglesham near Lechlade (Map 10) marks the point below which the Thames becomes navigable for boats (see p88, ©WA).

1: View of Isleworth from the path by Kew Gardens (©AU). 2 & 3: Chimney Meadows and Oxon Wildlife Trust's bird hide, ©WA. 4: The old (jetty) and the new (office blocks) near Thames Barrier (©AU). 5 & 6. The Magna Carta Monument and the Jurors sculpture at Runnymede (see p186, ©IH). 7: Pastoral scene below Richmond Hill (©AU). 8: The Thames Barrier (©AU).

Top: Once past Lechlade, you'll see numerous barges and other boats on the Thames (©HS).
Middle: Goring Lock (Map 30, ©WA). **Bottom**: Two barges using the lock at Brentford (©AU).

PLANNING YOUR WALK

1

Practical information for the walker

ROUTE FINDING

© AU

Your chances of getting lost on the Thames Path are slim. Along the length of the path, gates and signposts are marked with 'Thames Path National Trail' and the iconic **acorn symbol** of a National Trail; on the odd occasion the trail strays from the river these will ensure you stay on the path.

In London the route may be slightly less easy to follow but the maps in this book should help you keep to the trail, though the endless development does mean you may come across some new 'temporary' diversions; see also box on p219.

Using GPS with this book

Particularly given the above, modern Wainwrights will scoff at the idea of using GPS technology for navigation on this trail but, now built into most smartphones, it's an easily accessible if non-essential aid. In no time at all a GPS receiver with a clear view of the sky will establish your position and altitude.

The maps in the route guide include numbered waypoints; these correlate to the list on pp249-51, which gives the latitude/longitude position as well as a description. Where the path is vague, or there are several options, you'll find more waypoints. You can download the complete list of these waypoints free as a GPS-readable file (that doesn't include the text descriptions) from our website: 🖳 trailblazer-guides.com.

It's also possible to buy digital mapping (see p43) to import into your phone or GPS unit, assuming that you have sufficient memory capacity, but it's not always the most reliable way of navigating and the small screen will invariably fail to put places into context or give you the 'big picture'.

Bear in mind that the vast majority of people who tackle this trail do so perfectly well without GPS.

ACCOMMODATION

There are places to stay all along the Thames Path though particularly on the eastern side. However, it is always a good idea to book your accommodation in advance (see box on p20) especially as places tend to fill up quickly on national holidays and during any major festivals and events (see p16).

Camping

Camping is a glorious way to experience the Thames; you can camp pretty much all the way between the source and Chertsey, a distance of 139 miles. That said, such a journey will take some organisation as you will need to use public transport (see pp52-61) on occasions. Alternatively, you can save yourself the hassle and spend the odd night in a hostel, pub, or B&B.

Booking is recommended for all campsites in school holidays and at other peak times but is otherwise usually not necessary.

The Itineraries section suggests routes for campers (see box p36 if walking east & p38 for west). If planning to walk with a **dog** see p28 and pp255-6.

Campsites   The campsites along the Thames Path can be split into three types. Undoubtedly the best situated are those **run by the Environment Agency** (🖳 gov.uk/river-thames-bridges-locks-and-facilities-for-boaters) though at the time of research all their sites were closed due to Covid. Most of the sites are actually hidden away on islands that are separated from the riverbanks by locks. In other words, you couldn't possibly stay any closer to the river without being in it! These sites are generally open between April and September and they are quite basic with just a toilet and water supply, though a few also have showers which either operate with a token (and extra charge) or will be included in the price. Most require you to arrive within the lock-keeper's hours (approximately 9am-5/6pm) so you can pay (cards accepted) and pick up a key which will give access to the site. Pitches (usually for up to two people and one tent) cost around £12. Part 4 of this book provides the relevant details for each site.

Camping at one of the many **pubs** en route is also an option and sometimes a cheap one (about £8-12pp) – the exact amount depending to a large degree on the facilities. On the plus side you'll be as close to the pub as it's possible to be!

However, the most prevalent sites along the path are **privately run campsites**. These can vary drastically, from the serenity of small family-run sites to huge family-orientated sites including two (Oxford & Chertsey) run by The Camping and Caravanning Club (🖳 campingandcaravanningclub.co.uk/ukcampsites). Generally, the facilities are marvellous and most have small shops; indeed, some even have their own cafés and bars. However, some can be crowded and they aren't to everyone's taste. Some of these campsites charge per person and some per pitch but expect to pay £7-16pp.

Wild camping   The Thames Path is not really suited to wild camping. If you want to camp wild you should ask permission from whoever owns the land. Finding which farmhouse owns the field you want to camp in is no easy feat and you may find yourself trudging along miles of country lanes – only to be refused when you get there! Having said that, there will always be independent-minded souls who put up their tent as their spirit moves them. By pitching late in the day, leaving before anyone else is up and making sure you leave no trace of your ever having been there, it's unlikely you'll upset anyone.

Hostels

The Thames Path is not well served by hostels. Indeed, outside London there are only three (two YHA and one independent) and two of these are in Oxford. In London one independent hostel – Lambeth (see p226) – and two YHA hostels – YHA St Paul's (see p234) & YHA Thameside (Rotherhithe; see p240) – are well situated for the Thames. Other YHA hostel options are: YHA London Central, near Great Portland St & Goodge St; YHA Earls Court; YHA St Pancras; and YHA Oxford Street. However, at the time of research most of these YHA hostels were closed for individual bookings due to Covid though hopefully they will be open from March 2022 if not before.

Most offer private/family rooms, some with double beds, and (single-sex) dorm accommodation though at the time of research it wasn't certain if and when the latter would be available. Some have en suite rooms but generally shower/toilet facilities are shared. Rates vary a lot but in the low season a private room for up to two people starts from £28 and a dorm bed (all single sex) from £13pp; in the high season expect to pay double that.

Meals are available at most YHA hostels and some are licensed; some, but not all in London, have self-catering facilities. However, in general they always have a communal lounge area, internet access and wi-fi (in communal areas), laundry & drying facilities and 24hr access; card payment is also accepted.

YHA hostels always provide bedding and don't allow you to use a sleeping bag. Most independent hostels have bedding, although sometimes you have to pay an extra few quid for its hire. Towels are hardly ever provided, however, so it's worth remembering to pack one. If not, you can rent one at all YHAs.

Accommodation offering bed and breakfast

This accommodation is available along the length of the Thames Path in either B&Bs, guesthouses, pubs or hotels. In some places, particularly the chain hotels, the rate does not actually include breakfast though it is usually available.

The general concept of all these types of accommodation is the same: you book a room – a **single** with one bed for one person; a **double/twin** (one double/two single beds sleeping up to two people); or a **triple** or **quad** (sleeping up to three/four people with either a double and a single, or two double beds, or

---

❑ YOUTH HOSTELS ASSOCIATION (YHA)

You can join the YHA (☎ 01629-592700, 💻 yha.org.uk) directly or at any hostel. You don't need to be a youth to stay in a YHA hostel, nor do you need to be a member, though there are several benefits if you join including a monthly newsletter. Members are entitled to a 10% discount; this is applicable to both the rate and meals and is valid for a member booking for up to 16 people at the same time. The annual membership fee is £15/20 if paid by direct debit/credit card.

sometimes bunk beds or three/four single beds) for the night – and the next morning, often at a pre-arranged time if staying in a B&B, breakfast (see p22) is served to set you up for the day.

Wi-fi is available (usually free) in most accommodation. If planning to walk with a **dog** see p28 and pp255-6.

B&Bs and guesthouses B&Bs are a great British institution; they give you the opportunity to stay in a room in a family's home and you will often get a very friendly welcome, usually in the form of a cup of tea and cake/scone on your arrival. These days most rooms in B&Bs and guesthouses have **en suite** facilities, though staying in accommodation with shared facilities will save you a few quid. The shared facilities in many places are usually only a few steps from your room.

The main difference between a B&B and a guesthouse is that the latter offers evening meals and also has a sitting room (lounge) where you can go in the evenings and meet other guests.

Pubs The initial stages of the trail are not blessed with many traditional B&Bs. Fortunately numerous fantastic pubs make up for this peculiar anomaly by offering both decent accommodation and protein-replenishing breakfasts. Many are right on the river, and thus the path too. One advantage of staying in a pub is that most offer evening meals (see p23). However, they aren't always the most peaceful of places to stay, especially if your room is above the bar.

Hotels Apart from chain establishments (see opposite), many of the hotels en route tend to be upmarket, partly because they are in a wonderful location, and

PLANNING YOUR WALK

❑ BOOKING ACCOMMODATION IN ADVANCE

Booking ahead is a good idea for all types of accommodation as it guarantees a bed for the night, but also may mean you get a better rate. If you are walking alone it also means somebody is expecting you, which could prove a lifesaver if you go missing en route for some reason.

During the high season (July & August) you may need to book a few months ahead but note that many places do not accept single-night bookings in advance at peak times or, if they do, they charge more. In the winter, booking a few days or even the night before should suffice. If you are walking in the low season check that the proprietors provide an evening meal or that a local pub serves food. You may like to book through an online agency but do be aware that this may not be cheaper than booking direct and sometimes properties keep the best rooms for people who book direct; also agencies may exclude breakfast from their rates. Note that however you book you may have to pay a deposit.

Remember that even though it is possible to book chain hotels over the phone it will cost at least 10 pence per minute and you may have to pay a booking fee; you will find the best deals by booking online.

If the idea of booking all your accommodation yourself fills you with dread, you may want to consider booking a self-guided holiday (see pp25-8).

If you can't fulfil the booking do contact your host to cancel; it will save a lot of worry and allow them to provide a bed for somebody else.

a few may not welcome muddy trekkers darkening both their doors and their towels. Most, however, particularly in the smaller towns and villages, are used to seeing trekkers and make a good living from them. Rooms are virtually always en suite and services, such as restaurants, are available.

Your best options for cheap accommodation (as long as you book well in advance) in towns on/near the Thames Path are at the **hotel chains**, particularly Premier Inn and Travelodge, though there are some branches of (the more expensive) Holiday Inn/Holiday Inn Express and also a Crowne Plaza hotel. All rooms are en suite, some with a bath, and it is generally possible for up to two children to stay in a room with one/two adults, but not more than two adults. Most chain hotels have a restaurant and/or bar. These chain hotels have room rates only. Generally, there is a Saver rate which must be paid at the time of booking and is non refundable, and a Flexible rate which means bookings can be changed and cancelled up to 1pm on the day you are booked to stay. For all, booking online and well in advance is the way to get the best deal.

Rooms at **Premier Inn** hotels (🖥 premierinn.com) typically cost from £35 per night but can go up to £150 or more in the peak season or if an event is on nearby. **Premier Inn hotels do not allow dogs** though they do now offer **free wi-fi access**. Breakfast will cost at least an extra £7.50 (or from £9.50 for a full English). There are branches in or near many of the towns/cities en route and particularly so in London – for a full list see: 🖥 premierinn.com/gb/en/hotels/england/greater-london.html. Premier Inn's **Hub by Premier Inn** (🖥 premierinn.com/gb/en/hub.html) brand provides a few more options but expect the rooms to be compact.

The accommodation offered by their rivals **Travelodge** (🖥 travelodge.co.uk) is very similar – Saver rates start from £29 per room (£49 in London) per night but expect to pay double that in the summer months and even more in London. **Dogs are allowed** though they charge £20 per stay. Wi-fi is free for 30 minutes but if you want more than that you will have to pay (£3 for 24hrs). Breakfast is an additional cost and isn't available at all branches. **Holiday Inn** (🖥 ihg.com/holidayinn/hotels) also have branches in London and their Express brand (🖥 ihg.com/holidayinnexpress) offers the best rates. Some of Holiday Inn's accommodation is **apartment style** (🖥 ihg.com/staybridge/destinations/gb/en/united-kingdom/london-hotels); this would be a good option for the London stage of the walk as the hotels are geared for extended stays (see also box below).

❏ ACCOMMODATION OPTIONS IN LONDON

In addition to the hostels (see p19) and chain hotels (see above) already mentioned some university **halls of residence** are available, in the summer holiday period (July-August), for let as self-catering and/or serviced apartments; for suggestions see 🖥 visitlondon.com and click on Accommodation.

Aparthotels are a good option for people happy to self-cater. Providers in London include: Citadines (🖥 citadines.com); Staycity (🖥 staycity.com); and SACO (Serviced Apartment Company; 🖥 sacoapartments.com).

Other chains offering good-value accommodation in London, and with a few branches near the Thames, are: **ibis** (🖳 ibis.accor.com) and **Novotel** (🖳 novotel.accor.com).

Airbnb

The rise and rise of Airbnb (🖳 airbnb.co.uk) has seen private homes and apartments opened up to overnight travellers on an informal basis. While accommodation is primarily based in cities, the concept is spreading to tourist hotspots in more rural areas, but do check thoroughly what you are getting and the precise location. While the first couple of options listed may be in the area you're after, others may be far too far afield for walkers. At its best, this is a great way to meet local people in a relatively unstructured environment, but do be aware that these places are not registered B&Bs, so standards may vary, yet prices may not necessarily be any lower than the norm.

RATES

Because of the sheer variety of accommodation on offer along the river you'll find drastic differences in price. A night at a hostel in London can cost a similar amount per person to a double room in a B&B in a village. You should generally be able to source a double or twin room with breakfast for £35-55pp per night based on two people sharing, sometimes less, though sometimes significantly more. Single occupancy of double/twin rooms can be found for as little as £45 per night but will most likely be the room rate; single rooms start from about £65.

Many places offer a '**room-only**' rate, typically £10 less per person than the full B&B price; this is worth considering if you've had your fill of the 'full English' or if the café round the corner takes your fancy. Note as well that prices at certain times of the year, especially at times of festivals and events (see p15) in the local area, can soar.

FOOD AND DRINK

Breakfast, lunch and evening meals

The traditional **breakfast** is the celebrated 'full-English'. This consists of a choice of cereals and/or fruit juice followed by a plate of eggs, bacon, sausages, mushrooms, beans, fried bread and tomatoes, with toast and marmalade or jams to finish and all washed down with tea or coffee. This is good for a day's walking but, after a week or two, not so good for your cholesterol level. Some places offer a continental breakfast option or will charge less if all you want is a bowl of muesli or some toast.

For **lunch** there are several options. The easiest, if staying in a B&B, guesthouse or pub, is asking if they would make you a packed lunch as well as breakfast, or substitute a packed lunch in place of the breakfast – particularly useful if you want to make an early start. (Some of these places will also fill your flask with tea or coffee, often without charge.) Alternatively, buy a picnic lunch at one of the many shops or bakeries you'll pass. Otherwise you could eat out but, out of the London area, you need to plan ahead to make sure the pub or café is open and that you'll reach it in time.

For an **evening meal** a pub is often the best place. Most on the Thames Path have large beer gardens which roll down to the water's edge and have their own place in the Thames's history, with many of them being centuries old. Hearty menus are usually on offer: most pubs have a relatively standard bar 'pub grub' menu featuring such regulars as burgers, sausages, pies and battered fish – all usually served with chips – supplemented by one or two 'specials' such as fresh fish; many establishments also have an attached *à la carte* restaurant with more elaborate meals. Most menus now include at least one vegetarian/vegan option. A large number of the pubs en route offer real ales (see box below) too.

All the towns along the river have restaurants and takeaways offering fish & chips, Indian, Chinese and Italian/pizza. At the other end of the scale, if you want to splash out on fine dining there are lots of very nice restaurants, and one or two even bask under the radiance of a Michelin star or two; you'll have to plan and book well in advance if you want to eat at these places on your trip – and it would be wise to pack a smart set of clothes too.

Buying camping supplies

There are enough supermarkets/convenience stores and shops along the Thames Path to allow self-catering campers to buy **food** regularly along the way. See pp30-5 for general location information and Part 4 for details about the relevant shops. The longest you should need to carry food is for two days on the stretch between Lechlade and Oxford (unless you divert to Standlake).

Drinking water

Filling your water bottle or pouch from the river is not recommended. Meandering its way through agricultural fields, the Thames collects heavy metals, pesticides and other chemical contaminants from the surrounding land. **Tap**

❏ BEER AND PUBS

The two most common pub chains you'll come across on the Thames Path are those run by the **Young's** (🖳 youngs.co.uk) and **Fuller's** (🖳 fullers.co.uk) breweries. Real ales commonly available include **Bombardier** (4.1%) and **Young's London Gold** (4%). At Fuller's pubs, beers to sup from their core range include **London Pride** (4.1%) and the darker **London Porter** (5.4%).

The cheapest pubs you'll come across are typically those run by **Wetherspoon** (🖳 jdwetherspoon.com) or **Samuel Smith Brewery** (🖳 samuelsmithsbrewery.co .uk). There's generally a great range of organic lagers, ciders and ales; the lack of any TV or music keeps the price of both food and drink to a minimum.

Other pub chains include those run by: **Arkells** (🖳 arkells.com), **Brakspear** (🖳 brakspear.co.uk), **Greene King** (🖳 greeneking.co.uk), and **Nicholson's** (🖳 nicholsons pubs.co.uk). A smaller brewer you may encounter is **Rebellion Beer Company/ Marlow Brewery** (🖳 rebellionbeer.co.uk), whose Rebellion range of beers are particularly popular along certain stretches of the trail. A few pubs have their own microbreweries, such as *The Red Lion* in Cricklade (Hop Kettle Brewery; see p86).

water will be safe to drink unless a sign specifies otherwise; carry a two- or three-litre bottle or pouch and fill it up where you're staying. **Water taps** are marked on the maps but during the day cafés and pubs will often fill water bottles for you, especially if you have bought something. A three-litre 'platypus'-style bag (such as those made by Camelbak) should be sufficient for all but the hottest days.

MONEY

Many of the hotels, B&Bs, guesthouses, pubs and hostels along the Thames Path accept payment by debit/credit card (or bank transfer) but it is still worth having a sufficient amount of **cash** on you. When booking you should enquire whether cards are accepted, to save any last-minute dashes to an ATM. Campers would be wise to anticipate having to pay with cash.

You don't need to carry large amounts of money with you as all the towns have **banks** with **ATMs (cash machines)**; the latter are also often found in post offices, convenience stores, pubs and supermarkets though many are part of the Link chain (see box on p26) and often charge (£1.50-1.85) per withdrawal; there are clear signs warning you if this is the case. Alternatively, if a purchase has been made many shops and pubs will advance cash against a card ('**cashback**').

Use the Village and Town Facilities table (see pp30-5) to see where there is no ATM or post office (only ones near the path/river are included) and therefore where you may need to withdraw enough cash to last several days.

Getting cash from a post office

Many banks in Britain have agreements with the Post Office allowing customers using their debit card and PIN to make cash withdrawals at post office counters. For a full list of banks that are part of this scheme visit 🖳 www.post office.co.uk/everydaybanking. Alternatively, several of the post offices along the Thames Path have an ATM; the Post Office website (click on 'Branch finder') can also be used to search for these.

OTHER SERVICES

Most of the main settlements along the Thames Path have **food shops** and/or supermarkets that will provide all you need as well as **chemists/pharmacies** and tourist information centres (see box on p48). **Wi-fi** is commonplace though sometimes there is a charge. Some libraries offer free **internet access** (and wi-fi) but because of Covid this may be more limited.

Toilets are marked on the maps but a useful, though sometimes dated, resource is 🖳 toiletmap.org.uk.

WALKING COMPANIES

It is, of course, possible to simply rock up at either end of the path wearing your boots and carrying your backpack and set off with little planned apart perhaps from your first night's accommodation. The following companies, however, are in the business of making your holiday as stress-free and enjoyable as possible.

Baggage transfer

● **Move My Bags** (💻 movemybags.com) can arrange luggage transfer for walkers on the Thames Path. Bags must not weigh more than 20kg and must not have any daypack or other bag attached. Move My Bags doesn't book accommodation so you will have to do that yourself and then book the transfer. The cost of each transfer varies so you need to complete the enquiry form on the website. They can also arrange passenger transfers from or to a station or airport at the beginning or end of your walk.

● **Walk the Thames** (☎ 0118-466 4007, 💻 walkthethames.co.uk; Purley-on-Thames) Offer luggage transfer across the whole path and charge £15 per bag (not more than 23kg per bag); discounts for two bags or more. They can also arrange self-guided holidays (see p27).

If you would prefer not to commit to anything in advance, your B&B, or a local taxi company, may be willing to transfer luggage for you (for a fee) to your next destination.

Self-guided holidays

The following companies provide packages which usually include detailed advice and notes on itineraries and routes, maps, accommodation-booking, daily baggage transfer and transport arrangements at the start and end of your walk. Most companies offer a range of itineraries (taking 3-13 days) and offer the walk from west to east, though some also have east to west walks. However, **all will tailor-make your holiday** – generally in either direction and for however long or short you would like it to be.

Self-guided holidays can be started when you want to go but guided holidays (see p28) are operated only on specific dates.

● **Absolute Escapes** (☎ 0131-610 1210, 💻 absoluteescapes.com; Edinburgh) Offer self-guided itineraries in either direction: Kemble to Oxford (5-7 nights), Oxford to Windsor (7-8 nights) and Windsor to the Thames Barrier (6-7 nights).
● **British and Irish Walks** (☎ 01242-254353, USA toll-free ☎ 1-800-671-9863, 💻 britishandirishwalks.com; Cheltenham) Has an itinerary between the source and Pangbourne in 9 days/8 nights.
● **Celtic Trails Walking Holidays** (☎ 01291-689774, 💻 celtictrailswalkingholidays.co.uk; Chepstow) Offer the whole trail (west to east) and sections.
● **Contours Walking Holidays** (☎ 01629-821900, 💻 contours.co.uk; Derbyshire) The path in 12-15 nights as well as in sections (east & west).
● **Explore Britain** (☎ 01740-650900, 💻 explorebritain.com; Co Durham) The full route (17 nights) as well as options: Oxford to Goring/Windsor/Reading (4/6/7 nights) in either direction.
● **Footpath Holidays** (☎ 01985-840049, 💻 footpath-holidays.com; Wiltshire) Can arrange the whole of the trail in either direction; they also offer some centre-based holidays beside the Thames.
● **Freedom Walking Holidays** (☎ 07733 885390, 💻 freedomwalkingholidays.co.uk; Goring-on-Thames) The whole path and in sections (5-14 nights) in either direction. Can also include boat trips and horse-riding.

● **Hikes & Bikes** (☎ 0330 043 6843, 🖳 hikesandbikes.com; Warwickshire) The whole trail and in parts as well as highlights.

● **Let's Go Walking** (☎ 01837-880075, USA ☎ 646-233-1541, AUS ☎ 02-8006 0182, CAN ☎ 647-478-6251, 🖳 letsgowalking.com; Devon) The whole walk in 15 days, or parts in 6-11 days, all in either direction.

● **Macs Adventure** (☎ 0141-530 8886, US toll-free ☎ 1-(720)-487-9898, 🖳 macsadventure.com; Glasgow) Offer the whole path as well as in sections (west to east only).

❏ INFORMATION FOR FOREIGN VISITORS

● **Currency/money** The British pound (£) comes in notes of £100, £50, £20, £10 and £5, and coins of £2 and £1. The pound is divided into 100 pence (usually referred to as 'p', pronounced 'pee') which comes in silver coins of 50p, 20p, 10p and 5p, and copper coins of 2p and 1p. Debit/credit cards are accepted in many places but it is always worth having some cash. A charge is applied to use some **ATMs (cash machines)**, particularly those operated by Link (🖳 link.co.uk/consumers/locator); also these may not accept foreign-issued cards.

Up-to-date currency **exchange rates** can be found on 🖳 xe.com/currencycon verter, at some post offices, or at any bank or travel agent.

● **Business hours** Most **grocery shops, convenience stores and supermarkets** are open Monday to Saturday 8am-8pm (and sometimes 7am-11pm) and on Sunday from about 10/11am to 5/6pm, though again sometimes longer. Occasionally, especially in rural areas, you'll come across a local shop that closes at lunchtime on one day during the week, usually a Wednesday or Thursday, a throwback to the days when all towns and villages had an 'early closing day'.

Main **post offices** are open at least from Monday to Friday 9am-5pm and Saturday 9am-12.30pm. **Banks** typically open at 9.30am Monday to Friday and close at 3.30pm or 4pm though in some places they may open only two or three days a week and/or in the morning only; **ATMs** though are open all the time as long as they are outside; any inside a shop or pub will only be accessible when that place is open.

Pub hours are less predictable, although many open daily 11am-11pm; often in rural areas opening hours are Monday to Saturday 11am-3pm & 5 or 6-11pm, Sunday 11am/noon-3pm & 7-10.30pm. Last entry to most **museums and galleries** is half an hour, or an hour, before the official closing time.

● **National (Bank) holidays** Most businesses in the UK are shut on 1 January, Good Friday and Easter Monday (March/April), the first and last Monday in May, the last Monday in August, 25 December and 26 December.

● **School holidays** State-school holidays in England are generally as follows: a one-week break late October, two weeks over Christmas and the New Year, a week mid February, two weeks around Easter, one week at the end of May/early June (to coincide with the bank holiday at the end of May) and five to six weeks from late July to early September. Private-school holidays fall at the same time, but tend to be slightly longer.

● **Documents** If you are a member of a National Trust organisation in your country bring your membership card as you should be entitled to free entry to National Trust properties and sites in the UK.

● **Travel/medical insurance** Before Brexit the **European Health Insurance Card** (EHIC) entitled EU nationals (on production of an EHIC card) to necessary medical treatment under the UK's National Health Service (NHS) while on a temporary visit.

- **Mickledore** (☎ 017687-72335, 🖳 mickledore.co.uk; Cumbria) Also offer the whole path as well as in sections but in either direction.
- **Responsible Travel** (☎ 01273-823700, 🖳 responsibletravel.com; Brighton) The whole path in 15 days, The Cotswolds to Oxford in 8 days, and Oxford to London over a range of days (7-14). All available in either direction.
- **The Carter Company** (☎ 01296-631671, 🖳 the-carter-company.com; Bucks) Offer the whole trail and also in parts in either direction.
- **Walk the Thames** (see p25) Specialise in the Thames and offer tailor-made walks along the whole river in either direction.

However, this is not likely to be the case for EU nationals once their EHIC card has expired, though it would be worth checking either 🖳 myhealth.london.nhs.uk/help (click on advice for 'Overseas visitors to London'), or 🖳 nhs.uk/nhs-services (click on: 'Visiting or moving to England') before you come to the UK. But the EHIC card was never a substitute for proper medical cover on your travel insurance for unforeseen bills and for getting you home should that be necessary. Also consider getting cover for loss or theft of personal belongings, especially if you're staying in hostels, as there may be times when you'll have to leave your luggage unattended.

- **Weights and measures** Milk in Britain is still sometimes sold in pints (1 pint = 568ml), as is beer in pubs, though most other **liquids** including petrol (gasoline) and diesel are sold in litres. Most **food** is sold in metric weights (g and kg) but the imperial weights of pounds (lb: 1lb = 453g) and ounces (oz: 1oz = 28g) are often displayed too.

Road **distances** are given in miles (1 mile = 1.6km) rather than kilometres, and yards (1yd = 0.9m) rather than metres. The population remains divided between those who still use inches (1 inch = 2.5cm) and feet (1ft = 0.3m) and those who are happy with centimetres and millimetres; you'll often be told that 'it's only a hundred yards or so' to somewhere, rather than a hundred metres or so. The **weather** – a frequent topic of conversation – is also an issue: while most forecasts predict temperatures in °C, some people continue to think in terms of °F (see temperature chart on p14 for conversions).

- **Time** During the winter the whole of Britain is on Greenwich Mean Time (GMT). The clocks move one hour forward on the last Sunday in March, remaining on British Summer Time (BST) until the last Sunday in October.
- **Smoking** Smoking in enclosed public places is banned. The ban relates not only to pubs and restaurants, but also to B&Bs, hostels and hotels. These latter have the right to designate one or more bedrooms where the occupants can smoke, but the ban is in force in all enclosed areas open to the public – even in a private home such as a B&B. Should you be foolhardy enough to light up in a no-smoking area, which includes pretty well any indoor public place, you could be fined, but it's the owners of the premises who suffer most if they fail to stop you, with a potential fine of £2500.
- **Telephones** From outside Britain the international country access code for Britain is ☎ 44 followed by the area code minus the first 0, and then the number you require.

If you're using a **mobile (cell) phone** that is registered overseas, consider buying a local SIM card to keep costs down. Also remember to bring a universal adaptor so you can charge your phone. The Thames Path is pretty comprehensively covered by mobile phone reception.

- **Internet access** and wi-fi See p24.
- **Emergency services** For police, ambulance, fire brigade and coastguard dial ☎ 999 (or the EU standard number ☎ 112).

PLANNING YOUR WALK

● **Walkers' Britain** (formerly **Sherpa Expeditions**; ☎ 0800-008 7741 or ☎ 020-8875 5070, 💻 walkersbritain.co.uk; London)   From Henley-on-Thames to Greenwich in 9 days and in either direction; tailor-made west to east only.

Guided holidays
● **HF Holidays** (☎ 0345-470 8558, from outside the UK ☎ +44-20-8732 1250, 💻 hfholidays.co.uk; Herts) Offer a 7-night guided holiday from Oxford to the source based at their property in Bourton-on-the-Water.

WALKING WITH A DOG   [see also pp255-6]

Dogs are allowed on the Thames Path but must be kept on a lead whenever there are sheep or waterfowl in the vicinity. Considering much of the upper Thames is farmland it is well worth remembering that farmers are perfectly within their rights to shoot any dog they believe to be pestering their livestock.

Note that currents in the tidal part of the river (east of Teddington Lock) are very strong and therefore likely to be dangerous for a dog that goes for a swim.

DISABLED ACCESS

The Thames Path is relatively accessible for people with reduced mobility and the National Trail team have replaced all stiles with gates. The only place where access is a problem is Ashton Keynes (Map 4) because of a historic stone structure; on the map this is marked as a stile. Separately, due to the need for bridges to be positioned above the flood plain, there are places where there are steps though when bridges need to be replaced the National Trail team do their best to ensure they have ramps. Also due to flooding parts of the trail can get muddy!

The National Trail team and the Environment Agency have designed 12 walks suitable for a wheelchair; these cover from near Thames Head to Hampton Court (for details see 💻 visitthames.co.uk/things-to-do/walking/walks-for-all). Parts of London are accessible but some bridges have step access.

Budgeting

The UK is not a cheap place to travel in and accommodation providers on the Thames Path are more than accustomed to seeing tourists and charge accordingly. You may think before you set out that you are going to keep your budget to a minimum by camping every night and cooking your own food but it's a rare walker who sticks to this. Besides, the pubs are amongst the path's major attractions and it would be a pity not to sample the hospitality in at least some of them.

If the only expenses of this walk were accommodation and food, budgeting for the trip would be a piece of cake. Unfortunately, in addition there are all the little extras that push up the cost of your trip: actual cake, getting to and from the path, beer, snacks, museums/galleries, buses and trains, laundry, souvenirs ... it's surprising how much all of these things add up.

Camping

You can survive on about £20 per person (pp) if you use the cheapest campsites, never visit a pub, avoid all tourist attractions, cook all your own food from staple ingredients and generally have a pretty miserable time of it. Even then, unforeseen circumstances will probably nudge your daily budget above this figure. If you include the occasional pint and a pub meal every now and then the figure will be nearer to £30-35pp a day. And once in London you'll need to allow for the extra cost of a hostel (see p19) on at least two nights as there are no campsites.

Hostels

Assuming dorm beds are available expect to pay between £13pp (in the low season) and £35pp (peak times in London) per night. Some hostels offer private rooms, a few of which are en suite; 2-bed rooms typically cost £28-70 per night depending on the location and time of year. Rates do not include breakfast so allow for this as well as for other meals, unless you are self-catering. An amount for the extras mentioned above will need to be included in your budget.

B&Bs, guesthouses and hotels

On average, a night in a B&B will cost £30-55pp based on two people sharing a room (£65 for a single and often the room rate for single occupancy) per night.

Adding the cost of food and drink for both lunch and dinner as well as an allowance for the standard expenses mentioned above, you should reckon on an average of about £70-75pp per day, although other unexpected costs will likely mean you may need to budget slightly more. See also p78.

Itineraries

To help you plan your walk see the **colour maps** (at the end of the book); these show the walk divided into stages as in the route guide. The **Village and Town Facilities table** (p30-2 for walking east and pp33-5 if going west) provides a summary of the services en route. See p16 for the best **day and weekend walks** if you don't have time to do the whole walk in one go.

SUGGESTED ITINERARIES

The itineraries (for both directions) on pp36-9 are based on different accommodation types (camping/hostel and B&B-style), each divided into three options depending on your walking speed. They are only suggestions so feel free to adapt them. Don't forget to **add on your travelling time** before and after the walk. If using public transport a **map and service details** are on pp56-61.

Once you have an idea of your approach, turn to Part 4 for detailed information on accommodation, places to eat and other services in each village and town on the route. Also in Part 4 you will find summaries of the route to accompany the detailed trail maps.

(cont'd on p40)

VILLAGE AND TOWN FACILITIES
Thames Head to Woolwich Foot Tunnel – Walking East

PLACE*	DISTANCE* MILES KM		BANK (ATM)	POST OFFICE	TOURIST INFO*	EATING PLACE*	FOOD SHOP	CAMP-SITE	HOSTEL*	B&B* HOTEL
Kemble	0			✓		✓✓	✓	✓		✓✓
Ewen	2¾	4.4				✓				
Somerford Keynes	2¼	3.6				✓				
Ashton Keynes	2	3.2				✓	✓			✓
Cricklade	5¼	8.4	✓	✓	TIC	✓✓	✓			✓✓
Castle Eaton	4¼	6.8				✓		✓		✓
Lechlade	6½	10.5	✓	✓	VIC	✓✓	✓	✓		✓✓
St John's Lock	¾	1.2				✓				
Kelmscott	3¼	5.2				✓				✓✓
Radcot	2¾	4.4				✓		✓		
Rushey Lock	2¾	4.4				✓		✓		
Tadpole Br	1¼	2				✓				✓
Shifford Lock	3	4.8						✓		
Newbridge	3	4.8				✓✓				✓
(Standlake)				✓		✓	✓	✓		
Northmoor Lock	2	3.2						✓		
(Appleton)						✓				
Bablock Hythe	2	3.2				✓				✓
Pinkhill Lock	2½	4						✓		
Eynsham Lock	1	1.6				✓		✓		✓
King's Lock	2¾	4.4						(✓)		
(Lower Wolvercote)						✓				
(Binsey)						✓				
Oxford (Osney Br)	3¾	6	✓	✓		✓✓	✓	✓	H/YHA	✓✓
Iffley Lock	2½	4				✓				
Sandford-on-T	1¾	2.8				✓				
(Radley)						✓				
Abingdon	5½	9	✓	✓	VIC	✓✓	✓			✓✓
Culham	2¼	3.6								
Clifton Hampden	3	4.8		✓		✓	✓	✓†		✓
Day's Lock	2¾	4.4						✓†		
(Dorchester-on-Thames)						✓✓	✓			✓✓
Shillingford	2¼	3.6				✓				✓✓
Benson	2	3.2				✓				
(Crowmarsh Gifford)						✓	✓			✓
Wallingford	1¼	2	✓	✓	TIC	✓✓	✓			✓✓
Moulsford	4	6.4				✓				✓
Goring & Streatley	3	4.8	✓	✓		✓✓	✓		YHA	✓✓
Whitchurch-on-T	3½	5.6				✓✓				
Pangbourne	½	0.8	✓	✓		✓✓	✓			✓✓

NOTES

*PLACE Places in **bold** are on the path; those brackets are a short walk off the route
*DISTANCE = from the place above. Distances given are approximate and are between places directly on the route

VILLAGE AND TOWN FACILITIES
Thames Head to Woolwich Foot Tunnel – Walking East

PLACE*	DISTANCE* MILES KM	BANK (ATM)	POST OFFICE	TOURIST INFO*	EATING PLACE†	FOOD SHOP	CAMP-SITE	HOSTEL*	B&B* HOTEL
Mapledurham Lock	2¼ 3.6				✔				
Caversham (Rdng)	4¾ 3.2	✔			✔✔✔	✔	✔		✔✔✔
Sonning	3¼ 5.2				✔✔✔				✔✔✔
(Lower) Shiplake	3½ 5.6		✔		✔	✔			✔
Henley-on-T	3½ 5.6	✔	✔	VIC	✔✔✔	✔	✔		✔✔✔
Aston	3¼ 5.2				✔				✔
Hurley	3 1.2				✔✔✔	✔	✔		✔✔
Marlow	2¼ 3.6	✔	✔	TIC	✔✔✔	✔			✔✔✔
Bourne End	3¼ 5.2	✔			✔	✔			
Cookham	1¼ 2	✔			✔✔✔	✔			✔
Maidenhead	3¼ 5.2	✔			✔✔✔	✔			✔✔
Dorney Reach (Bray)	1½ 2.4				✔✔		(✔)†		
Eton/Windsor	5 8	✔	✔	VIC	✔✔✔	✔			✔✔✔
Datchet	2 3.2	✔			✔✔✔	✔			✔
Old Windsor	3 4.8				✔				
Runnymede	½ 0.8				✔✔✔				
Bell Weir Lock	2 3.2				✔				✔
Egham/		✔			✔	✔			✔
Staines	1 1.6	✔	✔		✔✔				✔
Laleham	2½ 4		✔		✔	✔	✔		
Chertsey (Br)	1 1.6	✔			✔✔	✔	✔		✔
Shepperton Lock	2 3.2				✔✔✔				
Shepperton	½ 0.8				✔✔				✔
Walton-on-T	1½ 2.4	✔	✔		✔✔✔	✔			✔
(or 1¼/2 by ferry from Shepperton Lock)									
Molesey Lock	4¼ 6.8				✔				
Hampton Crt/E Molesey	½ 0.8	✔			✔✔✔	✔			✔
Hampton Wick/			✔	✔	✔✔✔	✔			✔✔
Kingston	3¼ 5.2	✔	✔		✔✔✔	✔			✔✔✔
Southern bank (Kingston Bridge to Putney Bridge)									
Richmond	4¾ 7.6	✔	✔		✔✔✔	✔			✔
Mortlake	4¾ 7.6				✔✔✔	✔			
Barnes	¾ 1.2				✔✔				
Putney	3¼ 5.2	✔	✔		✔✔✔	✔		YHA (Earl's Court)	✔
Northern bank (Kingston Bridge to Putney Bridge)									
Teddington Lock	2 3.2				✔✔✔				
Twickenham	1½ 2.4	✔			✔✔✔	✔			✔

(cont'd overleaf)

B&B/HOTEL	✔ = one place W = two WW = three or more
HOSTEL	YHA = YHA hostel H = independent hostel
CAMPSITE	(✔) = no official campsite but a tent can be pitched ✔† = reopening uncertain
EATING PLACE	✔ = one place W = two WW = three or more
TOURIST INFO	TIC = Tourist information centre VIC = Visitor information centre

PLANNING YOUR WALK

PLANNING YOUR WALK

VILLAGE AND TOWN FACILITIES
Thames Head to Woolwich Foot Tunnel – Walking East

PLACE*	DISTANCE* MILES	KM	BANK (ATM)	POST OFFICE	TOURIST INFO*	EATING PLACE*	FOOD SHOP	CAMP- SITE	HOSTEL*	B&B* HOTEL
Northern bank (Kingston Bridge to Putney Bridge)(cont'd from p31)										
Richmond Br	2	3.2				✔				
Isleworth	1¼	2				✔				
Brentford	2¼	3.6	✔			✔	✔			✔✔
Strand on the Green	1¼	2				✔✔				
Hammersmith	3¼	5.2				✔✔				
Fulham (Putney)	2¾	4.4	✔			✔✔			YHA (Earl's Court)	✔
Southern bank (Putney Bridge to Tower Bridge)										
Wandsworth	1½	2.4	✔			✔	✔			✔
Battersea	2½	4	✔			✔✔	✔			✔
Vauxhall/Lambeth	2	3.2	✔			✔✔	✔		H	✔
Southwark/Blackfriars	2	3.2				✔✔				✔✔
Tower Br (S)	1¼	2					✔			✔
Northern bank (Putney Bridge to Tower Bridge)										
Impl Wharf/Chelsea	3½	5.6				✔				
Pimlico/Millbank	1¼	2	✔			✔✔	✔			
Westminster	2¼	3.6								
City of London	2	3.2				✔			YHA	
Tower Br (N)	1	1.6	✔			✔✔	✔			✔
Northern bank (Tower Bridge to Greenwich)										
Wapping	1¼	2				✔✔	✔			
Limehouse	1¼	2	✔			✔	✔			✔
Canary Wharf	1	1.6				✔✔				
Isle of Dogs	3¼	5.2 (to Greenwich Foot Tunnel)				✔				
Southern bank (Tower Bridge to Greenwich)										
Bermondsey	1	1.6				✔				
Rotherhithe	1	1.6				✔✔	✔		YHA	
Greenwich	3¾	6	✔		TIC	✔✔	✔			✔
Southern bank (Greenwich to Woolwich Foot Tunnel)										
Thames Barrier	4.5	7.2				✔(Charlton)				
Woolwich	1	1.6	✔	✔		✔✔				✔

SERVICE NOTES: In the **London** area only services mentioned in the route guide – because they are on or very near the path – are summarised in this table; there are plenty of additional ATMs, post offices, food shops and supermarkets as well as places offering accommodation and meals.

NOTES

*PLACE Places in **bold** are on the path; those brackets are a short walk off the route
*DISTANCE = from the place above. Distances given are approximate and are between places directly on the route

VILLAGE AND TOWN FACILITIES
Woolwich Foot Tunnel to Thames Head – Walking West

PLACE*	DISTANCE* MILES KM	BANK (ATM)	POST OFFICE	TOURIST INFO*	EATING PLACE*	FOOD SHOP	CAMP-SITE	HOSTEL*	B&B* HOTEL
Southern bank (Thames Barrier to Greenwich)									
Woolwich	0 0	✔	✔		✔✔	✔			✔✔
Thames Barrier	1 1.6				(✔Charlton)				
Southern bank (Greenwich to Tower Bridge)									
Greenwich	4.5 7.2	✔		TIC	✔✔	✔			✔✔
Rotherhithe	3¾ 6				✔✔	✔		YHA	
Bermondsey	1 1.6				✔				
Northern bank (Greenwich to Tower Bridge)									
Isle of Dogs	1 1.6				✔✔				
Canary Wharf	3¼ 5.2 (inc from Greenwich Foot Tunnel)								
					✔✔				
Limehouse	1 1.6	✔			✔✔	✔		✔	
Wapping	1¼ 2				✔✔	✔			
Southern bank (Tower Bridge to Putney Bridge)									
Tower Br (S)	1 1.6					✔			✔
Blackfriars/Southwark	1¼ 2				✔✔✔				✔✔✔
Lambeth/Vauxhall	2 3.2	✔			✔✔✔	✔		H	✔
Battersea	2 3.2				✔✔✔	✔			✔
Wandsworth	2½ 4	✔			✔✔	✔			✔
Northern bank (Tower Bridge to Putney Bridge)									
Tower Bridge (N)	1¼ 2	✔			✔✔✔	✔			✔✔
City of London	1 1.6				✔✔			YHA	
Westminster	2 3.2								
Millbank/Pimlico	2¼ 3.6	✔			✔✔✔	✔			
Chelsea/Impl Wharf	1¼ 2				✔✔				
Southern bank (Putney Bridge to Kingston Bridge)									
Putney	1½ 2.4	✔	✔		✔✔✔	✔		YHA (Earl's Court)	✔✔
Barnes	3¼ 5.2				✔				
Mortlake	¾ 1.2				✔✔✔	✔			
Richmond	4¾ 7.6	✔	✔		✔✔✔	✔			✔
Northern bank (Putney Bridge to Kingston Bridge) *(cont'd overleaf)*									
Fulham	3½ 5.6	✔			✔✔✔			YHA (Earl's Court)	✔
Hammersmith	2¾ 4.4				✔✔✔				

See also SERVICE NOTES in the box opposite

		PLANNING YOUR WALK
B&B/HOTEL	✔ = one place ✔✔ = two ✔✔✔ = three or more	
HOSTEL	YHA = YHA hostel H = independent hostel	
CAMPSITE	(✔) = no official campsite but a tent can be pitched ✔ † = reopening uncertain	
EATING PLACE	✔ = one place ✔✔ = two ✔✔✔ = three or more	
TOURIST INFO	TIC = Tourist information centre VIC = Visitor information centre	

VILLAGE AND TOWN FACILITIES
Woolwich Foot Tunnel to Thames Head – Walking West

PLACE*	DISTANCE* MILES KM	BANK (ATM)	POST OFFICE	TOURIST INFO*	EATING PLACE*	FOOD SHOP	CAMP-SITE	HOSTEL*	B&B* HOTEL
Northern bank (Putney Bridge to Kingston Bridge) *(cont'd from p33)*									
Strand on the Green 3¼ 5.2					✔✔				
Brentford 1¼ 2		✔			✔	✔			✔✔
Isleworth 2¼ 3.6					✔				
Richmond Br 1¼ 2					✔				
Twickenham 2 3.2			✔		✔✔	✔			✔
Teddington Lock 1½ 2.4					✔✔				
Kingston/ 4¾(S)7.6(S) 2(N)3.2(N)		✔	✔		✔✔	✔	✔		✔✔
Hampton Wick		✔	✔		✔✔	✔			✔
Hampton Crt/E Molesey 3¼ 5.2		✔			✔✔	✔			✔
Molesey Lock ½ 0.8					✔				
Walton-on-T 4¼ 6.8		✔	✔		✔✔				✔
Shepperton 1½ 2.4					✔✔				✔
Shepperton Lock ½/0.8 (1¼/2 by ferry from W-on-T)					✔✔				
Chertsey (Br) 2 3.2		✔			✔	✔	✔		✔
Laleham 1 1.6			✔		✔	✔	✔		
Staines/ 2½ 4		✔	✔		✔✔				✔
Egham		✔			✔	✔			✔
Bell Weir Lock 1 1.6					✔				✔
Runnymede 2 3.2					✔✔				
Old Windsor ½ 0.8					✔				
Datchet 3 4.8		✔			✔✔	✔			✔
Eton/Windsor 2 3.2		✔	✔	VIC	✔✔	✔			✔✔
Dorney Reach (Bray) 5 8					✔		✔		
Maidenhead 1½ 2.4		✔			✔✔	✔			✔✔
Cookham 3¼ 5.2		✔			✔✔	✔			✔
Bourne End 1¼ 2		✔			✔	✔			
Marlow 3¼ 5.2		✔	✔	TIC	✔✔	✔			✔✔
Hurley 2¼ 3.6					✔✔	✔	✔		✔
Aston 3 1.2					✔				
Henley-on-T 3¼ 5.2		✔	✔	VIC	✔✔	✔	✔		✔✔
Lower Shiplake 3½ 5.6		✔			✔				✔
Sonning 3½ 5.6					✔✔				✔✔
Caversham (Reading) 3¼ 5.2		✔			✔✔	✔	✔		✔✔
Mapledurham Lock 4¾ 3.2					✔				
Pangbourne 2¼ 3.6		✔	✔		✔✔	✔			✔

See also SERVICE NOTES in the box on p32

NOTES

*PLACE Places in **bold** are on the path; those brackets are a short walk off the route
*DISTANCE = from the place above. Distances given are approximate and are between places directly on the route

VILLAGE AND TOWN FACILITIES
Woolwich Foot Tunnel to Thames Head – Walking West

PLACE*	DISTANCE* MILES	KM	BANK (ATM)	POST OFFICE	TOURIST INFO*	EATING PLACE*	FOOD SHOP	CAMP-SITE	HOSTEL*	B&B* HOTEL
Whitchurch-on-T	½	0.8				✔✔				
Goring & Streatley	3½	5.6	✔	✔		✔✔✔	✔		YHA	✔✔✔
Moulsford	3	4.8				✔				✔
Wallingford	4	6.4	✔	✔	TIC	✔✔✔	✔			✔✔✔
(Crowmarsh Gifford)							✔	✔		✔
Benson	1¼	2				✔				
Shillingford	2	3.2				✔				✔✔
(Dorchester-on-Thames)						✔✔✔	✔			✔✔✔
Day's Lock	2¼	3.6						✔		
Clifton Hampden	2¾	4.4		✔		✔	✔	✔		✔
Culham	3	4.8								
Abingdon	2¼	3.6	✔	✔	VIC	✔✔✔	✔			✔✔✔
(Radley)						✔				
Sandford-on-T	5½	9			✔					
Iffley Lock	1¾	2.8				✔				
Oxford (Osney Br)	2½	4	✔	✔		✔✔✔	✔	✔	H/YHA	✔✔✔
(Binsey)						✔				
(Lower Wolvercote)						✔				
King's Lock	3¾	6					(✔)			
Eynsham Lock	2¾	4.4				✔		✔		✔
Pinkhill Lock	1	1.6				✔				
Bablock Hythe	2½	4				✔				✔
(Appleton)						✔				
Northmoor Lock	2	3.2						✔		
(Standlake)				✔		✔	✔	✔		
Newbridge	2	3.2				✔✔				✔
Shifford Lock	3	4.8						✔		
Tadpole Bridge	3	4.8				✔				✔
Rushey Lock	1¼	2						✔		
Radcot	2¾	4.4				✔		✔		
Kelmscott	2¾	4.4				✔				✔✔
St John's Lock	3¼	5.2				✔				
Lechlade	¾	1.2	✔	✔	VIC	✔✔✔	✔	✔		✔✔✔
Castle Eaton	6½	10.5				✔		✔		✔
Cricklade	4¼	6.8	✔	✔	TIC	✔✔✔	✔			✔✔✔
Ashton Keynes	5¼	8.4				✔	✔			✔
Somerford Keynes	2	3.2				✔				
Ewen	2¼	3.6				✔				
Kemble	2¾	4.4		✔		✔✔	✔	✔		✔✔

B&B/HOTEL	✔ = one place ✔✔ = two ✔✔✔ = three or more
HOSTEL	YHA = YHA hostel H = independent hostel
CAMPSITE	(✔) = no official campsite but a tent can be pitched ✔ † = reopening uncertain
EATING PLACE	✔ = one place ✔✔ = two ✔✔✔ = three or more
TOURIST INFO	TIC = Tourist information centre VIC = Visitor information centre

PLANNING YOUR WALK

CAMPING AND HOSTELS – WALKING EAST

Night	Relaxed Place	Approx Distance miles	km	Medium Place	Approx Distance miles	km	Fast Place	Approx Distance miles	km
0	Kemble			Kemble			Kemble		
1	Cricklade§	12¼	19.7	Cricklade§	12¼	19.7	Castle Eaton	16½	26.6
2	Lechlade	11	17.7	Lechlade	11	17.7	Radcot	13½	21.7
3	Radcot	6¾	10.9	Rushey Lock	9½	15.3	Northmr Lock	12¾	20.5
4	Shifford Lock	7	11.2	Northmoor Lock	10½	16.9	Oxford*		13.5	21.8
5	Northmoor Lock	5	8	Oxford*		13.5	21.8	Clifton Hampden†	13	20.1
6	Oxford*		13.5	21.8	Clifton Hampden†	13	20.1	Streatley(YHA)	15¼	24.5
7	Abingdon (bus back to Oxford)	7¾	12.5	Crowmarsh Gifford	8¼	13.3	Henley-on-T	21¼	34.2
8	Day's Lock† (Dorchester)	8	12.9	Pangbourne§ (train to Streatley YHA)	11	17.7	Dorney Reach†	17¼	27.7
9	Crowmarsh Gifford	5½	8.9	Caversham (Reading)	7	11.2	Chertsey	17½	28.2
10	Streatley (YHA)	7	11.2	Henley-on-T	10¼	16.5	Kingston§#	11¼	18.1
11	Caversham (Reading)	11	17.7	Hurley	6¼	10	Fulham§# (Putney§#	16¼ 13½	26.2 21.7)
12	Henley-on-T	10¼	16.5	Dorney Reach†	11	17.7	Tower Br N§• 10 (Tower Br S§• 9¼		16.1 14.9)
13	Hurley	6¼	10	Windsor§	5½	8.9	Woolwich N/S§° 12 (Woolwich S§° 11¼		19.3 18.1)
14	Dorney Reach†	11	17.7	Chertsey	12	19.3			
15	Windsor§	5½	8.9	Kingston§#	11¼	18.1			
16	Chertsey	12	19.3	Fulham§# (Putney§#	16¼ 13½	26.2 21.7)			
17	Kingston§#	11¼	18.1	Tower Br N§• 10 (Tower Br S§• 9¼		16.1 14.9)			
18	Brentford§# (Richmond§#	5½ 4¾	8.9 7.6)	Woolwich N/S§° 12 (Woolwich S§°11¼		19.3 18.1)			
19	Fulham§# (Putney§#	10¾ 8¾	17.3 14)						
20	Tower Br N§• (Tower Br S§•	10 9¼	16.1 14.9)						
21	Woolwich N/S§° (Woolwich S§°	12 11¼	19.3 18.1)						

Nearest hostel

\# = YHA London Earl's Court
• = YHA London St Paul's (**N**); Lambeth (**S**)
° = YHA London Thameside
Tower Br = Tower Bridge
N = northern bank; **S** = southern bank

Notes

Once past Kingston the places and distances in brackets are those on the southern (S) bank path; those not in brackets are for the northern (N) bank.

* Distances to/from Oxford include/deduct 2 miles from Osney Bridge to campsite turning.

† Campsite reopening uncertain; contact campsite to check

§ No hostel or campsite but alternative accommodation in B&B, pub or hotel.

Woolwich N/S = the route to Woolwich Foot Tunnel starts on the northern bank but ends on the southern.

STAYING IN B&B-STYLE ACCOMMODATION – WALKING EAST

Night	Relaxed Place	miles	km	Medium Place	miles	km	Fast Place	miles	km
0	Kemble			Kemble			Kemble		
1	Ashton Keynes	7	11.2	Cricklade	12¼	19.7	Cricklade	12¼	19.7
2	Cricklade	5¼	8.5	Lechlade	11	17.7	Lechlade	11	17.7
3	Lechlade	11	17.7	Tadpole Bridge	10¾	17.3	Newbridge	16¾	27
4	Tadpole Bridge	10¾	17.3	Newbridge	4	9.7	Oxford	14	22.5
5	Newbridge	4	9.7	Oxford	14	22.5	Dorch-on-T	17¾	28.6
							(¼ mile off path)		
6	Eynsham	7½	12	Abingdon	9¾	15.7	Pangbourne	16½	26.5
7	Oxford	6½	10.5	Wallingford	13½	21.7	Henley	17¼	27.7
8	Abingdon	9¾	15.7	Pangbourne	11	17.7	Marlow	8½	13.7
9	Shillingford	10¼	16.5	L Shiplake	13¾	22.1	Windsor	14¼	23
10	Goring/Streatley	10¼	16.5	Marlow	12	19.3	Shepperton	14½	23.3
11	Caversham	11	17.7	Windsor	14¼	23	Brentford	15	24.1
	(Reading)						(Richmond	14¼	23)
12	Henley-on-T	10¼	16.5	Chertsey	12	19.3	Fulham	10¾	17.3
							(Putney	8¾	14.1)
13	Marlow	8½	13.7	Kingston	11¼	18	Tower Br N	10	16.1
							(Tower Br S	9¼	14.9)
14	Maidenhead	7¾	12.5	Fulham	16¼	26.1	Woolwich N/S§°	12	19.3
				(Putney	13½	21.7)	(Woolwich S§° 11¼	18.1)	
15	Windsor	6½	10.5	Tower Br N	10	16.1			
				(Tower Br S	9¼	14.9)			
16	Staines	8½	13.7	Woolwich N/S§°	12	19.3			
				(Woolwich S§°11¼	18.1)				
17	Shepperton	6	9.7						
18	Kingston	9½	15.3						
19	Brentford	9	14.5						
	(Richmond	4¾	7.6)						
20	Fulham	7¼	11.7						
	(Putney	8¾	14.1)						
21	Tower Br N	10	16.1						
	(Tower Br S	9¼	14.9)						
22	Woolwich N/S§° 12	19.3							
	(Woolwich S§° 11¼	18.1)							

Notes

Once past Kingston the places and distances in brackets are those on the southern bank path; those not in brackets are for the northern bank.

Tower Br = Tower Bridge; **N** = northern bank; **S** = southern bank

Woolwich N/S = the route to Woolwich Foot Tunnel starts on the northern bank but ends on the southern.

PLANNING YOUR WALK

CAMPING AND HOSTELS – WALKING WEST

	Relaxed			Medium			Fast		
	Place	**Approx Distance**		**Place**	**Approx Distance**		**Place**	**Approx Distance**	
Night		miles	km		miles	km		miles	km
0	(Woolwich S§°) Woolwich S/N§°			(Woolwich S§°) Woolwich S/N§°			(Woolwich S§°) Woolwich S/N§°		
1	(Tower Br S§• Tower Br N§•	11¼ 12	18.1) 19.3	(Tower Br S§• Tower Br N§•	11¼ 12	18.1) 19.3	(Tower Br S§• Tower Br N§•	11¼ 12	18.1) 19.3
2	(Putney§# Fulham#	10 9¼	16.1) 14.9	(Putney§# Fulham§#	9¼ 10	14.9) 16.1	(Putney§# Fulham§#	9¼ 10	14.9) 16.1
3	(Richmond§ Brentford§#	4¾ 10¾	7.6) 17.3	Kingston§#	13½ 16¼	21.7 26.2	(Kingston§#	16¼ 13½	26.2) 21.7
4	Kingston§#	5½ 10¼	8.9 16.5	Chertsey	11¼	18.1	Chertsey	11¼	18.1
5	Chertsey	11¼	18.1	Windsor§	12	19.3	Dorney Reach	17½	28.2
6	Windsor§	12	19.3	Dorney Reach†	5½	8.9	Henley-on-T	18½	29.7
7	Dorney Reach†	5½	8.9	Hurley	6¼	10.1	Streatley	21¼	34.2
8	Hurley	11	17.7	Henley-on-T	11	17.7	C'ton Hampden†	15¼	24.5
9	Henley-on-T	6¼	10	Caversham	10¼	16.5	Oxford*	13	20.1
10	Caversham (Reading)	10¼	16.5	Streatley YHA	11	17.7	Northmoor Lock	13.5	21.8
11	Streatley (YHA)	11	17.7	Crowmarsh Gifford	7	11.2	Radcot	12	19.3
12	Crowmarsh G	7	11.2	Clifton Hampden†	8¼	13.3	Castle Eaton	13½	21.7
13	Day's Lock† (Dorchester-on-T)	5½	8.9	Oxford*	13	20.1	Kemble	16½	26.6
14	Abingdon (bus to Oxford)	8	12.9	Northmoor Lock	13.5	21.8			
15	Oxford*	7¾	12.5	Rushey Lock	9¼	14.9			
16	Northmoor Lock	13.5	21.8	Lechlade	9½	15.3			
17	Shifford Lock	5	8	Cricklade§	11	17.7			
18	Radcot	7	11.2	Kemble	12¼	19.7			
19	Lechlade	6¾	10.9						
20	Cricklade§	11	17.7						
21	Kemble	12¼	19.7						

Nearest hostel

° = YHA London Thameside

• = YHA London St Paul's (**N**); Lambeth (**S**)

= YHA London Earl's Court

Notes

Before Kingston the places and distances in brackets are those on the southern bank path; those not in brackets are for the northern bank.

† Campsite reopening uncertain; contact campsite to check

* Distances to/from Oxford include/deduct 2 miles from Osney Bridge to campsite turning.

§ In places where there is neither a hostel nor a campsite the only accommodation option will be a B&B, guesthouse, pub or hotel.

Tower Br = Tower Bridge; **N** = northern bank; **S** = southern bank

Woolwich S/N = the route from Woolwich Foot Tunnel starts on the southern bank but ends on the northern.

STAYING IN B&B-STYLE ACCOMMODATION – WALKING WEST

Night	Relaxed Place	Approx Distance miles	km	Medium Place	Approx Distance miles	km	Fast Place	Approx Distance miles	km
0	(Woolwich S) Woolwich S/N			(Woolwich S) Woolwich S/N			(Woolwich S) Woolwich S/N		
1	(Tower Br S	11¼	18.1)	(Tower Br S	11¼	18.1)	(Tower Br S	11¼	18.1)
	Tower Br N	12	19.3	Tower Br N	12	19.3	Tower Br N	12	19.3
2	(Putney	9¼	14.9)	(Putney	9¼	14.9)	(Putney	9¼	14.9)
	Fulham	10	16.1	Fulham	10¼	16.5	Fulham	10¼	16.5
3	(Richmond	4¾	7.6)	(Kingston	13½	21.7)	(Richmond	9¼	14.9)
	Brentford	9	14.5		16¼	26.1	Brentford	10	16.1
4	Kingston	9½	15.3	Chertsey	12	19.3	Shepperton	15	24.1
5	Shepperton	6	9.7	Windsor	11¼	18	Windsor	14½	23.3
6	Staines	8½	13.7	Marlow	14¼	23	Marlow	14¼	23
7	Windsor	6½	10.5	Henley-on-T	8½	13.7	Henley	8½	13.7
8	Maidenhead	10	16.1	Caversham (Reading)	10¼	16.5	Pangbourne	17¼	27.7
9	Marlow	7¾	12.5	Goring & Streatley	11	17.7	Dorch-on-T (¼ mile off path)	16½	26.5
10	Henley-on-T	9	14.5	Shillingford	10¼	16.5	Oxford	17¾	28.6
11	Caversham (Reading)	10¼	16.5	Abingdon	10¾	17.3	Newbridge	14	22.5
12	Goring & Streatley	11	17.7	Oxford	9¾	15.7	Lechlade	16¾	27
13	Shillingford	10¼	16.5	Newbridge	14	22.5	Cricklade	11	17.7
14	Abingdon	10¾	17.3	Tadpole Bridge	6	9.7	Kemble	12¼	19.7
15	Oxford	9¾	15.7	Lechlade	10¾	17.3			
16	Eynsham	6½	10.5	Cricklade	11	17.7			
17	Newbridge	7½	12	Kemble	12¼	19.7			
18	Tadpole Bridge	6	9.7						
19	Lechlade	10¾	17.3						
20	Cricklade	11	17.7						
21	Ashton Keynes	5¼	8.5						
22	Kemble	7	11.2						

Notes

Before Kingston the places and distances in brackets are those on the southern bank path; those not in brackets are for the northern bank.

Tower Br = Tower Bridge; **N** = northern bank; **S** = southern bank

Woolwich S/N = the route from Woolwich Foot Tunnel starts on the southern bank but ends on the northern.

PLANNING YOUR WALK

WHICH DIRECTION?

The route descriptions and trail maps are tailored to suit walking in either direction as there are advantages both ways. Following the Thames Path from west to east – ie downstream from source to sea – you would witness the river's growth and you'll also be walking against the flow of the river; it's often said, too, that by walking east you'll have the weather (the prevailing wind and the sun) on your back for most of the time. But many folk – those three men in that boat for example (see pp49-50) – have tackled the river by leaving London and following the waters westward, in search of the source. And the advantage that way is that you finish your walk surrounded by rural scenery.

What to take

What – and how much – you should take are very personal choices. For those who are new to long-distance walking the suggestions below will help you reach a balance of comfort, safety and minimal weight.

KEEP YOUR LUGGAGE LIGHT

When packing your rucksack it cannot be emphasised enough that the less weight you are carrying the more you will enjoy your walk. If you pack a lot of unnecessary items you will probably find yourself gradually discarding them as you go. If you are in doubt about taking something, be ruthless and leave it at home.

Rucksack

If you are staying in B&Bs or hostels you will need a medium-sized pack of about 40-60 litres' capacity; just big enough to hold several changes of clothes, a waterproof jacket, a few toiletries, a water bottle/pouch and a packed lunch. Hostellers may require a few extras such as a towel and food for cooking. However, if you have quick-drying clothes and wash them as you go a 20- or 30-litre pack would suffice.

Those camping are going to need a rucksack big enough to carry a tent, sleeping bag, towel, cooking equipment and food; a pack of about 70 litres should be ample in this case.

If you are walking with an organised tour (see pp25-8) you will be able to pack the bulk of your gear into a suitcase or holdall and carry just a daypack with you on the trail itself, containing a spare jumper, waterproof jacket, water bottle/pouch, this guidebook and lunch, though the fully equipped walker may also want to bring a camera, map, walking pole(s), binoculars and first-aid kit.

It's advisable to pack everything inside a large plastic bag for protection against the rain; there are few things worse than discovering at the end of the day that all your clothes and sleeping bag have got wet. Most outdoor shops stock large bags made from tough plastic or you can use bin bags instead.

FOOTWEAR

A comfortable, sturdy pair of leather or fabric **boots** is ideal for walking the Thames Path. If you don't already own a pair and the cost of purchasing them is prohibitive you could get by with a lightweight pair of trainers or trail shoes between late spring and early autumn. Certainly, if you're carrying a heavy rucksack, you would be wise to invest in boots although you do see people wearing trainers on the trail.

If you are walking in the winter you'll be much more comfortable if your boots are waterproof; wet feet equals cold feet and blisters are more of a concern too. These days most people opt for a synthetic waterproof lining (Gore-Tex or similar).

Gaiters are not really necessary but if you have a pair you may find them useful when it's wet (especially when the grass is long) and muddy.

CLOTHING

Even if you are just on a day walk you should always have suitable clothing to keep you warm and dry, however nice the weather is when you set out. Most walkers pick their clothes according to the versatile layering system, which consists of an outer layer or 'shell' to protect you from the wind and rain, a mid-layer or two to keep you warm, and a base layer to 'wick' (ie to remove) sweat away from your skin.

The most important item is a **waterproof/windproof jacket**. Even in summer it can rain for a week and if the sun isn't out any breeze can make it feel distinctly chilly. The most comfortable jackets are those made from breathable fabrics that let moisture (ie your sweat) out but don't let moisture (ie rain) in. (**Waterproof trousers** are also recommended, especially early in the year, as the grass is often very high because it hasn't been cut for a while.)

A polyester **fleece**, or **woollen jumper**, makes a good middle layer as they remain warm even when wet. The advantage of fleece is that it is lightweight and dries relatively quickly. In winter you may want to carry an extra jumper to put on when you stop or you may find yourself getting cold very quickly.

In summer, cotton T-shirts are fine for a **base layer** but at other times of the year you will be more comfortable wearing a **thin thermal layer**. Those made from synthetic material such as polypropylene are now less popular because they retain smells and there are several new, technical and natural fabrics available. One of the best is merino wool which is lightweight, high-wicking, quick-drying and washable. Cotton absorbs sweat, trapping it next to the skin which will chill you rapidly when you stop exercising. Modern synthetic fabrics on the other hand, 'wick' sweat away from the body and dry rapidly.

Shorts are great to walk in during the summer, although you'll probably want to bring a pair of **long trousers** for cooler days. Also, some sections of the path can become overgrown with stinging nettles and you may appreciate having your legs covered. Don't wear jeans; if they get wet they become incredibly heavy and stick uncomfortably to your skin and they take forever to dry.

How much **underwear** you bring comes down to personal preference. Women may find a **sports bra** more comfortable because a backpack can cause bra straps to dig into your shoulders.

If you haven't got a pair of the modern hi-tech walking **socks** the old system of wearing a thin liner sock under a thicker wool sock is just as good. Bring a few pairs of each.

A **hat** is always a good idea: during the summer a sunhat helps to keep you cool and prevent sunburn, in the winter a woolly hat can help to keep you warm. In the cooler months we would also recommend a pair of **gloves**.

You will also need a **change of clothing** for the evening. If you're staying in B&Bs and eating out you may feel more comfortable with something smart. A spare pair of shoes such as lightweight sandals or trainers is also worth carrying, even if they do add a bit of weight. There's nothing worse than having to put wet, dirty (not to mention smelly) boots back on after you've showered and changed. If you're camping, early spring and late autumn nights can be decidedly chilly so pack something warm.

TOILETRIES

Take only the minimum. Essentials are **toothbrush**, **toothpaste**, **soap** (especially if camping), **shampoo**, any **medication** you may need and, for women, **tampons/sanitary towels**.

Loo paper is generally provided in public toilets but bring a roll just in case and carry a small lightweight **trowel** for burying excrement if you get caught out far from a toilet (see p72 for the code of the outdoor loo).

Sunscreen and something to put on cracked lips is also a good idea. Deodorants, hair brushes, razors and so forth are up to you. If you are hostelling or camping you will also need a **towel**.

FIRST-AID KIT

Medical facilities in Britain are good so you need to take only a basic first-aid kit to deal with minor injuries. In a waterproof bag or container you should have: **scissors** for cutting tape and cutting away clothing; **aspirin** or **paracetamol** for treating mild to moderate pain; one or two **stretch bandages** for holding dressings or splints in place and for sprained ankles or sore knees; if you think your knees will give you trouble **elastic supports** are invaluable; a **triangular bandage** for broken/sprained arms; a small selection of **sterile dressings** for wounds and **porous adhesive tape** to hold them in place; **plasters/Band Aids** for minor cuts; a sturdier, preferably waterproof **adhesive tape** for blister prevention; **Compeed**, **Second Skin** or **Moleskin** for treating blisters; **safety pins**; **antiseptic cream** or **liquid**; **tweezers**; and possibly **Imodium** for acute diarrhoea – you never know when it might come in handy.

GENERAL ITEMS

Other **essential** items you should carry are: a **torch** (flashlight) in case you end up walking in the dark; a **compass**, assuming you can use one, to stop you getting lost; a **whistle** to attract attention if you do get lost, or find yourself in trouble (see pp75-6); a **water bottle or pouch** (two litres is the best size); a **watch**; and a **plastic bag** for carrying any rubbish you accumulate. You should also carry some emergency **food** with you such as chocolate, dried fruit and biscuits.

Walking poles are now widely used and can help in taking some of the weight off your feet. Using them requires some practice but once you get used to them they become a normal, indeed vital, part of your equipment.

Useful items to carry are: a **pen-knife**; a **camera**; a **notebook** to record your impressions; **sunglasses** to protect your eyes on sunny days; **binoculars**; something to **read**; and a **vacuum flask** for hot drinks (worth the investment if you're on a budget as buying all those cups of tea or coffee can get expensive). A **map-case** can be a useful extra for protecting your map and guidebook in the rain, which can very quickly reduce both to pulp.

MAPS

It would be perfectly possible to walk long stretches of the Thames Path unaided by map or compass: just keep the river alongside you and you can't go too far off track. The **hand-drawn maps in this book**, which cover the trail at a scale of 1:20,000, should provide sufficient aid in areas where navigation is slightly more problematic. Nevertheless, having other maps will paint a more

---

❏ DIGITAL MAPPING

Most smartphones have a GPS chip so you can see your position overlaid onto a digital map on your phone. There are numerous software packages that provide Ordnance Survey (OS) maps for a smartphone, tablet, PC or GPS unit. Maps are downloaded over the internet, then loaded into an app, also available by download, from where you can view them, print them and create routes on them.

It is important to ensure any digital mapping software on your smartphone uses pre-downloaded maps stored on your device, and doesn't need to download them on-the-fly, as this may be expensive and will be impossible without a signal. Note that battery life will be significantly reduced, compared to normal usage, when you are using the built-in GPS and running the screen for long periods.

Many websites have **free routes** you can download for the more popular digital mapping products; anything from day walks to complete Long Distance Paths.

Memory Map (🖳 memory-map.co.uk) currently sell OS 1:25,000 mapping covering the whole of the UK for £166. They also have annual subscriptions from £25.

For a subscription of £2.99 for one month, or £23.99 for a year (on their current offer) **Ordnance Survey** (see above) will let you download and then use their UK maps (1:25,000 scale) on a mobile or tablet without a data connection for a specific period.

Harvey Maps sell their digital Thames Path map for £20.49 for use on any device.

complete picture of your surroundings and will allow you to plan much more effectively for any accommodation or other facilities that lie off the trail.

The best option for walkers unconcerned by anything other than the path and its immediate environs is **AZ's Thames Path Adventure Atlas** (🖥 collins .co.uk/collections/az-adventure-maps). It is lightweight, cheap and includes the whole trail using Ordnance Survey's mapping on the same 1:25,000 scale as their Explorer series; it also includes an index.

Should you prefer to see the wider area **Ordnance Survey (OS**; 🖥 ord nancesurvey.co.uk) maps are best. They produce their maps to two scales: the 1:25,000 Explorer series in orange and the 1:50,000 Landranger in pink (which is less useful for walking purposes). Alongside the paper versions OS also produces 'Active' editions of both which are 'weatherproof' (ie covered in a lightweight protective plastic coating). Those needed for the Thames Path are as follows: **Explorer**: 168 Stroud, Tetbury & Malmesbury; 169 Cirencester &

☐ **FACTS AND FIGURES ABOUT THE THAMES**

The etymology of 'The Thames'

'Thames' is one of the most ancient names recorded in England. There are some interesting theories about its history: the Visit Thames website says the name may come from a Sanskrit word 'Tamas' meaning dark, as the water is dark/cloudy. It is also thought to derive from the Celtic words Tam and Isa (or possibly esa); the two put together describing something which is 'wide spreading' and consists of 'running water'. The Celts knew the river as Tamesas and the Romans called it the Tamesis, while the Anglo-Saxons who followed them knew it as the Temes or Temese. It seems it acquired the 'h' only in the mid 17th century.

In the Oxford area particularly it is given two names, **Thames** and **Isis**, both of which would seem to derive from the ancient Celtic words. However, it has been speculated that originally there were actually two separate rivers, the Isis being the waters that flow between the source and Dorchester, while the Thames was the name of the river between the River Thame – a tributary of the Thames – and the sea.

The Thames in numbers

The Thames, at 215 miles (346km) in length, is the longest river in England. (The title for being the longest river in the United Kingdom, by the way, goes to the Severn, which begins in Wales and is 220 miles/354km in length). But in a global context both the Thames and the Severn are short rivers as some are thousands of miles long.

Between its source and where the Thames meets the North Sea (often thought as the seaward limit of the Port of London Authority), the river falls 105m, its current moving at between 0.5 and 2.75 miles per hour (0.8-4.4kmph). The mean depth of the Thames is approximately 9 metres (30ft) and its mean width is 305m (1000ft), although this average is somewhat skewed by the fact that the river is 5½ miles wide at the Nore. At Lechlade, 191 miles away from the sea, the Thames becomes navigable and it becomes tidal at Teddington Lock – more accurately 'Teddington Locks' as there are three (barge, launch and skiff) locks; the barge lock is the largest of all the river's locks. On the non-tidal part there are 45 locks overall.

Along the length of the river there are over 200 (road, rail and foot) bridges, 27 tunnels, 6 ferry services and a cable car.

Swindon; 170 Abingdon, Wantage & Vale of White Horse; 180 Oxford –
Witney & Woodstock; 171 Chiltern Hills West; 172 Chiltern Hills East; 160
Windsor, Weybridge & Bracknell; 161 London South; 162 Greenwich &
Gravesend (162 covers just the final stretch to Woolwich so is not really neces-
sary). If you don't feel such precise cartography is needed the **Landranger** may
be sufficient: you will need: 163 Cheltenham & Cirencester; 164 Oxford; 175
Reading, Windsor, Henley-on-Thames & Bracknell; 176 West London; 177
East London. OS also offers **digital maps** (see box on p43).

Harvey Maps (⌨ harveymaps.co.uk) produce a series of waterproof maps
that cover all the designated National Trails to a scale of 1:40,000. Their paper
Thames Path map is also available digitally either from their website (⌨ harvey
maps.co.uk/acatalog/digital-mapping.html) or through various providers and
platforms.

The geography and pre-history of the Thames

The Thames can broadly be divided into three sections: the Upper Thames, between
the source and Goring Gap, a primarily rural landscape; the Middle Thames, between
Goring and Teddington, where the river is lined with commuter and tourist towns;
and the Lower Thames, where the river's tidal waters flow through London and
beyond, cutting through the Kent and Essex marshes and out to sea.

The river runs through nine counties: Gloucestershire, Wiltshire, Oxfordshire,
Berkshire, Buckinghamshire, Surrey, the Metropolitan county of Greater London
(historically Middlesex), Essex and Kent. In fact, it often acts as the border between
them, separating Wiltshire from Gloucestershire, for example, or Oxfordshire from
Berkshire, Surrey from Middlesex and Essex from Kent. Indeed, virtually since
Homo sapiens first came into contact with the Thames it has always acted as a border,
a geographical feature acting as both a separator and protector of man. Yet the river's
tale begins well before man's arrival.

The river was formed by the flow of the oceans of the Jurassic period, some 170
million years ago, though back then it followed a different route: the river's forerunner, the 'proto-Thames', actually flowed via the Vale of St Albans and into the North
Sea at Harwich. During this period Britain was still connected to the Continent and
the Thames was a tributary of a vast river (the Rhine) which ran across Europe; a
tropical river in which turtles paddled and crocodiles swam. But 250,000 years ago,
during an extreme Ice Age, the river, finding its course blocked by glaciers, pushed
southwards instead and burst through a weak point between the southern Downs and
the Chilterns (a point that today is known as **Goring Gap**; see p142) flowing along
the valleys, a course which it pretty much still follows to this day.

As the temperatures rose, following the end of the last Ice Age approximately
12,000 years ago, the improved climate attracted hippos and elephants to the river.
Mesolithic settlers, too, began to appear along the river's banks and ever since their
arrival the Thames Valley has been permanently occupied. This is true despite the
monumental events of c5500BC, when the rising waters submerged the land which
joined the continent to Britain, the English Channel met the North Sea – and Britain
became an island.

PLANNING YOUR WALK

CAMPING GEAR

Campers will need a decent lightweight **tent** able to withstand wind and rain; a **sleeping mat**; a two- or three-season **sleeping bag** (you can always wear clothes inside your sleeping bag if you are cold); a **camping stove** and **fuel**; **cooking equipment** (a pot with a pot-grabber and a frying pan that can double as a lid is enough for two people); a **bowl**, **mug**, **cutlery** (don't forget a can-opener), **pen-knife** and a **scrubber** for washing up.

MONEY

Debit and **credit cards** can be used to pay in larger shops, restaurants, most YHA hostels and hotels but as a result of Covid you now have to pay by card (or Apple/Google Pay) in many more places. However, it is still worth carrying some money as **cash** as not everywhere accepts cards; a debit card with a PIN is the easiest way to withdraw money either from banks, post offices or ATMs.

❏ **THE CULTURAL THAMES**

The Thames has been the muse of many an artist. The river has inspired painters and poets, sculptors... and punks. In their 1979 song *London Calling*, The Clash boasted how they 'live by the river.' Before them, in 1967 The Kinks sang of the sunsets over London's *Waterloo Bridge* making them 'feel fine.'

Rock and Punk **music** are both a far cry from the concert performed on a barge afloat the Thames for King George I in 1717, a highlight of which was a performance of Handel's *Water Music*, or the songs compiled by Alfred Williams in his book *Folk Songs of the Upper Thames* in 1923.

Though these works may differ in genre, they all clearly share an affinity for the river. And it is not just composers that the river has inspired. The Thames attracts **sculptors** too: there is a statue of *Old Father Thames* at St John's Lock (see box on p96) and in Runnymede (see box on p186) there are works which are meant to encourage the viewer to reflect on democracy. Meanwhile, situated at Rainham (Essex) – so beyond the Thames Path – is John Kaufman's 4.5-metre high steel statue, *The Diver*, completed in 2000. The only sculpture actually *in* the river, it is completely submerged by spring and neap tides. Apart from such extravagant pieces you'll pass numerous other smaller statues, metal-works and carvings.

Painters particularly associated with the river include the Italian, Canaletto (Giovanni Antonio Canal; *Westminster Bridge*, 1746; *Old Walton Bridge*, 1754); the American, James Abbott McNeill Whistler (*Nocturne: Blue and Silver – Chelsea*, 1871; *Nocturne: Blue and Gold – Old Battersea Bridge*, 1872); and the Frenchman, Claude Monet, who produced a series of paintings of the Houses of Parliament, with the river in the forefront, between 1901 and 1905.

The two painters most connected to the Thames, however, are British: Stanley Spencer and JMW Turner. Spencer dedicated much of his life to painting the river near Cookham (see box on p176); works include *Swan Upping at Cookham* (1915-19) and his unfinished painting *Christ Preaching at Cookham Regatta* (1952-9). Turner's images featuring the Thames include *The Thames from Richmond Hill* (c1815), *The Thames above Waterloo Bridge* (c1830-5) and *Windsor Castle from the Thames* (1805). These are worth stopping off to view at Tate Britain (see p230) in London and you'll also find several of Spencer's works there.

Always keep your money and documents in a safe place and in a waterproof container. In particular, those camping or staying in hostels should take care not to leave them lying around; it's much safer to carry them on you.

RECOMMENDED READING

The river has been muse for many a writer and numerous books have been penned which take the Thames either as their central subject or use it as a backdrop to their tale. What follows is a selection of those most useful and well known.

Guidebooks

There have been innumerable guidebooks published about the River Thames. One of the oldest is *The Royal River: The Thames, from Source to Sea*, first published in 1885. Newer editions are available in libraries but unfortunately the book is quite large so it's not really practical to take with you. It includes some wonderful illustrations and is beautifully written.

As for **literature**, the river has inspired many more books than the two mentioned on pp49-50 by Kenneth Grahame and Jerome K Jerome. It is aboard a boat ('a cruising yawl') anchored on the Thames that Joseph Conrad's Marlow narrates his tale of another river, the Congo, in *Heart of Darkness* (1899). The Thames also inspired Lewis Carroll's *Alice in Wonderland* (1865) and William Morris's *News from Nowhere* (1890; see box on p100). The river also features as the backdrop to a Sherlock Holmes mystery in Arthur Conan Doyle's *The Sign of Four* (1890) and, more recently, as the setting for a story of intrigue in William Boyd's *Ordinary Thunderstorms* (2009).

Perhaps the author who was most bewitched by the Thames, however, was Charles Dickens; he based scenes from several of his novels on the river. His last complete novel, *Our Mutual Friend* (1864-65), begins, rather morbidly, with a dead man being pulled from the river near London Bridge. It is along the Thames estuary that *Great Expectations* (1861) begins and amongst the slums along the southern bank of the river that his tale of an orphan, *Oliver Twist* (1838), ends. Indeed, Dickens even wrote a dictionary to the Thames (see p49).

Then there's **poetry**. As well as featuring in William Blake's *London* (1794), in which the poet wanders the 'charter'd streets, near where the charter'd Thames does flow', the river has also appeared in the work of many of England's other great poets. From the idyllic, 'silver streaming' Thames of Edmund Spenser (*Prothalamion*; 1596) and the riparian scene which made William Wordsworth purr, 'Ne'er saw I, never felt, a calm so deep' (*On Westminster Bridge*; 1802); to the river which makes Matthew Arnold crave for the days when 'life ran gaily as the Thames; before this strange disease of modern life' (*The Scholar Gypsy*; 1853), it has generally been used to summon a pastoral sense of contentment.

Possibly the most famous line of poetry penned about the river, however, comes from an American quill (though the owner of the quill was by this stage a naturalised Brit) and is more concerned with encroaching change. In TS Eliot's *The Waste Land* (1922) he begins a stanza by beseeching the river, 'Sweet Thames run softly, till I end my song.' Fearful of the consequences of industrialisation which he saw sweeping through the Western World, Eliot would hopefully be appeased by the efforts being made to conserve the river today.

❑ SOURCES OF FURTHER INFORMATION

Online Information

The most useful online resource for planning your journey is the official National Trail website (⌨ **nationaltrail.co.uk/thames-path**) which has a wealth of information and includes an interactive map, route descriptions (though for the London stretch there is a link to the TfL maps, see below, which at the time of writing hadn't been updated for a while), downloadable leaflets and information on geocaching.

The unofficial online guide, ⌨ **thames-path.org.uk**, may be of interest to those planning on walking the Thames Path from east to west as it includes route guides for that direction.

Useful information on facilities, river conditions, lock closures and much more can be found at the Environment Agency's website, ⌨ **gov.uk/government/organisations/environment-agency**, while lots of general information about the river can be found at the website of the River Thames Society (⌨ **riverthamessociety.org.uk**).

Another website which may be of interest for day walks in the London area is ⌨ **tfl.gov.uk/modes/walking/thames-path** as that has maps for the routes mentioned and basic public transport information.

Though not specifically for walkers ⌨ **visitthames.co.uk** includes practical information as well as facts and figures about the Thames. There is also an app for iPhone users.

Tourist information

Many of the towns and villages along the Thames Path have places where you can get information: **Tourist/visitor information centres (TICs/VICs)** provide all manner of locally specific information for visitors; most also have information about accommodation in the area (and some may book it) and public transport services. For details on where to find these consult the Village and town facilities table (see pp30-5), while in Part 4 of this book you'll find their location and the relevant contact details.

London's official **tourist board**, Visit London (⌨ visitlondon.com), can provide assistance for all aspects of your time in the capital. Other websites worth looking at are ⌨ experienceoxfordshire.org and ⌨ visitsoutheastengland.com/places-to-visit/berkshire.

Organisations for walkers

● **The Long Distance Walkers' Association** (⌨ ldwa.org.uk) An association for people with the common interest of long-distance walking in rural, mountainous and moorland areas. Membership includes a journal, *Strider,* three times per year giving details of challenge events and local group walks as well as articles on the subject. Membership costs £18 (£15 if paid by direct debit) per year for an adult.

● **Ramblers** (formerly Ramblers' Association; ⌨ ramblers.org.uk) Looks after the interests of walkers. Members receive their quarterly *Walk* magazine, have access to both the Ramblers Routes online library (short routes only for non members) and an app as well as group walks. Members also receive discounts at various stores. Individual/joint membership costs £36.60/49.

● **Backpackers' Club** (⌨ backpackersclub.co.uk) A club aimed at people who are involved or interested in lightweight camping through walking, cycling, skiing, canoeing, etc. They produce a quarterly magazine, provide members with a comprehensive advisory and information service on all aspects of backpacking, organise weekend trips and also publish a farm-pitch directory. Membership costs £20 per year.

Another 19th-century book which may be of interest is *Dickens' Dictionary of the Thames*, written by the great man himself and compiled by his son in 1887. Described as 'an unconventional handbook', Dickens' lovers should be warned that there are no orphans pleading for more, or convicts hiding in the marshes, in this tome.

Factual

For a magnificent introduction to the river try Peter Ackroyd's *Thames, Sacred River* (Vintage Books, 2008) and Andrew Sargent's *The Story of the Thames* (Amberley, 2013, paperback 2015). Both explore all facets of their topic. Ackroyd is also the author of *London, The Biography* (Vintage, 2001). A rather less academic work, Christopher Winn's *I never knew that about the River Thames* (Ebury Press, 2010) makes for an entertaining read.

In *Mudlark River* (2014) Simon Wilcox recounts his walk along the Thames using a Victorian map. (Mudlarks were what the Victorians called people who scavenged the banks of the river at low tide.) *Mudlark: In search of London's Past along the River Thames* by Lara Malkley (Liveright, 2020) is about the mudlarks who treasure hunt along the Thames and the history revealed through what they discover.

River Thames: From source to sea by Steve Wallis (Amberley, 2016) focuses on unusual and interesting features illustrated with colour photos.

There are numerous books specific to the Thames in London. A concise introduction is *London's Thames* by Gavin Weightman (John Murray, 2004). Concerned purely with traversing the river are *Cross River Traffic: A History of London's Bridges* (Roberts; Granta Books, 2005), *Crossing London's River* (Pudney; JM Dent & Sons, 1972) and *Crossing the River: The History of London's Thames River Bridges from Richmond to the Tower* (Cookson; Mainstream, 2006). This last one is especially good.

Also of interest may be *Front-Line Thames* by Michael Foley (The History Press, 2008), which takes the river's strategic significance as its central subject, or *Liquid History: A Photographic Guide to the Thames through Time* (Croad; Batsford, 2003), a book of black and white photos of the river accompanied by some explanatory text.

With the Thames having played such an important role in the country's history, it's certainly worth brushing up on your wars, kings and beheadings. *A Short History of England* by Simon Jenkins (Profile Books, 2018) is as concise as the title suggests.

Biography and fiction

Undoubtedly the two books most associated with the River Thames are Kenneth Grahame's *The Wind in the Willows* (1908; see boxes on p47 and p150), featuring Mr Toad of Toad Hall, Mole, Ratty and Badger, and Jerome K Jerome's *Three Men in a Boat*.

Originally published in 1889, the latter tells the comedic tale of three men – J (the narrator) and his two friends Harris and George – as they journey upriver from Kingston accompanied by the dog Montmorency. Many of the pubs mentioned by Jerome still exist and it's a rare walker who manages the whole trail without hearing the book mentioned at least once per day!

More recent Thames-side biographies which are particularly readable are the light-hearted *Boogie Up the River* (Mark Wallington; Arrow Books, 1990) and Pauline Conolly's witty and informative *All Along the River: Tales from the Thames* (Hale Books, 2013).

In *From source to sea: Notes from a 215-mile walk along the River Thames* Tom Chesshyre (2017) covers the journey he undertook just after the Brexit vote in Britain. The book covers the history of the various places he passes but he also describes the people he met and strange experiences he had as he walked the length of the River Thames.

For more information on the River Thames's cultural significance see the box on pp46-7.

Flora and fauna field guides

For identifying obscure plants and peculiar-looking beasties as you walk, Collins and New Holland publish a pocket-sized range to Britain's natural riches. The Collins Gem series are tough little books; current titles include guides to *Trees*, *Birds*, *Mushrooms*, *Wild Flowers*, *Wild Animals*, *Insects* and *Butterflies*. There is also a handbook to the stars for those who are considering sleeping under them.

In the Collins series, there's an adapted version of Richard Mabey's classic bestseller *Food for Free* – great for anyone intent on getting back to nature, saving the pennies, or just with an interest in what's available to eat without going into a shop.

New Holland's Concise range covers much the same topics as the Gem series; each one comes in a waterproof plastic jacket and includes useful quick reference foldout charts.

There are also several field guide **apps** for smartphones and tablets, including those that can aid in identifying birds (🖳 merlin.allaboutbirds.org) by their song as well as by their appearance.

Getting to and from the Thames Path

Travelling to the start of the Thames Path by public transport makes sense. There's no need to worry about the safety of your temporarily abandoned vehicle while you walk along the trail, there are no logistical headaches about how to return to your car afterwards and it's one of the biggest steps you can take towards minimising your ecological footprint. Quite apart from that, you'll feel your holiday has begun the moment you step out of your front door rather than having to wait until you've slammed the car door behind you.

❏ GETTING TO BRITAIN

● **By air** The best international gateway to Britain for the Thames Path is London with its five airports: **Heathrow** (the main airport), Gatwick, Stansted, Luton and **London City**. Both Tfl Rail (🖳 tfl.gov.uk/modes/tfl-rail; daily 2/hr) and Heathrow Express (🖳 heathrowexpress.com; daily 4/hr) provide train services from Heathrow to London Paddington). However, to reach the western end of the path you could take First's Railair 1 (RA1; 🖳 firstbus.co.uk/railair) bus service (1/hr; approx 60 mins) from Heathrow to Reading railway station and pick up a train to Kemble there.

Some airlines fly to **Bristol** (🖳 bristolairport.co.uk) and from there you can take a train to Swindon and then change to a train to Kemble.

London City Airport is the most convenient for the eastern end of the path, particularly for reaching Woolwich, as from the airport you can take the Docklands Light Railway to Woolwich Arsenal DLR station.

See box on pp56-7 for details about train services in Britain.

● **From Europe by train** Eurostar (🖳 eurostar.com) operates the high-speed passenger service via the Channel Tunnel between Paris/Brussels/Amsterdam and London. The terminal in London is St Pancras International. St Pancras station provides connections to the London Underground (tube) and all other main railway stations in London. Trains to many Thames Path destinations leave from both Paddington and Waterloo stations; see box on pp56-7.

For more information about rail services from the Continent to Britain contact your national rail operator, or Railteam (🖳 railteam.eu).

● **From Europe by coach** Eurolines (🖳 eurolines.com) have a wide network of long-distance bus services connecting over 500 destinations in 25 European countries to London's Victoria Coach Station. Visit their website for details of services from your country.

● **From Europe by ferry (with or without a car)** There are numerous ferries plying routes between the major North Sea ports as well as across the Irish Sea and the English Channel. A useful website for information about the routes and the ferry operators is 🖳 directferries.com.

● **From Europe by car** Eurotunnel (🖳 eurotunnel.com) operates 'le shuttle' (the shuttle) train service for vehicles via the Channel Tunnel between Calais and Folkestone taking just 35 minutes. Remember, though, that if you drive into the centre of London you're liable to pay a congestion charge.

PLANNING YOUR WALK

NATIONAL TRANSPORT

By rail

Most of the major stops along the Thames Path, other than in London, lie on either the main or branch line services run by **Great Western Railway** (**GWR**). Kemble, the nearest settlement to the source of the River Thames, is 80-100 minutes from London Paddington.

The trains to Woolwich – at the eastern end of the path – are run by **Southeastern** (Woolwich Arsenal and Dockyard) and **Thameslink** (Woolwich Arsenal only). Southeastern trains take less than half an hour to get to central London (stopping/terminating at either London Bridge & Cannon St, or London Bridge, Waterloo East & Charing Cross stations). Thameslink services go to London Bridge. From 2022 Elizabeth Line trains (see box below) should go to and from Woolwich (and also to Reading and other places on the path). Between Reading and London, and in south-west London, you will need to use **South Western Railway** to reach some destinations.

Other operators providing train services to places on or near the path include: **Southern**, **Chiltern Railway**, **Cross Country**, **c2c**, **London Overground**, **Tfl Rail** and **Docklands Light Railway** (**DLR**).

In the box on pp56-7 there is a list of the relevant destinations for these services along the path as well as contact details for the various operators.

Fare and timetable information Fares and timetable information can be found on the websites listed in the box on pp56-7 and at **National Rail Enquiries** (☎ 0345-748 4950, 🖥 nationalrail.co.uk). The best way to save some money is to book your train travel well in advance either at a railway station, or online through the relevant operator or via 🖥 thetrainline.com.

Most rail companies as well as National Rail and trainline have **apps** for smartphones which are worth downloading in order to keep up to date with train times and fares as well as any changes which may have occurred.

By coach

Both Stroud and Cirencester are just a short train or bus journey from Kemble, near the river's source, and both are connected to London via **National Express's** 445 service. National Express also has services from most major cities to Oxford, Heathrow Airport and London Victoria. For a selection of the

---

❑ ELIZABETH LINE

When fully open this new line will provide services right across London. One part of the line will start from Reading and another from Heathrow Airport; they will join at Hayes & Harlington and then divide again at Whitechapel with a southern spur going to Abbey Wood and a northern one to Shenfield. Stations served will include **Reading**, Twyford, **Maidenhead**, Taplow, Slough, Ealing Broadway, London Paddington, London Liverpool Street, **Canary Wharf** and **Woolwich**.

The Heathrow/Reading to Paddington sections are open (see Tfl Rail, box on p57), but the Elizabeth Line is not scheduled to be fully open till early/mid 2022. Services will operate approximately 2/hr from Reading but up to 12/hr in central London.

❏ COACH SERVICES

Not all stops are listed.

National Express (🖳 nationalexpress.com)
Note: at the time of research many services were not operating due to Covid; check the website for up-to-date information.
NX210 Heathrow Airport (T5) to Wolverhampton via **Oxford** & Birmingham, 4/day
plus 1/day to Birmingham
NX401 London to Bristol via Reading & Swindon, 2/day
NX445 London to Hereford via **Cricklade**, Cirencester, Stroud & Gloucester, 1/day
JL737 Stansted Airport to **Oxford** via Luton Airport, 4/day

Stagecoach Oxford Tube (🖳 oxfordtube.com)
London Victoria to **Oxford**, 1-5/hr, most frequently during the day

Oxford Bus Company (🖳 oxfordbus.co.uk)
● **the Airline** (🖳 airline.oxfordbus.co.uk) Heathrow & Gatwick airports to **Oxford** 2/hr between about 8am and 8pm, less frequently outside these hours
● **X90** (🖳 x90.oxfordbus.co.uk) London to **Oxford** 1-3/hr during the day, less frequently at night and at weekends

Green Line Coaches (operated by Reading Buses 🖳 reading-buses.co.uk)
702 London Victoria to Legoland via Slough & **Windsor**, daily 1/hr
703 Heathrow Airport to Bracknell via Slough & **Windsor**, daily approx 1/hr

---

services relevant to the Thames Path at the time of research, see the box above. For further details consult National Express's website. Megabus (🖳 uk.mega bus.com) also operates services to Oxford.

By car

With such an extensive public transport network there's really no need to drive; the risks of leaving a car somewhere (and probably having to pay to do so) surely outweighing the minor additional inconvenience typically suffered by those travelling by public transport. However, for accurate directions and timings from anywhere that you may wish to start your walk 🖳 theaa.com/route-planner is a wonderful resource.

LOCAL TRANSPORT

Getting to and from most parts of the Thames Path is generally pretty simple thanks to a relatively comprehensive public transport network.

The **public transport maps** (pp58-9) give an overview of routes which are of particular use to walkers. The **bus services and operators table** on pp60-1 gives the approximate frequency of bus services, the relevant stops and contact details for the operators; see box pp56-7 for details of **rail services**.

For public transport information for the whole of the UK contact **traveline** (🖳 traveline.info). Smartphone users can also download two traveline **apps** (South West and South East England) which may prove useful; there's also a National Rail app and a trainline app. Tourist information centres provide timetables and all other relevant details around the areas which they serve.

❏ OYSTER CARDS

The easiest way to pay a fare is with a **contactless debit card**, but if that isn't an option you should get an Oyster card (💻 tfl.gov.uk/oyster); this is a smart card which provides discounted travel on most of London's travel network. You can get an Oyster card from all tube (underground) and London Overground stations as well as at most TFL and some DLR stations; also at newsagents which are Oyster ticket stops. You must pay a £5 fee (refundable after a year) and put some credit on the card. You can then use it to swipe in and out of underground and DLR/railway stations and also on the buses and river buses. It can be topped up as and when required.

Apart from in London you will find **bus stops** either marked on the map, or their position described in the text. The nearest **railway stations** are also marked on the maps and relevant service details included in the text.

Transport in London

Between Hampton Court Bridge and Woolwich you have London's **extensive transport system** at your disposal. The combination of National Rail, Tfl Rail/London Overground, Docklands Light Railway (DLR) and London Underground (the 'Tube') trains, Uber by Thames Clipper river bus services, the city's famous red double-decker as well as single-decker buses means every point along the river can be accessed with relative ease.

London is divided into nine **zones** and other than for buses (see opposite) the **fare** you pay depends on the zone(s) you travel through. Hampton Court and Hampton stations, on the western side of London, are in Zone 6 and are the boundary stations for TfL; on the eastern side Charlton and Woolwich Dockyard are in Zone 3 and Woolwich Arsenal & Woolwich Zone 4, though at the time of writing there is a campaign to change Woolwich to Zone 3.

Holders of a Freedom pass/Oyster 60 card can travel as far as Reading on TfL Rail services, though do check you are on a TfL Rail train.

When it comes to paying for your journey (unless you are a London resident with a Freedom pass), you can use a debit card as long as it is contactless or an Oyster card (see box above). For the underground, or any train service, simply hold your card against the reader by the ticket gate and do the same as you exit the network, and you'll be charged the correct fare for your journey. If you forget to tap your card on the way out you'll be charged the maximum possible fare for your journey; the same applies if you inadvertently use a different card. For buses, you just need to tap your card against the reader on entering the bus. **It should also be noted that fares are cheaper outside the rush hour (off-peak times)**. 'Rush hour' times are Monday to Friday 6.30-9.30am and 4-7pm.

There are daily fare caps: Zones 1-6 £13.50 anytime and off peak; Zones 1 to 7/8/9 £14.70/17.40/19.30 anytime and £13.60 off peak. The equivalent weekly caps are £67.70/73.70/87/96.50. Caps for Zones 1-6 for paper tickets are £19.60/13.90. Caps are valid over 24 hours from 04.30.

For **information on all routes and services**, details of prices, timetables and up-to-date maps, visit the **Transport for London** (💻 tfl.gov.uk) website or get the **app**: TfI Go (⌨ tfl.gov.uk/maps_/tfl-go), available for both IoS and Android devices. It is worth checking especially for weekends as lines can often be closed due to engineering works.

Trains The nearest and most useful railway (overground), underground (tube) and DLR stations are marked on the maps and mentioned in the text which accompanies them. See also box on pp56-7 for rail and DLR routes.

Where a London Underground station is included, the text also states which line it is on: for example **Charing Cross** (Northern/Bakerloo lines).

Buses London buses do not take cash. If you intend to use buses and don't have a contactless debit card it is worth getting an Oyster card (see box opposite). Note also that the zone system does not apply to the bus network: you can travel by bus in Zones 1-6, with any Travelcard regardless of what zone it covers.

Anyone with a Freedom Pass or an 'English National Concessionary Travel Scheme bus pass' can travel for free on all buses except between 4.30am and 9am on weekdays, though at anytime at weekends and on public holidays.

Since there are almost always bus stops outside or near both underground and railway stations, as well as at many places in between, bus stops are not marked on the maps for London. Nor are bus service details included in the text as there are so many options.

River bus Uber Boat by Thames Clippers (⌨ thamesclippers.com) are a great way to see London from the river. River bus services are:
RB1 Battersea Power Station/London Eye (Waterloo) to/from Tower/Greenwich though some continue to Woolwich (Royal Arsenal) Pier, daily 2-3/hr

From spring 2022 services will go to/from Barking Riverside Pier.
RB2 Battersea Power Station to/from North Greenwich, Sat & Sun 2/hr
RB4 Doubletree Docklands (Rotherhithe) to/from Canary Wharf (daily 3-6/day)
RB6 Putney Pier to/from Blackfriars (though some services continue to Canary Wharf), Mon-Fri 1-2/hr but peak hours only (6.30-11.15am & 5.10-9pm).

Oyster cards (see box opposite) are valid and entitle you to a 10-20% discount (50% for Freedom Pass/60+Oyster Card holders); you can also get river bus tickets through the Uber app. Piers to access the river bus services are marked on the maps.

❏ BOATS ALONG THE THAMES

While they can't really be considered public transport, there are companies that offer boat trips along the Thames; a leisurely and scenic way of seeing the river as well as a fresh perspective on it. The main company behind these 'cruises' is Salters Steamers (⌨ salterssteamers.co.uk) which has been plying their trade on the river for over 160 years. They operated some round-trip cruises in 2021 but, due to Covid, not their scheduled services (routes covered Oxford to Windsor); check their website for an update.

Other services are provided by Turk Launches (⌨ turks.co.uk; Apr-end Oct; Hampton Court to Richmond) and Thames River Boats (⌨ wpsa.co.uk; Apr-end Oct; Kew to Hampton Court). See also River bus services above.

PLANNING YOUR WALK

❏ **TRAIN SERVICES** [see map pp58-9]

GWR (🖳 gwr.com)

- Paddington* ↔ Cheltenham Spa via **Reading**, Didcot Parkway, Swindon, **Kemble**, Stroud & Gloucester, Mon-Fri 13/day, Sat 11/day; additional services from Swindon and Sunday services only from there
- Paddington* ↔ Didcot Parkway via Slough, **Maidenhead**, Twyford, **Reading**, **Tilehurst**, **Pangbourne**, **Goring & Streatley** & Cholsey, daily 1-2/hr
- Didcot Parkway ↔ **Oxford**/Banbury, daily 1-2/hr (early morning and late after noon services call at **Appleford, Culham** & **Radley** but otherwise during the day there are limited services to these stations).
- Paddington* ↔ **Oxford** via **Reading**, Mon-Sat 2/hr, Sun 1/hr (some services stop at Slough and/or Didcot Parkway and some continue to Banbury)
- Slough ↔ **Windsor** & **Eton Central**, daily 1-3/hr
- Maidenhead ↔ **Marlow** via **Cookham** & **Bourne End**, daily 1-2/hr
- Twyford ↔ **Henley-on-Thames** via Wargrave & **Shiplake**, daily 1-2/hr

South Western Railway (**SWR**; 🖳 southwesternrailway.com)

- **Waterloo***, **Vauxhall**, Clapham Junction, Earlsfield, Wimbledon:
  ↔ **Hampton Court** via Raynes Park, New Malden & Surbiton, daily 2-3/hr
  ↔ **Shepperton** via Raynes Park, New Malden, Norbiton, **Kingston**, **Hampton Wick**, **Teddington**, Fulwell, **Hampton** & Sunbury, daily 1-2/hr
  ↔ **Strawberry Hill** via Raynes Park, New Malden, Norbiton, **Kingston**, **Hampton Wick** & **Teddington**, daily 1-2/hr
  ↔ Woking via Surbiton, Esher, **Walton-on-Thames** & Weybridge, daily 2-4/hr
- **Waterloo***, **Vauxhall**, **Queenstown Road**, Clapham Junction, Wandsworth Town, **Putney**, Barnes:
  ↔ **Kingston** via **Mortlake**, **Richmond**, St Margarets, Twickenham, **Strawberry Hill**, **Teddington** & **Hampton Wick**, daily 1-2/hr (Kingston Loop)
  ↔ **Barnes Bridge**, **Chiswick**, **Kew Bridge**, Brentford, **Syon Lane**, Isleworth & Hounslow, daily 1-2/hr, some services continue to Twickenham
  ↔ **Shepperton** via **Mortlake**, **Richmond**, St Margarets, Twickenham, **Strawberry Hill**, Fulwell, Hampton & Sunbury, peak hour services only 3/hr
  ↔ **Hounslow** via (*not Queenstown Road*), **Mortlake**, North Sheen, **Richmond**, St Margarets, **Twickenham**, daily 1-2/hr (Hounslow Loop)
  ↔ Weybridge via (*not Queenstown Road*), **Barnes Bridge**, **Chiswick**, **Kew Bridge**, Brentford, **Syon Lane**, Isleworth, Hounslow, **Staines**, Egham, Virginia Water & **Chertsey**, daily 1-2/hr
- **Waterloo***, **Vauxhall**, Clapham Junction to/from:
  ↔ **Windsor & Eton Riverside**, **Putney**, **Richmond**, **Twickenham**, **Staines**, Sunnymeads & **Datchet**, daily 2/hr
  ↔ **Reading** via **Richmond**, **Twickenham**, Feltham, **Staines**, Egham, Virginia Water, Ascot, Bracknell & Wokingham, daily 2/hr

Southeastern (🖳 southeasternrailway.co.uk)

- **Cannon Street***, **London Bridge**:
  ↔ Crayford via **Deptford**, **Greenwich**, **Charlton**, **Woolwich Dockyard**, **Woolwich Arsenal**, Abbey Wood & Erith, daily 2/hr
  ↔ circular route via Lewisham, Sidcup, Bexley, Crayford, Erith, Abbey Wood, **Woolwich Arsenal**, **Woolwich Dockyard**, **Charlton** & **Greenwich**, daily 1-2/hr

Southeastern *(cont'd)*
- **Charing Cross***, **Waterloo East**, **London Bridge**,
  - ↔ Dartford via Lewisham, Blackheath, **Charlton**, **Woolwich Dockyard**, **Woolwich Arsenal**, Abbey Wood & Erith, daily 2/hr
  - ↔ Gravesend via New Eltham, Sidcup, Crayford & Dartford, daily 2/hr

Southern (🖥 southernrailway.com)
- Victoria* ↔ Epsom Downs via **Battersea Park**, Clapham Junction, Balham, West Croydon & Sutton, daily 2/hr plus 2/hr to Sutton
- **London Bridge** ↔ Epsom via West Croydon & Sutton, Mon-Sat 2/hr

Chiltern Railway (🖥 www.chilternrailways.co.uk)
- Marylebone* ↔ **Oxford** via High Wycombe, daily 1-2/hr

Cross Country (🖥 crosscountrytrains.co.uk)
- Manchester Piccadilly to **Reading** via Birmingham, Banbury & **Oxford**, daily 1/hr

Thameslink Railway (🖥 thameslinkrailway.com)
- Bedford ↔ Brighton via Luton, Luton Airport Parkway, West Hampstead Thameslink, St Pancras International, Farringdon, **Blackfriars**, **London Bridge** (some services), East Croydon, Gatwick Airport & Haywards Heath, Mon-Sat 1-2/hr, Sun 12/day
- Luton ↔ Rainham (Kent) via Luton Airport Parkway, West Hampstead Thameslink, St Pancras International, Farringdon, City Thameslink, **Blackfriars***, **London Bridge**, Deptford, **Greenwich**, **Charlton** & **Woolwich Arsenal**, Mon-Sat 1-2/hr, Sun St Pancras International to Rainham only 2/hr

c2c (🖥 c2c-online.co.uk)
- Fenchurch Street* to Shoeburyness via **Limehouse**, daily 2-4/hr

Tfl Rail (🖥 tfl.gov.uk/modes/tfl-rail) (see also box on p52)
- London Paddington ↔ **Reading** via Ealing Broadway, Hayes & Harlington, West Drayton, Slough, Taplow & **Maidenhead**, daily 1-3/hr

London Overground (🖥 tfl.gov.uk/modes/london-overground/)
- Highbury & Islington ↔ Crystal Palace/West Croydon via Dalston Junction, Shadwell, **Wapping**, **Rotherhithe**, Canada Water & Surrey Quays, Mon-Sat 3/hr (2/hr to West Croydon), Sun 2/hr (1/hr to West Croydon)
- Dalston Junction ↔ Clapham Junction via **Wapping**, **Rotherhithe**, Canada Water Surrey Quays & Wandsworth Road, daily 1-2/hr
- Clapham Junction ↔ Stratford via **Imperial Wharf**, daily 3-4/hr
- **Richmond** ↔ Stratford via **Kew Gardens** & Willesden Junction, daily 3-4/hr

Docklands Light Railway (**DLR**; 🖥 tfl.gov.uk/modes/dlr)
- Stratford International ↔ **Woolwich Arsenal** via Canning Town & London City Airport, daily approx 6/hr
- Bank ↔ **Woolwich Arsenal** via **Limehouse**, Canning Town & London City Airport, daily approx 6/hr
- Bank ↔ Lewisham via **Limehouse**, **Canary Wharf**, **Island Gardens**, **Cutty Sark for Maritime Greenwich** & Greenwich, daily approx 6/hr

NOTES Not all stops are listed and only the main services are included

* Paddington = London Paddington; Waterloo = London Waterloo; Victoria = London Victoria, Charing Cross = London Charing Cross, Waterloo East = London Waterloo East, Blackfriars = London Blackfriars, Cannon St = London Cannon St

PLANNING YOUR WALK

PLANNING YOUR WALK

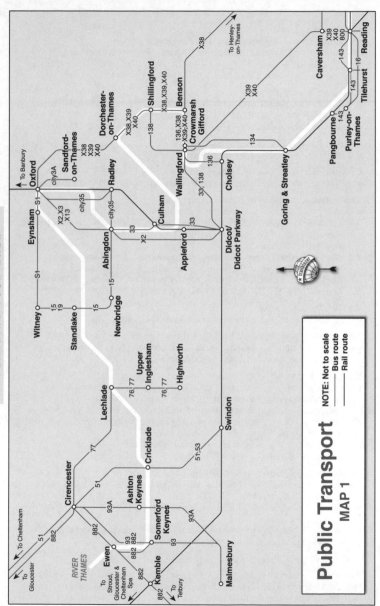

Public Transport
MAP 1

NOTE: Not to scale
— Bus route
— Rail route

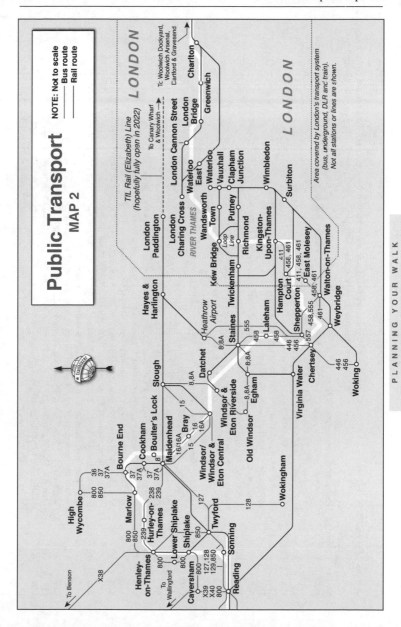

PLANNING YOUR WALK

☐ BUS SERVICES & OPERATORS

Note: not all stops are listed and a few limited frequency services are not listed here but mentioned only in the route guide section under the relevant village/town

No	Operator	Route and frequency details
882	PC	Gloucester to Tetbury via Cirencester & **Kemble**, Mon-Fri 7/day plus 1/day from Cirencester stopping at **Somerford Keynes** (school days only) & **Ewen**; Sat 3/day
93	CS	Malmesbury to Cirencester via **Somerford Keynes**, Mon-Sat 3/day
93A	CS	Malmesbury to Cirencester via **Ashton Keynes**, Mon-Sat 1/day
51	SC	Cheltenham to Swindon via Cirencester & **Cricklade**, Mon-Sat 1/hr, Sun 5/day
53	SC	Swindon to **Cricklade**, Mon-Sat 7/day
76	SC	**Lechlade** to Highworth via **Upper Inglesham** & Fairford, Mon-Fri 2/day, Sat 1/day from Cirencester
77	SC	Cirencester to Highworth via **Lechlade** & **Upper Inglesham**, Mon-Fri 5/day, Sat 3/day
S1	SC	Witney to **Oxford** via North Hinksey & **Eynsham**, Mon-Sat 4/hr, Sun 3/hr
15	SC	Witney to Abingdon via **Standlake** & **Newbridge**, Mon-Sat 5/day
19	SC	Witney to Carterton via **Standlake** & Aston, Mon-Sat 8/day
city 3A	SC/OB	**Oxford** to Sandford-on-Thames, Mon-Sat 2/hr (Stagecoach & Oxford Bus Company each provide an hourly service)
X3/X13	OB	**Oxford** to **Abingdon**, Mon-Fri 6/hr
city 35	OB	**Oxford** to Abingdon via Kennington & **Radley**, Mon-Sat 3/hr, Sun 2/hr
X2	TT	**Oxford** to Didcot Parkway via **Abingdon**, Mon-Sat 3/hr, Sun 2/hr
33	TT	**Abingdon** to **Wallingford** via Culham, Sutton Courtenay & Didcot Parkway, daily 1/hr
X38	TT	(River Rapids) **Oxford** to **Henley-on-Thames** via Nuneham Courtenay, Berinsfield Layby (for **Dorchester-on-Thames**), Shillingford, Benson, Crowmarsh **Gifford** & **Wallingford**, daily 1/hr
X39	TT	(River Rapids) **Oxford** to **Reading** via Nuneham Courtenay, Berinsfield Layby (for **Dorchester-on-Thames**), Shillingford, Benson, Crowmarsh, **Wallingford** & **Caversham**, Mon-Sat 1/hr
X40	TT	(River Rapids) **Oxford** to **Reading** via Nuneham Courtenay, Berinsfield Layby (for **Dorchester-on-Thames**), Shillingford, Benson, Crowmarsh, **Wallingford**, Woodcote & **Caversham**, daily 1/hr
136	TT	Benson to Cholsey via Crowmarsh **Gifford** & **Wallingford**, Mon-Sat 1/hr
143	TT	Pangbourne to Reading via **Purley on Thames** & Kentwood Circle for **Tilehurst station**, Mon-Sat 4-5/day
134	GF	Goring to **Wallingford** via Cleve, South Stoke, North Stoke & Crowmarsh **Gifford**, Mon-Fri 3-4/day
138	GF	**Wallingford** to **Shillingford**, Mon, Wed & Fri 3/day, Tue 2/day, Mon 1/day continues to **Didcot Parkway**
16	RB	**Purley-on-Thames** to central **Reading** via & Kentwood Circle for **Tilehurst station**, Mon-Sat 3/hr, Sun 2/hr

800	AB	Reading to High Wycombe via Caversham, Shiplake, Lower Shiplake, Henley-on-Thames, daily 1-2/hr
850	AB	Reading to High Wycombe via Sonning, Twyford, Wargrave, Henley-on-Thames & Marlow, Mon-Sat 1/hr
127	CB	Maidenhead to Reading via Twyford & Sonning, Sat 4/day plus 1/day to Twyford
128	TV	Wokingham to Reading via Twyford & Sonning, Mon-Fri 8/day, Sat 6/day
129	TV	Twyford to Reading via Sonning, Mon-Fri 5/day
238	CB	Maidenhead to Cookham Dean via Hurley-on-Thames & Bisham, Tue & Thur 3/day
239	CB	Maidenhead to Hurley-on-Thames, Mon-Fri 5/day (on Mon, Wed & Fri 3/day continue to Henley), Maidenhead to Henley via Hurley, Sat 2/day
36	Crl	High Wycombe to Bourne End, Mon-Sat 2/hr
37/37A	AB	High Wycombe to Maidenhead via Bourne End & Cookham, Mon-Sat 1/hr, Sun 1/hr to Bourne End
8	CB	Maidenhead to Boulter's Lock, Mon-Sat 11/day
15	CB	Maidenhead to Slough via Dorney, Eton Wick & Eton, Mon-Sat 4/day plus to Eton Wick 1/day
16/16A	CB	Maidenhead to Windsor via Bray & Dedworth, daily approx 1/hr
8/8A	FB	Slough to Heathrow Airport Terminal 5 via Windsor, Old Windsor, Egham & Staines, Mon-Fri 2/hr, Sat & Sun 1/hr
458	DB	Staines to Kingston via Laleham, Shepperton & Walton-on-Thames, daily 1/hr plus Mon-Sat 1/hr to Walton-on-Thames
446	WB	Woking to Staines via Chertsey, Mon-Sat 1/hr plus Mon-Fri 1/hr to Chertsey
456	FA	Woking to Staines via West Byfleet, Addlestone & Chertsey, Mon-Sat 1/hr
555	DB	Heathrow Airport to Whiteley Village via Ashford, Sunbury, Shepperton, Walton-on-Thames & Hersham, daily 1/hr
557	DB	Addlestone to Sunbury via Chertsey, Shepperton & Upper Halliford, Mon-Sat 1/hr
461	AS	Addlestone to Kingston via Walton-on-Thames, East Molesey, Hampton Court & Hampton Wick, Mon-Sat 2/hr
411	LU	West Molesey to Kingston via East Molesey & Hampton Court, Mon-Sat 3-4/hr, Sun 1-2/hr

Operator contact details: (some operators are part of a group so have the same phone number)
PC (Pulham's Coaches; ☎ 01451-820369, 🖳 pulhamscoaches.com); CS (Coachstyle; ☎ 01249-782224, 🖳 www.coachstyle.ltd.uk);
SC (Stagecoach; ☎ 01865-772250, 🖳 stagecoachbus.com); OB (Oxford Bus Company; ☎ 01865-785400, 🖳 city.oxfordbus.co.uk);
TT (Thames Travel; ☎ 01865-785400, 🖳 www.thames-travel.co.uk); GF (Going Forward Buses; ☎ 07484 605888, 🖳 goingforwardbuses
.com); RB (Reading Buses; ☎ 0118-959 4000, 🖳 reading-buses.co.uk); AB (Arriva in Beds & Bucks; ☎ 0344 800 4411, 🖳
arrivabus.co.uk); CB (Courtney Buses; ☎ 0118-973 3486, 🖳 courtneybuses.com); TV (Thames Valley Buses; ☎ 0118-973 3486, 🖳 thames
valleybuses.com); Crl (Carousel; ☎ 01494-450151, 🖳 carouselbuses.co.uk); FB (First Bus; firstbus.co.uk/berkshire-thames-valley); WB
(White Bus; ☎ 01344-882612, 🖳 whitebus.co.uk); FA (Falcon Buses; ☎ 01932-787752, 🖳 falconbuses.co.uk); DB (Diamond Buses; ☎
01784-425621, 🖳 www.diamondbuses.com/south-east); LU (London United; ☎ 020-8400 6665, 🖳 ratpdevlondon.com).

2

THE ENVIRONMENT & NATURE

Flora and fauna

The following is not in any way a comprehensive guide – if it were, you would not have room for anything else in your rucksack – but merely a brief rundown of the more commonly seen flora and fauna on the trail, together with some of the rarer and more spectacular species.

BIRDS

A common occurrence – especially while walking in the upper Thames – is the sudden scattering of waterfowl, shocked into action by your unexpected appearance as you make your way along the bank. Whilst birds are almost omnipresent on the river it's also worth keeping your eyes on the trees which line the shore as well as on the skies above as there are plenty to be spotted there too.

Worth visiting as you pass is the new **bird hide** at Chimney Meadows Nature Reserve (see p97; 💻 bbowt.org.uk/nature-reserves/chimney-meadows); it is 10 metres from the path.

Waterfowl

Most of the waterfowl happily mingle and they are generally quite easy to identify. Needing no introduction, it's highly likely that the first bird you'll see gracefully gliding on the water is a **mute swan** (*Cygnus olor*, see Swan Upping on p16). Be wary of getting too close, especially if they have cygnets in tow. If you do invade their territory you'll soon discover that they're not actually mute at all as they'll warn you off with a threatening hiss. Often to be seen socialising with the swans are **mallard** (*Anas platyrhynchos*) – say the word 'duck' and it's a mallard most people immediately envisage with their shimmering green heads – and **tufted duck** (*Aythya fuligula*). The commonest diving duck, the tuft on the back of their heads (which gives them their name), along with their grey black-tipped bill, makes them easily identifiable. Tufted ducks are especially prevalent in winter.

Never ones to shy away from any form of riverborne congregation are **Canada geese** (*Branta canadensis*). Introduced to the estates of wealthy landowners approximately 300 years ago, the population has exploded since and they're now the most common goose in southern Britain. Their large brown bodies, black necks and distinctive white 'chinstraps' make them easy to spot. You'll also see the **greylag goose** (*Anser anser*), sometimes mixed in with the flocks of Canada geese. The greylag is the ancestor of the domestic goose. A more recent introduction is the pinkish-brown **Egyptian goose** (*Alopochen aegyptica*).

Likely to be spotted about the river during the winter months are **black-headed gull** (*Larus ridibundus*) and **pochard** (*Aythya ferina*), while other birds which may make an appearance include the **wigeon** (*Anas penelope*) – brown with a white belly and small pale blue-grey bill – and the **long-tailed duck** (*Clangula hyemalis*). A small sea duck, it's unusual for them to make a foray inland but they might be seen on the Thames. Another rare visitor – it is reckoned that fewer than 100 make the trip between November and March each year from Scandinavia and Siberia – is the **smew** (*Mergus albellus*). The male is distinguishable by its black 'bandit' mask whilst the females have red heads.

Waders observed along the river include the **snipe** (*Gallinago gallinago*), with its extremely long and straight bill, the larger **curlew** (*Numenius arquata*), and the **lapwing** (*Vanellus vanellus*). Sightings of all of these are rather uncommon but one bird you'll definitely spot, thanks in part to its tendency to stand motionless and pose on riverbanks and mooring posts, watching for prey, is the **grey heron** (*Ardea cinerea*). Related to it, but much rarer, is the **bittern** (*Botaurus stellaris*); a type of heron, by 1997 they were nearly extinct but major conservation efforts since mean that there are estimated to be about 80 breeding males in England. On a still night the males' distinctive 'booming' mating call can be heard for up to five kilometres – meaning you're much more likely to hear it than see it.

Other birds you may see enjoying the river are: **moorhen** (*Gallinula chloropus*), comparable in size to a pigeon but black in colour and with a yellow-tipped red bill and long legs; similarly sized and shaped **coots** (*Fulica atra*), which are all black but for their white bill; the long thin neck and pinkish bills of the **great-crested grebe** (*Podiceps cristatus*); **cormorant** (*Phalacrocorax carbo*), which are dark-coloured with a hook-tipped bill; and, during summer, the **common tern** (*Sterna hirundo*).

In the woods and trees

A sure sign of spring and easily identifiable by its song is the **cuckoo** (*Cuculus canorus*), which will often give your journey along the river's upper reaches a musical accompaniment. Also resident on the Thames are: Britain's largest woodpecker, the **green woodpecker** (*Picus viridius*), which has a red head, black 'moustache' and a greenish-yellow lower back; and the commonest, the black, white and red **great spotted woodpecker** (*Dendrocopos major*).

You may also see **swallows** (*Hirundo rustica*); their smaller relative, the **sand martin** (*Riparia riparia*), which is usually one of the earliest summer visitors to arrive; and Britain's most exotically coloured bird, the **kingfisher** (*Alcedonatthis*). They can be hard to spot, but with their iridescent blue colouring they're unmistakable once you do. Introduced from Asia and more commonly seen the closer you get to London are **ring-necked parakeets**

(*Psittacula krameri*). Britain's only parrot is green, certainly offering competition to the kingfisher in the colour stakes. First recorded in the wild in 1969, you're most likely to see them perched in a tree top or hear their squawk (*kree, kree, kree, kree*); we saw our first one in Runnymede, but they're pretty ubiquitous east from there to Richmond and beyond. Indeed, they have become so common that one pub, The Anglers at Walton (see p196), now has one on one of its signs – a sure indication that they've become part of the landscape and fabric of this part of the country.

Common birds that are generally resident in Britain and which you should see on your walk include **blue tits** (*Cyanistes caeruleus*), the slightly larger but no less colourful **great tit** (*Parus major*) and the rarer – at least along the river – **long-tailed tit** (*Aegithalos caudatus*).

Near to the water you may spot the sedentary **reed bunting** (*Emberiza schoeniclus*), clinging to a branch or singing from the top of a bush, or the **grey wagtail** (*Motacilla cinerea*), which breeds along tree-lined sections of the river and commonly nests close to weirs.

A relatively uncommon summer visitor to the meadows is the **yellow wagtail** (*Motacilla flava*), identifiable by its bright yellow underparts and brownish wings, whilst the black and white **pied wagtail** (*Motacilla alba*) also nests near water but is equally associated, especially in winter, with urban areas.

Other birds often spotted include Britain's smallest, the **goldcrest** (*Regulus regulus*), the **goldfinch** (*Carduelis carduelis*), the **bullfinch** (*Pyrrhula pyrrhula*), usually seen in woodland, as well as the sparrow-like **dunnock** (*Prunella modularis*), **skylark** (*Alauda arvenis*), **house sparrow** (*Passer domesticus*), and of course, the very common **robin** (*Erithacus rubecula*) and **blackbird** (*Turdus merula*). Then there are the **warblers**.

Sometimes spotted on their summer vacation are **blackcap** (*Sylvia atricapilla*), as well as the **garden** (*Sylvia borin*), **reed** (*Acrocephalus scirpaceus*) and **sedge warblers** (*Acrocephalus schoenobaenus*). You may also hear **chiffchaff** (*Phylloscopus collybita*), their olive-green feathers identifying them as they stand on branches and rather arrogantly sing their own names ... *chiff chaff chiff chaff chiff chaff* ... as if boasting of their successful migration from the Mediterranean or West Africa.

Birds of prey

One bird which today you'll probably see hunting over the farmland, woodland and meadows which line the river – but which just 25 years ago you most definitely wouldn't – is the **red kite** (*Milvus milvus*). Persecuted almost to the point of extinction by the start of the 20th century, young birds from Spain and Sweden were reintroduced to parts of England in 1989, since when numbers have been increasing exponentially; see also box on p161.

Similar in size to the **buzzard** (*Buteo buteo*), the kites are distinguishable by their 'scooped' tail and more graceful, 'shapely' silhouette than the rather clumsy, galumphing buzzard. They are also of a more russet/orange colour compared to the rather dull brown plumage of the buzzard – though it's doubtful you'll be able to distinguish this while they are in flight.

Above, clockwise from top left: Grey heron (©AU), red kite, chaffinch, reed bunting, coot, skylark, pied wagtail, black-headed gull (©BT).

Above, clockwise from top left: Pochard (©BT), mallard (©HS), Egyptian geese (©HS), family of greylag geese (©WA), Canada goose (©HS), curlew (©BT).

Himalayan Balsam
Impatiens glandulifera

Red Admiral butterfly (*Vanessa atalanta*) on
Hemp Agrimony (*Eupatorium cannabinum*)

Common Vetch
Vicia sativa

Herb-Robert
Geranium robertianum

Red Campion
Silene dioica

Lousewort
Pedicularis sylvatica

Meadow Cranesbill
Geranium pratense

Common Dog Violet
Viola riviniana

Common Knapweed
Centaurea nigra

Common Centaury
Centaurium erythraea

Old Man's Beard
Clematis vitalba

Common Ragwort
Senecio jacobaea

Yarrow
Achillea millefolium

Hogweed
Heracleum sphondylium

Gorse
Ulex europaeus

Meadow Buttercup
Ranunculus acris

Marsh Marigold (Kingcup)
Caltha palustris

Bird's-foot trefoil
Lotus corniculatus

St John's Wort
Hypericum perforatum

Tormentil
Potentilla erecta

Primrose
Primula vulgaris

Cowslip
Primula veris

Honeysuckle
Lonicera periclymemum

Harebell
Campanula rotundifolia

Foxglove
Digitalis purpurea

Rosebay Willowherb
Epilobium angustifolium

Rowan (tree)
Sorbus aucuparia

Dog Rose
Rosa canina

Forget-me-not
Myosotis arvensis

Scarlet Pimpernel
Anagallis arvensis

Self-heal
Prunella vulgaris

Germander Speedwell
Veronica chamaedrys

Ramsons (Wild Garlic)
Allium ursinum

Bluebell
Hyacinthoides non-scripta

Ox-eye Daisy
Leucanthemum vulgare

Peacock
Inachis io

Small Tortoiseshell
Aglais urticae

Common Blue
Polyommatus icarus

Large Garden/Cabbage White
Pieris brassicae

Small Heath
*Coenonympha
pamphilus*

Red
Admiral
Vanessa atalanta

Painted Lady
Cynthia cadui

Small Garden/Cabbage White
Pieris rapae

Small Copper
Lycaena phlaeas

Meadow
Brown
Maniola jurtina

Brimstone
*Gonepteryx
rhamni*

Smaller birds of prey you may spot standing on telephone wires or swooping down on their unexpecting prey include **kestrels** (*Falco tinnunculus*). There's also a chance, if wandering along in the evening, that you'll see – or, at least hear the distinctive 'snoring' or screeching calls of – a **barn owl** (*Tyto alba*).

BUTTERFLIES

One of the most pleasant sights whilst walking anywhere in the spring and summer is that of the butterfly which will suddenly appear, flitting about in the air, appearing to dance alongside you as you pace along the trail.

The meadows and waterside pathways of the Thames Path are rich in many species. You'll frequently see the **common** (*Polyommatus icarus*) and **adonis blue** (*Polyommatus bellargus*), the **large** and **small white** (*Pieris brassicae/Pieris rapae*), **small copper** (*Lycaena phlaeas*), **meadow brown** (*Maniola jurtina*) and, in early summer only, the **orange tip** (*Anthocharis cardamines*). These are all relatively easy to distinguish thanks to their descriptive names.

Others commonly spotted but without such self-explanatory monikers include the striking lemon-yellow **brimstone** (*Gonepteryx rhamni*), the **gatekeeper** (*Pyronia tithonus*), which has orange wings rimmed with brown, the light-brown **small heath** (*Coenonympha pamphilus*) and the migrant **painted lady** (*Cynthia cardui*), the multicoloured wings of which will have carried it approximately 800 miles from North Africa; meaning, you'd imagine, that you're more likely to see it resting on a leaf, and probably asleep.

WILD FLOWERS AND SHRUBS

The river's waters are vital to the life of the local flora, of course, and many plants and wild flowers thrive along the banks and in the meadows lining the Thames.

By the river

Close to the water you're likely to come across an array of colours: **yellow iris** (*Iris pseudacorus*), the pink flowers of the **flowering rush** (*Butomus*), the lilac of the **water violet** (*Hottonia palustris*), an abundance of white-flowered **water crowfoot** (*Ranunculus aquatilis*) – and all watched over by **purple loosestrife** (*Lythrum salicaria*), which can grow up to 1.5m tall. You may also see **hemp-agrimony** (*Eupatorium cannabinum*), the reddish stem of which displays small dull pink flowers; whilst below them reside the dark green kidney-shaped leaves of **marsh-marigold** (*Caltha palustris*); the blue petals of **water forget-me-nots** (*Myosotis scorpioides*) and the floating oval leaves of **yellow water-lilies** (*Nymphaea lutea*), a good sign of nutrient-rich water.

Finally, if walking between June and October, perhaps the most common plant you'll see are the pink flowers of the non-native **Himalayan balsam** (*Impatiens glandulifera*) dotted along the bank.

Meadows and woodland

Synonymous with spring and the start of the walking season are **bluebells** (*Hyacinthoides non-scripta*), the bluish-purple bell-shaped flowers which carpet the woodland and hedgerows about the Thames. Appearing at a similar time of year are **cowslips** (*Primula veris*), **cuckooflower** (*Cardamine pratensis*), aka Lady's Smock, and **meadow buttercups** (*Ranunculus acris*); the latter can grow up to one metre in height.

By June the pinkish-lilac petals of the **common valerian** (*Valeriana officinalis*) should be on display in the meadows, as should the yellow-centred white-petalled **oxeye daisies** (*Leucanthemum vulgare*), the purple florets of the **common** (*Centaurea nigra*) and **greater knapweed** (*Centaurea scabiosa*), **bird's foot trefoil** (*Lotus corniculatus*), the tall and fragrant **meadowsweet** (*Filipendula ulmaria*), the golden-yellow **lady's bedstraw** (*Galium verum*), and the highly poisonous bright yellow flowers of the invasive **common ragwort** (*Senecio jacobaea*), which, sensibly avoided by grazing animals, thrives, particularly in pastures.

A relatively rare wild flower which is particularly exciting to see is the **purple snakeshead fritillary** (*Fritillaria meleagris*); this can be found carpeting North Meadow NNR (Map 5), Iffley Meadows (Map 20) and Clifton Meadow (Map 25) in April. A plant you're unlikely to see any further north than the

Thames is the **summer snowflake** (*Leucojum aestivum*), which can be spotted amongst the meadows and along the banks from April; complimenting the two, you may also come across **yellow meadow vetchling** (*Lathyrus pratensis*), **red clover** (*Trifolium pratense*), **adder's tongue fern** (*Ophioglossum*), and a range of **orchids** such as the pink **southern marsh** (*Dactylorhiza praetermissa*) and **pyramidal orchids** (*Anacamptis pyramidalis*). Especially worth looking out for is the **bee orchid** (*Ophrys apifera*), the flowers of which are a mixture of pink, maroon, yellow and green; a distinctive colour scheme that is believed to attract a particular species of bee (*Andrena hattorfiana*) that pollinates the flowers.

TREES

The tree most associated with the river is the **willow** (*Salix*) and a number of varieties thrive along the banks of the Thames. The most easily identified is the **weeping willow** (*Salix x sepulcralis*), the leaves of which you'll often find yourself

Left: London plane tree, Fulham (©AU)

wandering beneath as they hang lazily over the river. Other varieties encountered include the **white willow** (*Salix alba*), which can be easily identified by its long and narrow leaves which taper to curled tips and are hairy underneath, and the **crack willow** (*Salix fragilis*), with its bright green leaves.

As well as **black poplar** (*Populus nigra*), **silver birch** (*Betula pendula*) and **ash** (*Fraxinus excelsior*) – the only native tree of the olive family – you may also come across **whitebeam** (*Sorbus aria*) and **elder** (*Sambucus nigra*) along the banks. **Hawthorns** (*Crategus monogyna*) are common as, especially along the Chiltern stretch of the river, are **beech** (*Fagus sylvatica*). If walking in August you may see the tiny bright scarlet fruits of the **rowan** (*Sorbus aucuparia*) tree. And in London you'll see numerous London plane trees (see below).

MAMMALS

The character of Ratty in *The Wind in the Willows* (see box p49) is based on a **water vole** (*Arvicola terrestris*), and along with the other mammalian heroes and villains of Kenneth Grahame's tale, **badgers** (*Meles meles*), **moles** (*Talpa europaea*), **stoats** (*Mustela ermine*) and **weasels** (*Mustela nivalis*), all – with a little luck – can still be seen in the vicinity of the river.

The 'plop' of the water vole diving into the Thames nearly became a thing of the past as they suffered a devastating drop in population due to the arrival in the English countryside of the **American mink** (*Neovison vison*), which had successfully adapted to living in the wild after escaping from fur farms. Unfortunately, the mink not only hunts water voles but is small enough to slip inside their burrows, thus being able to wipe out an entire river's population in a matter of months. The consequences of the mink's arrival made the survival and protection of **otters** (*Lutra lutra*) along the Thames all the more important as they are believed to hunt mink. Shy and nocturnal, so spotting an otter is unlikely but not impossible, thanks in large part to the huge conservation efforts to reintroduce them following a steep decline in their numbers during the middle of the

---

❏ THE CAPITAL'S GENTLE GIANTS – THE LONDON PLANE TREE

It's a little-known fact that the London plane (*Platanus x Hispanica,* photo opposite) is the most common tree in the capital. Most easily distinguished by its olive, grey, cream and brown bark that forms a camouflage-like pattern on the tree, the plane is particularly common in London parks, and you'll walk through avenues of them in Wandsworth and Battersea parks (on the Thames's southern side) as well as Bishop's Park in Fulham (on the northern side).

Believed to be a hybrid between the American sycamore and the Oriental plane, the London plane is thought to have first appeared in the renowned nursery of John Tradescant the Younger, in Vauxhall, in the 17th century. But it really found popularity in the 18th and 19th centuries thanks to the unique property of its bark. London at the time was filled with soot and smog as the Industrial Revolution reached its peak, and many trees were unable to cope with the pollution. The plane tree, however, could shed large patches of its bark when it became too clogged with soot – thereby 'cleansing' itself of pollutants.

THE ENVIRONMENT & NATURE

20th century. While still seldom spotted, their distinctive pad and toe prints are sometimes seen in the mud and their musk-scented droppings are occasionally seen left on prominent rocks to mark their territory. The shells of depressed river mussels (*Pseudanodonta complanata*) are often found on the riverbank, particularly around Wolvercote, which is perfect for otters as they love them.

Usually measuring 60-90 centimetres in length, the otter would be the largest mammal living by the Thames if it weren't for the introduction in 2005 of six **Eurasian beaver** (*Castor fiber*) to the lake at Lower Mill Estate in Gloucestershire (see Map 3, p83). Likely to be watching the beaver's gnawing with trepidation from the branches above, a number of **bat** species frequent the habitat about the river, including the **soprano pipistrelle** (*Pipistrellus pygmaeus*), **Natterer's bat** (*Myotis nattereri*), and **Daubentons's bat** (*Myotis daubentonii*). This last will fly along the surface of the river foraging for food before using their webbed feet to catch prey.

Back on all fours, common mammals that are more likely to be encountered include **foxes** (*Vulpes vulpes*), **hares** (*Lepus europaeus*), **hedgehogs** (*Erinaceus europaeus*), **grey squirrels** (*Sciurus carolinensis*), **rabbits** (*Oryctolagus cuniculus*) and any number of species of **mice**, **voles** and **shrews**.

Aquatic mammals

Whales generally stick to deeper sea water than in the Thames but in recent years there have been some sightings: most have only reached the eastern parts of the Thames (Greenhithe and Gravesend) but in January 2006 a female **bottle-nosed whale** (*Hyperoodon ampullatus*) was seen swimming in the river as far upstream as Chelsea; sadly attempts to rescue the whale were unsuccessful. In May 2021 a baby **minke whale** (*Balaenoptera*) was seen near Barnes Bridge but then made it as far as Richmond Lock where it got stuck; after being freed it moved on to Teddington Lock where it got trapped again and as a result was put down.

Though you're extremely unlikely to see whales from the banks of the London Thames, there is a slim chance of catching a glimpse of a **harbour porpoise** (*Phocoena phocoena*). Also occasionally spotted are **grey seal** (*Halichoerus grypus*), **harbour seal** (*Phoca vitulina*) and **bottlenose dolphins** (*Tursiops truncatus*).

INSECTS

Of course, while you walk there is another world in existence all about you of which you'll largely be oblivious: that of the insect. Whizzing past your ears will be the **dragonfly** (*Anisoptera*) and the smaller **damselfly** (*Zygoptera*), the brilliant-green **banded demoiselle** (*Calopteryx splendens*) and the rare and relatively slow-flying **club-tailed dragonfly** (*Gomphus vulgatissimus*).

Also airborne are the splendidly named **marmalade hoverfly** (*Episyrphus balteatus*), the amber-winged **brown hawker** (*Aeshna grandis*), **mayfly** (*Ephemeroptera*) and the ubiquitous **bees** and **wasps**. Meanwhile, on the ground you may come across one of the 70 species of **longhorn beetle** (*Cerambycidae*) native to Britain, the yellow and black **caterpillar** of the **Cinnabar moth** (*Tyria jacobaeae*) and **yellow meadow ants** (*Lasius flavus*).

The singing of grasshoppers and crickets is ubiquitous in summer; those you'll possibly see springing about in the grass include **meadow grasshoppers** (*Chorthippus parallelus*), **field grasshoppers** (*Chorthippus brunneus*) and **Roesel's bush-crickets** (*Metrioptera roeseli*).

REPTILES AND AMPHIBIANS

The amphibians you're most likely to come across during the day are **frogs** (*Rana temporaria*), whilst at dusk **toads** (*Bufo bufo*) become more conspicuous.

The only poisonous snake in Britain is the **adder** (*Vipera berus*). They pose very little risk to walkers – indeed, you should consider yourself extremely fortunate to see one, providing you're a safe distance away, of course. They bite only when provoked, preferring to hide instead. The venom is designed to kill small mammals such as mice, voles and shrews, so deaths in humans are very rare but a bite can be extremely unpleasant and occasionally dangerous to children or the elderly. You are most likely to encounter them in spring when they come out of hibernation and during the summer when pregnant females warm themselves in the sun. They are easily identified by the striking zigzag pattern on their back. Should you encounter one, enjoy it but leave it be.

Locks are the perfect habitat for **grass snakes** (*Natrix natrix*) and you may see one swimming in the river. They're harmless but if you touch them it's likely to leave a nasty smell on your hand, the foul odour being their choice of defence rather than venom.

A treat for **gastropod** enthusiasts will be Kew Riverside Park Snail Reserve (Map 57, p212), home to the **two-lipped door snail** (*Balea biplicata*).

FISH

Unless you've a trained eye, it's unlikely you'll be able to identify many of the fish which exist in the Thames from the quick glimpse that you may catch of them as they swim by. Indeed, you're probably more likely to experience one on a plate than in the river. The following, however, are there beneath the surface and thrive in today's cleaner Thames (see box on p71).

Smaller fish (usually 15-30cm) include **ruffe** (*Gymnocephalus cernua*), **gudgeon** (*Gobio gobio*), **dace** (*Leuciscus leuciscus*), **roach** (*Rutilus rutilus*), **grayling** (*Thymallus thymallus*), **rudd** (*Scardinius erythrophthalmus*), **perch** (*Perca fluviatilis*), **bullhead** (*Cottus gobio*), and the jawless **brook lamprey** (*Lampetra planeri*).

Common medium-sized fish (usually 30-60cm) include **chub** (*Squalius cephalus*), **bream** (*Abramis brama*), **tench** (*Tinca tinca*), **barbel** (*Barbus barbus*), **brown trout** (*Salmo trutta*) and **carp** (*Cyprinus carpio*).

Larger fish (usually 60cm or above) to frequent the river include **salmon** (*Salmo salar*), **pike** (*Esox lucius*) and **eel** (*Anguilla anguilla*), some of the latter growing up to two metres long. The crown, however, for the largest freshwater fish to frolic in the river's waters goes to the **Wels catfish** (*Silurus glanis*), which can be anything between one and three metres in length.

THE ENVIRONMENT & NATURE

MINIMUM IMPACT & OUTDOOR SAFETY

ENVIRONMENTAL IMPACT

A walking holiday in itself is an environmentally friendly approach to tourism. The following are some ideas on how you can go a few steps further in helping to minimise your impact on the environment while walking the Thames Path.

Use public transport whenever possible
Public transport along the Thames Path is readily available (though it can be a little infrequent at times along the upper reaches). Public transport is always preferable to using private cars as it benefits everyone: visitors, locals and the environment.

Never leave litter
'Pack it in, pack it out'. Leaving litter is antisocial so carry a degradable plastic bag for all your rubbish, organic or otherwise (you could even pick up other people's too) and pop it in the first bin you see. Or better still, reduce the amount of litter you take with you by getting rid of packaging in advance.
● **Is it OK if it's biodegradable?** Not really. Apple cores, banana skins, orange peel and the like are unsightly, encourage flies, ants and wasps and ruin a picnic spot for others; they can also take months to decompose. In high-use areas such as the Thames Path either bury them or take them away with you.

Buy local
Look and ask for local produce to buy and eat. Not only does this cut down on the amount of pollution and congestion that the transportation of food creates (so-called 'food miles'), it also ensures that you are supporting local farmers and producers.

Erosion
● **Stay on the main trail** The effect of your footsteps may seem minuscule but when they're multiplied by several thousand walkers each year they become rather more significant. Avoid taking shortcuts, widening the trail or taking more than one path, especially across meadows and ploughed fields.
● **Consider walking out of season** Maximum disturbance by walkers coincides with the time of year when nature wants to do most of

its growth and repair. In high-use areas, like that along much of the Thames Path, the trail is often prevented from recovering.

Walking at less busy times eases this pressure while also generating year-round income for the local economy. Not only that but it may make the walk a more relaxing experience with fewer people on the path and less competition for accommodation.

Respect all flora and fauna

Care for all wildlife you come across along the path; it has as much right to be there as you. Tempting as it may be to pick wild flowers, leave them so the next

---

❑ THE ENVIRONMENT AND CONSERVATION

Throughout much of its history the Thames and its tributaries acted as natural sewers for the industrial and domestic waste created by the settlements which had sprung up alongside it. For generations, the river's natural cycle had dispersed this waste, aerating the waters before flushing them out on the tides. By the 18th century the population bulge in the Thames Valley (and especially in London) had overwhelmed the river's innate ability to self-heal and pollution had become endemic. In the early 19th century a dramatic decline in the amount of fish in the river (always a good indicator of a river's condition) was followed by four significant cholera epidemics in London (1832, 1849, 1854, 1865). Despite evidence that linked the 1854 epidemic with the city's water, it would take the Great Stink of 1858 (during which the smell seeped in through the windows of the House of Commons) before Parliament finally acted and sewage systems were constructed to divert the city's waste away from the metropolis and further out towards the sea. Even with such efforts, however, by the 1950s there were still 28 sewage works emptying into the Thames and much industrial waste continued to leak into the river. Levels of oxygen in the water were at an all-time low; the lower Thames was dying.

The closure of London's docks (see box on p239) along with increased investment and the application of higher water-quality standards have, since the 1960s, led to the natural life of the river going through something of a renaissance and today it is healthier than at any point in the past half-millennium. A good indicator of an unpolluted environment is the presence of otters (see p67), and their return to the river in around 2001 – along with the recent identification of over 125 species of fish – is testament to the ongoing conservation efforts of the organisations responsible for the enduring health of the River Thames. A feature of the path in the London area now is the construction work for the **Thames Tideway Tunnel** (🖳 www.tideway.london), a 15-mile (25km) sewer being bored under the Thames to take the raw sewage (and excess rainfall) to sewage treatment works where it will be cleaned – thus meaning a much healthier river. Work is scheduled to finish in 2025.

Today, a variety of bodies watch over the river and its immediate environs. Legally responsible for taking care of the stretch between the source and Teddington is the **Environment Agency** (see box on p48), whilst the Thames in London is the responsibility of the **Port of London Authority** (🖳 pla.co.uk). Other organisations heavily involved in the river's upkeep include the **National Trust** (🖳 nationaltrust .org.uk) and **Natural England** (🖳 gov.uk/government/organisations/natural-england). The latter is responsible for managing the **National Nature Reserves** (NNRs) – such as North Meadow (p82) and Chimney Meadows (see p97) – and the many **Sites of Special Scientific Interest** (SSSIs) that exist within three miles of the Thames.

people who pass can enjoy them too. Don't break branches off trees. If you come across wildlife keep your distance and don't watch for too long. Your presence can cause considerable stress, particularly if the adults are with young, or in winter when the weather is harsh and food is scarce. Young animals are rarely abandoned. If you come across young birds keep away so that their mother can return.

The code of the outdoor loo

'Going' in the outdoors is a lost art worth reclaiming, for your sake and everyone else's. As more and more people discover the joys of the outdoors this is becoming an important issue. In some parts of the world where visitor pressure is higher than in Britain, walkers and climbers are required to pack out their excrement. This might one day be necessary here. Human faeces are not only offensive to our senses but, more importantly, can infect water sources.

● **Where to go** Wherever possible **use a toilet**. Public toilets are marked on the trail maps in this guide and you'll also find facilities in pubs, cafés, libraries and campsites along the path. Many pubs in London and other businesses have signed up to the 'Community Toilet Scheme' – this means they are happy for anyone to use their toilet facilities without making a purchase. There are also toilet (and water tap) facilities at some of the locks.

If you do have to go outdoors, avoid ruins which can otherwise be welcome shelter for other walkers, as well as sites of historic or archaeological interest, and choose a place that is at least **30 metres away from running water**. Use a stick or trowel to **dig a small hole** about 15cm (6") deep to bury your excrement. It decomposes quicker when in contact with the top layer of soil or leaf mould. Stirring loose soil into your deposit speeds up decomposition. Do not squash it under rocks as this slows down the composting process. If you have to use rocks to cover it make sure they are not in contact with your faeces.

● **Toilet paper and tampons** Toilet paper takes a long time to decompose whether buried or not. It is easily dug up by animals and may then blow into water sources or onto the path.

The best method for dealing with it is to **pack it out**. Put the used paper inside a paper bag which you then place inside a recyclable bag. Then simply empty the contents of the paper bag at the next toilet you come across and throw the bag away. If this is too much bother, light your used toilet paper and watch it burn until the flames are out – you don't want to start a wild fire. Pack out **tampons** and **sanitary towels**; they take years to decompose and may also be dug up and scattered about by animals.

ACCESS

Britain is a crowded island with few places where you can wander as you please. Most of the land is a patchwork of fields and agricultural land and the terrain through which much of the Thames Path flows, at least outside London, is no different. However, there are countless public rights of way, in addition to the Thames Path, that criss-cross the land.

Right to roam

The Countryside & Rights of Way Act 2000 (CRoW), or 'Right to Roam' as dubbed by walkers, came into effect in 2005 after a long campaign to allow greater public access to areas of countryside in England and Wales deemed to be uncultivated open country; this essentially means moorland, heathland, downland and upland areas. Some land is covered by restrictions (ie high-impact activities such as driving a vehicle, cycling and horse-riding are not permitted) and some land is excluded (such as gardens, parks and cultivated land). Full details are given on the Natural England website (see box on p71).

With more freedom in the countryside comes a need for more responsibility from the walker. Remember that wild open country is still the workplace of farmers and home to all sorts of wildlife. Have respect for both and avoid disturbing domestic and wild animals.

❏ THE COUNTRYSIDE CODE

Respect everyone
● Be considerate to those living and working in the countryside
● Leave gates and property as you find them
● Take special care on roads without pavements
● Follow local signs and keep to marked paths, even if they're muddy.

Protect the environment
● Take all your litter home
● Do not light fires
● Always keep dogs under control and in sight (see also p28 and pp255-6).
● Care for nature – do not cause damage or disturbance

Enjoy the outdoors
● Check your route and local conditions
● Follow advice and local signs
● Make no unnecessary noise

For more information visit: 🖥 www.gov
.uk/government/publications/the-coun
tryside-code

Outdoor health and safety

STAY HEALTHY

You will enjoy your walk more if you have a reasonable level of fitness. Carrying a pack for 5-7 hours a day is demanding and any preparation you have done beforehand will pay off.

Water

You need to drink lots of water while you're walking: 2-4 litres per day, depending on the weather. If you start to feel tired, lethargic or get a headache it may be that you are not drinking enough. Thirst is not a good indicator of when to drink; stop and have a drink every hour or two at the very least. A good indication of whether you are drinking enough is the colour of your urine – the lighter the better. If you are not needing to urinate much and/or your urine is dark yellow you need to increase your fluid intake.

Blisters

It's essential to try out new boots before embarking on your long trek. Make sure they're comfortable and once on the move try to avoid getting them wet on the inside and remove any small stones or twigs that get in the boot. Air and massage your feet at lunchtime, keep them clean, and change your socks regularly. As soon as you start to feel any hot spots developing, stop and apply a few strips of low-friction zinc oxide tape. Leave them on until the foot is pain free or the tape starts to come off. If you're walking continuously the chances are it won't get better – but it won't get worse so quickly either. If you know you have problems apply the tape pre-emptively. If you've left it too late and a blister has developed you should apply a plaster such as Compeed (or the slightly cheaper clone now made by Boots). Many walkers have Compeed to thank for enabling them to complete their walk. Popping a blister reduces the pressure but can lead to infection. If the skin is broken keep the area clean with antiseptic and cover with a non-adhesive dressing material held in place with tape.

Blister-avoiding strategies include rubbing the prone area with Vaseline or wearing a thin and a thick sock as well as adjusting the tension of your laces. All are ways of reducing rubbing and foot movement against the inside of the boot.

Hypothermia, hyperthermia and sunburn

Also known as **exposure**, **hypothermia** occurs when the body can't generate enough heat to maintain its normal temperature, usually as a result of being wet, cold, unprotected from the wind, tired and hungry. Hypothermia is easily avoided by wearing suitable clothing, carrying and consuming enough food and drink, being aware of the weather conditions and checking the morale of your companions. Early signs to watch for are feeling cold, tired and shivering involuntarily. If allowed to worsen, erratic behaviour, slurring of speech and poor co-ordination will become apparent and the victim can very soon progress into unconsciousness, followed by coma and death. Of course, on the Thames Path you're seldom far from civilisation and your first action should be to seek help or call the emergency services. But if for some reason this isn't possible, find some shelter as soon as possible and warm the victim up with a hot drink and some chocolate or other high-energy food. If possible give them another warm layer of clothing and allow them to rest until feeling better. Quickly get the victim out of wind and rain, improvising a shelter if necessary. Rapid restoration of bodily warmth is essential and best achieved by bare-skin contact: someone should get into the same sleeping bag as the patient, both having stripped to the bare essentials, placing any spare clothing under or over them to build up heat.

Not an ailment that you would normally associate with southern England, hyperthermia (heat exhaustion and heatstroke) is a serious problem nonetheless. Symptoms of **heat exhaustion** include thirst, fatigue, giddiness, a rapid pulse, raised body temperature, low urine output and, if not treated, delirium and finally a coma. The best cure is to drink plenty of water. **Heatstroke** is another matter altogether and even more serious. A high body temperature and an absence of sweating are early indications, followed by symptoms similar to hypothermia (see above) such as a lack of co-ordination, convulsions and coma. Death will follow if treatment is not given instantly. Sponge the victim down, wrap them in wet towels, fan them – and get help immediately.

Sunburn can happen, even in England, and even on overcast days. The best ways to avoid it are either to stay wrapped up or smother yourself in sunscreen (with a minimum factor of 15), reapplying it regularly throughout the day. Don't forget your lips, nose, the back of your neck and even under your chin to protect you against rays reflected from the ground.

SAFETY

Sadly every year people are injured walking along the trail, though usually it's nothing more than a badly twisted ankle. Parts of the upper reaches of the River Thames are pretty remote, and it certainly pays to take precautions when walking. Abiding by the following rules should minimise the risk.

● Avoid walking on your own if possible.

● Make sure that somebody knows your plans for every day you're on the trail. This could be a friend or relative whom you have promised to call every night, or your accommodation at the end of each day's walk. That way, if you fail to turn up or call that evening, they can raise the alarm.

● If the weather closes in suddenly and fog or mist descends while you're on the trail and you become uncertain of the correct path, do not be tempted to continue. Just wait where you are and you'll find that mist often clears, at least for long enough to allow you to get your bearings. If you're still uncertain, and the weather does not look like improving, return the way you came to the nearest point of civilisation. If it is misty or foggy be careful you don't fall in the river.

● Fill up with water at every opportunity and carry some high-energy snacks.

● Always carry a torch, compass, map, whistle, phone and waterproofs with you.

● Wear sturdy boots or shoes, not trainers.

● Be extra vigilant if walking with children.

Walking alone

If you are walking alone you must appreciate and be prepared for the increased risk. Take note of the safety guidelines above.

Swimming

The laws regarding swimming outdoors are a little ambiguous in England and Wales. Currently, as long as you are not trespassing, you are fine to swim in 'navigable' waters such as the **non-tidal Thames**. This does not mean that you should just dive in anywhere. It cannot be stressed highly enough that when choosing to have a dip you must do so with both the upmost respect for the river and highest regard for your own **personal safety**.

An informative online resource for potential Thames swimmers is 🖳 out doorswimmingsociety.com.

It is only legal to swim in the **tidal Thames** between Teddington Lock and Putney Bridge but even so the dangers are significant; as you walk you may notice memorials to people who have lost their lives swimming in the Thames. For further information see 🖳 pla.co.uk/Safety/Swimming-in-the-Tidal-Thames.

Top safety tips include:
● Do not swim alone
● Wear a bright coloured hat (preferably red) so that you can easily be seen
● If possible, ask local advice first before plunging in
● Acclimatise to cold water gradually
● Have warm clothes available for when you get out
● Make sure you know your exit point
● Always step in; whether you can see the bottom or not, do not jump in.

Avoidance of hazards

With good planning and preparation most hazards can be avoided. This information is just as important for those out on a day walk as for those walking the entire Thames Path. Always make sure you have suitable **clothing** (see pp41-2) to keep you warm and dry, whatever the conditions when you set off, and a change of inner clothes too. Carrying plenty of food and water is vital too.

Dealing with an accident

● Use basic first aid to treat the injury to the best of your ability.
● Try to attract the attention of anybody else who may be in the area. The **international distress (emergency) signal** is six blasts on a whistle, or six flashes with a torch; both are best done when you think someone might see the light flashes or hear the whistle blasts.
● If possible leave someone with the casualty while others go to get help. If there are only two people, you have a dilemma. If you decide to get help leave all spare clothing and food with the casualty.
● In an emergency dial ☎ 999 (or the EU standard number ☎ 112); report the position of the casualty and their condition. However, before you call work out exactly where you are; on the app What3words (💻 what3words.com) the world is divided into three-metre squares and each has its own three-word geocode so it makes it easy to tell people where you are.

WEATHER FORECASTS

The weather along the Thames Path is as unpredictable as the rest of England and you'd be well advised to always prepare for the worst. Along the river's upper reaches, and especially during winter, **flooding** can be an issue. Before you set off for the day, look at the Government's flood information page (💻 flood-warning-information.service.gov.uk) should you have concerns about the area in which you plan to go walking. Flooding along the tidal Thames in London is an issue and it would be worth consulting 💻 tidetimes.org.uk before you set out, although diversion signs are in place anywhere when flooding occurs regularly.

Most hotels, some B&Bs and tourist information centres will have a summary of the **weather forecast** somewhere. Alternatively you can get a forecast either through 💻 bbc.co.uk/weather, or 💻 metoffice.gov.uk/public/weather.

Pay close attention to the weather forecast and alter your plans for the day accordingly. That said, even if the forecast is for a fine sunny day, this is the British Isles and you should always pack some wet-weather gear.

Using this guide

This route guide has been divided according to logical start and stop points. However, these are not intended to be strict daily stages since people walk at different speeds and have varying interests. The maps can be used to plan how far to walk each day but note that these are walking times only (see box below). With so much accommodation available you can pretty much divide your walk into as few or as many days as you want. See pp36-9 for some suggested itineraries.

To provide further help, practical information is provided on the trail maps, including walking times, places to stay and eat, public toilets as well as shops and supermarkets. Further service details are given in the text under the entry for each settlement. For a condensed overview of this information see the **village and town facilities table** on pp30-2 (walking eastward) or pp33-5 (walking west).

For cumulative **distance charts** see pp252-4; and for **overview maps** and **map profiles** see the colour pages at the end of the book.

TRAIL MAPS [see key map inside cover; symbols key p251]

Direction

(See p40 for a discussion of the pros and cons of either walking west to east or east to west.) In the text that follows, look for the **E➜** symbol for a route summary for those walking **from Thames Head to Woolwich (Foot Tunnel)** and the **W ←** symbol with shaded text for those walking **from Woolwich to Thames Head**.

Scale and walking times

The trail maps are drawn to a scale of 1:20,000 (1cm = 200m; 3¹/₈ inches = 1 mile). Walking times are given along the side of each map and the arrow shows the direction to which the time refers. Black triangles indicate the points between which the times have been taken.

The time bars are a tool and are not there to judge your walking ability. There are so many variables that affect walking speed, from

---

☐ **IMPORTANT NOTE – WALKING TIMES**

Unless otherwise specified, **all times in this book refer only to the time spent walking.** You should add 20-30% to allow for rests, photos, checking the map, drinking water etc, not to mention time simply to stop and stare. When planning the day's hike count on 5-7 hours' actual walking.

the weather conditions to how many beers you drank the previous evening. After the first hour or two of walking you will be able to see how your speed relates to the timings on the maps.

Up or down?

The trail is shown as a **dashed red line** on all the maps. An arrow across the trail indicates the gradient; two arrows show that it's steep. If, for example, you are walking from A (at 80m) to B (at 200m) and the trail between the two is short and steep it would be shown thus: A— — — >> — — – B. However, as there is only one gradient of note on this entire trail you will only see this symbol (two arrows) on one map. Note that the arrow points uphill, the opposite of what OS maps use on steep roads. Reversed arrow heads indicate a downward gradient.

Other features

Features are marked on the map when of possible interest or pertinent to navigation. In order to avoid cluttering the maps not all features have been marked each time they occur. The numbered **GPS waypoints** refer to the list on pp249-51.

ACCOMMODATION

Apart from larger towns (and especially for the London area) where some selection of places has been necessary, almost every place to stay that is on, or very close to, the actual trail is marked on the map. Details of each place are given in the accompanying text.

The number of **rooms** of each type is stated, ie: **S** = Single, **T** = Twin room (with two single beds), **D** = Double room (with one bed), **Tr** = Triple room and **Qd** = Quad. Note that most of the triple/quad rooms have a double bed and one/two single beds (or bunk beds); thus for a group of three or four, two people would have to share the double bed, but it also means the room can be used as a double or twin. See pp19-20.

Rates quoted for B&B-style accommodation are **per person (pp) based on two people sharing a room** for a one-night stay; rates are usually discounted for longer stays. Where a **single room (sgl)** is available the rate for that is quoted if different from the rate per person. The rate for **single occupancy (sgl occ)** of a double/twin may be higher, and the per person rate for three/four sharing a triple/quad may be lower. Unless specified, rates are for bed and breakfast. At some places the only option is a **room rate**; this will be the same whether one or two people (or more if permissible) use the room. See p22 for more on rates.

Unless otherwise stated you can assume that the accommodation described has **en suite facilities** in all its rooms. The text only mentions where places have **private**, or **shared, facilities** (in either case this may be a bathroom or shower room just outside the bedroom). In the text ☛ signifies that at least one **bath** is available – either in an en suite room or in a separate bathroom – for those who prefer a relaxed soak at the end of the day.

Also noted is whether the premises have **wi-fi** (WI-FI) and if **dogs** (🐾 – see also pp255-6) are welcome in at least one room (often places have only one room suitable for dogs), or at campsites, subject to prior arrangement.

The route guide

E ➡ FROM THAMES HEAD If you're doing this walk in an **easterly direction** (from west to east starting at Thames Head and ending in Woolwich) follow the maps in an ascending order (from 1 to 65) and the text as below, looking for the **E➡ symbol** on overview text.

⬅ W FROM WOOLWICH If you're walking in a **westerly direction** (Woolwich to Thames Head) follow the maps in a descending order (from 65 to 1) and the text with a **red background**, looking for the **⬅W symbol** on overview text. **Turn to p246 to start your walk in this direction**.

KEMBLE [Map 1, p80]

The source of the River Thames (see box below) – and thus the start/end of the Thames Path itself – is approximately 1¾ miles (2.8km; 35-45 mins) from the village of Kemble; for directions between Kemble and the source see p81. We have also marked on the map the route from The Thames Head Inn (see Map 1).

The site of 7th-century Anglo-Saxon cemeteries and, before them, where the Romans buried their dead too, Kemble's name has evolved from *Kemele*, meaning boundary. The village sits at a junction of several historical transport routes including the Thames, the Roman Fosse Way (which links Exeter with Bath and Lincoln) and the

Great Western Railway. A local politician, Robert Gordon, was so affronted by the arrival of the railway at Kemble that he insisted that the new line be hidden from view when it passed in front of his house. A tunnel was thus built over the track to conceal it from his view. The main attraction, the **church** on its southern edge, has a Norman door and tower dating from 1250.

On Windmill Rd, **Kemble Stores** (Mon-Sat 8.30am-1pm & 2-6pm, Sun 9am-noon) provides the essentials; the **post office** (Mon, Tue, Thur & Fri 9am-1pm & 2-5pm, Wed & Sat 9am-1pm) is part of the shop and cash can be withdrawn depending on what debit card you have (see p24).

ROUTE GUIDE AND MAPS

❑ THE SOURCE OF THE RIVER THAMES

Approximately one mile north from Kemble the source of the river Thames is hidden deep in a Gloucestershire field known as **Trewsbury Mead**. Lying 105 metres (356ft) above sea level, the river's origin is marked by an **inscribed stone** next to an ancient ash tree. Thought to be two centuries old, the tree once had the initials 'TH' (Thames Head) carved in its bark; letters some beady-eyed folk still claim to be able to see. Despite photos from the 1960s showing young boys canoeing beneath the tree's boughs you will most likely see no water. Fear not though; deep in the earth below, the river's journey *is* beginning – as yours may be, though at ground level.

There is some dispute over the source of the River Thames, an alternative origin being Seven Springs at the head of the River Churn. Joining the Thames at Cricklade (Map 5) this would make the Thames 12 miles longer and 91 metres further above sea level. Historically, however, the Churn has always borne its own name so it is considered to be merely a tributary rather than the river itself. The honour of being the official source of the Thames thus goes to Thames Head.

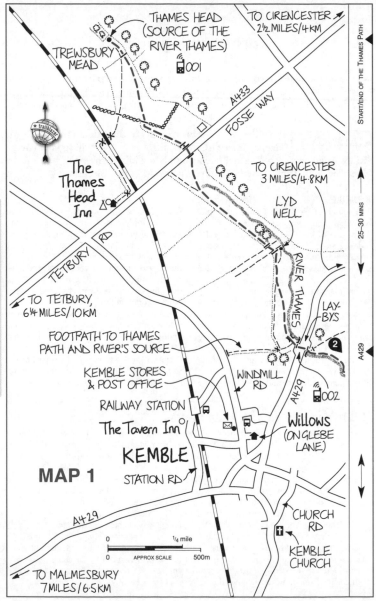

THAMES HEAD (SOURCE OF THE RIVER THAMES)

TREWSBURY MEAD

TO CIRENCESTER 2½ MILES/4KM

001

START/END OF THE THAMES PATH

A433

FOSSE WAY

The Thames Head Inn

TO CIRENCESTER 3 MILES/4.8KM

LYD WELL

25-30 MINS

RIVER THAMES

TETBURY RD

TO TETBURY, 6¼ MILES/10KM

LAY-BYS

A429

FOOTPATH TO THAMES PATH AND RIVER'S SOURCE

KEMBLE STORES & POST OFFICE

WINDMILL RD

A429

2

002

RAILWAY STATION

The Tavern Inn

KEMBLE

STATION RD

Willows (ON GLEBE LANE)

MAP 1

A429

CHURCH RD

KEMBLE CHURCH

TO MALMESBURY 7 MILES/6.5KM

0   ¼ mile

0   500m
APPROX SCALE

ROUTE GUIDE AND MAPS

For **B&B** in the village, *Willows* (☎ 01285-770667; 1T en suite shower/1D private bathroom; ☞; WI-FI) is tucked away down a quiet cul-de-sac at 2 Glebe Lane. The rate is £35-40pp (sgl occ from £65).

Between the village and the river source, there's no more appropriate place for Thames Path trekkers to stay and eat than *The Thames Head Inn* (☎ 01285-770259, ☐ thamesheadinn.co.uk; fb; 3D/1T; ☞; WI-FI; ☜). **B&B** costs from £45pp (sgl occ £60); room-only rates are also available. **Camping** (from £20 per pitch) is an option and shower/toilet facilities are available. **Food** is served daily (Mon-Sat 11am-9.30pm, Sun from noon), Bob's bubble & squeak (£12.95) being particularly popular, and the homemade steak, kidney & ale pie (£14.50) is terrific.

The other option is *The Tavern Inn* (☎ 01285-770216, ☐ arkells.com/pub; fb; ☜;

WI-FI), situated next to the railway station, an inviting family-friendly pub with a lovely garden. **Food** (Tue-Sat noon-2pm & 5.30-8pm, Sun noon-3pm) is available: at lunch you'll get a sandwich or baguette and chips for £7.50, and plenty more to choose from.

Kemble is a stop on GWR's (Paddington–Cheltenham Spa; see box on pp56-7) **train** service and on **bus** service No 882 (see pp58-61).

A few **taxi firms** operate in the Kemble area, including Reliance Taxis (☎ 07787-790644, ☐ reliancetaxiscirences ter.co.uk). Cirencester is a 10-minute drive away, but they can arrange to pick you up either at the Thames Head pub, or at the layby on the A429, just outside the town; these are both good places to have friends pick you up or drop you off, as the A433 (Fosse Way) is a narrow road with fast traffic.

E → THAMES HEAD TO CRICKLADE [MAPS 1-5]

Your first day on the Thames Path is a tranquil **12¼-mile (19.7km, 4¼-5hrs)** stroll from Thames Head (see box on p79), through meadows and farmland to the village of Cricklade. From **Kemble** you'll have to do some walking just to get to the start of the trail, and if you're starting from the railway station it's easiest to walk along the National Trail to the source, then turn around and walk back towards the village again!

The official stage begins with scarcely any water to be seen (unless it's raining, of course), but it is not long before you pass **Lyd Well** – the spring from

ROUTE GUIDE AND MAPS

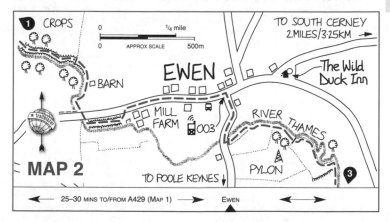

which, after rainfall, the nascent Thames often introduces itself (if it hasn't already done so); it seems strange to think that almost every footstep from now on is accompanied by the river as its now crystal-clear waters slowly deepen and spread. Cotswold meadows lead you through the hamlet of **Ewen** (see below; Map 2) and on to **Cotswold Water Park** (⌨ waterpark.org), a huge expanse of man-made lakes rich in flora and fauna. As the trail cuts its way through the lakes the roar of the speedboats of the water-skiers is replaced by the traffic noise from the busy A419.

You pass the outskirts of **Somerford Keynes** (Map 3) before arriving at **Ashton Keynes** (see below; Map 4), both of which offer good options for lunch. The path continues past **Cleveland Lakes Nature Reserve** (Map 5) and then through the ancient and uncultivated **North Meadow NNR** – abundant in butterflies and wild flowers – and finally to **Cricklade** (see pp84-7).

EWEN [Map 2, p81]

Once the site of the first mill on the Thames – now called Mill Farm – Ewen provides an attractive alternative to a first night in Kemble. It is home to the 16th-century *Wild Duck Inn* (⌨ thewildduckewen.com; **fb**; WI-FI; 🐾). It is now part of the Lucky Onion group (⌨ theluckyonion.com) and at the time of writing was undergoing substantial renovation. They hope to reopen in 2022 and will be offering boutique accommodation, so check the website(s) for further details.

The 882 **bus** service (Mon-Fri 1/day) stops in Ewen in the morning en route from Kemble and in the afternoon en route from Cirencester (see pp58-61).

SOMERFORD KEYNES [Map 3]

The site of a 'summer ford' (ie where the river was fordable during the summer months when it was at its lowest), the village was originally in Wiltshire, but in 1897 the villagers opted to join neighbouring Gloucestershire instead. The village's 'surname' derives from Sir Ralph de Keynes, the local landowner in the time of King John (1199-1216). Near its northern end lies **All Saints Church** which has a number of interesting features including a Saxon doorway and a Viking carving.

Of more interest to thirsty ramblers may be *The Baker's Arms* (☎ 01285-861298, ⌨ bakerarmssomerfordkeynes.co.uk; **fb**; WI-FI; 🐾; **food** Mon & Wed-Sat noon-2.30pm & 5.30-8.30pm, Sun noon-4pm). A 10-minute walk from the path, this 17th-century pub is a friendly place with a good-sized beer garden which can get busy at weekends. The food can be described as superior pub fare though we suspect that most trekkers would prefer it if the food was less refined and more hearty. Still, it *is* undoubtedly tasty and the menu may include such mouth-watering prospects as pan-fried rump lamb (£22), or at the cheaper end foraged mushroom & wild garlic risotto (£11).

The 93 **bus** service calls here (see pp58-61).

ASHTON KEYNES [Map 4, p85]

Walking east, as you leave Gloucestershire for Wiltshire you arrive at the first village actually on the river: Ashton Keynes has over 20 bridges that cross the infant Thames as it flows through the village. Those with time to loiter may be interested in visiting the remains of four 14th-century 'preaching crosses' scattered about the village, though each one was damaged by Cromwell's Roundheads during the Civil War.

On High Rd both the **village shop** (Mon-Sat 7.30am-7pm, Sun 9am-3pm) and *The White Hart Inn* (☎ 01285-861247, ⌨ thewhitehartashtonkeynes.com; **fb**; **food** Tue-Sat noon-3pm & 5-9pm, Sun noon-3pm; WI-FI; 🐾 bar area) provide sustenance for walkers. At the pub the lunch menu includes soup with crusty bread (£5) and ham, eggs & chips (£10); the dinner menu consists largely of pub classics including fish & chips (£14). Note that on a Monday the bar is only open from 5pm and food is not served. **B&B** is available close to the

path at friendly *The Long House* (☎ 01285-861317, 🖥 thelonghouse-ashtonkeynes.co .uk; 1S/2D/1T, shared bathroom; ▼; WI-FI), a Grade II-listed building constructed in the 17th century. The rate (from £35pp, sgl/sgl occ £50) includes a continental breakfast.

The 93A **bus** calls here (see pp58-61).

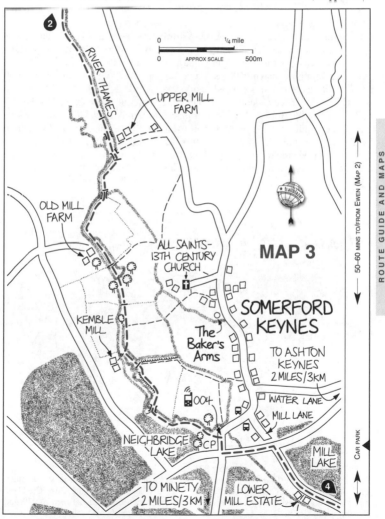

W ← CRICKLADE TO THAMES HEAD   [MAPS 5-1]

[Route section begins on Map 5, p87] Your final day on the Thames Path is a tranquil **12¼-mile (19.7km, 4¼-5hrs)** stroll from the village of Cricklade, through meadows and farmland to Thames Head (see box p79).

A wander through the ancient and uncultivated **North Meadow NNR** – abundant in butterflies and wild flowers – takes you towards **Cleveland Lakes Nature Reserve**. As the path threads its way between the lakes, the traffic noise from the busy A491 begins to recede, replaced perhaps by the roar of the speed boats of the water skiers. Both **Ashton Keynes** (see pp82-3; Map 4) and later the outskirts of **Somerford Keynes** (see p82; Map 3) in Gloucestershire offer good options for lunch. Although many of the lakes are hidden, you are passing through **Cotswold Water Park** (🖥 waterpark.org), a huge expanse of man-made lakes rich in flora and fauna.

Cotswold meadows lead you through the hamlet of **Ewen** (see p82; Map 2). The river varies from a clear flow in places to barely a trickle in the grass in others. Eventually you pass **Lyd Well** (Map 1) – the spring from which, after rainfall, the nascent Thames often introduces itself. The official stage ends in **Trewsbury Mead** (see p79) but now with scarcely any water to be seen. From Thames Head take the path back to **Kemble** (see p79 & p81).

ROUTE GUIDE AND MAPS

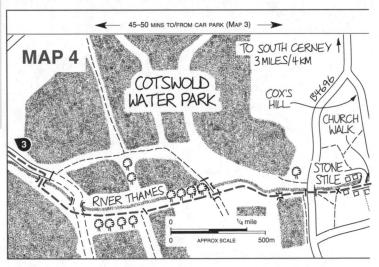

CRICKLADE   [map p87]

The first *town* on the Thames Path, and the only one in Wiltshire, Cricklade started out as a small Anglo-Saxon community back in the 9th century. Alfred the Great fortified

the town against the Danes in AD890, and a century later it became the site of Cricklade Mint, which operated between AD979 and 1100 and produced coins bearing such well-known figures from England's past as King Cnut (AD995-1035).

The four corner pinnacles of Cricklade's mighty **St Sampson's Church** are the town's dominant feature. There has been a church on this site since the 9th century, though the current edifice, including the tower, is 16th century in origin.

In addition to its illustrious history, there are some legends about Cricklade that survive to this day. For one thing, there are suggestions that the town is located on the site where St Augustine converted Wessex's Anglo-Saxons to Christianity in AD597; while some folk believe that the town's name originates from 'Greeklade' and espouse the theory that Cricklade is actually the site of England's first university, having been founded by the Mercians in AD650 – making it a mere 600 years older than any of Oxford's venerable colleges. Oddly, or possibly not, attempts to prove either claim has thus far proved inconclusive.

Services

The **tourist information point** (Mon-Fri 10am-12.30pm & 1.30-4pm) is in the town council building (☎ 01793-751394, 🖥 crickladetowncouncil.gov.uk; **fb**) at 113 High St. An **ATM** can be found at the Tesco **supermarket** (Mon-Sat 6am-11pm, Sun 7am-10.30pm) which also hosts the local **post office** (Mon-Fri 9am-5.30pm, Sat to 12.30pm). On the other side of High St you'll find **Cricklade Stores** (Mon-Sat 6am-8pm, Sun to 2pm) and a **Boots the Chemist** (Mon-Fri 9am-6.30pm, Sat to 2pm). There are **toilets** in the car park.

The 51 & 53 **buses** (see pp58-61) call here as does National Express's 445 coach service (see box on p53).

Where to stay

You have three accommodation options in Cricklade, all reasonably priced pubs within easy walking distance of the trail. Indeed, the path goes past the front door of

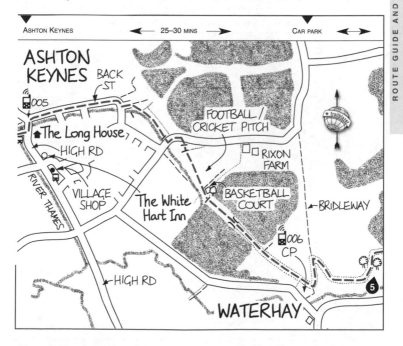

ASHTON KEYNES ← 25–30 MINS → CAR PARK ↔

ASHTON KEYNES BACK ST

005

♠ The Long House

HIGH RD

RIVER THAMES

VILLAGE SHOP

The White Hart Inn

FOOTBALL / CRICKET PITCH

RIXON FARM

BASKETBALL COURT

← BRIDLEWAY

006 CP

HIGH RD

WATERHAY

5

The *Red Lion* (☎ 01793-750776, 🖳 theredlioncricklade.co.uk; **fb**; 3D/2D or T; 🛏; WI-FI; 🐾; from £50pp, sgl occ room rate), which is brimming with character and also serves delicious food (see Where to eat and drink).

Further along High St, *The White Hart Hotel* (☎ 01793-750206, 🖳 thewhitehartcricklade.co.uk; **fb**; 1S/7D/4T/1Tr/1Qd; 🛏; WI-FI; 🐾) is another fine option which also serves food (see Where to eat). The rate, including breakfast, is from £40pp (sgl/sgl occ £70).

At 101 High St, *The Old Bear Inn* (☎ 01793-750005, 🖳 theoldbearinn.com; **fb**; 3D/2D/2T; WI-FI; 🐾) charges from £32.50pp (sgl occ £50) for room only. Breakfast costs from £8.50pp and they are happy to cater for vegetarians. The bar is open daily (Mon-Fri 4-11pm, Sat & Sun noon to 11pm), but unlike the other two pubs in the town there is no other food served here.

Where to eat and drink

If you opt for a room-only rate at one of the pubs you have the perfect opportunity to visit *Cricklade Café/Stacey's Kitchen* (☎ 01793-750754; Mon-Fri 8am-12.30pm, Sat to noon; 42 High St). It's an unpretentious place but the food is nonetheless pretty tasty, with a 6-item cooked breakfast for £5 (served all day).

For a **pub meal** both *The White Hart Hotel* (see Where to stay; food Mon-Sat noon-2.30pm & 6-9pm, Sun noon-3pm), with items such as a 10oz rare-breed rump steak (£17.50) on the menu together with vegetarian, vegan and other dietary sensitive items, and *The Red Lion* (see Where to stay; food Mon-Sat noon-2pm, Sun to 4pm, Mon-Sat 5.30-8.30pm; Sat also pizzas only 2-5.30pm) are decent options. The latter has a **micro brewery** (🖳 hop-kettle.com; **fb**) so not surprisingly serves real ales; it also has a big beer garden. It dishes up

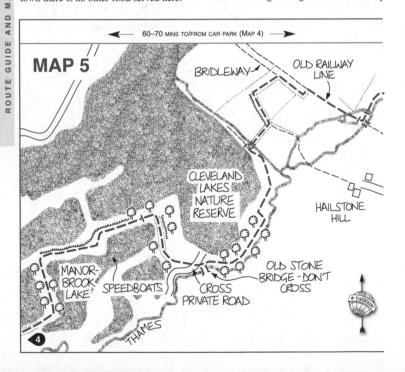

←— 60–70 MINS TO/FROM CAR PARK (MAP 4) —→

MAP 5

BRIDLEWAY

OLD RAILWAY LINE

CLEVELAND LAKES NATURE RESERVE

HAILSTONE HILL

MANOR-BROOK LAKE

SPEEDBOATS

OLD STONE BRIDGE - DON'T CROSS

CROSS PRIVATE ROAD

THAMES

4

hearty food such as fried buttermilk chicken with cajun mayo & fries (£14.50) and red wine poached cod loin (£20). This is a very popular place and one that isn't averse to putting on a bit of live music now and then.

Spicier morsels can be found at both *Jicsaw Thai* (☎ 01793-752838, 🖳 jicsaw .oo.uk; **fb**; Tue-Sun & Bank Holiday Mon noon-2.30pm & 5-9.30pm; wi-fi; 32 High St), with a chicken Thai green curry costing £7.99; and *The Ancient Raj* (☎ 01793-752242; food Mon-Fri 5.30-9.30pm, Sat & Sun to 11pm; 47 High St), with either sit-down or **takeaway** Indian meals.

Takeaway food is also available from *The Harbour Fish and Chips* (☎ 01793-751827; **fb**; Mon 4.30-10pm, Tue-Sat 11.30am-2pm & 4.30-10pm), which does decent fish & chips, and the longstanding *Cricklade Kebab House* (*Sammy's Kebabs*; ☎ 01793-751177; daily 4-9pm).

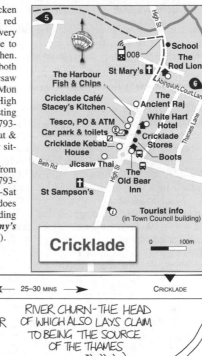

Cricklade

CRICKLADE SEE TOWN PLAN

E → CRICKLADE TO LECHLADE [MAPS 5-10]

As with yesterday's stage, this **10¾-mile (17.3km, 3¾-4¾hrs)** section of the trail primarily consists of agrarian rambling through flora-rich meadows, although it has to stray from the river a couple of times.

As the four 'spirelets' of St Sampson's Church bid you farewell, so the swans and meadows welcome you back and accompany you to the village of **Castle Eaton** (see opposite; Map 8), from which a short jaunt along a country lane returns you to the banks of the Thames, with **St Mary's Church, Kempsford**, visible on the opposite bank.

A further spell spent deep in the meadows of Wiltshire (the northern bank, incidentally, is in Gloucestershire) leads you safely to **Inglesham** (Map 10), where the 13th-century **Church of St John the Baptist** is well worth a visit. The path used to follow the busy A361, but the only reason to go to Upper Inglesham now is to take **bus** 77 (see pp58-61).

Much to the chagrin of the waterfowl that live along here, the final, sublime stretch to **Lechlade** (see pp91-3) has the first boats on the river since you started your walk. On the opposite bank a **roundhouse** marks the Thames's **head of navigation** (the point at which the river becomes navigable for boats) as well as one end of the ill-fated **Thames-Severn Canal** (see box on p90). The circular abode was the accommodation for the lock-keeper, who would have controlled the traffic between the two waterways.

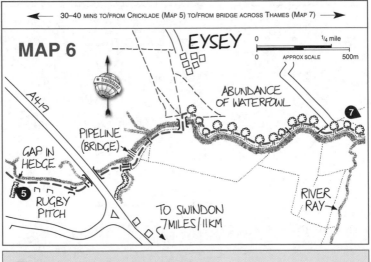

30–40 MINS TO/FROM CRICKLADE (MAP 5) TO/FROM BRIDGE ACROSS THAMES (MAP 7)

MAP 6

EYSEY

ABUNDANCE OF WATERFOWL

0   ¼ mile
0   APPROX SCALE   500m

PIPELINE (BRIDGE)

A419

GAP IN HEDGE

5 RUGBY PITCH

TO SWINDON 7 MILES / 11KM

RIVER RAY →

7

❑ **IMPORTANT NOTE – WALKING TIMES**
All times in this book refer only to the time spent walking. You will need to add 20-30% to allow for rests, photography, checking the map, drinking water etc.

CASTLE EATON [Map 8, p90]

Shortly before you leave the village the 12th-century **Church of St Mary**, tucked away down a footpath, is worth a peek.

Far harder to miss is the first pub to line the Thames's banks: *The Red Lion* (☎ 01285-706533, 🖳 theredlioncastleeaton.co .uk; **fb**; WI-FI; 🐾 bar only), built around

1730, has a **shepherd's hut** sleeping 2 (en suite; from £125, inc pastries for breakfast) and home-cooked **food** (Wed-Thur noon-3.30pm & 6-9pm, Fri & Sat noon-9pm, Sun to 4pm). If you are here on a winter Sunday it would be a shame to miss out on one of their roast dinners (£9.25). Note that the

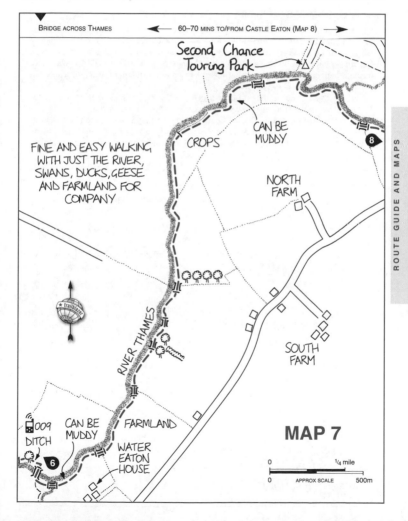

BRIDGE ACROSS THAMES

◄─── 60-70 MINS TO/FROM CASTLE EATON (MAP 8) ───►

Second Chance Touring Park

CROPS

CAN BE MUDDY

FINE AND EASY WALKING WITH JUST THE RIVER, SWANS, DUCKS, GEESE AND FARMLAND FOR COMPANY

NORTH FARM

8

RIVER THAMES

SOUTH FARM

009 DITCH

CAN BE MUDDY

FARMLAND

WATER EATON HOUSE

6

MAP 7

0 ¼ mile

0 APPROX SCALE 500m

ROUTE GUIDE AND MAPS

pub closes at 6pm on Sunday and all day Monday and Tuesday; accommodation is only available on Wednesday to Saturday nights.

The first **campsite** along the Thames Path is on the opposite side of the river. *Second Chance Touring Park* (Map 7; ☎ 01285-810939, 🖥 secondchanceholiday park.co.uk; 🐕 on lead; Mar-end Nov) charges from £7pp including use of shower/toilet/washing up facilities and is a half-mile stroll from the village. The site has some lodges and chalets but these are for longer stays.

❏ THE THAMES-SEVERN CANAL

Opened in 1789, the Thames-Severn Canal was part of a system of waterways linking London with Bristol. Thirty miles long, the canal carved its way through the landscape from **Lechlade to Stroud**, from where it went on to connect with the River Severn. Passing just to the north of the Thames's source, the canal also travelled through Sapperton Tunnel which, at just over two miles in length, was, for a spell at least, the longest tunnel in Britain.

Beset by leaks due to the porous nature of the Cotswold limestone and struggling to compete with the nascent railway network the canal was last used commercially in 1911, and the last (non-commercial) boat made the journey between the two rivers in 1927. Many blame the lack of water at the Thames's source on the canal; the waterway's pumping station, so it is alleged, drew all the water away from the underground springs that had once risen in Trewsbury Mead (Map 1).

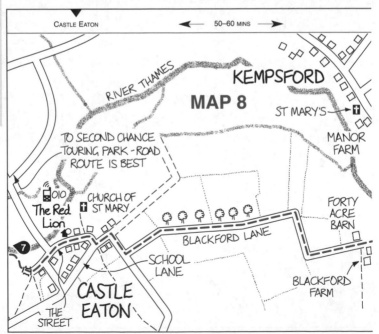

W ← LECHLADE TO CRICKLADE [MAPS 10-5]

[Route section begins on Map 10, p94] This **10¾-mile (17.3km, 3¾-4¾hrs)** section of the trail primarily consists of agrarian rambling through flora-rich meadows, although it has to stray from the river a couple of times.

On the first stretch out of Lechlade, you'll see the last boats on the river. On the opposite bank a **roundhouse** (see p88) marks the Thames's **head of navigation** as well as one end of the ill-fated **Thames-Severn Canal** (see box opposite).

At **Inglesham**, the 13th-century **Church of St John the Baptist** is well worth a visit. The path used to follow the busy A361, but the only reason to go to Upper Inglesham now is to take **bus** 77 (see pp58-61).

A further spell is spent deep in the meadows of Wiltshire (the northern bank, incidentally, is in Gloucestershire) with **St Mary's Church, Kempsford** (Map 8), visible on the opposite bank; here a short jaunt along a country lane leads you safely to the village of **Castle Eaton** (see pp89-90), where you return to the banks of the Thames.

Finally the four 'spirelets' of St Sampson's Church welcome you to **Cricklade** (pp84-7; Map 5). *[Next route overview on p84]*

LECHLADE [map p93]

So named because of its proximity to the River Leach, this market town used to be a bustling port due to its privileged location as the first place from which large commercial barges could head downstream carrying their wares to Oxford and London.

One of the primary commodities traded was sage cheese, whilst the stone required to construct the dome of London's St Paul's Cathedral was also loaded here.

The town's two main features are: **Halfpenny Bridge**, opened in 1792 to help deal with the influx of traders following the creation of the Thames-Severn Canal and taking its name from the toll taken from walkers who wished to cross; and **St**

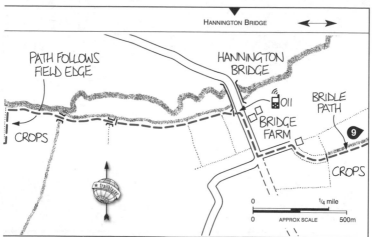

HANNINGTON BRIDGE ←→

PATH FOLLOWS FIELD EDGE

HANNINGTON BRIDGE

☎ 011

BRIDLE PATH

CROPS

BRIDGE FARM

❾

CROPS

0   ¼ mile

0   APPROX SCALE   500m

★ trailblazer

Lawrence Church, the view of which from the opposite bank is one photographers will not want to miss.

Services

All services can be found on High St. The **visitor information centre** is staffed by volunteers and is in the same building as the community-run library (☎ 01367-252631; Mon & Sat 10am-1pm, Wed 1-4pm); information is also available on 🖥 lechladeonthames.co.uk.

If you're planning on a picnic (not a bad idea given the paucity of eateries going eastwards) *Cutler & Bayliss* (☎ 01367-252451, 🖥 cutlerandbayliss.co.uk; **fb**; Mon-Fri 8am-5pm, Sat to 4pm; 4 Oak St) are a family-run butcher and greengrocer who also sell homemade pies and scotch eggs.

The **post office** (Mon-Fri 8.30am-4pm, Sat to noon) is nearby, and on the other side of the road are: **Lechlade Pharmacy** (Mon-Fri 9am-6pm, Sat to 5pm); and a Londis **shop** (daily 6.30am-10pm) with **ATM**.

The 77 **bus** links Lechlade with Cirencester (see pp58-61).

Where to stay

Campers need not cross the river. *Bridge House Campsite* (Map 10; ☎ 01367-252348, 🖥 bridgehousecampsite.co.uk; **fb**; 🐾 on lead; Apr-Oct; reception Mon-Wed 1-7pm, Thur-Sun 9am-7pm) is a friendly, clean and efficiently run place. The cost is from £9pp; payment must be in cash, or by cheque with the relevant debit card number.

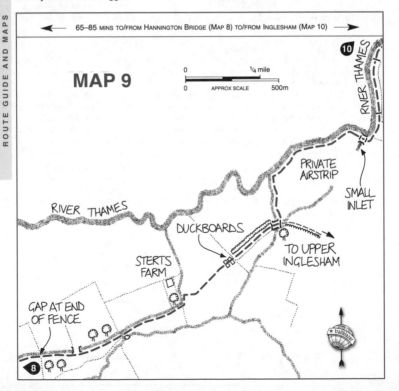

← 65–85 MINS TO/FROM HANNINGTON BRIDGE (MAP 8) TO/FROM INGLESHAM (MAP 10) →

RIVER THAMES

MAP 9

0 — 1/4 mile
0 — APPROX SCALE — 500m

10

PRIVATE AIRSTRIP

SMALL INLET

RIVER THAMES

DUCKBOARDS

TO UPPER INGLESHAM

STERTS FARM

GAP AT END OF FENCE

8

B&B is available at *Vera's Kitchen and B&B* (☎ 01367-252677, 🖳 veras kitchenlechlade.co.uk; **fb**; 3D with private facilities; WI-FI; 🐾; from £45pp, sgl occ £75; 10 Burford St).

A few pubs also offer **B&B**. Wonderfully situated right on the riverbank and next to the bridge is *The Riverside* (☎ 01367-252534, 🖳 riverside-lechlade.com; **fb**; 1S private facilities, 1D/1T/2Tr/3Qd; 🛁; WI-FI). Rates vary, but expect to pay around £45pp (sgl £70-80, sgl occ room rate). Another option is *The New Inn Hotel* (☎ 01367-252296, 🖳 newinnhotel.co.uk; **fb**; 3S/27D or T; 🛁; WI-FI; 🐾) which enjoys both a frontage on High St and a huge beer garden which backs directly on to its own private section of the river. Rates here also depend on demand but £32.50-60pp (sgl £65-90, sgl occ from £75) is a guideline.

Away from the Thames on Burford St, *The Swan Inn* (☎ 01367-253571, 🖳 swan innlechlade.co.uk; **fb**; 3D/1T; 🛁; WI-FI; 🐾) not only has four-poster beds but also real ales, and some parts of the pub date from the 16th century. Rates (£39-49pp, sgl occ £68-88) do not include breakfast though it is available – a full English costs £9.

Where to eat and drink

At *The Tea Chest* (☎ 01367-253015, **fb**; Tue-Sun 10am-4pm, but hours are variable; 🐾) sandwiches, soups, salads and toasties cost less than £5; the coffee is great and dogs are welcome.

If you're prepared to walk a bit further into the centre of Lechlade the smart *Lynwood & Co Café* (☎ 01367-253707, 🖳 lynwoodandco.com; food Mon-Sat 8am-3pm, Sun to 2pm; WI-FI; 🐾) does the best breakfasts of anyone in town.

A short walk round the corner takes you to *Vera's Kitchen and B&B* (see Where to stay; food daily 8.30am-3.30pm)

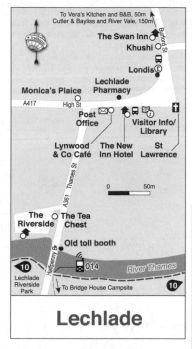

Lechlade

which serves delicious fresh juices, tasty salads, homemade sweet treats and cakes.

The menus at the town's pubs are not unimaginative and include the usual pub classics. *The New Inn Hotel* (see Where to stay) serves pub standards (daily noon-2pm & 6-8.45pm) including steak & ale pie for £13. Other pub options include *The Riverside* (see Where to stay; Mon-Fri noon-2.45pm & 6-9pm, Sat noon-9pm, Sun to 5pm, pizzas daily until 8pm; 🐾), which, given its location and name may be the most appropriate place to enjoy salmon fillet & salad (£10.95).

ROUTE GUIDE AND MAPS

Symbols used in text (see also p78)
🛁 Bathtub in, or for, at least one room
WI-FI means wi-fi is available
fb signifies places that post their current opening hours on their Facebook page
🐾 Dogs allowed; if for accommodation this is subject to prior arrangement (see p255)

At *The Swan Inn* (see Where to stay; food Mon-Sat noon-3pm & 6-9pm, Sun noon-5pm) you will find pub grub such as scampi & chips (£11.50).

Traditional Indian meals can be enjoyed at *Khushi* (☎ 01367-252956, 🖥 lechladekhushi.com; **fb**; daily 5.30-10.30pm) and Chinese meals at *River Vale* (☎ 01367-250033; Tue-Sun 5-10pm; 6 Oak St). Both offer a **takeaway** option.

Fish & chips for about a fiver can be purchased at *Monica's Plaice* (☎ 01367-250050, 🖥 monicasplaice.com; **fb**; Mon-Thur 11.30am-2pm & 4.30-9.30pm, Fri-Sun 11.30am-9.30pm).

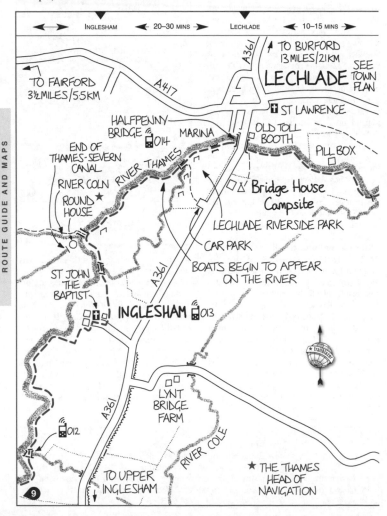

E → LECHLADE TO NEWBRIDGE [MAPS 10-15]

This **16¾-mile (26.7km, 5-6½hrs)** stage is the longest and most splendidly isolated along the whole path. Also the path now hugs the river close, holding on tight to every twist and time-consuming turn. Apart from the occasional riverside pub or lock, your only companionship is likely to be provided by the swans, with the call of the cuckoo a constant presence in the background.

The relative wildness of this stretch of the river also means **a paucity of services**. There *are* several pubs on the trail that serve food but unless you're willing to add some (otherwise unnecessary) mileage walking to the shop in Standlake you should purchase any supplies in Lechlade – as the next shop on the path is over thirty miles and two days away in Oxford!

From Lechlade the Thames becomes navigable and locks and weirs (see box on pp98-9) become a frequent point of reference. The first you encounter

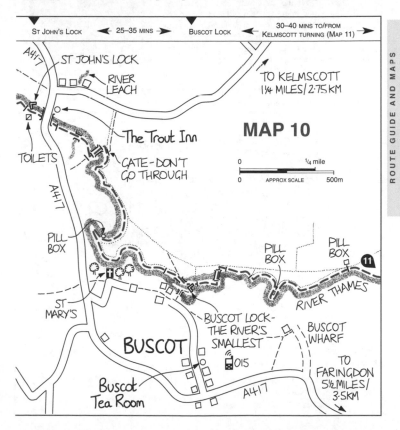

ST JOHN'S LOCK ← 25-35 MINS → BUSCOT LOCK ← 30-40 MINS TO/FROM KELMSCOTT TURNING (MAP 11) →

A417
ST JOHN'S LOCK
RIVER LEACH
TO KELMSCOTT 1¼ MILES/2·75 KM
The Trout Inn
GATE - DON'T GO THROUGH
TOILETS
A417
MAP 10
0   ¼ mile
0   APPROX SCALE   500m
PILL BOX
PILL BOX
PILL BOX
11
ST MARY'S
RIVER THAMES
BUSCOT LOCK - THE RIVER'S SMALLEST
015
BUSCOT WHARF
BUSCOT
TO FARINGDON 5½ MILES/ 3·5KM
A417
Buscot Tea Room

ROUTE GUIDE AND MAPS

is **St John's Lock** (see opposite); be careful not to miss the **statue of Old Father Thames** (see box below). As well as locks you'll also notice the ubiquity of another new feature on the river from here all the way to Pangbourne: **the pill box**. The result of a panic in 1940 over a presumed imminent invasion by the Germans, these small concrete buildings are just one way that the river – the 'artery of England' – has been defended and are a reminder of its

❑ OLD FATHER THAMES

The statue of Old Father Thames, at St John's Lock (see above) near Lechlade, is by the Italian sculptor Rafaelle Monti and one of several originally commissioned to adorn the fountains at the Crystal Palace in Sydenham in 1854. When fire destroyed the palace in 1936 the statue was rescued, eventually finding a new home at Thames Head, the river's source, in 1958. A victim of vandalism, it was moved to St John's Lock in 1974; thus, whilst Old Father Thames guards the river, the statue itself can be kept under the watchful eye of the lock-keeper.

© WA

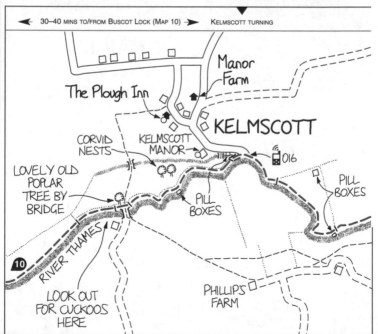

← 30–40 MINS TO/FROM BUSCOT LOCK (MAP 10) → KELMSCOTT TURNING

Manor Farm

The Plough Inn

KELMSCOTT

CORVID NESTS

KELMSCOTT MANOR

📱 016

LOVELY OLD POPLAR TREE BY BRIDGE

PILL BOXES

PILL BOXES

10

RIVER THAMES

LOOK OUT FOR CUCKOOS HERE

PHILLIP'S FARM

strategic significance. From St John's Lock you get the sense that the Thames seems to know that it is now navigable and begins to indulge in some rather intense meandering, passing **Buscot** on the opposite bank, its 13th-century **St Mary's Church** visible amongst the trees. *Buscot Tea Room and Village Shop* (☎ 01367-250329; Tue-Sun and Bank Hol Mon 10am-4.30pm; 🐾; WI-FI) is on the opposite side of the river and serves salad lunches, teas with home-made cakes. However, note that the shop part is more for postcards and the like than groceries.

For a break along the way you have the option of a visit to **Kelmscott** (see p101; Map 11) and the estate of William Morris (see box p100). There are pubs worthy of a lunch stop by both **Radcot Bridge** (see p101; Map 12) and **Tadpole Bridge** (see p102; Map 13).

Having visited the 1000-acre **Chimney Meadows National Nature Reserve** (Map 13; see also p62) with a fine bird hide (Map 14; always open; free) offering a wealth of information, and **Shifford Lock** (see p102), you then pass the hamlet of **Shifford** – the site at which the Anglo-Saxon King Alfred held the first recorded English Parliament in AD890 – before the river leads you to **Newbridge** (see p104; Map 15) and your first night in Oxfordshire.

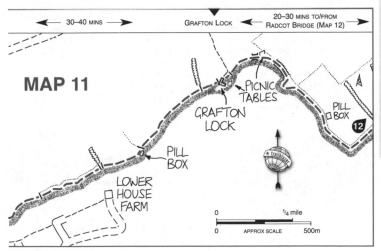

ST JOHN'S LOCK [Map 10, p95]

Across the bridge from the trail, *The Trout Inn* (☎ 01367-252313, 🖳 thetroutinn.com; fb; **food** Tue-Sat noon-2pm, Sun to 2.30pm, Tue-Sun 5.30-8pm; WI-FI; 🐾 bar only) has a history almost as long as the river. Once a priory's almshouse, it was converted to an inn in 1472, gaining its current name in 1704. Today you'll find snacks, pizzas and burgers as well as dishes with locally sourced meat and a good selection of responsibly sourced fish, including local Bibury trout, grilled and served with potatoes & vegetables for around £15. Note that at the time of research the pub was closed all day on Monday.

ROUTE GUIDE AND MAPS

❏ LOCKS AND WEIRS

While small boats can journey downriver from Cricklade, the Thames becomes navigable for larger craft only from Lechlade. Between here and Teddington (from where the Thames becomes tidal), the Thames falls approximately 70 metres and there are 45 **locks** along the way, each with at least one accompanying **weir**.

Weirs are nothing more than a barrier placed across a waterway to alter the river's flow. They have existed on the Thames in one form or another for centuries, used by fishermen to persuade fish towards nets and by millers to power their mills.

Goring Lock

© JN

By blocking the river, however, the millers and fishermen created problems for the boats that needed to travel round them. An early solution to this was the introduction of the **flash lock**, where several boards (or a gate) are placed in the weir which, when a boat approached, could be removed, thus allowing the vessel to be swept through on the resulting surge – or 'flash' – of water.

Unfortunately, this method only really worked for those travelling downstream; those travelling upriver, of course, would need to be winched or towed through the gap against the flow. Furthermore, flash locks were hazardous for everyone involved. So eventually, in the 17th century, these flash locks were replaced by **pound locks**, which is the type of lock you see to this day on the river. Pound locks operate by using two gates, one at either end of a 'pound' or chamber of water.

The water level within the pound can thus be controlled by removing one of the gates (ie it can be raised by removing the gate upstream of the chamber, or lowered by removing the 'downstream gate').

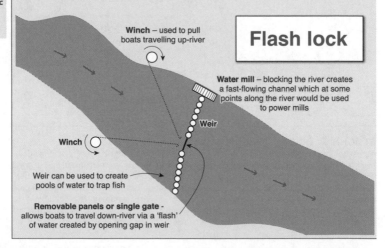

Winch – used to pull boats travelling up-river

Flash lock

Water mill – blocking the river creates a fast-flowing channel which at some points along the river would be used to power mills

Weir

Winch

Weir can be used to create pools of water to trap fish

Removable panels or single gate - allows boats to travel down-river via a 'flash' of water created by opening gap in weir

Once a boat has manoeuvred its way into the lock the two gates are then closed, thereby trapping the boat in the pound. The water in the pound is then raised or lowered, depending on which way the boat is travelling, using 'paddles' in the gates; so that the water level within the pound is equal to the water level above the lock (if the boat is travelling upstream) or below it (if travelling downstream). The first locks of this kind to be used on the Thames were constructed in 1633 and located at Iffley, Sandford and Abingdon, while the last, King's and Eynsham locks, were installed in 1928.

The pound lock is still the main design used on the river. All locks are run by the Environment Agency, and many have tearooms and campsites nearby. For a list of the facilities available at each lock see 🖳 gov.uk/river-thames-bridges-locks-and-facilities-for-boaters#facilities-at-river-thames-locks.

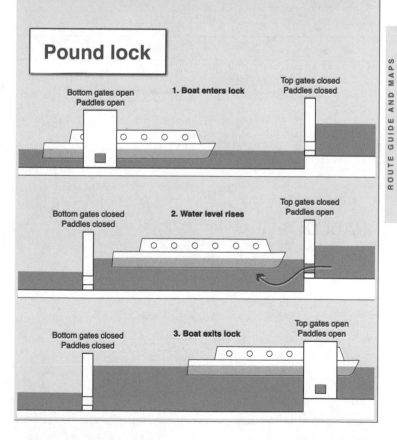

Pound lock

Bottom gates open
Paddles open

1. Boat enters lock

Top gates closed
Paddles closed

Bottom gates closed
Paddles closed

2. Water level rises

Top gates closed
Paddles open

Bottom gates closed
Paddles closed

3. Boat exits lock

Top gates open
Paddles open

ROUTE GUIDE AND MAPS

ROUTE GUIDE AND MAPS

❑ WILLIAM MORRIS AND KELMSCOTT MANOR

Poet, novelist, translator, textile designer, social reformer and founder of the Victorian Arts and Crafts movement, William Morris (1834-96) was a man of many talents. Though he owned several homes during his lifetime; he will forever be most associated with Kelmscott Manor, which was first built in 1570 as a farmhouse. Morris first laid eyes on the Manor in 1871; believing it to be the perfect retreat from his hectic life in London, he began renting it the same year, entertaining such guests as George Bernard Shaw and WB Yeats. But the building itself also inspired him to found the Society for the Protection of Old Buildings – a forerunner to the National Trust – in 1877.

Kelmscott Manor (Map 11, p96; 🖥 sal.org.uk/kelmscott-manor; **fb**; Apr-Oct Thur-Sat 11am-5pm, last entry 4pm; £12.50) will reopen to the public after extensive conservation and improvement works on 1st April 2022. The Manor displays collections of furniture, furnishings and artwork owned by Morris as well as other former occupants. There is also a *tearoom* (Thur-Sat 10.30am-5pm) which serves lunches (noon-2.30pm), teas and cakes and a gift shop.

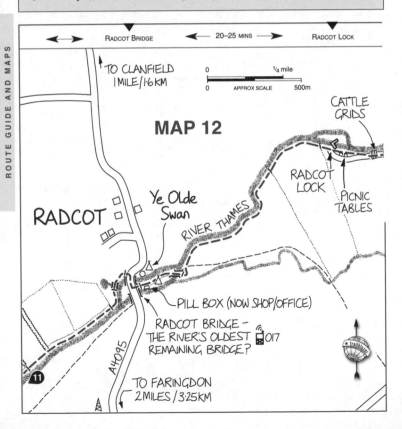

KELMSCOTT   [Map 11, p96]

For those considering breaking this lengthy stage a stop in Kelmscott is an option.

B&B (£55-73.50pp, sgl £90-110, sgl occ room rate) is available at *The Plough Inn* (☎ 01367-253543, 🖳 theploughinn kelmscott.com; **fb**; 1S/6D/1D or T; 🛏; WI-FI; 🐾). You'll also discover some splendid **food** here (Tue 6-8.30pm, Wed-Thur noon-2.30pm & 6-8.30pm, Fri & Sat noon-3pm & 6-8.30pm, Sun noon-6.30pm); their menu is constantly changing but always imaginative (eg slow-cooked shoulder of lamb, crispy haggis, braised pearl barley & swede purée for £16). *Manor Farm* (☎ 01367-252620, 🖳 kelmscottbandb.co.uk; **fb**; 2D/1Tr; 🛏; WI-FI; from £45pp (sgl occ £55) offers B&B in a 17th-century National Trust farmhouse.

☐ IMPORTANT NOTE – WALKING TIMES

All times in this book refer only to the time spent walking. You will need to add 20-30% to allow for rests, photography, checking the map, drinking water etc.

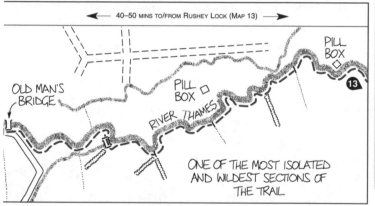

← 40–50 MINS TO/FROM RUSHEY LOCK (MAP 13) →

OLD MAN'S BRIDGE

PILL BOX

PILL BOX

RIVER THAMES

13

ONE OF THE MOST ISOLATED AND WILDEST SECTIONS OF THE TRAIL

ROUTE GUIDE AND MAPS

RADCOT   [Map 12]

The **bridge** here lays reasonable claim to being the oldest over the Thames, with much of the stone that makes up its pointed Gothic arches dating from approximately 1200. Indeed, there is even evidence of there being a bridge here as far back as the 10th century, Radcot having been an important crossing point between the Saxon kingdoms of Mercia and Wessex.

Ye Olde Swan (☎ 01367-810220, 🖳 yeoldeswan.co.uk; **fb**; WI-FI) offers **camping** (Apr-end Sep; 30 pitches; £8-12pp; 🐾) with good showers and toilet facilities.

They also have **glamping tipis** and **shepherds huts** but these are only for two-night stays; see their website for details. All camping/glamping must be booked online. The **food** (Mon-Fri noon-4pm & 6-8.30pm, Sat noon to 9pm, Sun to 8pm; see the menu on their website or **fb**) is tasty, the portions generous and the large beer garden, which extends down to the river, is a lovely spot to eat or drink. The **pill box** on the river island is now the campsite office and shop for Ye Olde Swan.

RUSHEY LOCK [Map 13]

Rushey Lock Campsite (☎ 01367-870218; 🐾 on lead; Apr-end Oct) is the western-most on the river that is run by the Environment Agency. There are 10 pitches, each costing £12 for up to two people; the site was closed at the time of research due to Covid but, assuming it is open, booking is recommended. Water and a toilet are always available, but access to the showers is limited to when the lock-keeper is on duty (hours variable but generally 9am-6pm) as that's who you need to pay (£3.50 per token). Note there is no road access to the site. For food, the nearest pub, The Trout at Tadpole Bridge (see below), is one mile downstream.

TADPOLE BRIDGE [Map 13]

The setting of the award-winning *The Trout at Tadpole Bridge* (☎ 01367-870382, 🖥 troutinn.co.uk; **fb**; 2D/3D or T/1Tr; 🍺; WI-FI; 🐾) is pure Thames-side splendour, with a beer garden rolling down to a river-bank lined with barges. The cost of **B&B** (approx £50-125pp, sgl occ room rate) reflects both the standard of the location and the exquisite establishment itself. Their **food** (Mon-Fri noon-3pm & 6-9pm, Sat noon-9pm, Sun to 7.30pm) is not for those keeping an eye on their bank balance. The menu changes regularly but if it is on the menu it's doubtful you'll rue the day you ate their roast river trout fillet (£17.50); always on the menu though are fish (usually haddock) & chips (£14.50).

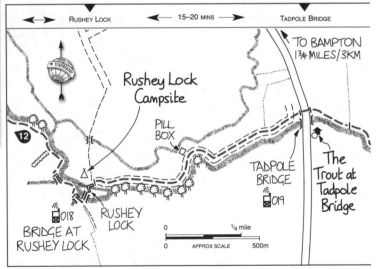

← RUSHEY LOCK — 15–20 MINS → TADPOLE BRIDGE

TO BAMPTON 1¾ MILES/3KM

Rushey Lock Campsite

PILL BOX

TADPOLE BRIDGE

The Trout at Tadpole Bridge

RUSHEY LOCK

BRIDGE AT RUSHEY LOCK

0 — ¼ mile
0 — APPROX SCALE — 500m

SHIFFORD LOCK [Map 14, p104]

If you wish to stay at *Shifford Lock Campsite* (☎ 01367-870247; well-behaved 🐾 and on lead; Good Friday to end Sep/Oct) you'll need to carry your food as there's no shop or pub within reasonable walking distance. The five pitches available on the island cost £12 each (for up to two people and a tent), there are shower (£1.75) and toilet facilities. Booking is recommended.

W → NEWBRIDGE TO LECHLADE [MAPS 15-10]

[Route section begins on Map 15, p106] This **16¾-mile (26.7km, 5-6½hrs)** stage is the longest and most splendidly isolated on the whole path. The path also hugs the river close, holding on tight to every twist and time-consuming turn. Apart from the occasional riverside pub or lock, your only companionship is likely to be provided by the swans, with the call of the cuckoo a constant presence in the background.

From Newbridge the path takes you past the hamlet of **Shifford** (see p97; Map 14) and then **Shifford Lock** (see opposite). Having visited the 1000-acre **Chimney Meadows National Nature Reserve** (Map 13; see also p62) with a fine bird hide (always open; free), you continue through the peaceful countryside and will find pubs worthy of a lunch stop by both **Tadpole Bridge** (see opposite) and **Radcot Bridge** (see p101; Map 12).

For a break along the way you have the option of a visit to **Kelmscott** (see p101; Map 11) and the estate of William Morris (see box p100). The Thames continues to indulge in some rather intense meandering, passing **Buscot** (Map 10) on the opposite bank, its 13th-century **St Mary's Church** visible amongst the trees. *Buscot Tea Room and Village Shop* (see p97) is on the opposite side of the river and serves teas. However, note that the village shop part is more for postcards and the like than groceries.

Beyond **Lechlade** (see pp91-4), where you enter Wiltshire, the Thames is not navigable except to very small boats, so you find the first of its 45 locks and weirs (see box pp98-9) at **St John's Lock** (p97); be careful not to miss the **statue of Old Father Thames** (see box p96). *[Next route overview on p91]*

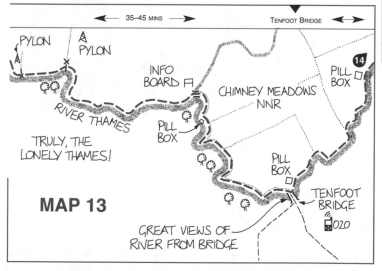

← 35–45 MINS → TENFOOT BRIDGE ←→

PYLON

PYLON

INFO BOARD

CHIMNEY MEADOWS NNR

PILL BOX 14

RIVER THAMES

PILL BOX

TRULY, THE LONELY THAMES!

PILL BOX

MAP 13

TENFOOT BRIDGE 020

GREAT VIEWS OF RIVER FROM BRIDGE

NEWBRIDGE [Map 15, p106]

This is the second oldest bridge over the Thames, its name deriving from the fact that it is 'new' compared to its venerable neighbour in Radcot – though even then it's only younger by 50 years. Originally built by monks to carry Cotswold wool across to customers in the south, the bridge now carries the A415 – a road on which you should be careful.

There are a couple of places to rest and have a drink here. *The Maybush* (☎ 01865-300101, 🖥 themaybushnewbridge.co.uk; **fb**; food Mon-Thur noon-9pm, Fri & Sat to 10pm, Sun to 8pm; WI-FI; 🐕) provides a varied menu including small bites and kids' portions (small fish & chips with peas £7, for example).

Crossing the bridge, the Path drops you at *The Rose Revived* (☎ 01865-300221, 🖥 greeneking-pubs.co.uk; **fb**; 7D; WI-FI; 🐕 bar area only), with B&B varying in price but from around £55pp (sgl occ room rate). **Food** is served (daily brunch from 9-11am, main menu noon-9pm); a gourmet beefburger will set you back £11.99.

Rather than walk along the busy A415, **campers** would be well advised to take the No 15 **bus** service (see pp58-61) to get to **Standlake** (see opposite), five minutes' ride away. The No 15 also travels to Abingdon (see pp127-9), which provides the closest B&B accommodation should The Rose Revived be full.

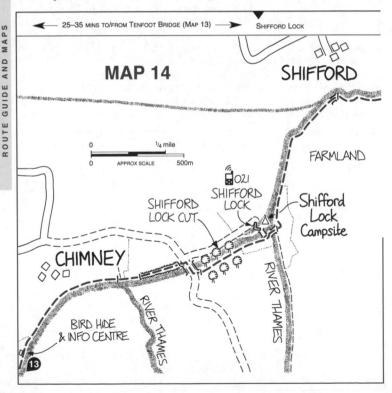

← 25–35 MINS TO/FROM TENFOOT BRIDGE (MAP 13) → SHIFFORD LOCK

MAP 14 SHIFFORD

FARMLAND

0 ¼ mile
0 APPROX SCALE 500m

SHIFFORD LOCK CUT

📱021 SHIFFORD LOCK

Shifford Lock Campsite

CHIMNEY

RIVER THAMES

RIVER THAMES

BIRD HIDE & INFO CENTRE

13

STANDLAKE [Map 15, p106]

Lincoln Farm Park (☎ 01865-300239, 🖳 lincolnfarmpark.co.uk; WI-FI; 🐾; Feb-early Nov) is the best option in the area for **campers** but it is aimed at families so walkers should book in advance; the standard pitch price is £24, or £29 using full facilities. The staff are friendly and informative; there's a shop too.

The No 15 **bus** service (see pp58-61) calls here; many trekkers will find this convenient especially as services operate in the late afternoon and also early in the morning (though Mon-Sat only). Their No 19 bus service also stops here.

A short walk from the site is the village **General Stores** (Mon-Sat 8am-6pm, Sun to 4pm) which includes a **post office** (Mon-Fri 9am-1pm & 2-5pm, Sat 9am-1pm).

Next to the campsite's entrance, *The Black Horse* (☎ 01865-300307, 🖳 the blackhorsestandlake.com; **fb**; WI-FI; 🐾; **food** Wed-Fri noon-2.30pm & 6-9pm, Sat noon-3pm & 6-9.30pm, Sun noon-5pm; also Sun-Tue 6-8.30pm pizzas only; 81 High St) is a typical country boozer, full of joviality and hearty 'modern British food with a global influence'. Note that the pub opens at 5pm on Monday and Tuesday.

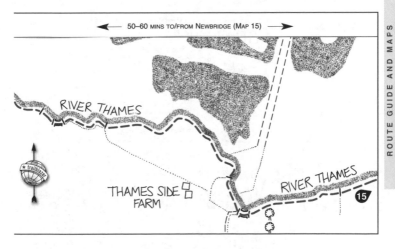

ROUTE GUIDE AND MAPS

E → NEWBRIDGE TO OXFORD (OSNEY BRIDGE) [MAPS 15-19]

This **14-mile (22.5km, 4½-5½hrs)** hike is as wonderfully riparian as yesterday's stage, the path continuing to hug the riverbanks closely. The route scythes its way through meadows, passing **Northmoor Lock** (see p107 & p110; Map 15) before arriving at **Bablock Hythe** (see p110; Map 16).

From here, there is a brief diversion from the river before you return to pass **Pinkhill Lock** (see p110; Map 17) and arrive at **Swinford Toll Bridge**, one of just two such bridges remaining on the Thames (the other being at Whitchurch); don't let the toll put you off – walkers cross for free. Crossing the bridge (and a bit of a walk from the trail) will bring you – eventually – to the southern part of the historic village of **Eynsham**, once home to a great 11th-century abbey, which – like most of its age – was a victim of Henry VIII's dissolution. On the trail you will soon reach **Eynsham Lock** (see p110).

Continuing on, the river toys with the edge of **Wytham Woods** (Map 18), the last resting place for at least one victim in the *Inspector Morse* novels. The river and trail now wend their way via **King's Lock** (Map 18) – the northernmost point on the Thames – and onwards past the turn-off to **Lower Wolvercote** (see p111) and right by **Godstow Lock** and the remains of its nearby **Abbey** (see box p111; Map 18).

It's a lovely end to the day with the vast vista of **Port Meadow** (see box on p114) opening up on the opposite bank and Oxford's rowers accompanying you onwards. **Binsey** (see p111) offers the last chance for a pub-stop before you arrive in **Oxford** (see p114 & pp116-21; Map 19) which, if you plan for a rest

ROUTE GUIDE AND MAPS

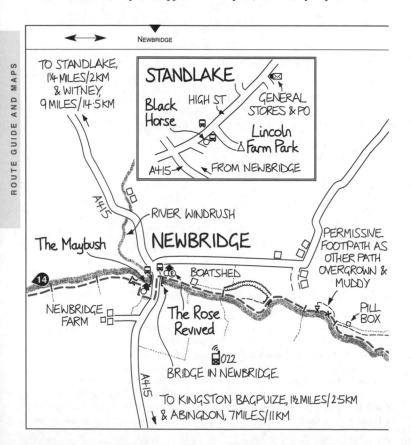

NEWBRIDGE

TO STANDLAKE, 1¼ MILES/2KM & WITNEY, 9 MILES/14·5KM

STANDLAKE

HIGH ST

Black Horse

GENERAL STORES & PO

Lincoln Farm Park

A415

FROM NEWBRIDGE

A415

RIVER WINDRUSH

The Maybush

NEWBRIDGE

14

BOATSHED

PERMISSIVE FOOTPATH AS OTHER PATH OVERGROWN & MUDDY

NEWBRIDGE FARM

The Rose Revived

PILL BOX

022

BRIDGE IN NEWBRIDGE

A415

TO KINGSTON BAGPUIZE, 1½ MILES/2·5KM & ABINGDON, 7 MILES/11KM

day, is an absorbing place to take one. Where you plan to stay in Oxford might determine which route you should take to enter into the city (see box on p114).

NORTHMOOR LOCK [Map 15]

Northmoor Lock Paddocks (🖳 barefoot campsites.co.uk; **fb**; 🏕 campers only; late May-Aug) is as splendidly isolated a **campsite** as you'll find along the River Thames. However, sadly, tent pitches are now only available 28 days a year on Fri and Sat due to planning permission issues related to flooding. There is also a minimum 2-night booking policy, though single-night booking may be possible on restricted pitches for walkers depending on campsite capacity.

A pitch costs £14pp per night. You can also hire one of their two **wooden cabins** called '**log pods**' (sleep up to four; £35 per night plus £14pp). Bedding is not provided so you need to have an air-bed or sleeping mat. People staying have access to a fire pit for open fires; firewood must be bought on site. With cars being banned the atmosphere is one to be relished. Booking is essential. There is also a **water tap** here.

(cont'd on p110)

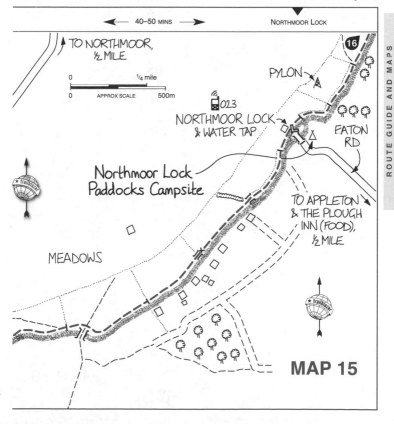

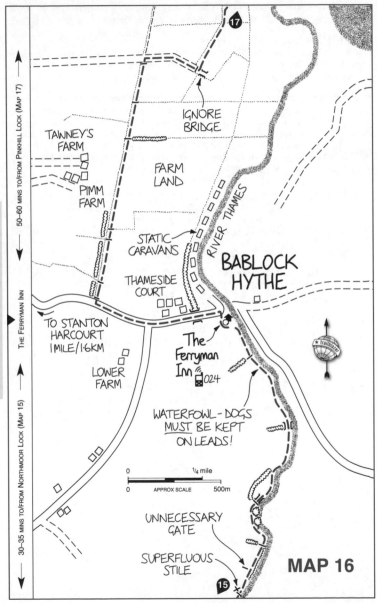

50-60 MINS TO/FROM PINKHILL LOCK (MAP 17)

THE FERRYMAN INN

30-35 MINS TO/FROM NORTHMOOR LOCK (MAP 15)

ROUTE GUIDE AND MAPS

17

IGNORE BRIDGE

TAWNEY'S FARM

PIMM FARM

FARM LAND

STATIC CARAVANS

RIVER THAMES

BABLOCK HYTHE

THAMESIDE COURT

TO STANTON HARCOURT 1 MILE/1·6KM

LOWER FARM

The Ferryman Inn 024

WATERFOWL - DOGS MUST BE KEPT ON LEADS!

0   ¼ mile
0   APPROX SCALE   500m

UNNECESSARY GATE

SUPERFLUOUS STILE

15

MAP 16

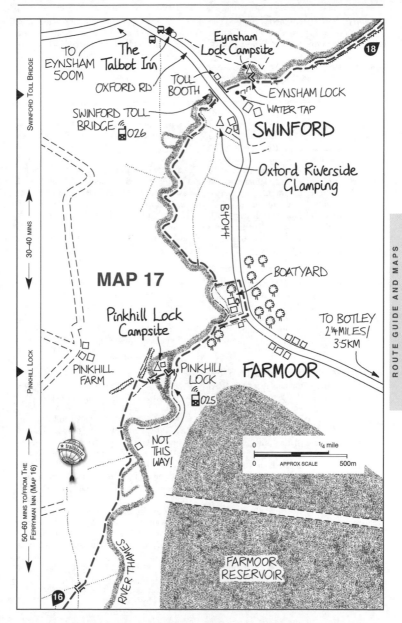

(cont'd from p107) For food, a civilised pub meal can be had approximately half-a-mile away in **Appleton** at *The Plough Inn* (☎ 01865-863535, 💻 appleton-eaton.org/ amenities/the-plough; **fb**; WI-FI; 🐾 on lead and bar only; **food** Tue-Sat 5.30-9.30pm,

Sat & Sun noon-3pm), where you'll find real ales and home-cooked meals. At the time of research the pub opened at 4pm during the week (but is closed on Mon) and noon at the weekend; they hope to serve food more in 2022.

BABLOCK HYTHE [Map 16, p108]

Situated at what was once an important crossing point between Oxford and the West Country, Bablock Hythe is said to have played host to a ferry across the Thames for almost a thousand years, with the earliest record of one dating back to 1279. Before then, the Romans are known to have forded the river here too.

Despite such history the closest you'll get to a helping hand over the Thames these days is through the name of the local pub. *The Ferryman Inn* (☎ 01865-880028, 💻

theferrymaninn.co.uk; **fb**; 2D/2T/2Tr; WI-FI; 🐾 in Fisherman's bar only) provides **B&B** and meals. For £50pp (sgl occ room rate) you get a room and a breakfast of toast and cereal; a full English is an extra £5pp. The pub is open for lunch and dinner (**food** daily noon-2.30pm & 7-9pm). A free house, there are plenty of real ales to sip as you succumb to the smell of a home-made steak & ale pie (£13.75), or on Sundays a 2-/3-course lunch (£15.50/19.50).

PINKHILL LOCK [Map 17, p109]

Pinkhill Lock Campsite (☎ 01865-881452; 🐾 on lead; Apr-Oct) is run by the Environment Agency and like all of these was closed at the time of research but hopes to be open in 2022. A pitch (tent and up to

two people) costs from £12 (inc the cost of a shower); toilet facilities are available. Note that there is no vehicle access. The nearest pub is The Talbot Inn (see below), in Eynsham, about 1½ miles away.

EYNSHAM LOCK [Map 17, p109]

Another of the Environment Agency's (EA) sites, *Eynsham Lock Campsite* (☎ 01865-881324; well-behaved 🐾 on lead) has 10 pitches (from £8.50 per pitch irrespective of the number of people or tent size). The toilets are available 24 hours a day, though a code from the lock-keeper is required, obtainable during working hours; the showers (£3.50) operate on a token basis. There is a water tap and a firepit is also available. Like all EA campsites this was closed in 2021 due to Covid but generally it is open year-round unless the site is flooded. Booking is recommended at weekends and in July & August.

Right by the path, *Oxford Riverside Glamping* (💻 oxfordriversideglamping.co .uk; **fb**; end Mar-early Oct) has 10 fully fitted **bell tents** sleeping up to four people and complete with electric heater, though

there's a 2-night minimum stay (£180 for two people for the two nights plus £10pp).

Approximately 250 metres along Oxford Rd, between the lock and Eynsham, *The Talbot Inn* (☎ 01865-881348, 💻 talbot oxford.co.uk; **fb**; 🍺; WI-FI; 🐾) provides **B&B** in either the original part of the pub (1D/1T share bathroom, 1T; from £27.50pp, sgl occ room rate) or in a new building called Wharf Side (2D/6D or T; from £37.50pp, sgl occ room rate). There's also **food** (Mon-Sat noon-2pm & 6-9pm, Sun noon-4pm & 6-9pm). The menu includes such delights as homemade lasagne, garlic bread and dressed seasonal salad (£12.50).

For information about Eynsham visit 💻 eynsham-pc.gov.uk.

The frequent S1 **bus** service (see pp58-61) stops by The Talbot.

KING'S LOCK [Map 18, p113]

If you wish to stay here (☎ 01865-553403; 🐾 on lead; Apr-Oct) you can put up a **tent** (a pitch costs £8.50) but the term 'basic' is taken to a new extreme: there's a water tap but no showers or toilets – and there's no vehicle access either. Booking is recommended. The nearest pub on the Path is The Trout Inn (see below) approximately one mile further along the river.

LOWER WOLVERCOTE
[Map 18, p113]

As you cross **Godstow Bridge** (see also box below) you'll come to *The Trout Inn* (☎ 01865-510930, 🖥 thetroutoxford.co.uk; **fb**; **food** Mon-Sat noon-9pm, Sun to 8.30pm; WI-FI; 🐾); it has a lovely terrace on which to relax and indulge in such exotic delights as goat's cheese, caramelised red onion chutney, mozzarella & rocket pizza (£12.50) or, for evening dining, spit-roast chicken (£14.50).

❑ GODSTOW ABBEY [Map 18, p113]

In between Godstow Bridge and Lock are the **remains of Godstow Abbey**. Established in 1133 and once a magnificent nunnery, the outer walls and ruins of the abbess's chapel are all that now remain. Young girls of the nobility were often sent here for 'finishing' and it is thought to be where Henry II met Rosamund Clifford. Famed for her beauty, 'Fair Rosamund' would go on to become the king's mistress and, according to rumour, bear him two children. Following her death in 1176 and burial here, the abbey grew in size due to the significant endowments lavished on it by the bereft king.

In 1541 Henry VIII's dissolution saw most of the buildings destroyed. Those that remained found themselves involved in a political rather than a religious conflict a century later when the Royalists used them in the English Civil War to assist in their defence of Godstow Bridge.

ROUTE GUIDE AND MAPS

BINSEY [Map 19, p115]

Following a signposted and magnificent willow-arched path, illuminated by fairylights, away from the river will bring you to *The Perch* (☎ 01865-728891, 🖥 the-perch .co.uk; **fb**; **food** daily noon-9.30pm; WI-FI; 🐾), certainly one of the trail's quirkier places. Sitting beneath one of their huge weeping willows on a sunny day, this is a lovely place to eat lunch; the menu is imaginative, and you might try their quail's eggs with celery salt (£4.95). The location and ambience make it an essential stop.

OSNEY LOCK [Map 19, p115]

There was a flash weir (see box pp98-9) at Osney (or Oseney), recorded as far back as 1227 when Henry III was King of England. The neat, efficient lock you see today was built in 1790 by the inmates of Oxford Prison; it cost the mere sum of £750. Right alongside the lock you will now see **Osney Lock Hydro**, 🖥 osneylockhydro.co.uk) which proudly announces itself as the first community-owned power station on the Thames. Set up and financed by a group of local residents in 2021, it uses the power of the river flowing through an Archimedes screw to generate clean electricity which is sold to the local grid, with zero carbon emissions.

W ← OXFORD (OSNEY BRIDGE) TO NEWBRIDGE [MAPS 19-15]

[Route section begins on Map 19, p115] This **14-mile (22.5km, 4½-5½hrs)** hike is wonderfully riparian, the path hugging the riverbanks closely, although the relative wildness of this stretch of the river also means a paucity of services. Several pubs on the trail serve food, but unless you're willing to add some (otherwise unnecessary) mileage walking to the shop in Standlake you should purchase any supplies in Oxford – as the next shop is over thirty miles and two days away in Lechlade!

A delightful walk away from the busyness of Oxford takes you to **Binsey** (see p111), which offers the day's first chance for a pub-stop before the vast vista of **Port Meadow** (see box on p114) opens up on the opposite bank; Oxford's rowers accompany you up to **Godstow Lock** and the remains of its nearby **Abbey** (see box on p111; Map 18). Just after this is the turn-off to **Lower Wolvercote** (see p111) and another of the day's possible pub-stops.

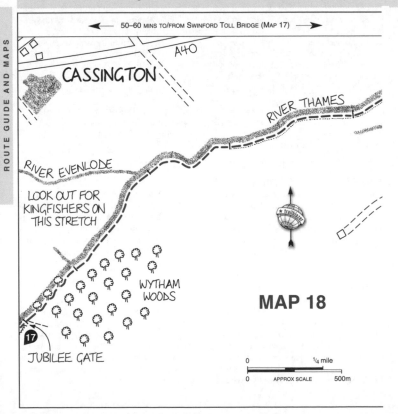

ROUTE GUIDE AND MAPS

50–60 MINS TO/FROM SWINFORD TOLL BRIDGE (MAP 17)

A40

CASSINGTON

RIVER THAMES

RIVER EVENLODE

LOOK OUT FOR KINGFISHERS ON THIS STRETCH

WYTHAM WOODS

MAP 18

JUBILEE GATE

17

0   ¼ mile
0   APPROX SCALE   500m

You continue to **King's Lock** (see p111, Map 18) – the northernmost point on the Thames – and then the river works its way round the meadows to the edge of **Wytham Woods**, the last resting place for at least one victim in the *Inspector Morse* novels. You will soon reach **Eynsham Lock** (see p110; Map 17) and **Swinford Toll Bridge** (see pp105-6). Crossing the bridge (and a bit of a walk from the trail) will bring you to another pub and – eventually – to the historic village of **Eynsham** (see p110). At **Pinkhill Lock** (see p110) you cross the Thames, and there is a diversion from the river before arriving at **Bablock Hythe** (see p110; Map 16) and another pub. The final section is through lovely meadows passing **Northmoor Lock** (see p107 & p110; Map 15) before arriving at **Newbridge** (see p104) where you have the choice of two good pubs!

[Next route overview on p103]

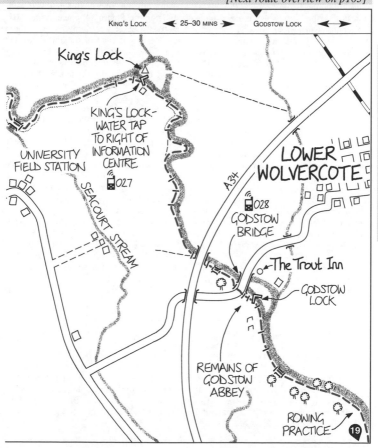

KING'S LOCK ◄ 25–30 MINS ► GODSTOW LOCK ◄►

King's Lock

KING'S LOCK – WATER TAP TO RIGHT OF INFORMATION CENTRE
📱027

UNIVERSITY FIELD STATION

SEACOURT STREAM

LOWER WOLVERCOTE

A34

📱028 GODSTOW BRIDGE

The Trout Inn

GODSTOW LOCK

REMAINS OF GODSTOW ABBEY

ROWING PRACTICE

19

ROUTE GUIDE AND MAPS

❏ **PORT MEADOW** [Map 19]

Thought to have been grazed for over 4000 years and never touched by plough or pesticide, this 350-acre area of land was gifted to Oxford by Alfred the Great for the locals' help in resisting the Danes in the 10th century. The liberty to graze animals freely on the meadow was recorded in the *Domesday Book* in 1086 and has remained in place ever since. The cows quenching their thirst in the river obviously know their rights as they continue to stubbornly sup, unbothered by the endless stream of rowers who scull past on the water.

OXFORD [map p119]

Originally the site of a simple Saxon 'ford' used to guide 'oxen' across the river, 'modern' Oxford's story begins early in the 8th century with the founding of a priory. In AD872, while journeying upstream, King Alfred rested at the priory and fell into discussions with the resident monks. The debate purportedly lasted a few days, and Oxford gained a reputation as a place where people could learn. Over the coming centuries a fortified settlement developed, a mint was built, and the fledgling city would host councils between the Saxons and the Danes, with the latter also opting to raid it as and when they felt the need. Heavily fought over during the Norman Conquest, William ordered a castle to be built to control the town. Originally wooden but gradually modified in stone, the Norman fortification would be Matilda's base during the Anarchy of 1141 (see box on p138) and also the primary fortification of the Royalists who would make Oxford their capital during the English Civil War.

The university's origins are as rooted in conflict as the city itself; specifically, Henry II's troublesome relationship with his archbishop Thomas Becket. In 1167 Henry ordered English students who were studying in France to come home. His motive? Becket was living in exile there and Henry was concerned that the students would side with the archbishop against him. Attracted by Oxford's reputation as a centre of learning the scholars headed there and, on arrival, established halls of learning akin to the ones they had recently experienced in France. This led to the founding of Oxford's oldest college, **University College**, in 1249 – the first university in the English-speaking world. The **University Church of St Mary the Virgin** (see box on p116) became the university church as the scholars needed a central meeting place: the church was used for academic lectures as well as services.

Oxford today is a constant hive of activity and it's a great place to stroll amongst the throngs of students, locals and tourists who happily mingle beneath the 'dreaming spires'. An excellent way to see the sights is on a **walking tour**. Thoroughly recommended, the guides at Footprints Tours (🖥 footprints-tours.com/oxford; **fb**)

❏ **ACCESSING OXFORD**

Depending on where you are staying in Oxford (and which direction you are walking from) there are different ways to reach your accommodation from the trail. Those staying near Osney Bridge and Oxford railway station, or in the city centre, should leave the path at Osney Bridge (Map 19), while those staying on Abingdon Rd should leave the river at Folly Bridge (Map 20), but this also provides a convenient access point for anyone staying in the city centre (especially if coming from the east). **Campers** should continue (or leave the path) two miles from Folly Bridge and follow the directions on Map 20.

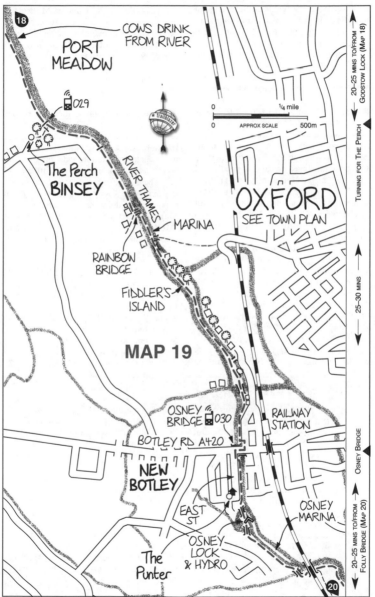

18

PORT MEADOW

COWS DRINK FROM RIVER

📱029

The Perch
BINSEY

RIVER THAMES

MARINA

RAINBOW BRIDGE

FIDDLER'S ISLAND

MAP 19

OXFORD
SEE TOWN PLAN

0   1/4 mile
0   APPROX SCALE   500m

OSNEY BRIDGE 📱030

BOTLEY RD A420

RAILWAY STATION

NEW BOTLEY

EAST ST

OSNEY LOCK & HYDRO

The Punter

OSNEY MARINA

20

20-25 MINS TO/FROM Godstow Lock (MAP 18)

TURNING FOR THE PERCH

25-30 MINS

OSNEY BRIDGE

20-25 MINS TO/FROM Folly Bridge (MAP 20)

ROUTE GUIDE AND MAPS

are knowledgeable, enthusiastic and great at adding the necessary sense of drama to the city's turbulent past. They operate a range of tours: options include a two-hour tour of the city (daily 11am, 12.30pm, 2pm, Sat also 3.30pm) which is free, though tips are appreciated. Guides can be found at 5 Broad St shortly before each tour begins.

Similar **tours** are available from City Sightseeing Oxford (☎ 01865-790522, 💻 citysightseeingoxford.com; **fb**), who will also provide a wealth of information at their Visitor Information Point (daily 9.30am-5pm) at 44-45 High St. If you'd rather see Oxford's attractions at your own pace you'll find many marked on the map on p119.

The city's number one tourist attraction is **Ashmolean Museum of Art and Archaeology** (☎ 01865-278000, 💻 ashmolean.org; **fb**; daily 10am-5pm; free) on Beaumont St; it was established in 1683 and is the oldest museum in England. Another history house is the **Museum of Oxford** (☎ 01865-252334, 💻 museumofoxford.org; **fb**; Mon-Sat 10am-5pm, closed on Bank Hol Mons; free; St Aldates), whilst **Oxford Castle and Prison** (☎ 01865-260666, 💻 oxfordcastleandprison.co.uk; **fb**; Mon-Thur 10.30am-5pm, Fri-Sun 10am-5.30pm; guided tour only; £14.45) offers the best panorama of the city from its Saxon St George's Tower. Not to be missed

is the legendary 1770s **Covered Market** (💻 oxford-coveredmarket.co.uk) with its artisan grocers, boutique clothing and buzzing cafés; nor should **Blackwell's Bookshop** (☎ 01865-792792, 💻 blackwells.co.uk; **fb**; 48-51 Broad St) be, even though it is hardly a tourist attraction.

Services

Sadly, the tourist information centre has closed, but the official Experience Oxfordshire (💻 experienceoxfordshire.org; **fb**) website has information about everything including accommodation booking and tickets for local events and attractions.

There are two branches of Sainsbury's **supermarket** (daily 7am-9pm or 10pm depending on the store; St Aldates and also Magdalen St) and **Boots the Chemist** (Mon-Sat 8am-8pm, Sun 11am-5pm; Cornmarket St). The **post office** (Mon & Wed-Sat 9am-5.30pm, Tue from 9.30am) is on St Aldates. Oxford has branches of all major High St banks and plentiful **ATMs**.

The closest **food shop** to Osney Bridge is Westgate Stores (daily 8am-9.30pm; Botley Rd).

● On Abingdon Rd (Map 20) there are several **food stores** including a Tesco (daily 6am-11pm) with a free **ATM**.

For **camping supplies** visit Go Outdoors (💻 gooutdoors.co.uk/oxford; 426

❑ THE VIRGIN MARY CHURCHES

As you wander past the great churches and spires which watch over the river you may notice that many of them have more in common than just their fluvial location. For Cricklade, Castle Eaton, Buscot, Oxford, Wallingford, North Stoke, Streatley, Hurley, Henley-on-Thames, Putney and Lambeth all have a church dedicated to the Virgin Mary. Indeed, the list above is far from exhaustive, and there are more than 50 religious institutions devoted to St Mary along the banks of the Thames, an amount which equates to approximately one for every four-mile stretch of water! And of the few churches which no longer bear the name of Jesus's mother, several have been renamed and originally were St Mary's too – the Church of St Lawrence in Lechlade being one such example.

So why the fascination? Well, throughout history, water and rivers have long been associated with fertility. Indeed, women used to bathe in the Thames's waters believing that the river's power would increase their ability to produce offspring. Whether these riparian dips worked is unclear – but it did lead to numerous churches along the banks being dedicated to the most famous mother of them all – Mary, mother of the son of God.

Abingdon Rd; Mon-Fri 9am-8pm, Sat to 6pm, Sun 10.30am-4.30pm).

Transport

Buses (see pp58-61) connect the city with many of the towns and villages along the Thames Path. The services most likely to be of use are the: S1, X2, city 3A, X3/X13, city35, X38, X39 & X40; the 'X' services run via stops along St Aldates and Abingdon Rd.

Oxford is easily accessed by **coach** (National Express, Oxford Tube, and Oxford Bus Company; see box on p53) from airports in southern England as well as many other places in the UK. Most services operate to and from Gloucester Green Bus Station.

Oxford **railway station** is a short walk from the path and is served by GWR, Chiltern Railways and Cross Country (see box on pp56-7).

Where to stay

There are loads of accommodation options in Oxford. In addition to the places listed below, in the summer months you can stay in some of the colleges (🖳 university rooms.com/en-GB/city/oxford/home).

Camping and hostels The city has two **hostels**; both are clean and comfortable. Next to the railway station is *YHA Oxford* (☎ 0345-371 9131 or ☎ 01865-727275, 🖳 yha.org.uk/hostel/yha-oxford; **fb**; 203 beds, 1-, 2-, 3-, 4- & 6-bed rooms, some en suite; WI-FI communal areas; 2a Botley Rd). Dorm beds cost from £18pp, private rooms (for up to two sharing) from £28; see also p19. At the time of research the hostel was still closed due to Covid and there is even the possibility of the hostel moving to a new site so contact the YHA or the hostel to check.

The other hostel is a short stroll towards the centre of town: *Central Backpackers* (☎ 01865-242288, 🖳 central backpackers.co.uk; **fb**; 4-, 6-, 8- & 12-bed mixed dorms, 1 x 6- & 1 x 8-bed female-only dorm; shared facilities; WI-FI; 13 Park End St) charges £15-28pp for a dorm bed; 4- & 6-bed rooms can be booked as private rooms (£80-130); breakfast is not provided,

but there is a fully equipped kitchen for guests' use.

● **On Abingdon Rd (Map 20) Camping** is available at *Oxford Camping & Caravanning Club Site* (☎ 01865-244088, 🖳 campingandcaravanningclub.co.uk/ oxford; **fb**; WI-FI; 🐾 on lead); the campsite is conveniently hidden behind a branch of Go Outdoors (see Services). It does lack charm but it's the only option in town; the official backpacker rate for non-members is £9.65-10.70pp but in the summer season, a tent for two non-members costs from £32. Booking is recommended in the peak season. Buses to/from central Oxford, Abingdon and Wallingford run from the stops outside the site.

B&Bs

● **On Abingdon Rd (Map 20)** Most of Oxford's B&Bs are on Abingdon Rd, amongst them *Newton House* (☎ 01865-240561, 🖳 newtonhouseoxford.co.uk; **fb**; 8D/2T/2D or T/2Tr; WI-FI; from £45pp, sgl occ room rate; Nos 82-84); *The Oxford Townhouse* (☎ 01865-511122, 🖳 theox fordtownhouse.co.uk; **fb**; 2S/2T/11D; WI-FI; from £84pp, sgl occ £158; Nos 88-90); and the delectable *Lakeside Guest House* (☎ 01865-244725, 🖳 lakeside-guesthouse.com; **fb**; 1S/3D/2D or T/1D in Studio; WI-FI; £45-70pp, sgl from £80, sgl occ room rate; No 118).

Overlooking Folly Bridge is *The Head of the River* (☎ 01865-721600, 🖳 headof theriveroxford.co.uk; **fb**; 19D; 🍷; WI-FI; 🐾; from £62.50pp, sgl occ room rate). Owned by Fuller's Brewery and situated on the site at which – it is thought – the ancient ford that gave the town its name was located, this is urban Thames accommodation at its finest. Food is also available (see Where to eat).

Hotels For those who want to stick near the river, accommodation is available at two hotels near Osney Bridge – neither will linger long in the memory but they won't break the bank either: *River Hotel* (☎ 01865-243475, 🖳 riverhotel.co.uk; **fb**; 2S/8D/2T/5Tr, 1S/1D private bathroom; 🍷; WI-FI; 17 Botley Rd) charges from £60pp (sgl/sgl occ from £99), and there is a minimum two-night stay at weekends in the peak season; for a single-night stay it is best to call them in case they have availability. *Westgate Hotel* (☎ 01865-726721, 🖳 west gatehoteloxford.co.uk; **fb**; 6S/5D/4T/3Tr/ 2Qd, mix en suite and shared facilities; 🛏; WI-FI; 1 Botley Rd) is on two sites: the main building has most of the en suite rooms (and baths) and there is a separate annex across the road where most rooms have shared facilities. If you want a room with a bath it is best to call them as that can't be requested online or if booked through an agency. B&B (continental breakfast) costs from £55pp (sgl £85-100, sgl occ room rate); cooked breakfast extra £5pp.

Hotels can also be found centrally. Between river and city is *Royal Oxford Hotel* (☎ 01865-248432, 🖳 royaloxford hotel.co.uk; **fb**; 1S/10T/13D/2Tr; 🛏; WI-FI; Park End St), where the room-only prices vary depending on demand but begin from approximately £70pp (sgl from £75, sgl occ room rate; breakfast £9.50pp); while on St Michael's St (20-24) is the plush boutique *Vanbrugh House Hotel* (☎ 01865-244622, 🖳 vanbrughhousehotel.co.uk; **fb**; 1S/3D or T/18D; 🛏; WI-FI). Rates here are also very flexible, but expect to pay at least £100pp (sgl from £180, sgl occ room rate).

Surreptitiously tucked away just off Holywell St is the well-established *Bath Place Hotel* (☎ 01865-791812, 🖳 bath place.co.uk; **fb**; 12D/3D or Tr/1Qd; 🛏; WI-FI; 🐾; 4 & 5 Bath Place). Hiding practically next door to the famous Turf Tavern pub (see Where to eat, Pubs), this establishment

OXFORD – MAP KEY

Where to stay
2 River Hotel
5 Westgate Hotel
6 YHA Oxford
8 Royal Oxford Hotel
10 Central Backpackers
18 Vanbrugh House Hotel
51 Bath Place Hotel

Where to eat & drink
1 The Punter
3 The One
7 The Jam Factory
9 Yellow Submarine
12 Café from Crisis
13 Kebab King
14 George Street Social
15 Chutneys
16 Eagle and Child
20 The Nosebag
21 The Three Goats Heads
32 The Bear
52 The Turf Tavern

Services
4 Westgate Stores
19 Sainsbury's
23 Sainsbury's
24 Post Office
26 Footprint Tours meeting place (5 Broad St)
27 Boots
35 Blackwell's Bookshop
56 City Sightseeing Information Point

Other
11 Oxford Castle and Prison
17 Ashmolean
22 Carfax Tower
25 Pembroke College
28 Balliol College
29 Jesus College
30 Covered Market
31 Museum of Oxford
33 Christ Church College & Cathedral
34 Trinity College
36 Exeter College
37 Lincoln College

Other *(cont'd)*
38 Museum of the History of Science
39 New Bodleian Library
40 Sheldonian Theatre
41 Brasenose College
42 Wadham College
43 Clarendon Building
44 Bodleian Library
45 Radcliffe Camera
46 University Church of St Mary the Virgin
47 Oriel College
48 Corpus Christi
49 Bridge of Sighs
50 Hertford College
53 All Souls College
54 University College
55 Merton College
57 New College
58 The Queen's College
59 St Edmund Hall
60 Magdalen College

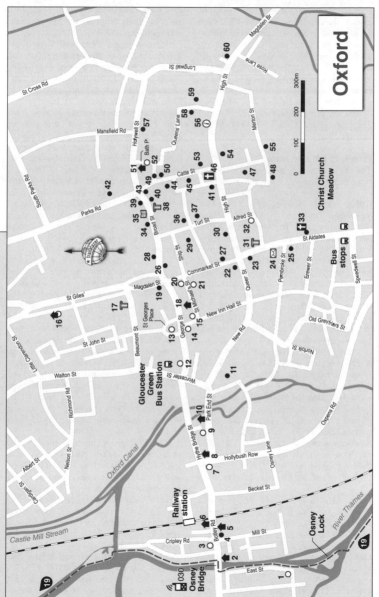

Oxford

ROUTE GUIDE AND MAPS

is in a great central location from which to explore the city. The rate (from £72.50pp, sgl occ £120) includes a continental buffet; a cooked breakfast costs extra. Advance bookings for a single-night stay are not taken for Friday or Saturday nights year-round but nearer the time may be considered.

● **On Abingdon Rd (Map 20)** There's a branch of **Travelodge** (see p21; Oxford Abingdon Road; ☎ 08715-591877, 🖳 tra velodge.co.uk).

Where to eat and drink
The city also has innumerable eateries of all types, amongst them ...

Cafés and takeaways
Yellow Submarine (☎ 01865-236119, 🖳 yellow submarineshop.org; **fb**; Mon-Fri 8.30am-3pm; WI-FI; 🐾 if OK with manager; 12 Park End St) employs people with autism and learning difficulties. There's a limited breakfast but they prepare toasties (£2.90-4.10) at lunchtime as well as smashing coffees and cakes. **Café from Crisis** (☎ 01865-263972; **fb**; Tue-Fri 9am-3pm; WI-FI; 40 George St) supports the homeless and provides decent breakfast options and has daily specials at lunch.

Takeaway is available centrally at **Kebab King** (☎ 01865-200121, 🖳 kebab kingoxford.com; **fb**; Mon-Sat 11.45am-3.55am, Sun noon-2.55am) at 36 George St.

● **On Abingdon Rd (Map 20)** **Paper Boat Café** (Tue-Sat 8am-5pm, Sun 9am-5pm) has baguettes (from £5.30), biscuits and cakes (from £1.50) for both eat-in and takeaway. **Mediterranean Fish Bar** (☎ 01865-243822; **fb**; Mon-Sat 11am-9pm, Sun noon-8pm) claims to serve the best fish & chips in Oxford but also has kebabs & burgers.

Pubs
'My happiest hours are spent with three or four old friends in old clothes, tramping together and putting up in small pubs.' CS Lewis.

There are almost as many pubs in Oxford as academics; indeed, you could almost drown in the variation of ales, organic lagers and high-voltage ciders available. **They all also serve food** though in some cases almost as an afterthought – ale is definitely the priority at most of these establishments.

Ever-popular, **The Turf Tavern** (☎ 01865-243235, 🖳 greeneking-pubs.co.uk; **fb**; WI-FI; 🐾; food daily 10am-9pm; Bath Place) has been a stalwart of Oxford's pub-scene for centuries and the section of old town wall which borders its back garden has witnessed many a peculiar event, from Bob Hawke (once prime minister of Australia) downing a yard of ale in eleven seconds to Bill Clinton 'not inhaling' something someone had lit. Other famous customers include Margaret Thatcher, Elizabeth Taylor and Oscar Wilde – the pub even claims to have a ghost, Rosie, who hangs around the glass wash area, apparently still awaiting her husband's return from the English Civil War. There's a decent menu with some interesting sharing platters (from £10.99).

Despite The Turf Tavern's claims, it seems most likely that the title of oldest watering hole in Oxford goes to **The Bear** (☎ 01865-728164, 🖳 bearoxford.co.uk; **fb**; food Wed-Sat noon-4pm & 5-8pm, Sun noon-6pm; WI-FI; 🐾). A mainstay of the city's walking tours, beverages were first served here in 1242. The pub has an interesting interior, the walls being adorned with club and college ties donated by alumni from all over England. Now owned by Fuller's Brewery there is their normal range of ales on tap as well as a menu which always includes bar snacks and pub classics with a Caesar salad for £8, £11.25 with chicken.

Sadly closed for renovation at the time of writing, but hoping to re-open in early 2022 as a hotel as well as a pub, **The Eagle and Child** (49 St Giles) was once the favoured drinking venue of The Inklings, a group of writers including JRR Tolkien and CS Lewis, who would regularly meet here. It will be managed by Young & Co (🖳 youngs.co.uk) so check their website for details.

For **cheap pub-grub and drinks**, **The Three Goats Heads** (☎ 01865-721523; **fb**; food Mon-Fri noon-3pm & 5-9pm, Sat noon-9pm, Sun to 5pm; 🐾 on lead) serves

Samuel Smith beer. There's no music or TV but the lack of such distractions keeps prices low – indeed, you'll get a plate of Cumberland sausage & mash for just £8.95.

Though not strictly a pub, *George Street Social* (☎ 01865-204735, ☐ george streetsocial.com; **fb**; food Mon 9am-7.45pm, Tue-Sun to 10pm; WI-FI) is a lively place that's open all day to feed and water the masses. If you really feel like indulging they do a 'bottomless brunch' for £29pp, where you can choose any item off their brunch menu and twin it with as much prosecco or bloody Mary as you can within a two-hour slot! Their mains are more reasonable, with pasta dishes from £10 and burger with fries for £12.

Right on the trail, *The Punter* (☎ 01865-248832, ☐ thepunteroxford.co.uk; **fb**; food Mon-Fri noon-2.30pm & 5-9pm, Sat & Sun noon-9pm; WI-FI; 🐾) is unusual in that its menu has only vegetarian and vegan dishes, though it's reasonable value with main dishes at £13-14.

● **On Abingdon Rd (Map 20)** Libations by the Thames can be sunk at *The Head of the River* (see Where to stay; WI-FI; 🐾; food Mon-Sat noon-9pm, Sun to 8pm). There's plenty of outdoor seating peering out over the water and a decent menu (main courses £12-25) but it can get very busy, especially in the summer months, so it is worth booking in advance then.

Campers and those residing on Abingdon Rd in particular may be interested in *The Duke of Monmouth* (☎ 01865-240294, ☐ greeneking-pubs.co.uk; **fb**; food daily noon-9pm); WI-FI; 🐾 bar area; No 260), another Greene King pub. The prices are particularly reasonable including sandwiches from £4.99 and 8oz rump steak with chips for £9.99.

Restaurants Nearest to Osney Bridge is jack-of-all-trades *The One* (☎ 01865-240018, ☐ theoneoxford.co.uk; **fb**; food daily noon-10pm; WI-FI; 2 Botley Rd), where you'll find not just Chinese, Thai and Western food but also tapas and takeaway.

The Jam Factory (☎ 01865-244613, ☐ thejamfactoryoxford.com; **fb**; food Mon-Fri 10am-3pm & 5-9.30pm, Sat 10am-10pm, Sun to 4pm) is a characterful place on Hollybush Row and a restaurant, bar and gallery all rolled into one. Food-wise, they do a wide range of burgers (£11.50-15) and a varied menu too.

Based at 6-8 St Michael's St, *The Nosebag* (☎ 01865-721033, ☐ nosebag oxford.co.uk; **fb**; daily 9am-9pm) is a well-regarded independent place that's been serving great home-cooked food for almost fifty years. Though they do cater for carnivores they are best-known for their vegetarian food; consider their porcini & mushroom (£11.50) or, if you need the meat, the warm chicken, peach & feta salad (£12.95).

At the end of the street, for Indian lovers, *Chutneys* (☎ 01865-724241, ☐ chutneysoxford.co.uk; **fb**; food daily noon-2.30pm, Sun-Thur 5.30-10pm, Fri & Sat to 10.30pm; 36 St Michael's St) is a must. Tandoori dishes (£9.95-14.95) and all the usual suspects are available at the city's oldest-surviving Indian restaurant.

● **On Abingdon Rd (Map 20)** On an island in the river is *The Folly* (☎ 01865-201293, ☐ no1-folly-bridge.co.uk; **fb**; food daily lunch noon-2.30pm, afternoon tea 2.30-3.45pm, dinner 6pm to late). The restaurant offers riverside dining on an outdoor floating pontoon. The menu changes regularly but may include fish of the day with caramelised onion gnocchi (£23.95) and roasted pepper & aubergine polenta (£21.50).

Symbols used in text (see also p78)
🛁 Bathtub in, or for, at least one room
WI-FI means wi-fi is available
fb signifies places that post their current opening hours on their Facebook page
🐾 Dogs allowed; if for accommodation this is subject to prior arrangement (see p255)

E ➜ OXFORD (OSNEY BRIDGE) TO ABINGDON   [MAPS 19-23]

This **9¾-mile (15.5km, 3¼-3¾hrs)** stretch retains the sense of isolation from the previous stages, the bustle of Oxford notwithstanding; although the size and style of the houses that occasionally spring up on the opposite bank suggest that the solitude one finds downstream of Oxford is in a decidedly more affluent setting than that you've already encountered upstream.

Having left the spires and students behind, this is a straightforward and relatively short stroll along the riverbank. Passing **Iffley Meadows Nature Reserve** (Map 20) – host to thousands of snake's-head fritillaries in spring – you arrive at **Iffley Lock** (see below), the first 'pound' lock built on the Thames (see box on pp98-9). **Sandford Lock** (Map 21) follows with its accompanying, infamous weir, known as 'the Lasher' (see box below). You'll find decent opportunities for food at both locks.

After the turning to **Radley** (see p125; Map 22) you come across the 18th-century **Nuneham House** (and also Carfax Conduit Building, see p126) on the eastern bank; a Grade II-listed Palladian Villa, it was built in 1756 by the 1st Earl Harcourt. During WW2 the house and grounds were requisitioned by the Ministry of Defence and it was known as RAF Nuneham Park. After its return, in the mid 1950s, to the Harcourt family they sold it to Oxford University who now lease it to Brahma Kumaris World Spiritual University. Shortly before you arrive at **Abingdon Lock** (Map 23), on the opposite bank are the two entrances of **Swift Ditch** (or Short Cut), also labelled as **Back Water** on OS maps. It is thought that this was enlarged from an existing channel by the monks of Abingdon in the 10th century in order to divert the river away from the abbey's doors. Following the lock, a pleasant amble sees you arrive in **Abingdon** (see pp127-9).

IFFLEY LOCK   [Map 20]

Shortly before the lock, *Isis (River) Farmhouse* (☎ 01865-243854, 🖥 theisis farmhouse.co.uk; **fb**; **food** Sun-Thur noon-8.30pm, Fri & Sat to 9pm; 🐾) is set in a magnificent location and often has live music in the evenings such as jazz on Sunday evenings (7-9.30pm). Note there is no vehicle access to the pub.

SANDFORD-ON-THAMES
[Map 21, p124]

Kings Arms (☎ 01865-777095, 🖥 chefand brewer.com; **fb**; WI-FI; 🐾 bar area) serves **meals** such as Caesar salad (£9.99) and slow-cooked steak & red wine (£12.49) all day (daily 11.30am-9.30pm) and you can eat out in the garden that looks over the lock and river.

The city 3A **bus** service (see pp58-61) stops on Henley Rd.

❏ THE SANDFORD LASHER   [Map 21, p124]

North of Sandford Lock is an infamous weir known as 'the Lasher.' Described by Jerome K Jerome in *Three Men in a Boat* as 'a very good place to drown yourself', the weir's dramatic title has been gained due to the number of unfortunate souls who have lost their lives to this particular section of the river's fast and deadly undercurrents. Rather ironically, one of the Lasher's victims was the adopted son of JM Barrie and the inspiration for Peter Pan – not, alas, a boy who would live for ever.

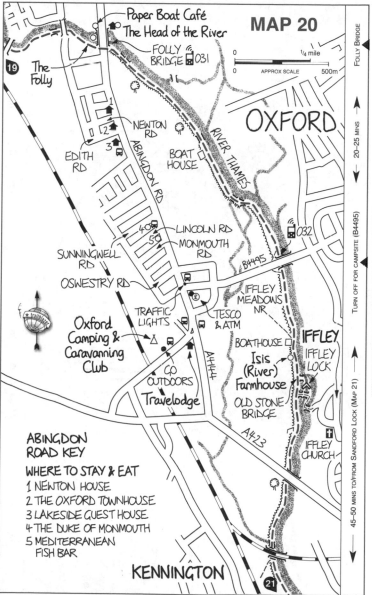

MAP 20

Paper Boat Café
The Head of the River

FOLLY BRIDGE 031

The Folly

19

0 — ¼ mile
0 — 500m
APPROX SCALE

FOLLY BRIDGE

OXFORD

1
NEWTON RD
2
3
EDITH RD

ABINGDON RD

BOAT HOUSE

RIVER THAMES

20-25 MINS

4
5
LINCOLN RD
MONMOUTH RD

032

SUNNINGWELL RD

OSWESTRY RD

B4495

TURN OFF FOR CAMPSITE (B4495)

IFFLEY MEADOWS NR

TRAFFIC LIGHTS

TESCO & ATM

IFFLEY

Oxford Camping & Caravanning Club

GO OUTDOORS
Travelodge

A4144

BOATHOUSE

Isis (River) Farmhouse

OLD STONE BRIDGE

A423

IFFLEY LOCK

IFFLEY CHURCH

45-50 MINS TO/FROM SANDFORD LOCK (MAP 21)

ABINGDON ROAD KEY

WHERE TO STAY & EAT
1 NEWTON HOUSE
2 THE OXFORD TOWNHOUSE
3 LAKESIDE GUEST HOUSE
4 THE DUKE OF MONMOUTH
5 MEDITERRANEAN FISH BAR

KENNINGTON

21

ROUTE GUIDE AND MAPS

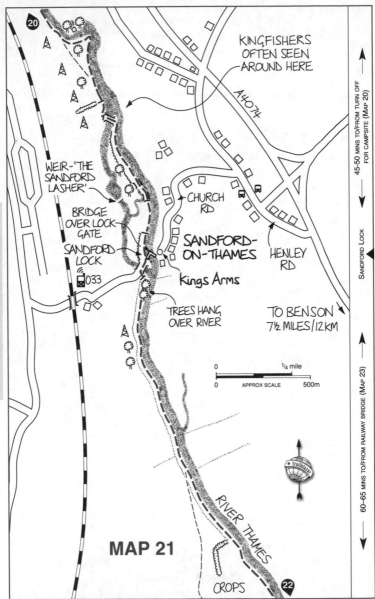

20

KINGFISHERS
OFTEN SEEN
AROUND HERE

A4074

WEIR-'THE
SANDFORD
LASHER'

BRIDGE
OVER LOCK-
GATE

SANDFORD
LOCK

📞033

CHURCH
RD

SANDFORD-
ON-THAMES

Kings Arms

HENLEY
RD

TREES HANG
OVER RIVER

TO BENSON
7½ MILES/12 KM

0 ——— ¼ mile
0 ——— 500m
APPROX SCALE

★ trailblaze

RIVER THAMES

CROPS

MAP 21

22

45-50 MINS TO/FROM TURN OFF FOR CAMPSITE (MAP 20)

SANDFORD LOCK

60-65 MINS TO/FROM RAILWAY BRIDGE (MAP 23)

RADLEY [Map 22]

Just shy of a mile away from the path, there is no need to divert to Radley unless you are desperate for a railway station, bus or pub; the latter, *Bowyer Arms* (☎ 01235-523452, 💻 greeneking pubs.co.uk; **fb**; **food** daily noon-8.45pm; WI-FI; 🐾 bar area only and on lead; Foxborough Rd) provides good standard pub classics from £11.49. Rump steaks for £7 on Steak Thursday!

Some GWR **services** (see box on pp56-7) on the Didcot Parkway to Oxford line call at the **railway station**; the city 35 **bus** also calls at the station (see pp58-61).

W ← ABINGDON TO OXFORD (OSNEY BRIDGE) [MAPS 23-19]

[Route section begins on Map 23, p126] This **9¾-mile (15.5km, 3¼-3¾hrs)** stretch introduces a sense of isolation contrasting with the previous stages, the bustle of Oxford notwithstanding. The day begins with a pleasant walk to **Abingdon Lock**, shortly after which on the opposite bank are the two

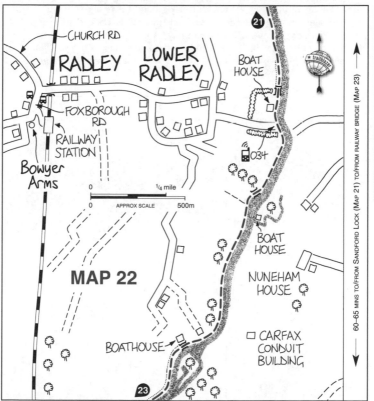

ROUTE GUIDE AND MAPS

60–65 MINS TO/FROM SANDFORD LOCK (MAP 21) TO/FROM RAILWAY BRIDGE (MAP 23)

entrances to **Swift Ditch** (or Short Cut), also labelled as **Back Water** on OS maps. Before you reach the turning to **Radley** (see p125; Map 22), you come across 18th-century **Nuneham House** (see p122), staring down at you from the eastern bank; just as it comes into sight you may also see the **Carfax Conduit Building** in the trees to the right, though originally in Oxford itself. The conduit used to bring clean water from the nearby hills to the centre of Oxford. Unfortunately, by 1787 it had become too much of an obstacle for the ever-increasing traffic of the city and the decision was taken to demolish it and replace it with a smaller cistern. It was at this point that Earl Harcourt stepped in and brought the building to Nuneham, where it stands today.

Sandford Lock (Map 21) follows with its accompanying, infamous weir, known as 'the Lasher' (see box on p122); and next you come to **Iffley Lock** (see p122; Map 20), the first 'pound' lock built on the Thames (see box on pp98-9). You'll find decent opportunities for food at both locks.

Passing **Iffley Meadows Nature Reserve** – host to thousands of snake's-head fritillaries in spring – a straightforward and relatively short stroll along the riverbank brings you to the spires and students of **Oxford** (see pp114-21; Map 19), which, if you plan for a rest day, is an absorbing place to take one. Where you plan to stay in Oxford might determine which route you should take to enter into the city (see box on p114).   *[Next route overview on pp112-13]*

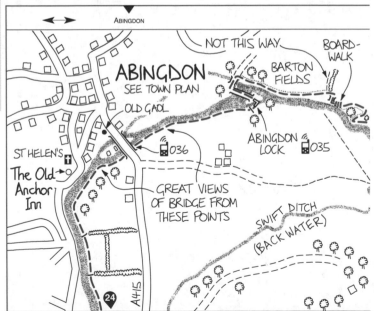

ABINGDON [map p129]

With excavations uncovering evidence of Iron Age, Roman and Saxon communities, Abingdon (its official name is Abingdon-on-Thames) can lay reasonable claim to being the oldest continuously inhabited settlement in England. Wonderfully, this market town is as pretty as it is historic.

The town originally grew prosperous in the 7th century thanks to its abbey and continued to thrive even after Henry VIII's dissolution of the monasteries in 1538. In 1556 it was named the county town of Berkshire, though reorganisation of local government led to the town becoming part of Oxfordshire in 1974.

The grandeur of Abingdon's sights means that they tend to introduce themselves. In the centre is **St Nicolas Church**, parts of which date back to the 11th century; the archway next door was once the Abbey Gateway though now it leads to **Abbey Gardens**. Dominating one side of Market Place is **County Hall**, in which you'll find the town's **museum** (☎ 01235-523703, 🖳 abingdon.gov.uk/abingdon-county-hall-museum; **fb**; Tue-Sun & Bank Hol Mons 10am-4pm; free but donation appreciated).

A climb up on to the hall's roof (Mar-Nov daily but closed if the weather is bad; £2) presents magnificent views out over the town and back down towards the river. You'll not be able to miss the tower and spire of the 10th-century **St Helen's Church**, which together with the town's **bridge** offer great photo opportunities. Close to the bridge is the town's imposing former **Old Gaol**, completed in 1812 to a then modern radial design; it now houses serviced apartments.

Services

The **visitor information centre** (☎ 01235-522711, 🖳 abingdon.gov.uk/discover-abingdon; Mon-Fri 10am-4pm, weekends from the museum) is in Guildhall. On West St Helen St there is a Co-op **supermarket** (daily 7am-10pm) which includes a **post office** (Mon-Fri 9am-5.30pm, Sat to 2pm), while on Bury St is a **Boots the Chemist** (Mon-Sat 8.30am-5.30pm). Market Place has a branch of NatWest **bank** with **ATMs** outside; there are many others too.

Numerous **bus** services run between here (city 35, X2, X3/X13) and Oxford; the

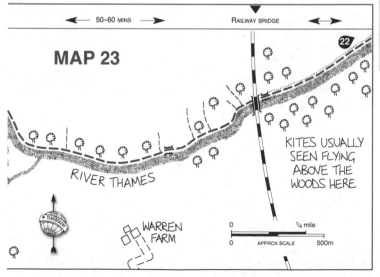

MAP 23

◄— 50–60 MINS —►   RAILWAY BRIDGE ◄—►

22

RIVER THAMES

KITES USUALLY SEEN FLYING ABOVE THE WOODS HERE

WARREN FARM

trailblazer

0   ¼ mile

0   APPROX SCALE   500m

15 and 33 also call here; see pp58-61 for details. Relevant bus stops are situated on Bridge St and High St.

Where to stay

Abingdon is not overrun with **B&B**-style accommodation but the two nearest to the path more than make up for this: both are on East St Helen St.

At No 22 is *Susie Howard* (☎ 07811-293310, 🖳 abingdonbedandbreakfast.com; 1T shared bathroom, 1D; ☛; WI-FI), a colourful house with beamed ceilings. The owner has been in the business for over 30 years. Room-only rates are from £37.50pp (sgl occ £45-75); breakfast is no longer served here. A little further along the road, *St Ethelwold's House* (☎ 01235-555486, 🖳 ethelwoldhouse.com; **fb**; 3S/3D/room sleeping up to six; shared bathroom; ☛; WI-FI; No 30) is a unique establishment. The building is made up of a mixture of medieval and Georgian architecture and the gardens run down to the Thames. 'A place to find stillness in the world' according to the brochure and there are several 'quiet rooms' throughout the building, and meditation sessions are held regularly. Prices vary but the majority of guests pay from £35pp (sgl £40, sgl occ room rate); a continental breakfast is £8pp but this must be requested in advance. A couple of the rooms have some kitchen facilities so guests can prepare their own meals.

There are other accommodation options near to the river with the first a particularly quirky one. Hidden away from the town and set in its own magnificent grounds is the rather secretive *Coseners House* (☎ 01235-523198, 🖳 thecosenershouse.co.uk; **fb**; 15S/19D/1T/15D or T, most en suite, some share shower facilities; ☛; WI-FI; 15-16 Abbey Close). B&B costs from £55pp (sgl £70, sgl occ room rate) and evening meals are available (see Where to eat).

Hotel-wise, *The Crown & Thistle* (☎ 01235-522556, 🖳 crownandthistleabingdon.co.uk; **fb**; 2D or T/14D/2Tr; ☛; WI-FI; 🐾; 18 Bridge St) offers the most expensive accommodation in town. It has some stunning rooms with the price for B&B reflecting the standard of the accommodation. The rate varies according to demand but is in the range of £64.50-72pp (sgl occ negotiable but room rate in peak season).

Where to eat and drink

Centrally located and locally owned **cafés** include *Throwing Buns* (☎ 01235-533656, 🖳 throwingbuns.com; **fb**; daily 8am-5pm) and *Java & Co* (☎ 01235-526957, 🖳 javaandco.co.uk; **fb**; Mon 8am-5.30pm, Tue-Sat until 6pm, Sun 9am-6pm; WI-FI; 🐾). At both you'll find friendly service and sandwiches and other typical café fare costing around £5.

Nearby, spacious *R&R* (☎ 01235-528472; **fb**; WI-FI; Mon-Sat 8am-5.30pm, Sun from 9am) offers paninis (from £5.50), jacket potatoes (from £5.75), cakes and snacks. Cheap baguettes (around £3) can be found at – where else? – *La Baguette* (**fb**; Mon-Sat 9am-4.30pm; 14 Bath St).

The nearest **pub** to the path is actually on the island in the middle of The Thames. A winner of CAMRA awards, *The Nag's Head* (☎ 01235-524516, 🖳 thenagsheadonthethames.co.uk; **fb**; food Mon-Sat noon-9pm, Sun to 8pm; WI-FI; 🐾) stocks a wide range of local real ales and has a large outside riverside dining area. In the summer months (though this depends on the weather) you can sit by the water's edge and ponder the outdoor menu which includes grilled dishes using locally sourced produce, pizza (from £9.95) cooked in a pizza oven (Mon-Sat noon-9pm, Sun to 8pm).

At 10 East St Helen St, in what was once a 16th-century coaching inn, *Kings Head and Bell* (☎ 01235-525362, 🖳 kingsheadandbell-abingdon.com; **fb**; food Mon-Fri noon-3pm & 5-8.30pm, Sat noon-8.30pm, Sun to 7.30pm; WI-FI; 🐾) has an imaginative menu including a £6.50 lunch deal burger, pizza or salad and a soft drink.

By the river and recently refurbished, *The Old Anchor Inn* (☎ 01235-352607; **fb**; WI-FI; 🐾; bar Tue & Thur from 5pm, Wed & Fri-Sun from noon), 1 St Helen's Wharf, is beautifully set in the shadow of the church and worth a visit for its location. A good lunch is available on Wednesday (hot meal lunch club; 12.30-2.30pm); otherwise food is served only at the weekend (Fri & Sat is pie & mash and Sun a roast). Booking essential for lunch club.

Another restaurant worth considering for its locality is *Cosener's House* (see Where to stay) where meals are served noon-10pm. The menu at *The Crown & Thistle* (see Where to stay; food Mon-Thur 8am-10pm, Fri & Sat to 10.30pm, Sun to 9pm) has everything from eggs Benedict for breakfast (£4.75/8.50) to super-food salads for the health conscious (from £13.50), pizzas, burgers and a delicious slow-cooked belly of pork (£16.50) during the day.

Gargantuan servings of Chinese food can be found at *Parasol* (☎ 01235-520700; **fb**; Mon-Sat noon-2pm & 5.30-11.30pm, Sun noon-10pm) where they have an eat-as-much-as-you-can deal (Sun-Thur £17.99 plus service) as well as set menus (£10-13.50pp) and **takeaway**.

On Bath St is an Indian, *Tiffins* (☎ 01235-537786, ☐ tiffinsabingdon.com; **fb**; daily 5-10pm) with a vegetarian curry from £7. A couple of doors away there's a Lebanese, *Mezzeh House* (☎ 01235-533551, ☐ mezze-house.co.uk; **fb**; Mon-Sat noon-3pm & 5-11pm, Sun 6-11pm) with tapas-style Middle Eastern dishes for around £5, as well as mains for £10-15.

Round the corner on High St, *Chaba Thai* (☎ 01235-525540, ☐ chabathai .co.uk; **fb**; Tue-Sun 6-10pm) is open in the evenings only; a chicken green curry is £8.95. Finally, there are a couple of Italian eateries, including *Bella Napoli* (☎ 01235-537676, ☐ bellanapoliabingdon.co.uk; **fb**; Tue 5-10pm, Wed-Fri noon-3pm & 5-10pm, Sat noon-10pm, Sun noon to 9pm; 29a Broad St), and a branch of the national chain *ASK Italian* (☎ 01235-529699, ☐ askitalian.co.uk; **fb**; daily 11.30am-10pm) on The Square.

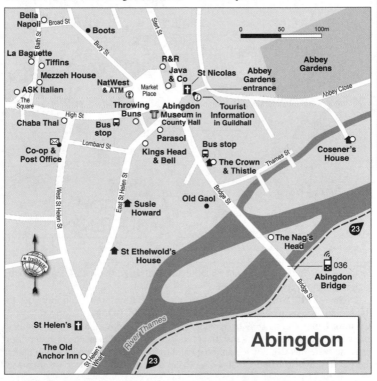

ROUTE GUIDE AND MAPS

E → ABINGDON TO WALLINGFORD [MAPS 23-27]

This quite lengthy **13½-mile (22km, 4½-5½hrs)** stage is blessed. Not only does the trail start and end in two of the most picturesque of Thames-side towns but it also passes through a number of smaller settlements of interest. Furthermore, there's some wonderful scenery as you amble on through meadows between

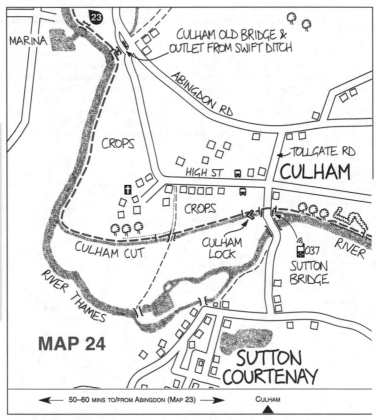

locks and hamlets, past ancient churches and villages, the path keeping to the water's edge for most of the stage.

Where **Swift Ditch** (Map 24) flows into the Thames, take a short detour to the left to see the medieval (1416-22) **Culham Old Bridge**. Having followed **Culham Cut** – dug in 1809 to bypass a section of the river that was notoriously awkward to navigate – you cross the road leading to **Culham**; the only services there now are bus (No 33; see pp58-61) and train (see box on pp56-7). Go under the railway line to reach **Clifton Cut** (Map 25) which in turn delivers you to

Clifton Hampden (see p132 & p134), ideally situated for lunch. As you approach you are treated to one of the finest vistas along the length of the river, with the hamlet's tiny 12th-century church nestled behind its red-brick bridge.

At **Day's Lock** (see p135) you cross the river and have the option of exploring the ancient settlement of **Dorchester-on-Thames** (see pp135-6; Map 26). Dorchester lies across the river from **Sinodun Hills** (Map 25), more commonly known as **Wittenham Clumps** (see box on p134), the second of two major landmarks – after the remaining towers of Didcot Power Station – that dominate the views to the south of the trail today. As you leave the clumps behind you cross the confluence of the rivers Thames and Thame (see box on pp44-5; Map 26). The only brief diversion from the river is on the approach to **Shillingford** (see p136).

Benson (see p137; Map 27) is both the last settlement and final lock you pass by – and, on this occasion, cross – before the day's concluding stretch, flanked by river and peaceful meadow. The ground here has not always known such serenity, however, for until 1652 this (peaceful) meadow was **the site of Wallingford Castle** (see box on p138), one of the largest and most formidable fortifications in pre-Civil War England. At Wallingford Bridge you can decide to turn left for **Crowmarsh Gifford** (see p137) – really a viable option for campers only – or continue for **Wallingford** town (see pp138-41).

ROUTE GUIDE AND MAPS

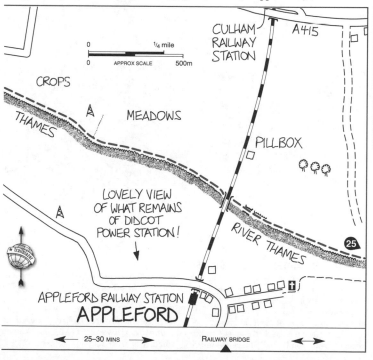

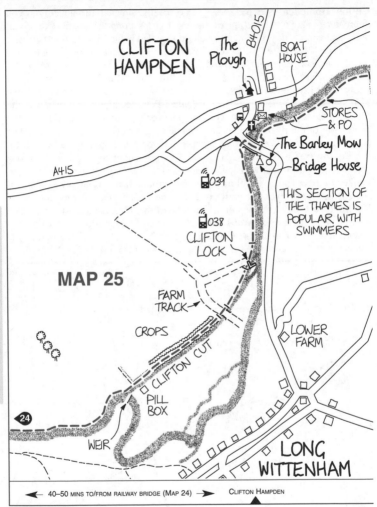

CLIFTON HAMPDEN   [Map 25]

Here the river passes over sandstone, the 'clif' in the village's name being made up of such. The village's 'surname' derives from John Hampden, cousin of Oliver Cromwell and one-time owner of the local manor.

In amongst the thatched cottages on the western bank you'll find **Stores** (Mon-Fri 7am-5pm, Sat to 2.30pm, Sun 8am-noon) with a **post office** (Mon-Fri 9am-5pm, Sat to 12.30pm).

Until 2021, **campers** were able to pitch up at *Bridge House Caravan & Campsite*. However, it is not known whether or when they will reopen.

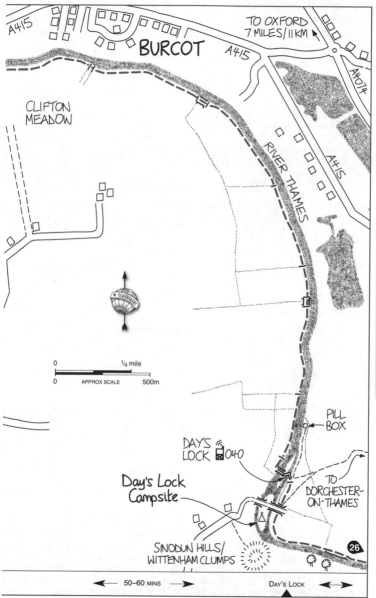

A415

TO OXFORD
7 MILES/11 KM

BURCOT

A415

A415

A4074

CLIFTON
MEADOW

RIVER
THAMES

trailblazer

0 ___ 1/4 mile
0 ___ APPROX SCALE ___ 500m

PILL
BOX

DAY'S
LOCK 040

Day's Lock
Campsite

TO
DORCHESTER-
ON-THAMES

SINODUN HILLS/
WITTENHAM CLUMPS

26

ROUTE GUIDE AND MAPS

◄── 50–60 MINS ──►   DAY'S LOCK ◄──►

❑ WITTENHAM CLUMPS [Map 25, p133]

These twin chalk hills are part of **Little Wittenham Nature Reserve**, the 'clumps' being the small huddles of beech trees which cap them. Wittenham Clumps is the most common moniker used to refer to the **Sinodun Hills**; others being the Berkshire Bubs (the redrawing of the county boundaries in 1974 making this name somewhat redundant as they are now in Oxfordshire) and Mother Dunch's Buttocks, so named after the unpopular local Lady Dunch who was Oliver Cromwell's aunt. The name 'Sinodun' possibly derives from the Celtic *Seno-Dunum* meaning 'old fort' and indeed on top of one of the twin clumps, Castle Hill, there was an Iron Age hill fort, built in approximately 500BC.

Archaeological digs have also unearthed Bronze Age and Roman settlements so it would seem that the hills' strategic vantage point over the surrounding lands has long been exploited. Today the clumps are one of the most visited sites in Oxfordshire.

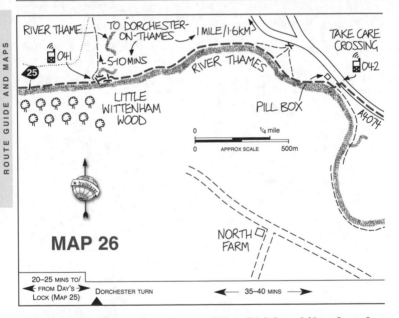

MAP 26

CLIFTON HAMPDEN (*cont'd*)
The Plough (☎ 01865-409976, 🖥 ploughbnb.com; **fb**; 6D; 🍺; WI-FI), on the A415, offers **B&B** (from £39pp, sgl occ £75) including a cooked breakfast.

On the opposite side of the river, *The Barley Mow* (☎ 01865-407847, 🖥 chefand brewer.com; **fb**; **food** Mon-Thur noon-

8.30pm, Fri & Sat to 9.30pm, Sun to 8pm; WI-FI; 🐾 bar area) has the usual Chef & Brewer menu, so you may know what to expect. This place can get busy in the evenings so you may have to wait for the usual pub fare, which is of variable quality and value; expect to pay £7.29 for fish & chips at lunchtime.

DAY'S LOCK   **[Map 25, p133]**
Campers staying on the island (☎ 01865-407768; Good Friday-end Sep; well-behaved 🐾) here must arrive during the lock-keeper's working hours (from Good Friday/Mar by 4pm, Apr-Jun by 5pm, July-Aug by 6.30pm, Sep by 6pm) in order to collect a key for the site, for which there is a deposit (£10). A pitch (one tent and up to two people) costs £12 including use of the

showers. Booking is recommended as the maximum number of people (inc children) allowed to stay on the site each night is only 10. However, at the time of research, it wasn't certain if and when it would re-open as there were lots of repairs to do to the site.

The nearest shop and pub are in Dorchester-on-Thames (see below).

DORCHESTER-ON-THAMES
                       [Map 26]
Entering sleepy Dorchester-on-Thames, you'll find it hard to imagine that it was once a great city, home to a Roman garrison and entertained by an amphitheatre. The pretty village was – preceding Winchester – the primary city of Wessex and it was on

the banks of the River Thame here that Bishop Birinius, sent by Pope Honorius I to convert the Saxons, baptised King Cynegils of Wessex (AD611-643). Converting Cynegils in the presence of the already Christian King Oswald of Northumbria united the two kingdoms against the pagan

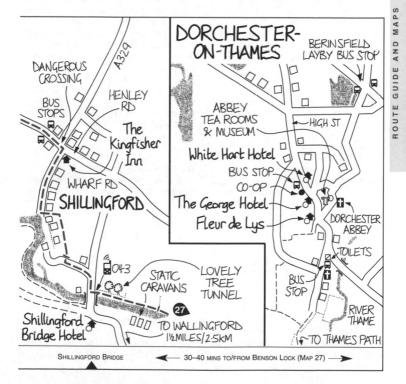

SHILLINGFORD BRIDGE   ◄— 30–40 MINS TO/FROM BENSON LOCK (MAP 27) —►

Mercians and established England as a Christian nation. A more recent claim to fame for the village occurred in 2017, when the local cricket side managed the unlikely feat of scoring 41 runs off the final over to win a game against a nearby village, an achievement that's particularly noteworthy when one considers that the maximum number of runs that one can normally score off an over is 36!

If, on entering the village, you get the feeling you've visited Dorchester before, that's probably not evidence that you are the reincarnation of King Cynegils of Wessex, but is instead more likely an indication that you've been watching *Midsomer Murders* recently; many of the TV drama's episodes were filmed in and around the village.

Dorchester Abbey (🖳 dorchester-abbey.org.uk; fb; summer daily 8am-6pm, winter 8am to dusk) was founded in 1140 and was spared the worst of Henry VIII's wrath during the dissolution of the monasteries. Just outside the abbey there is a **museum** (early Apr-end Sep daily 2-5pm; free) housed in the medieval Abbey Guest House; this isn't a guest house at all but it describes itself as a 'place of hospitality' and does have a **tearoom** (Apr-Sep Wed-Thur 3-5pm, Sat, Sun & Bank Holiday Mon 2.30-5pm).

For services, on the High St there's a Co-op **supermarket** (Mon-Sun 7am-9pm) that can provide **cashback**. The X38, X39 & X40 **bus** services (see pp58-61) stop at Berinsfield Layby, but some school and other limited services call in the village.

The place closest to the Thames offering both **accommodation and food** is *Fleur de Lys* (🕿 01865-661865, 🖳 fleurdelys-dorchester.co.uk; fb; 4D; 🛆; 🐾 bar area; WI-FI; food daily noon-3pm & 6-9pm); B&B costs £37.50-67.50pp (sgl occ room rate). The menu changes regularly but a two/three-course evening meal costs from £25/30.

On either side of High St are *The George Hotel* (🕿 01865-340404, 🖳 his toricinnz.co.uk/dorchester-on-thames; fb; 3S/18D/1D or T/2T; 🛆; WI-FI; 🐾 in garden only; £35-70pp, sgl from £65, sgl occ room rate), a traditional 15th-century coaching inn which serves some delicious dishes (**food** Mon-Sat noon-3pm & 6-9pm, Sun noon-4pm) including the landlord's moussaka (£14.50); and *White Hart Hotel* (🕿 01865-340074, 🖳 white-hart-hotel-dorchester.co.uk; fb; 2S/6D or T/14D; 🛆; WI-FI; 🐾; from £47.50pp, sgl/sgl occ £75/85. The menu (**food** Mon-Sat noon-2.30pm & 6.30-9.30pm, Sun noon-8pm) here is varied but in the evening may include Cotswold Lamb Chump Boulanger (£19.50).

SHILLINGFORD [Map 26]

At the western entrance to the village is *The Kingfisher Inn* (🕿 01865-858595, 🖳 kingfisher-inn.co.uk; 5D/1T; 🛆; WI-FI; from £47.50pp, sgl occ £75; 27 Henley Rd); it offers **B&B** but is more a guesthouse than a pub; evening meals for residents are available if requested in advance.

Fortunately, across the water, *Shillingford Bridge Hotel* (🕿 01865-858567, 🖳 shillingfordbridgehotel.co.uk;

fb; 4S/31D or T; 🛆; WI-FI; 🐾) *does* provide victuals for non-residents (daily noon-9pm) and the **food** is reasonably priced too, with mains from £13, rising to £23 for the best steaks. Some rooms have four-poster beds and/or river views; the tariff (from £42.50pp, sgl £72, sgl occ room rate) includes breakfast.

Bus services 138, X38 and X39/X40 stop here (see pp58-61).

Symbols used in text (see also p78)
🛆 Bathtub in, or for, at least one room
WI-FI means wi-fi is available
fb signifies places that post their current opening hours on their Facebook page
🐾 Dogs allowed; if for accommodation this is subject to prior arrangement (see p255)

BENSON [Map 27, p139]

The site of a Saxon battle between the king-doms of Wessex and Mercia, somnolent Benson offers little such excitement today.

Bus services 136, X38 and X39/X40 stop on the B4074 (see pp58-61).

Run by **Benson Waterfront** (🖳 benson waterfront.co.uk) are the riverside *Waterfront Café* (☎ 01491-833732, 🖳 waterfrontcafe.co.uk; **fb**; Sun-Wed 9am-7pm, Thur-Sat to 8pm; WI-FI; 🐾 in conservatory only) – where a very varied menu includes light bites (£5.25-6.95) and gourmet burgers (£11.75-13.95) – and a campsite, though sadly from 2022 this will only have touring pitches.

CROWMARSH GIFFORD [Map 27, p139]

The nearest **food shop** is Crowmarsh Stores (Mon-Fri 7am-6pm, Sat 8am-4pm).

Bus services X38, X39, X40, 134 & 136 stop on The Street (see pp58-61).

Campers have two choices here: by the river is *Riverside Park Campsite* (🖳 better.org.uk/leisure-centre/south-oxford shire/riverside-park-and-pools; **fb**), run by South Oxfordshire District Council, which has 18 pitches, 15 of which have electricity, and all have use of showers and washing facilities (pitch £17-20). Booking is available through the website (Online chat).

Further along the street is *Bridge Villa* (☎ 01491-836860, 🖳 bridgevilla.co.uk; **fb**; WI-FI; 🐾 on leads; Feb to end Dec), a camping & caravan park charging £10-14/15-27 for a tent and a walker/two walkers. The facilities are very good and include a little shop. Also available on the site is one en suite twin **room** (year-round; from £27.50pp, sgl occ £50; WI-FI) with tea- and coffee-making facilities – though breakfast is not included in the price.

W ← WALLINGFORD TO ABINGDON [MAPS 27-23]

[Route section begins on Map 27, p139] This quite lengthy **13½-mile (22km, 4½-5½hrs)** stage is blessed. Not only does the trail start and end in two of the most picturesque of Thames-side towns but it also passes through a number of smaller settlements of interest. Furthermore, there's some wonderful scenery, the path keeping to the water's edge for most of the stage.

Until 1652 this peaceful meadow north of Wallingford was **the site of Wallingford Castle** (see box p138). The first settlement and lock you pass by – and, on this occasion, cross – is **Benson** (see above). After **Shillingford** (see opposite; Map 26) there is a brief diversion from the river, but you then return to the waterside and soon cross the confluence of the rivers Thames and Thame (see box pp44-5). Here you have the option of exploring the ancient settlement of **Dorchester-on-Thames** (see pp135-6). Dorchester lies across the river from **Sinodun Hills** (Map 25) more commonly known as **Wittenham Clumps** (see box p134), the second of two major landmarks – after the remaining towers of **Didcot Power Station** – that dominate the views to the south of the trail today.

At **Day's Lock** (see p135; Map 25) you cross the river and follow the curve round to the hamlet of **Clifton Hampden** (see p132 & p134), ideally situated for lunch. As you leave, look back to see one of the finest vistas along the length of the river, with the hamlet's tiny 12th-century church nestled behind its red-brick bridge. After the lock you go along **Clifton Cut** and pass under the railway line to cross the road leading to **Culham** (Map 24); the only services there now are bus (No 33; see pp58-61) and train (see box on pp56-7).

Having followed **Culham Cut** – dug in 1809 to bypass a section of the river that was notoriously awkward to navigate – you swing round to the right to find the outlet from **Swift Ditch** (or Short Cut; see p130), also labelled as **Back Water** on OS maps. Take a detour of a few yards to the left here to see the medieval (1416-22) **Culham Old Bridge** before the pleasant walk into **Abingdon** (see pp127-9; Map 23). *[Next route overview on pp125-6]*

WALLINGFORD [map p141]

Steeped in history, Wallingford is the finest-surviving example of a Saxon *burh* (a fortified town) in England. Having previously been the site of a Roman settlement, the town's 9th-century importance is reflected by the defences whose construction was ordered by King Alfred to resist the Danes. Once as large as the Wessex capital of Winchester, by the time the Normans invaded in 1066 Wallingford was Berkshire's primary town (although, as with Abingdon, the town is now in Oxfordshire).

Deemed a safer place to cross the Thames than London Bridge, William the Conqueror led his freshly victorious army over the river here and in 1067 the Normans began the construction of **Wallingford Castle** (see box below). More recently,

Wallingford has been perhaps better known for its association with Agatha Christie, who lived with her husband just outside the town at Winterbrook House for over forty years until her death in 1976. A blue plaque sits on the wall of her unremarkable home, which is still a private house, though **Wallingford Museum** (☎ 01491-651127, 🖥 wallingfordmuseum.org.uk; **fb**; Mar-end Nov Tue-Fri & Bank Hols 2-5pm, Sat 10.30am-5pm, Jun-Aug also Sun 2-5pm; £5; 52 High St) tells the town's tale and has an exhibition on Mrs Christie's associations with the town.

Services

Wallingford Town Tourist Information (☎ 01491-826972, 🖥 wallingford.co.uk;

❑ SITE OF THE FORMER WALLINGFORD CASTLE [Map 27]

The castle here was one of three built by the Normans to control the Thames Valley, the others being at Windsor and Oxford. The first castle was built between 1067 and 1071 and was made of wood. As the castle was passed down the Norman lineage it was gradually rebuilt with stone and would develop into one of the great royal castles of the 12th and 13th centuries. During The Anarchy (1135-54), a civil war fought between Stephen (the nephew of Henry I) and Matilda (Henry I's daughter), who both laid claim to the English throne, the castle was one of Matilda's strongholds and one which would never be taken.

The lengthy war would end with Henry II – Matilda's son – on the throne and the castle converted into a luxurious royal residence. The castle went into decline after Henry VIII's reign but would be refortified in 1643 during the English Civil War (1642-51) when it became a Royalist stronghold and part of a defensive ring surrounding the escaping king's Oxfordshire base.

Repeated Parliamentarian attacks and a 16-week siege failed to penetrate the castle's defences and it became the last Royalist stronghold to surrender, finally doing so only by royal command. So fierce and impenetrable had the defence of the castle been that Cromwell, never wishing to have to lay siege to such a formidable fortress again, ordered it destroyed in 1652.

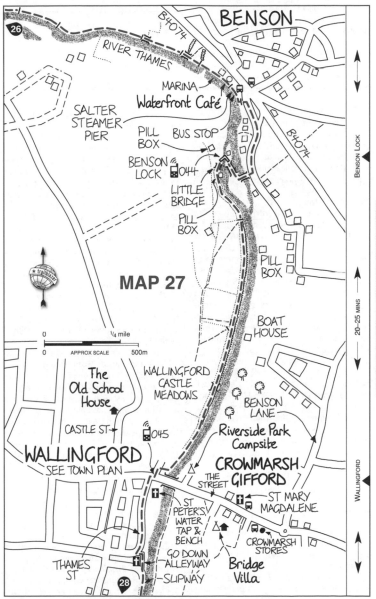

MAP 27

Mar-Nov Mon-Fri 9.30am-12.30pm & 1-3.30pm, Sat 9.30am-1.30pm, Dec-Feb Mon-Sat 9.30am-1.30pm) is in the town hall on Market Place.

There's also a **post office** with **ATM** (Mon-Fri 9am-5.30pm), a **Boots the Chemist** (Mon-Fri 9am-6pm, Sat to 5.30pm, Sun 10am-4pm), other **ATMs** and branches of several **banks**. On High St there is a Waitrose **store** (Mon-Fri 8am-9pm, Sat to 8pm, Sun 10am-4pm).

Wallingford is well connected by **bus**: the X38, X39, X40, 33, 133 (see p142), 134, 136 & 138 call in at various destinations along the Thames Path (see pp58-61). Buses run from Market Place.

Where to stay

A short walk from the town centre at 23 Castle St (Map 27) is a decent option for **B&B**, namely *The Old School House* (☎ 01491-839571, 🖥 bbwallingford.co.uk; 1D private bathroom/1D; 👝; WI-FI; from £50pp, sgl occ room rate). Note that weekend bookings between May and September must be for two nights but it's always worth enquiring to see if they are willing to provide a last-minute booking for a single night. In addition to the two advertised rooms they also offer a third double to family and friends of residents, and they charge £180 for all four people.

If you want to stay more centrally, a **pub** may be your best bet and *The Coach Makers Arms* (☎ 01491-838229, 🖥 coach makersarms.com; **fb**; 1D/2Tr; 👝; WI-FI; 🐾; £40-50pp, sgl occ room rate; 37 St Mary's St) has rooms. Situated on the edge of the town centre, it provides a friendly atmosphere and reasonably peaceful night's sleep.

Right on the path, *The Town Arms* (☎ 020-3887 0391, 🖥 thetownarmswalling ford.com; **fb**; 5D/1Tr; WI-FI; 🐾 small and not moulting(!); 102 High St) is one of the friendlier places in town. Closed Mon and (at the time of research) Tue, B&B check-ins are accepted Tue-Sat with rooms for £45-65pp (sgl occ room rate); breakfast (£3-6) is an additional charge.

Just up the road is *The George Hotel* (☎ 01491-836665, 🖥 peelhotels.co.uk/

george-hotel; **fb**; 9S/26D/4T; 👝; WI-FI; 🐾; High St), though it's not cheap: they charge £65-75pp (sgl/sgl occ from £95).

Where to eat and drink

Food at *The Dolphin* (☎ 01491-837377, 🖥 thedolphinwallingford.co.uk; **fb**; food Mon 8am-3pm, Tue-Sat 8am-9pm, Sun 9am-2pm; WI-FI; 🐾 bar area) is amongst the best value in the town, with a great Full English breakfast (£6).

Their near-neighbour *Shellfish Cow* (☎ 01491-832807, 🖥 shellfishcow.co.uk/wallingford; food Tue-Fri noon-2pm & 6-9pm, Sat noon-9.30pm; WI-FI; 🐾 ground floor only; 28 High St) offers for lunch ¼ kilo Fowey mussels (£7.50) or a sirloin steak baguette (£12); for dinner you might try an 8oz Aberdeen Angus sirloin steak (£19.50).

Pub food and locally brewed ales can be found at *The Town Arms* (see Where to stay; food Wed-Sat noon-9pm, Sun to 3pm). Before that, the first place you come to on entering Wallingford walking downstream is *The Boat House* (☎ 01491-834100, 🖥 greeneking-pubs.co.uk/pubs/oxfordshire/boat-house; WI-FI; 🐾; food daily 10am-10pm), right on the riverbank and with a sunny outdoor area. It's not the most characterful of places – and we could have done without the music piped throughout the place, and with faster service – though the food is cheap enough for such an idyllic and convenient location, with sandwiches and wraps from £5.89, burgers from £8.99.

Away from the water at the *Tavern Bar* (see **The George Hotel**, Where to stay; food daily noon-3pm & 6-9pm), mains cost from £12.95 and there is sport on the telly. Food is also served in the *bistro* (daily 6-9pm).

Pub food is also on offer at *The Coach Makers Arms* (see Where to stay; WI-FI; 🐾 in bar; food Mon-Sat 5.30-9pm, Sat 1-9pm, Sun to 4.30pm); they offer a range of burgers or pizzas (£6-13.50).

More good-value Eastern fare is available at *Thai Corner* (☎ 01491-825050; Mon-Sat 5-9.30pm) and, nearer to the river, *Wallingford Tandoori* (☎ 01491-833133, 🖥 wallingfordtandoori.com; **fb**; Mon-Sat 5.30-11.30pm, Sun noon-11pm; 4 High St), with some dishes costing less than £10.

The favoured Italian of local folk is *Avanti* (☎ 01491-835500, 🖥 avantiitalian .com; **fb**; food Tue-Sat 4.30-9pm; WI-FI; 85 High St), where, unsurprisingly, there's plenty of pizzas (£8.50-13) and pasta dishes (£9.80-15). Flashier – but still serving good grub – *The Old Post Office* (☎ 01491-836068, 🖥 opowallingford.co.uk; food Mon-Sat 8am-9pm, Sun 9am-9pm; WI-FI; 🐾 in bar area) serves food all day. The outside tables are the perfect spot to watch the world of Wallingford go by whilst enjoying a pizza (from £7). There's also a branch of the national chain *Pizza Express* (☎ 01491-

833431, 🖥 pizzaexpress.com/wallingford; daily 11.30am-10.30pm) at 12 St Mary St.

For **takeaway** try *The Pizza Café* (Mon-Fri 9am-2.30pm & 5-10pm, Sat 9am-3pm & 5-10.30pm, Sun 5-10pm; 2 The Arcade), or the kebabs and burgers at *USA Chicken* (daily 3-11pm); a branch of *Greggs* (Mon-Sat 6.30am-5.30pm, Sun 8.30am-4pm), the bakery; and a couple of Chinese takeaways including *Hong Kong House* (☎ 01491-835453, 🖥 hongkong house.org.uk; Sun-Wed 5-9pm, Thur to 9.30pm, Fri noon-1.30pm & 5-10pm, Sat 5-10pm).

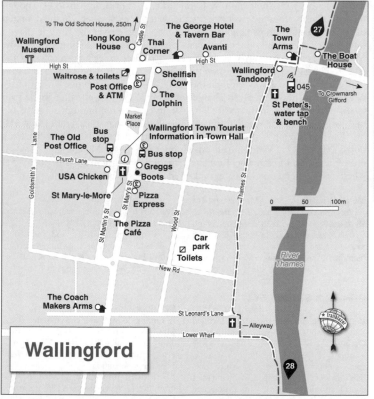

E → WALLINGFORD TO PANGBOURNE [MAPS 27-32]

The centrepiece of this **11-mile (17.7km, 3¾-4¾hrs)** stage is **Goring Gap**. It was here, during an Ice Age a quarter of a million years ago, that the ancient course of the river (see box on p45), finding its route blocked by glaciers, instead penetrated its way through the chalk at a weak spot between the Chiltern Hills and the Berkshire Downs, so forcing the river through the valley – the 'Gap' – and thereby permanently changing the river's course to that which it roughly follows today. The riverscapes surrounding the Gap are some of the finest along the whole length of the river.

This is also a day on which something most unfamiliar occurs: a **hill**.

Before you reach the Gap, the route keeps to the Thames as far as **Moulsford** (see below; Map 29) passing **Cholsey Marsh Nature Reserve** (🖳 bbowt.org.uk/nature-reserves/cholsey-marsh) with The Ridgeway following a parallel path on the opposite bank. You walk beneath two magnificent **double-arched railway viaducts** built by Isambard Kingdom Brunel in 1839. Though the path diverts from the river briefly, the water lures you back to the doorstep of one of the path's most famous pubs before a simple riverside stroll leads you into Berkshire, towards the twin towns of **Streatley** and **Goring** (see below; Map 30), the path first arriving in Streatley (in Berkshire) before crossing the river to Goring (in Oxfordshire) on the opposite bank. Having spent half a million years eroding its way through the chalk the Thames continues victoriously onwards. You, however, divert away from its banks for a while though the path is still rewarding as it flirts with The Chilterns, passing through some of the only woodland on the whole trail before heading up that solitary hill (Map 31).

The final stretch is an unremarkable road walk, eventually guiding you back down to the river at **Whitchurch-on-Thames** (see p147; Map 32) and across it out of Oxfordshire and into Berkshire again at **Pangbourne** (see pp149-51) where tales of a rat, toad, badger and mole await (see box on p150).

ROUTE GUIDE AND MAPS

MOULSFORD [Map 29, p144]
At the end of Ferry Lane, *The Beetle & Wedge* (☎ 01491-651381, 🖳 beetleand wedge.co.uk; **fb**) deals in both **B&B** (4D; 🛏; WI-FI; 🐾; £62.50pp, sgl occ room rate, breakfast £15pp) and **food** (Mon-Sat noon-3pm & 5.30-9pm, Sun noon-8pm).

The lunch menu offers sandwiches from £8.50 and mains from £15.50.

Going Forward's 133 (Goring–Wallingford; Tue, Wed, Thur & Fri 1-2/day) **bus** service calls on the A329. The Wednesday service now goes to Didcot.

GORING & STREATLEY [Map 30, p145]
Both the ancient Ridgeway and Icknield Way – Britain's oldest road – pass through Goring Gap, the 'street' in Streatley referring to either of these paths, although there is some ambiguity over exactly which one. Such ancient features suggest the area was of considerable importance to early Britons and the twin villages are certainly worth a stop.

Services
In Goring, as well as a **convenience store**, McColls (Mon-Sat 6am-10pm, Sun from 7am), which includes a **post office**, there is also a branch of Tesco Express (daily 7am-11pm) by the station.

Lloyds **pharmacy** (Mon-Fri 9am-6pm, Sat to 5pm) and an **ATM** are on the High St. *(cont'd on p146)*

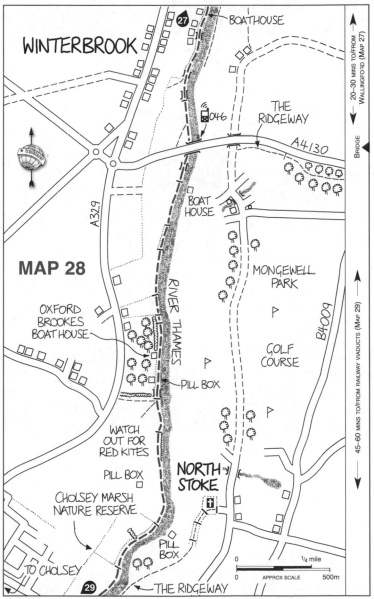

WINTERBROOK

BOATHOUSE

27

046

THE RIDGEWAY

A4130

A329

BOAT HOUSE

MAP 28

MONGEWELL PARK

B4009

OXFORD BROOKES BOAT HOUSE

RIVER THAMES

GOLF COURSE

PILL BOX

WATCH OUT FOR RED KITES

PILL BOX

NORTH STOKE

CHOLSEY MARSH NATURE RESERVE

PILL BOX

TO CHOLSEY

29

THE RIDGEWAY

0   ¼ mile
0   APPROX SCALE   500m

BRIDGE

ROUTE GUIDE AND MAPS

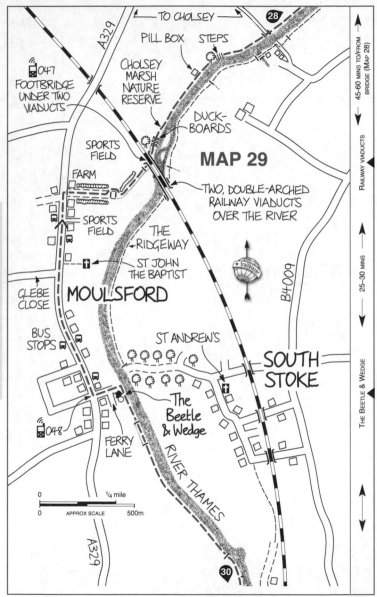

To Cholsey

PILL BOX   STEPS

📱047
FOOTBRIDGE
UNDER TWO
VIADUCTS

CHOLSEY
MARSH
NATURE
RESERVE

DUCK-
BOARDS

MAP 29

SPORTS
FIELD

FARM

TWO, DOUBLE-ARCHED
RAILWAY VIADUCTS
OVER THE RIVER

SPORTS
FIELD

THE
RIDGEWAY

ST JOHN
THE BAPTIST

GLEBE
CLOSE

MOULSFORD

BUS
STOPS

ST ANDREW'S

**SOUTH
STOKE**

📱048

**The
Beetle
& Wedge**

FERRY
LANE

RIVER
THAMES

0   ¼ mile
0   APPROX SCALE   500m

A329

45-60 MINS TO/FROM
BRIDGE (MAP 28)

RAILWAY VIADUCTS

25-30 MINS

THE BEETLE & WEDGE

B4009

ROUTE GUIDE AND MAPS

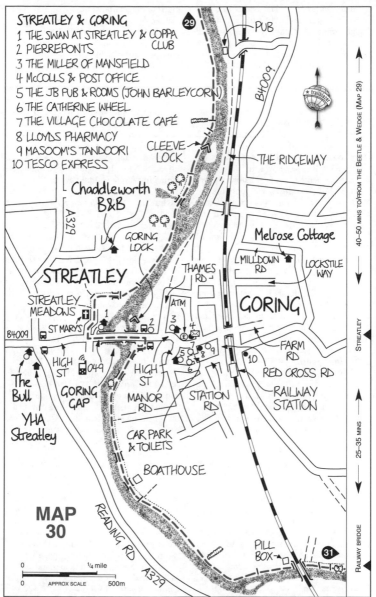

STREATLEY & GORING
1 THE SWAN AT STREATLEY & COPPA CLUB
2 PIERREPONTS
3 THE MILLER OF MANSFIELD
4 McCOLLS & POST OFFICE
5 THE JB PUB & ROOMS (JOHN BARLEYCORN)
6 THE CATHERINE WHEEL
7 THE VILLAGE CHOCOLATE CAFÉ
8 LLOYDS PHARMACY
9 MASOOM'S TANDOORI
10 TESCO EXPRESS

40-50 MINS TO/FROM THE BEETLE & WEDGE (MAP 29)

ROUTE GUIDE AND MAPS

29

PUB

B4009

THE RIDGEWAY

CLEEVE LOCK

Chaddleworth B&B

A329

GORING LOCK

Melrose Cottage

MILLDOWN RD

LOCKSTILE WAY

STREATLEY

THAMES RD

GORING

STREATLEY MEADOWS

ATM

B4009

ST MARY'S

1

2

3

4

7

9

FARM RD

HIGH ST

049

5

8

6

10

RED CROSS RD

The Bull

GORING GAP

HIGH ST

MANOR RD

STATION RD

RAILWAY STATION

YHA Streatley

CAR PARK & TOILETS

BOATHOUSE

MAP 30

READING RD A329

PILL BOX

31

0   1/4 mile
0   APPROX SCALE   500m

STREATLEY

25-35 MINS

RAILWAY BRIDGE

(cont'd from p142) GWR **trains** (see box on pp56-7) run regularly from Goring to Pangbourne and Reading as well as other Thames Path destinations. **Bus** service 134 (see pp58-61) connects the twin villages with various towns on the path. Going Forward's 133 (see Moulsford, p142) and limited 142 (to Reading; Tue 2/day) services also call here.

Where to stay and eat

Goring If an extra 15- to 20-minute walk doesn't put you off and you'd rather not stay above a pub, *Melrose Cottage* (☎ 01491-873040, 🖳 howarthr523@gmail .com; 1D en suite, 2T shared bathroom; ▼; WI-FI; 36 Milldown Rd) is your only option; **B&B** is very reasonably priced (from £37.50pp, sgl occ from £54) and all the rooms have a fridge and a microwave.

As for the pubs, *The Miller of Mansfield* (☎ 01491-872829, 🖳 millerof mansfield.com; **fb**; 13D; ▼; WI-FI; 🐾) has some glorious rooms although the price (£64.50-104.50pp, sgl occ room rate) may put some off. The **food** (Wed-Sat noon-2pm & 6-9pm, Sun noon-4pm) is as magnificent as the rooms but you're unlikely to get a meal in the evening for much less than £28 (eg grilled Cornish brill on the bone £28.50).

Cheaper, *The JB Pub & Rooms (The John Barleycorn)* (☎ 01491-871813, 🖳 jbpubgoring.co.uk; **fb**; 3D; ▼; WI-FI; 🐾 on lead, bar/garden only) charges from £45pp (sgl occ room rate) for **B&B** and their traditional pub menu (**food** Mon-Sat noon-3pm & 6.30-9pm, Sun noon-4pm) includes fish & chips (£12.95) and burgers/pies (from £11.95).

Other food options include the unpretentious *The Village Chocolate Café* (☎ 01491-874264, 🖳 chocolatecafegoring.co .uk; daily 10am-4pm; WI-FI; 🐾) – note that the sign still says The Village Café, its previous incarnation. They sell a decent range of sandwiches, baguettes and breakfasts, their wonderful breakfast baguette (sausage, egg & bacon) costing £8. Other than their hot chocolate (from £3), made using Belgian chocolate, the menu is light on chocolate. Nearer to the bridge, *Pierreponts Café* (☎ 01491-874464, 🖳

pierrepontsgoring.co.uk; **fb**; Wed-Sat 8.30am-5pm, Sun to 3pm; 🐾 dog hooks outside; WI-FI) cooks up full-English breakfasts (£11.50) and has lots of homemade sausage rolls and cakes.

The Catherine Wheel (☎ 01491-872379, 🖳 tcwgoring.co.uk; **fb**; food Mon & Tue 6-8pm, Wed-Fri 1-3pm & 5-8pm, Sat noon-3pm & 4-8pm, Sun 1-3pm & 4pm till the pizza dough runs out; WI-FI; 🐾) serves pizzas (evenings only Wed-Sun; £9-13) as well as a menu that changes regularly; while *Masoom's Tandoori* (☎ 01491-875078, 🖳 masooms.co.uk; Mon-Thur 5.30-10.30pm, Fri & Sat to 11pm, Sun to 10pm) is an Indian restaurant and **takeaway**.

Streatley YHA *Streatley* (☎ 0345-371 9044, or ☎ 01491-872278, 🖳 yha.org .uk/hostel/yha-streatley-thames; 2 x 2-, 3 x 4-, 2 x 5- & 3 x 6-bed rooms; WI-FI communal area; Mar-Oct & midweek Nov-Feb) is on Reading Rd. Note that the hostel may be booked for exclusive hire (and this was the only option in 2021) so it's advisable to book well in advance. Dorm beds cost from £13pp and private/family rooms from £29/25. See also p19.

The Swan at Streatley (☎ 01491-878800, 🖳 theswanatstreatley.com; **fb**; 31D/16D or T; ▼; WI-FI; 🐾; from £40pp room only, sgl occ room rate) has luxurious rooms on a lovely riverside site. **Food** is served at *Coppa Club* (☎ 01491-529315, 🖳 coppaclub.co.uk/streatley;   Mon-Fri 7.30am-11pm, Sat & Sun from 8am); the breakfast menu offers buckwheat & rye pancakes (£9.50), and the comprehensive all-day menu includes a corn-fed half chicken with tomato salad & skinny fries (£15). It is a nice place to go even just for a drink, though is popular so it is worth booking.

The Bull at Streatley (☎ 01491-872392, 🖳 bullinnpub.co.uk; **fb**; 1D/2T/ 1Tr; ▼; WI-FI; best in pub; 🐾; from £35pp, sgl occ room rate) is also on Reading Rd but nearer to the crossroads. It provides **B&B** and also serves standard pub **food** (Mon-Sat noon-9pm, Sun to 7pm).

On the edge of Streatley, and only a few minutes from the path, is the beautiful *Chaddleworth B&B* (☎ 07711-420586, chaddleworthbedandbreakfast.com; 1D/ 1D or T both en suite, 1D or T private bathroom: ▼; WI-FI; from £50pp, sgl occ £75). Cake is served on arrival and they have a

lovely garden where you can relax after a long day on the trail. Breakfast is cooked on an Aga. It is on a private road called Cleeve Court.

Symbols used in text (see also p78)
▼ Bathtub in, or for, at least one room
WI-FI means wi-fi is available
fb signifies places that post their current opening hours on their Facebook page
🐕 Dogs allowed; if for accommodation this is subject to prior arrangement (see p255)

WHITCHURCH-ON-THAMES
[Map 32, p148]

Whitchurch is possibly best known for its **toll bridge**; drivers still have to pay but it is free for walkers.

There are two **pubs** here serving food: *The Greyhound* (☎ 0118-343 3016, 🖥 greyhoundwhitchurchonthames.co.uk; **fb**; WI-FI; 🐕 on lead; food Wed-Sat noon-3pm & 5-9pm, Sun noon-4pm) serves standard pub food; *The Ferryboat* (☎ 0118-984

2161, 🖥 theferryboatwhitchurch.com; **fb**; WI-FI; 🐕 on lead and in bar area only; food Tue-Sat noon-2.15pm & 6-9.15pm, Sun noon-2.15pm) has a similar menu but a bit more extensive and expensive. Note that it is closed all day on Monday.

Whitchurch is a stop on the 142 **bus** (Going Forward; Tue 2/day) service between Goring & Reading.

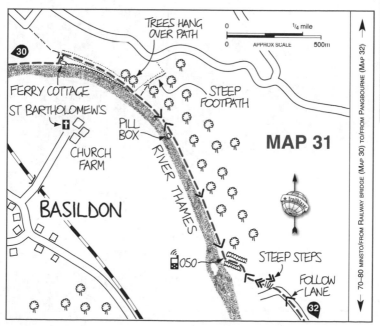

W← PANGBOURNE TO WALLINGFORD   [MAPS 32-27]

[Route section begins on Map 32, below] The centrepiece of this **11-mile (17.7km, 3¾-4¾hrs)** stage is **Goring Gap** (see p142 and box on p45) but this is also a day on which something most unfamiliar occurs: a **hill**.

From **Pangbourne** you cross into Oxfordshire and pass uphill through **Whitchurch-on-Thames** (see p147; Map 32), after which there is a gentle road walk; then (on Map 31) after some steep steps down and a sharp pull up again, you find yourself high above the banks of the river. The path is rewarding as it flirts with the Chilterns, passing through some of the only woodland on the whole trail. Here you'll notice a new feature on the river: **the pill box** (see pp96-7) which becomes ubiquitous all the way up to Lechlade.

The path arrives in **Goring** (Map 30) before crossing the river to its twin town **Streatley** (for both see p112 & pp126-7); you are now briefly in Berk-

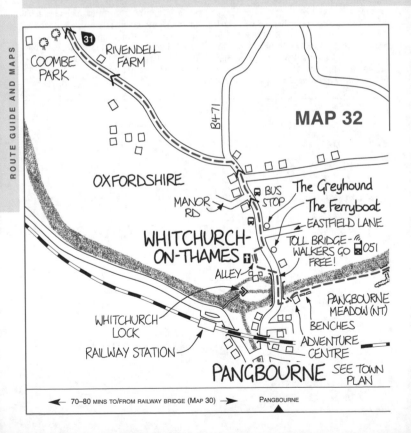

ROUTE GUIDE AND MAPS

31

COOMBE PARK

RIVENDELL FARM

MAP 32

OXFORDSHIRE

B4-71

MANOR RD

🚌 BUS STOP

The Greyhound

The Ferryboat

EASTFIELD LANE

WHITCHURCH-ON-THAMES

TOLL BRIDGE – WALKERS GO FREE!

051

ALLEY

PANGBOURNE MEADOW (NT)

WHITCHURCH LOCK

BENCHES

RAILWAY STATION

ADVENTURE CENTRE

PANGBOURNE SEE TOWN PLAN

◄— 70–80 MINS TO/FROM RAILWAY BRIDGE (MAP 30) —►   PANGBOURNE

shire again, but soon you walk into Oxfordshire which has extended south of the river. A simple riverside stroll leads you to the doorstep of one of the path's most famous pubs in **Moulsford** (see p142; Map 29). Here sadly the path diverts from the river but on its return you pass beneath two magnificent **double-arched railway viaducts** built by Isambard Kingdom Brunel in 1839.

From here the path keeps to the Thames (Map 28) and part of the time you walk along the edge of **Cholsey Marsh Nature Reserve** (🖳 bbowt.org.uk/nature-reserves/cholsey-marsh), with The Ridgeway a parallel path on the other side of the river, before reaching **Wallingford** (see pp138-41; Map 27). If you are camping you might continue on to Wallingford Bridge and cross to **Crowmarsh Gifford** (see p137). [Next route overview on pp137-8]

PANGBOURNE [map p151]

So named due to the village's location on the River Pang, Kenneth Grahame, author of *The Wind in the Willows*, lived here following the death of his son (see box on p150). A cultural hotspot, Jimmy Page – guitarist in Led Zeppelin – also resided in the village. Indeed, it is said that in 1968, during a visit from Robert Plant, the powerhouse rockers' vocalist, it was actually here that the band formed.

Services

There is a Co-op **store** with **ATM** (daily 7am-10pm), **post office** (Mon-Wed, Fri 8.30am-5pm, Thur & Sat to 2pm, and Lloyds **pharmacy** (Mon-Fri 9am-6pm, Sat to 5.30pm).

Pangbourne is a stop on some of GWR's **train** services (see box on pp56-7). The 143 **bus** service (see pp58-61) also calls here as does the 142 (Going Forward; Tue 2/day) Goring to Reading service.

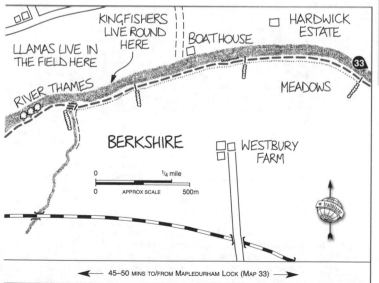

KINGFISHERS LIVE ROUND HERE

LLAMAS LIVE IN THE FIELD HERE

RIVER THAMES

BOATHOUSE

HARDWICK ESTATE

33

MEADOWS

BERKSHIRE

WESTBURY FARM

0   ¼ mile

0   APPROX SCALE   500m

← 45-50 MINS TO/FROM MAPLEDURHAM LOCK (MAP 33) →

ROUTE GUIDE AND MAPS

Where to stay and eat

On the corner of Whitchurch Rd is *The George Hotel* (☎ 0118-984 2237, 🖥 george hotelpangbourne.com; **fb**; 3S/12D/4T/3Tr/3Qd; 🛏; WI-FI; room rates from £32.50pp, sgl/slg occ £50). Breakfast (booked in advance) costs an extra £8pp; food (Tue-Thur noon-3pm & 6-9pm, Fri & Sat noon-9pm, Sun to 4pm; 🐾 in bar only) is available in both the bar and the restaurant.

You can expect to pay from £42.50pp (sgl/sgl occ £37.50) for B&B in a classic room at *The Elephant* (☎ 0118-984 2244, 🖥 elephanthotel.co.uk; **fb**; 2S/18D/2D or T; 🛏; WI-FI; 🐾). **Fine dining** (restaurant Fri-Sat noon-2.30pm, Sun to 4pm, Mon-Sat 6-9pm, Sun 5-8pm) is available; an 8oz sirloin steak is £21. They also serve food in the bar (Fri-Sun noon-2.30pm). Note that

reception is unmanned noon-3pm and they prefer queries by email. The best location for **pub food** is next to the river at *The Swan* (☎ 0118-984 4494, 🖥 swanpang bourne.co.uk; **fb**; WI-FI; 🐾 in bar area; Shooters Hill). Famous as the location where Jerome K Jerome's three men finally ditched their comedic boat, the setting is grand and the food (Mon-Thur 10am-9pm, Fri & Sat to 10pm, Sun to 8pm) great too. The menu changes regularly but features both classic and contemporary dishes.

Equally imaginative meals such as chargrilled Cajun tuna steak (£12) are on the menu at *The Cross Keys* (☎ 0118-984 3268, 🖥 crosskeyspangbourne.com; **fb**; food Mon-Sat noon-2pm & 6-9pm, Sun noon-3pm). Their menu also includes a grilled halloumi salad (£10.50).

❑ KENNETH GRAHAME & *THE WIND IN THE WILLOWS*

Born in Edinburgh in 1859, Kenneth Grahame spent most of his formative years living with his grandmother in the Thames-side village of Cookham – his mother having died of scarlet fever when he was very young, and his father being an alcoholic. During this early period of his life he would get to learn about the river, go boating and explore the countryside of the upper reaches of the Thames. His family could not afford for him to go to university so instead he moved to London where he worked at the Bank of England. Progressing swiftly through the ranks, it was during this period that he would begin to write. His early essays and short stories were much acclaimed – though they would all be overshadowed by what was to come.

Grahame married Elspeth Thomson in 1899 and their only son – Alastair – was born the following year. Unfortunately, Alastair was a sickly child, blind in one eye and of poor health, so his father created bedtime stories to help his disabled son to sleep. These anthropomorphic stories recounting the riverside adventures of Mole, Ratty, Badger and the troublesome Mr Toad were undoubtedly influenced to a large degree by Grahame's early childhood at Cookham. Eventually the tales were collected together and published in 1908 under the title *The Wind in the Willows*.

The book would, of course, go on to become one of the best loved in the English language. One particular fan who was instrumental in its mass publication was Theodore Roosevelt, then President of the United States, who on visiting Oxford in 1910 was so taken with the tales that he requested an audience with the author.

Tragedy struck the Grahames in 1920 when Alastair Grahame committed suicide. His devastated parents fled abroad, though they eventually returned to England – and the banks of the river – a few years later in 1924, moving into **Church Cottage** in Pangbourne, where Kenneth Grahame lived until his death in 1932.

It wasn't just the stories that were influenced by the scenery surrounding Pangbourne and Cookham; the book's illustrations, too, especially those completed by EH Shepard for the 1931 edition, were inspired by the area. Indeed, both Hardwick Estate (Map 32) and Mapledurham House (Map 33), across the water from the path en route to Henley, lay claim to being the inspiration for Shepard's Toad Hall.

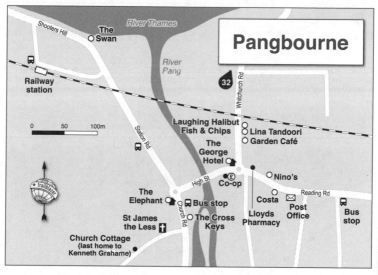

For pasta (£11-14) or pizza (from £9) look no further than *Nino's* (☎ 0118-984 1333, 🖥 ninos-trattoria.co.uk; **fb**; Tue-Sat noon-2pm, Mon-Sat 6-10pm). *Lina Tandoori* (☎ 0118-984 5577, 🖥 linatandoori.co.uk; daily noon-2.30pm & 5-11pm) is a standard Indian restaurant with chicken masala for £8.95. For traditional British fare, *Laughing Halibut* (☎ 0118-984 1614; Mon-Sat 11.30am-2.30pm & 5-11pm, Sun

& Bank Hols 4.30-11pm; 18 Whitchurch Rd) has **takeaway** fish & chips for £7.90. For early risers, across the road there's a branch of the national chain *Costa* (Mon-Sat 7am-6pm, Sun 8am-6pm); while back on Whitchurch Rd is *Garden Café* (☎ 0118-984 1114; **fb**; WI-FI; 🐾; Mon-Sat 9am-4pm, Sun 10am-3pm), which does a good line in food and hot and cold drinks including iced teas and frappés (both £2.80).

E → PANGBOURNE TO HENLEY-ON-THAMES   [MAPS 32-38]

This **17¼-mile (27.7km, 5½-6½hrs)** section boasts some impressive locks which bookend a long and surprisingly peaceful jaunt – surprising, as for much of it you'll be accompanied by the Great Western Railway line and red kites compete with the aeroplanes for dominance of the skies. The latter are inflicted on the area by Heathrow, a timely reminder that the nation's capital gets ever closer.

As you follow the river out of Pangbourne the opposite bank is dominated by the Chilterns, as well as **Hardwick Estate** and **Mapledurham House** (Map 33), both of which claim to have been the inspiration for EH Shepard's illustrations for Kenneth Grahame's Toad Hall (see box opposite).

The café at **Mapledurham Lock** (see p153) appears to be permanently closed now. Either here, or after walking a little further round to the next café (along a lovely 5-minute stretch of river bank, which is recommended), you sadly have to leave the river and take a suburban walk through **Purley-on-Thames** before a bridge over the railway and steep steps down take you back

ROUTE GUIDE AND MAPS

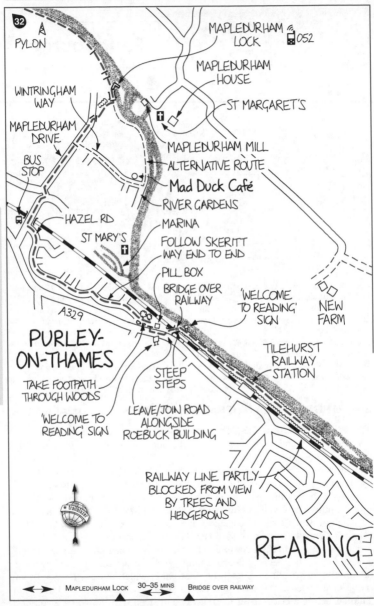

32
PYLON

MAPLEDURHAM LOCK 📱052

MAPLEDURHAM HOUSE

ST MARGARET'S ✝

WINTRINGHAM WAY

MAPLEDURHAM DRIVE

BUS STOP

MAPLEDURHAM MILL

ALTERNATIVE ROUTE

Mad Duck Café

RIVER GARDENS

HAZEL RD

ST MARY'S ✝

MARINA

FOLLOW SKERITT WAY END TO END

PILL BOX

BRIDGE OVER RAILWAY

'WELCOME TO READING' SIGN

NEW FARM

A329

PURLEY-ON-THAMES

TILEHURST RAILWAY STATION

TAKE FOOTPATH THROUGH WOODS

STEEP STEPS

'WELCOME TO READING' SIGN

LEAVE/JOIN ROAD ALONGSIDE ROEBUCK BUILDING

RAILWAY LINE PARTLY BLOCKED FROM VIEW BY TREES AND HEDGEROWS

READING

MAPLEDURHAM LOCK ←→ 30–35 MINS BRIDGE OVER RAILWAY

to the water's edge shortly before **Tilehurst railway station**; here a sign welcomes you to Reading. Tilehurst is a stop on some of GWR's train services (see box on pp56-7). The 143 & 16 **bus** services stop in Tilehurst and also call in at **Purley-on-Thames** (see pp58-61).

The path skirts around the outer reaches of **Reading** (p155; Map 33), though the trail is usually separated from its companions by the obligatory meadow. Central Reading (🖳 livingreading.co.uk/visit) is a fair hike from the river, and walkers will likely be more than happy with the food and accommodation options near **Caversham Bridge** (see p156; Map 34).

Having left Caversham and Reading a lovely stretch follows through the **Thames Valley Nature Reserve** (🖳 thamesvalleypark.com) and then a shady walk along the river into **Sonning** (see pp157-8; Map 35), where you switch counties again (from Berkshire to Oxfordshire). The path now takes you past the boathouse and playing fields of Shiplake College to **Shiplake Lock** (Map 36).

A little further on there is another diversion inland, passing under the railway line and then through a residential area into **Lower Shiplake** (see p158; Map 36); you cross the railway line at the station and are then led past more houses back to the river shortly before **Marsh Lock**. A final stretch along a path draped in willows to **Henley-on-Thames** (see pp161-3; Maps 37 & 38) ensues, a suitably pleasant reward for what has been a long day.

MAPLEDURHAM LOCK   [Map 33]

This lock made history in 1956 when it became the first mechanical lock on the River Thames; it was using an early type of electro-mechanical system, although this wasn't very successful, and it was converted to hydraulic operation in 1974. The weir next to the lock supplies a head of water which powers the nearby 15th-century **water mill**, the only water mill working on the Thames today. The mill appears in

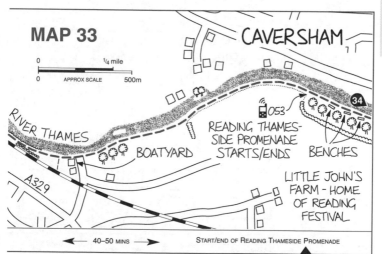

MAP 33

0 — ¼ mile
0 — APPROX SCALE — 500m

RIVER THAMES

A329

BOATYARD

053

READING THAMES-
SIDE PROMENADE
STARTS/ENDS

CAVERSHAM

34

BENCHES

LITTLE JOHN'S
FARM - HOME
OF READING
FESTIVAL

← 40–50 MINS →   START/END OF READING THAMESIDE PROMENADE the Domesday book, so clearly there was a dam or weir here in 1086, one of the earliest recorded on the river; sadly, the mill is not accessible from this side of the river. Also sadly, the former Mapledurham Lock Café is now permanently closed, though if you are ready for a coffee or refreshments you might try walking 500 metres downstream to find the *Mad Duck Café* (☎ 07429-232316, 🖥 themadduckcafe.co.uk; **fb**; WI-FI; 🐾; Mon & Thur-Sat 9.30am-5.30pm, Sun to 4pm, closed Tue & Wed) at 82-4 Wintringham Way, where they do breakfasts (from £4.50) and light lunches. You can then return to the path in Mapledurham Drive (or do the detour in reverse if you are walking east to west).

❑ FISH LADDERS

Weirs are as much a hindrance to fish as they are to boats as they prevent the former from swimming upriver in their search for new waters in which to feed and breed. Since the 1980s fish ladders have been added to weirs in order to allow the fish such passage. Using metal plates to slow the water down at the edge of the weir allows fish the chance to bypass the weirs and continue their journey upstream.

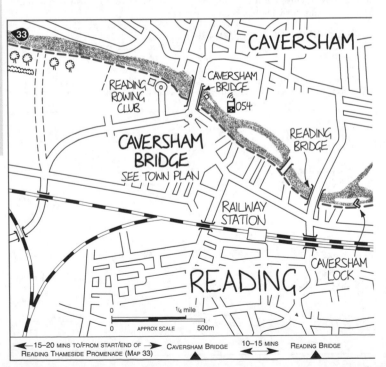

ROUTE GUIDE AND MAPS

CAVERSHAM (READING)
[map p156]

Though Reading is widely believed to have been settled since Roman times, the first irrefutable evidence of its existence dates back 'only' to the 8th century when it was known as *Readingum*, a name which originated from Reada, a Saxon leader whose tribe had settled here. The Victorian era – and the arrival of the Great Western Railway – saw the town prosper due to the manufacturing of what famously became known as the **Three Bs**: **beer**, at Simond's Brewery; **bulbs**, at Suttons Seeds; and **biscuits**, at Huntley & Palmers who once ran the world's largest biscuit factory. Today, however, the town is perhaps most famous/notorious as the place where in 1895 **Oscar Wilde** was incarcerated for 'committing acts of gross indecency with other male persons', his time immortalised in his poem *The Ballad of Reading Gaol*.

There is a BP petrol station with a **shop** (24hrs) and **ATM** on Richfield Ave. Just off the path by King's Meadow is a Tesco (Mon-Sat 6am-midnight, Sun 10am-4pm).

The only option for **campers** is *Wokingham Waterside Centre* (Map 34; ☎ 0118-926 8280, 🖥 wokinghamwaterside centre.com/camping; **fb**; 🐾); the centre has a small field where tents can be pitched (£10pp). A fob (available from reception) provides access to showers and toilets. There is also a kitchen with microwave ovens, a hob and a kettle. Booking is recommended as they can get full with groups.

For **accommodation** with a roof, by the bridge and with a terrace onto the river is the plush *Crowne Plaza* hotel (see p21; Crowne Plaza Reading; ☎ 0118-925 9900, 🖥 cp-reading.co.uk); at times prices can be very reasonable. Cheaper accommodation might be found at the Reading (Caversham

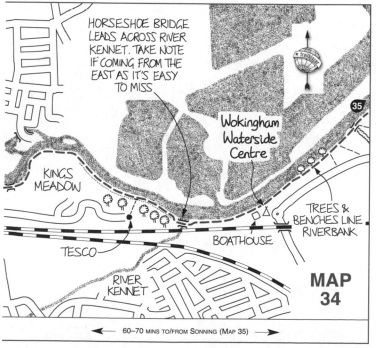

HORSESHOE BRIDGE LEADS ACROSS RIVER KENNET. TAKE NOTE IF COMING FROM THE EAST AS IT'S EASY TO MISS

trailblazer

Wokingham Waterside Centre

KINGS MEADOW

35

TREES & BENCHES LINE RIVERBANK

BOATHOUSE

TESCO

RIVER KENNET

MAP 34

← 60–70 MINS TO/FROM SONNING (MAP 35) →

Bridge) branch of *Premier Inn* (see p21; ☎ 0333-321 8344, 💻 premierinn.com).

You can also find a **bed** at *Caversham Lodge* (☎ 0118-961 2110 or ☎ 07971-391133; 1T/2Tr/1Qd, shared facilities; ☛; WI-FI), 133a Caversham Rd (on the corner of Swansea Rd). Online booking is only through 💻 booking.com but for the best rate book by phone. A room costs from £35pp (sgl occ £55) but breakfast isn't included; however, they'll sell you a voucher for £4pp for *The Gorge Café* (☎ 0118-950 3446; **fb**; Mon-Fri 8am-3pm, Sun from 9am) on the corner of Caversham Rd and Richfield Ave which also provides 'early bird' breakfasts (until 10am) for £4.60.

You can also try *Richfields Deli & Grill* (☎ 0118-939 1144, 💻 richfields deli.com; **fb**; Mon-Fri 8.30am-3pm, Sat-Sun from 9am; WI-FI; 211 Caversham Rd), where you'll find breakfasts from £4.50.

Thai food is on the menu at *The Moderation* (☎ 0118-375 0767, 💻 themod reading.com; **fb**; food Mon-Sat noon-3pm & 6-9.30pm, Sun noon-4pm & 6-9pm; 213 Caversham Rd), where you'll get a *nasi goreng* for £12; and more traditional pub food at *Toby Carvery Caversham Bridge* (☎ 0118-950 5044, 💻 tobycarvery.co.uk; **fb**; food Tue-Sun 8am-10pm, Mon from noon; WI-FI), which, like all branches of Toby Carvery, is very good value, their midweek carvery costing just £8.29.

River Spice (☎ 0118-950 3355, 💻 riverspice.co.uk; **fb**; Mon-Sat noon-2.30pm & 5.30-11.30pm, Sun noon-10pm) is the local Indian restaurant. Located right next to the river there are seafood specialities such as tandoori monkfish masala (£15.95).

Takeaway can be found on Caversham Rd at *Mr Cod* (☎ 0118-957 4731; daily 11am-10pm; No 155) and *Marmaris Kebabs* (☎ 0118-959 0363; Sun-Thur noon-1am, Fri & Sat to 2am; No 169). From both you'll be able to eat for less than a tenner.

Caversham Rd is linked to central Reading by the X39/X40 **bus** service. Services from central Reading include the 16, 127, 128/129, 143, 800 & 850. See pp58-61 for details. The limited 142 (Going Forward; Tue 2/day) service to Goring also calls here. Reading is also well connected by **train** (GWR, SWR, Cross Country and TfL Rail; see box on pp56-7).

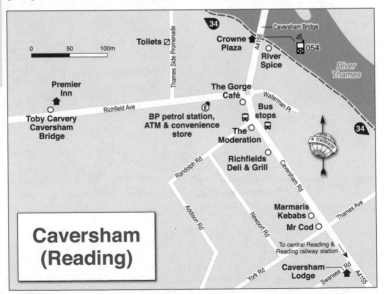

Caversham (Reading)

SONNING [Map 35]

One of the Thames's most eye-catching villages, there is evidence of there being a bridge here back in the Saxon era, though the current stone one was erected only in 1775. There is also evidence of a settlement as far back as the Palaeolithic and Mesolithic eras: our predecessors must have seen the site as Jerome K Jerome described it as 'the most fairy-like little nook on the river'.

Sonning is a stop on the 127, 128, 129 & 850 **bus** services (see box pp58-61).

Three establishments provide **B&B** and **food**. Tucked away along a footpath just to the south of the bridge is *The Bull Inn* (☎ 0118-969 3901, 💻 bullinnsonning .co.uk; 6D/1D or T; WI FI; 🐕; High St). It's a very well-kept and popular place partly because of its mention in Jerome's *Three Men in a Boat*. B&B costs from £44.50pp (sgl occ room rate). Food is served daily (Mon-Fri noon-3pm & 6-9pm, Sat & Sun noon-9pm).

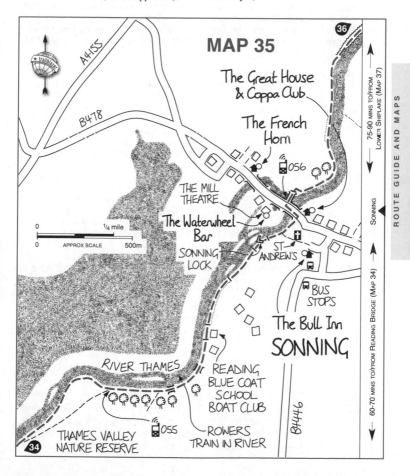

MAP 35

75-90 MINS TO/FROM LOWER SHIPLAKE (MAP 37)

60-70 MINS TO/FROM READING BRIDGE (MAP 34)

ROUTE GUIDE AND MAPS

SONNING

A4155

B478

36

The Great House & Coppa Club

The French Horn

056

THE MILL THEATRE

The Waterwheel Bar

SONNING LOCK

ST ANDREW'S

BUS STOPS

The Bull Inn
SONNING

0   1/4 mile
0   500m
APPROX SCALE

RIVER THAMES

READING BLUE COAT SCHOOL BOAT CLUB

B4446

THAMES VALLEY NATURE RESERVE

055

ROWERS TRAIN IN RIVER

34

The Great House (☎ 0118-969 2277, 🖥 greathouseatsonning.co.uk; **fb**; 36D/7T; 🍴; 🐾) is yet another fine establishment near to the water's edge. B&B costs from £42.50pp (sgl occ room rate); the food in their restaurant/bar called *Coppa Club* (☎ 0118-207 8971; **fb**; WI-FI; 🐾; food daily 7.30am-10pm, Sat & Sun from 8am) is surprisingly reasonable with flash steak & fries for £15.50. Coppa Club is part of same chain as at The Swan in Streatley (see p146).

Across the road bridge is *The French Horn* (☎ 0118-969 2204, 🖥 thefrenchhorn .co.uk; **fb**; 5D/3 suites/4 cottages; 🍴; WI-FI; from £90pp, sgl occ £145). The rooms and meals (Wed-Sat noon-2pm & 7-9pm, Sun noon-4pm & second sitting from 4.30pm) are simply staggering but the prices reflect this. At dinner half a spit-roasted Aylesbury duck costs £34.

Nearer **Sonning Lock**, and part of the Mill Theatre complex, is *The Waterwheel Bar* (☎ 0118-969 6039, 🖥 millatson ning.com; WI-FI; 🐾; Tue-Sun 11am-5pm) which offers artisan coffee, home-made cakes, a range of sandwiches (from £5.50) and delicious bar food including fish & chips (£13.50) in a beautiful riverside setting, with indoor and outdoor seating. If staying the night in Sonning you may also want to fit in a performance at this theatre.

SHIPLAKE, LOWER SHIPLAKE
[Map 36; Map 37, p160]

Shiplake itself is hidden from the trail by trees; its main claim to fame is that the author Eric Blair, aka George Orwell, grew up here. Another literary behemoth – Alfred, Lord Tennyson – got married in the church (**St Peter & St Paul**), paying the vicar for his services with a poem rather than a fee. You're unlikely to get away with that in the **corner shop** (Map 37; Mon-Fri 7.30am-5.30pm, Sat 8am-12.30pm, Sun 8-11am) or **post office** (Mon-Fri 9am-5.30pm, Sat to 12.30pm) which share a building on Station Rd, Lower Shiplake.

At 7 Station Rd is *The Baskerville* (☎ 0118-940 3332, 🖥 thebaskerville.com; 3D/1Tr; WI-FI; 🐾). B&B costs from around £60pp (sgl occ £100) and the **food** in their award-winning restaurant (Tue-Sat noon-2.30pm & 6-9.30pm, Sun noon-4pm) – such as pan-fried monkfish, butternut purée, candied beets, cherry tomatoes, hot house vegetable salsa & seasonal vegetables (£28) – starts from £10.50.

Shiplake **railway station** is a stop on GWR's services (see box on pp56-7) from Twyford to Henley; the 800 **bus** service (see pp58-61) calls here and in Shiplake.

W ←HENLEY-ON-THAMES TO PANGBOURNE [MAPS 37-32]

[Route section begins on Map 37, p160] This **17¼-mile (27.7km, 5½-6½hrs)** section of the path boasts some impressive locks which bookend a long and surprisingly peaceful jaunt – surprising, as for much of it you'll be accompanied by the Great Western Railway line and red kites compete with the aeroplanes for dominance of the skies, the latter inflicted on the area by Heathrow. However, the trail is usually separated from its companions by the obligatory meadow.

The path out of **Henley** passes Mill Meadows and then goes under the willow trees to **Marsh Lock**. Sadly, you are soon led away from the river and through a residential area of **Lower Shiplake** (see above), crossing the railway line at Shiplake station; you are then led past more houses and turn left, going under the railway line to rejoin the river before you walk round to **Shiplake Lock** (Map 36). You pass the boathouse and playing fields of Shiplake College before approaching the bridge at **Sonning** (Map 35), where you cross back into

Berkshire. A lovely stretch now follows – a shady walk along into **Thames Valley Nature Reserve** (🖥 thamesvalleypark.com) before you hit the edge of Reading and the busier riverside of **Caversham**. Central Reading (🖥 living reading.co.uk/visit) is a fair hike from the river and walkers will likely be more than happy with the food and accommodation options near **Caversham Bridge**

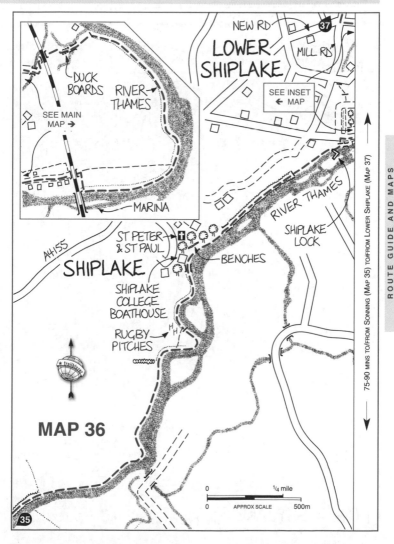

MAP 36

75-90 MINS TO/FROM SONNING (MAP 35) TO/FROM LOWER SHIPLAKE (MAP 37)

ROUTE GUIDE AND MAPS

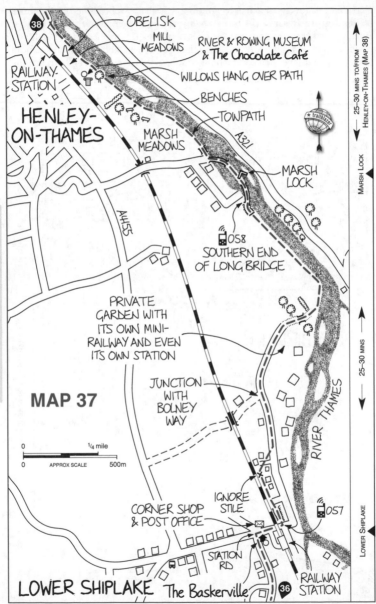

OBELISK
MILL MEADOWS
RIVER & ROWING MUSEUM & The Chocolate Café
WILLOWS HANG OVER PATH
BENCHES
TOWPATH
MARSH MEADOWS
MARSH LOCK
A321
RAILWAY STATION
HENLEY-ON-THAMES
A4455
058 SOUTHERN END OF LONG BRIDGE
PRIVATE GARDEN WITH ITS OWN MINI-RAILWAY AND EVEN ITS OWN STATION
JUNCTION WITH BOLNEY WAY

MAP 37

0   ¼ mile
APPROX SCALE
0   500m

RIVER THAMES

CORNER SHOP & POST OFFICE
IGNORE STILE
057
STATION RD
LOWER SHIPLAKE   The Baskerville
RAILWAY STATION

25–30 MINS TO/FROM HENLEY-ON-THAMES (MAP 38)
MARSH LOCK
25–30 MINS
LOWER SHIPLAKE

38

36

★ trailblazer

(see pp155-6; Map 34) before continuing along **Reading**'s Thames-side Promenade (Map 33) and on past **Tilehurst railway station**. Tilehurst is a stop on some of GWR's **train** services (see box on pp56-7). The 143 & 16 **bus** services (see pp58-61) stop in Tilehurst, also calling in at Purley-on-Thames. You have to cross the railway and take a suburban walk through **Purley-on-Thames** (Map 33) before returning to the water's edge at **Mapledurham Lock** (see pp153-4); you may, however, choose to return to the river shortly before this to visit a café, then enjoy a 5-minute walk along a lovely stretch of river bank to reach the lock.

As you follow the river towards **Pangbourne** (pp149-51; Map 32) the opposite bank is dominated by the Chilterns, with views of **Mapledurham House** and the **Hardwick Estate**, both of which claim to have been the inspiration for EH Shepard's illustrations for Kenneth Grahame's Toad Hall (see box on p150). *[Next route overview on pp148-9]*

HENLEY-ON-THAMES [map p163]

Host to the world-famous Henley Royal Regatta (see box on p164), the path's most stylish Thames-side town is not cheap; its sheer beauty, however, goes some way to compensating you.

A market town since 1269, the town's most photogenic feature is its bridge, built in 1786. While admiring its arches note the sculpted faces of **Old Father Thames** (see box on p96) peering downstream and of Isis staring back towards the source.

Facing Mill Meadows to the south of the town there is a **River and Rowing Museum** (Map 37; ☎ 01491-415600, 🖳 rrm.co.uk; Thur-Mon 10am-4pm; £9).

Fans of The Beatles probably know that George Harrison lived at Friar Park, to the west of town; Dusty Springfield has a gravestone marker in **St Mary's** churchyard.

Services

Henley **Visitor Information Centre** (☎ 01491-576982, 🖳 visit-henley.com; Easter to end Oct Mon-Fri 9am-4pm, Sat 10am-4pm, Sun 11am-3pm, Nov-Easter Mon-Fri same, Sat 10am-noon) is in the town hall.

On Bell St there is a **pharmacy**, Boots (Mon-Sat 9am-6pm, Sun 10.30am-4.30pm), and for provisions Sainsbury's (daily 7am-11pm); a larger **supermarket**, Waitrose (Mon-Sat 8am-9pm, Sun 10am-4pm) is located just off the same street.

The **post office** (Mon-Fri 9am-5.30pm, Sat to 12.30pm) is on Reading Rd. Henley has branches of most high street banks, and **ATMs** can be found on Hart St.

Henley **railway station** (Map 37) is at the end of the branch line from Twyford; **train** services are operated by GWR (see box on pp56-7). **Bus** services X38, 239, 800 & 850 call here; see pp58-61.

❑ RED KITE ALERT

As you walk the path, the sight of red kites magnificently soaring in the sky is a delight. Known to Shakespeare as rather pesky scavengers, these birds of prey were hunted to near extinction, but were reintroduced to this country from Spain and Sweden in the '90s, and it is thought that there are now up to 1000 breeding pairs in the Thames area. The problem is that some people have been feeding them (unnecessarily, as the RSPB says that they have plenty of natural food sources) to get close-up pictures, and they have developed a taste for picnic and barbecue food, with the result that several very unpleasant attacks have been reported in Henley-on-Thames, including some injuries. Bearing in mind that they have sharp talons and a wingspan of up to 1.5 metres, you should be on the look-out for them.

Where to stay

Note that during certain times of year – and especially during Henley Royal Regatta (late June to early July) – accommodation prices rise to astronomical levels and it is essential to book months in advance.

Campers have a short amble out of town to reach *Swiss Farm Touring & Camping* (Map 38; ☎ 01491-573419, ⌨ swissfarmcamping.co.uk; **fb**; WI-FI; ✻; Apr/May-end Oct but weather dependent). Walkers should ask for the walkers' rate (from £15pp). Note that in the Henley Regatta period they only accept bookings of seven nights. It's a large family site where the staff are friendly and the facilities – including a **shop** (daily 9am-5pm) and a (seasonal) **café** – good.

Accommodation in **pubs** can be found centrally. *The Catherine Wheel* (☎ 01491-848484, ⌨ jdwetherspoon.com; 4S/16D/6T/4Tr; ✆; WI-FI; 7-15 Hart St) has plenty of rooms but some of them can be quite noisy, especially on Friday and Saturday nights. Rates (£25-42pp, sgl occ room rate) don't include breakfast but this is available (£3-6) from the restaurant downstairs, as is food throughout the day (see Where to eat).

For a more peaceful forty winks, *The Row Barge* (☎ 01491-572649, ⌨ brakspear.co.uk/pub-finder/row-barge; **fb**; 3D/1T; ✆; WI-FI; £45-50pp, sgl occ room rate; 37 West St) is a better bet and food is also available (see Where to eat) but no breakfasts.

The big hotels in Henley are pricey, but *Rioshouse Henley* (☎ 07485-753367, ⌨ rioshousehenley.co.uk; **fb**; 2D/4T/1 x 5-bed apartment; ✆; WI-FI; 38 Hart St) is a few steps away from the bridge. Rooms cost from £99.50 (sgl occ room rate) without breakfast. This is a No Reception Hotel: the day before your arrival you will receive on your mobile all the information for check-in.

Should you really want to push the boat out, you could treat yourself to *The Relais Henley* (⌨ therelaishenley .com) which stands next to the bridge overlooking the Thames. There's also a deli if you want to pick up some posh sandwiches or takeaway treats.

Where to eat and drink

Henley has numerous eateries. For **breakfast** go straight to *Café Buendia* (☎ 01491-573706; WI-FI; food Mon-Thur 8am-9pm, Fri & Sat to 10pm, Sun 9am-9pm; 8 Bell St). Primarily a pizza and pasta restaurant, it also cooks up a splendid full-English breakfast (from £6.10). If you can't be bothered to walk that far, *The Chocolate Café* (☎ 01491-411412, ⌨ chocolatecafe henley.co.uk; WI-FI; Mon-Fri 10am-4pm, Sat & Sun 9.30am-5pm) is right on the path and the riverfront. There is now **another branch** (Map 37; ☎ 01491-415602, ⌨ rrm .co.uk/visit/cafe; WI-FI; ✻ outside; Thur-Mon 10am-4pm) in the same building as the rowing museum (see p161). The menu at both is similar: paninis for £8.95, cakes from £2.75 as well as breakfasts and main courses.

Ten of Henley's **pubs** are owned by Brakspear Brewery (⌨ brakspear.co.uk). Best located for a pint after a hard day's walk is *The Angel on the Bridge* (☎ 01491-410678, ⌨ theangelhenley.com; **fb**; WI-FI; ✻; food Mon-Sat 11.30am-9pm, Sun to 7pm; in winter Mon-Fri noon-3pm & 6-9pm, Sat 11.30am-9pm, Sun to 7pm), which is ... by the bridge. Mains are good value, starting at £11.50 for a leek & feta tart and rising to £15.50 for venison in port and Guinness with celeriac mash & spiced red cabbage.

For an evening meal, the town's locals rave about a trio of the Brakspear pubs. Preeminent amongst them, *The Bull on Bell St* (☎ 01491-576554, ⌨ bullonbell.co.uk; **fb**; food Mon-Sat noon-10pm, Sun to 9pm; WI-FI; ✻ bar only; Nos 57-59), which is more restaurant than pub; mains cost from £9.95 and the lunch menu may include such dishes as pan-fried sea bream (£14.95).

The other two are: *The Three Tuns* (☎ 01491-410138, ⌨ threetunshenley.co.uk; **fb**; food Mon-Sat noon-9.30pm, Sun to 8pm; 5 Market Place), where tart of the day with house salad costs £12.95 and a provençal fish stew is £16.25; and *The Row Barge* (see Where to stay; ✻ in bar on lead; food Wed-Sat noon-2pm & 7-9pm,

Sun noon-3pm), which has a beer garden to relax in.

Focusing on meat and fish dishes from South Africa, Germany and Switzerland, *Hof's Bar & Dining* (☎ 01491-529313, 🖳 hofshenley.co.uk; **fb**; food Tue-Sat noon-10pm, Sun to 9pm; 38 Market Place) offers light dishes from £6.50 and signature dishes from £12.50, for which you will get an African chicken curry with coriander on saffron rice.

The Anchor (☎ 01491-574753, 🖳 theanchorhenley.co.uk; **fb**; Tue-Sat noon-2.30pm & 6-7.30pm, Sun noon-2.30pm; WI-FI), at 58 Friday St, has a sunny garden restaurant with a good and reasonable menu, and a simpler take-away menu from its beer garden.

Cheapest for standard pub food is *The Catherine Wheel* (see Where to stay; food daily 7am-10pm), although, being Henley, the food prices are slightly inflated above those of your average Wetherspoon's.

Nearby, heat-seekers should consider *Giggling Squid* (☎ 01491-411044, 🖳 gigglingsquid.com/restaurant/henley; **fb**; Mon-Thur noon-10pm, Fri & Sat to 10.30pm, Sun to 9.30pm; 40 Hart St), for chicken & cashew nut stir-fry (£8.50 at lunch) and other spicy Thai dishes; or *Café Le Raj* (☎ 01491-573337, 🖳 cafeleraj.co.uk; **fb**; food daily 6-11.30pm; 17 Reading Rd) which provides some of the best-value meals in Henley, with a chicken vindaloo for £6.75.

Takeaway is also available at *Domino's Pizza* (☎ 01491-577666, 🖳 dominos.co.uk; daily 11am-9.30pm; 55 Bell St), *Istanbul Kebabs* (☎ 01491-411810, 🖳 istanbulkebabhenley.restajet.com; Mon-Thur 11.30am-11pm, Fri-Sat noon-midnight, Sun 1-11pm; 7 Greys Rd) and *JK's Fish and Chips* (Mon-Sat 11.30am-2.30pm & 4.30-9.30pm, Sun & Bank Hols 4.30-9.30pm; 54 Kings Rd).

ROUTE GUIDE AND MAPS

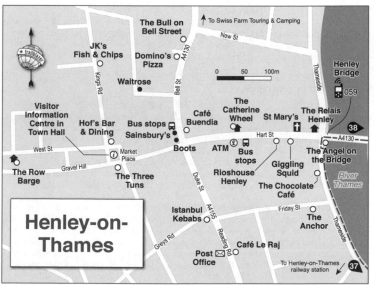

Henley-on-Thames

E ➔ HENLEY-ON-THAMES TO MARLOW   [MAPS 38-40]

This short **8½-mile (13.5km, 3-3¾hrs)** stage begins by following the same stretch of river used by the races during the Henley Regatta (see box below) – albeit in reverse – to **Temple Island** (Map 38). From here the river sweeps swiftly round to **Hambleden Lock** (Map 39), the starting point for the first-ever University Boat Race (see box on p211). Leaving the Thames at **Aston** (see below; Map 39) the trail cuts its way past the 18th-century **Culham Court** (lovely cowslips in the meadows in the spring) and through a **deer park** before reuniting itself with the river. At **Hurley Lock** (Map 40) a footpath can be taken to **Hurley** village (see below). After you've crossed the river to Buckinghamshire – your third county of the day (at Henley you crossed from Oxfordshire into Berkshire) – **Temple Lock** is the last lock encountered before you follow the towpath to **Marlow** (see p169). As you wander along be sure not to miss the view of **Bisham Church** on the opposite bank.

ASTON   [Map 39, p166]

The Flower Pot (☎ 01491-574721, 🖳 brak spear.co.uk/pub-finder/flowerpot; **fb**; 1T shared bathroom, 2D; 🛏; WI-FI; 🐕 bar only) charges £40-60pp (sgl occ from £60) for **B&B**. The menu (**food** Mon-Fri noon- 2.30pm & 6-9pm, Sat noon-9pm, Sun to 2.30pm) includes staples such as chicken curry with rice & naan (£12.50) as well as a long list of specials. Possibly one of the most characterful pubs on the entire walk.

HURLEY   [Map 40, p168]

There are two options for **campers** here. On the island is *Hurley Lock Campsite* (☎ 01628-824334; pitch £12 up to two people; 🐕 if on a lead and any messes cleaned up; Apr-end Sep). As with other Environment Agency campsites it is gated so you'll need to arrive within the lock-keeper's hours (generally 9am-5pm) to get the key.

❏ HENLEY ROYAL REGATTA

Attracting rowers from all over the globe, The Royal Regatta at Henley is held annually over the first weekend in July and lays fair claim to being the world's most famous festival of rowing and boat races. Established in 1839, the event predates any form of national or international rowing organisation so abides by its own rules and regulations.

Attempts to make the course as fair as possible have led to the route changing over time and the advantages once offered – by, for example, bends in the river, riverside features which offered shelter from the wind and areas which had a stronger current – have all been eradicated. Since 1924, however, the course has remained fairly constant, the rowers setting off from **Temple Island** before crossing the finishing line just short of **Henley Bridge** (both on Map 38), a distance of one mile and 550 yards – the longest naturally straight stretch of river in Britain. The patronage of Prince Albert enhanced its prestige and it became a royal regatta in 1851; since that time it has been one of the most popular occasions of the English social season. Beginning as a one-day event in 1839, the regatta has grown in length as well as popularity down the years and since 1986 has been spread over five days. The regatta's most prestigious event is the Grand Challenge Cup, raced by Men's Eights, which – the war years aside – has taken place every year since 1839 and has been won by crews from all over the world. For further information on the regatta visit 🖳 hrr.co.uk.

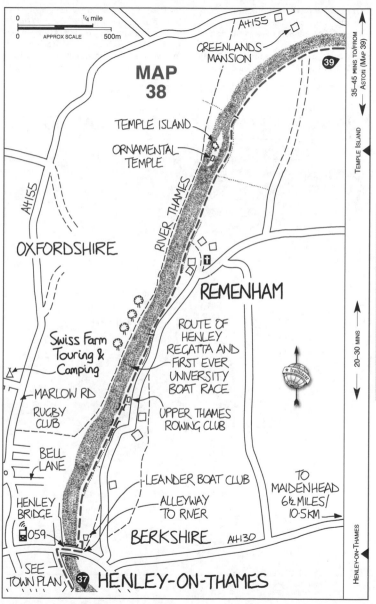

There are shower and toilet facilities. Booking is recommended especially for a weekend. Refreshments are available at a *tea shop* (Apr-end Sep Tue-Sun & Bank Hol Mon 11am-5pm), serving pasties, rolls and cakes and biscuits (£8 for a cream tea

for two). The toilets are always open. You can also camp at the gargantuan *Hurley Riverside Park* (☎ 01628-824493, 🖳 hurleyriversidepark.co.uk; pitch £15-32; WI-FI; 🐾; Mar-Oct), the main entrance to which is on High St. There is a key-coded back

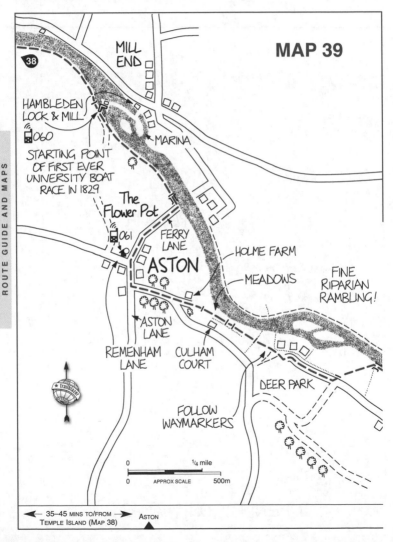

MAP 39

MILL END

38

HAMBLEDEN LOCK & MILL
📱060

STARTING POINT OF FIRST EVER UNIVERSITY BOAT RACE IN 1829

The Flower Pot
📱061

MARINA

FERRY LANE

ASTON

HOLME FARM

MEADOWS

FINE RIPARIAN RAMBLING!

ASTON LANE

REMENHAM LANE

CULHAM COURT

DEER PARK

FOLLOW WAYMARKERS

0   ¼ mile
0   500m
APPROX SCALE

ROUTE GUIDE AND MAPS

← 35-45 MINS TO/FROM → ASTON
TEMPLE ISLAND (MAP 38)

entrance gate on to the Thames Path for campers who have already checked-in (last check-in is 8pm).

Hidden from the river, Hurley's **St Mary's Church** is built on the foundations of its Saxon predecessor which was founded by St Birinus – the first bishop of Dorchester – in AD635. Beneath the Norman nave rest the remains of Edward the Confessor's sister.

Opposite the church is the **Village Shop** (☎ 01628-824271; daily summer Mon-Sat 8am-1pm & 2-5pm, Sun 9am-1pm & 2-5pm; winter Mon-Sat 8am-2pm, Sun 9am-2pm) with limited **post office** services (Tue & Thur 9am-noon only).

The closest *indoor* accommodation to the path is at *Crazy Fox* (☎ 01628-825086, 🖳 crazyfoxhurley.com; **fb**; 4D; ➡; WI-FI), a 'boutique' bed and breakfast with luxury king-size rooms; rates depend on demand but are from £100pp (£150pp at weekends), sgl occ room rate. One of the many historic pubs you'll come across on your Thames

journey, *The Olde Bell* (☎ 01628-969790, 🖳 theoldebell.co.uk; **fb**; WI-FI; 🐾 bar and some rooms) has both fine **rooms** (48D; ➡), a bar with **food** (Mon-Thur noon-3pm, Fri-Sun to 5pm) and a restaurant (Mon-Sat noon-2.30pm & 6-9.30pm, Sun noon-6.30pm). As you munch on seared trout fillet with garlic spinach, celeriac fondant and blushed tomatoes (£22), it's worth contemplating that their rooms have hosted Benedictine monks (there was a Benedictine abbey nearby and the pub was used as a guesthouse for its visitors) and even Winston Churchill and Dwight D Eisenhower as they planned the liberation of Europe.

The Rising Sun (🖳 risingsun hurley.co.uk; **fb**) was being taken over by new owners in November 2021 and at the time of research it was unclear what services they would provide but hopefully they will still serve Rebellion Beer and food.

The 239 **bus** stops on Hurley High St; see pp58-61.

ROUTE GUIDE AND MAPS

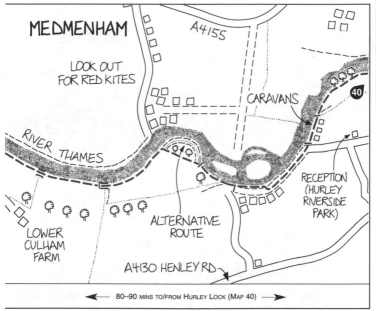

MEDMENHAM

LOOK OUT FOR RED KITES

A4155

CARAVANS

40

RIVER THAMES

RECEPTION (HURLEY RIVERSIDE PARK)

LOWER CULHAM FARM

ALTERNATIVE ROUTE

A4130 HENLEY RD

← 80–90 MINS TO/FROM HURLEY LOCK (MAP 40) →

W ← MARLOW TO HENLEY-ON-THAMES   [MAPS 40-38]

[Route section begins on Map 40, below] This **8½ mile (13.5km, 3-3¾ hours)**
stage begins by following the towpath out of **Marlow**, with views of **Bisham
Church** on the opposite bank, as far as **Temple Lock**.

Shortly after this you cross the river, leaving Buckinghamshire and entering
Berkshire. Further on, a bridge leads to an island accessing **Hurley Lock**, after
which a footpath can be taken to **Hurley** village (see p164). The river path continues alongside the campsite, with chalk cliffs on the opposite side.

Beyond the Hurley Riverside Park campsite (Map 39) the path joins a residential road, but after a while don't miss the sign guiding you to a path right
by the waterside. Further on, the path turns away from the river through a **deer
park** past the 18th-century **Culham Court** (lovely cowslips in the meadows in
the spring) and then into **Aston**, where it re-joins the river.

You pass **Hambledon Lock**, the starting point for the first ever University
Boat Race (see box on p211), and then the river sweeps round to **Temple
Island** (Map 38), after which there is the straight stretch of river into **Henley-
on-Thames** (see pp161-3; Maps 38 & 37) used by the races during the Henley
Regatta (see box on p164). Here you enter your third county of the day –
Oxfordshire. *[Next route overview on p158]*

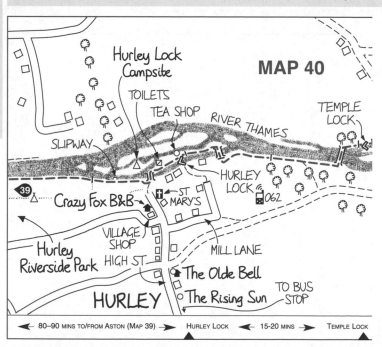

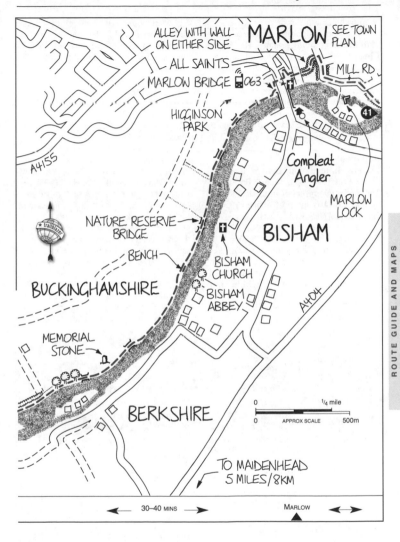

ALLEY WITH WALL ON EITHER SIDE

MARLOW SEE TOWN PLAN

ALL SAINTS

MILL RD

MARLOW BRIDGE ☎063

HIGGINSON PARK

41

Compleat Angler

NATURE RESERVE BRIDGE

MARLOW LOCK

BISHAM

BENCH

BISHAM CHURCH

BUCKINGHAMSHIRE

BISHAM ABBEY

MEMORIAL STONE

BERKSHIRE

0   ¼ mile

0   APPROX SCALE   500m

TO MAIDENHEAD 5 MILES/8KM

← 30–40 MINS →

MARLOW ← →

MARLOW   [map p170]

Rich in literary association, this laidback market town is where Thomas Love Peacock's *Nightmare Abbey* and Mary Shelley's *Frankenstein* were both composed; the latter's husband, the poet Percy Bysshe Shelley, also wrote *The Revolt of Islam* whilst floating on the river nearby and post-WW1 the town was the home of TS Eliot (see box on p47). It may be time to start scribbling in your diary – there must be something in the air here.

The town's significant features are its **19th-century bridge** and **All Saints Church**, the two combining to form yet another splendid riparian scene. **Marlow Museum** (☎ 01628-485474, 🖳 marlowmuseum.uk; **fb**, Mar-Oct Wed 2-5pm, Sat & Sun 1-5pm, Nov-Feb Sun 2-4pm; free), on Pound Lane, gives an interesting insight into the history of the town and surrounding area.

Services

Marlow Information Centre is in the library (Tue 10am-6pm, Wed & Fri to 5pm, Thur & Sat to 4pm) on Institute Rd; also on the same road is the **post office** (Mon-Fri 9am-5.30pm, Sat to 12.30pm).

On the High St are both **Marlow Pharmacy** (Mon-Fri 8.30am-5.30pm, Sat 9am-5pm, Sun 11am-4pm; No 62) and a Sainsbury's **supermarket** (daily 7am-11pm), near to which you'll find an **ATM**. There is also a branch of the **trekking outfitters** Mountain Warehouse (☎ 01628-487823; Mon-Sat 9am-6pm, Sun 10.30am-4.30pm) at 36-38 High St.

Marlow is at the end of the branch **railway** line from Maidenhead; services are operated by GWR (see box on pp56-7). **Bus** services 800 & 850 (see pp58-61) also call in town.

Where to stay

Nearest to the river on the northern side is a branch of the *Premier Inn* (Marlow; see p21; ☎ 0333 321 1325, 🖳 premierinn.com; The Causeway) chain.

Three **pubs** also offer accommodation. Close to the railway station is *The Prince of Wales* (☎ 01628-482970, 🖳 prince-of-wales@hotmail.co.uk; **fb**; 1S/2D/3T; 🛏; WI-FI; 🐾; from £58.50pp, sgl/sgl occ from £85.50/room rate; 1 Mill Rd). Contact them for details of their special offers.

The Chequers (☎ 01628-482053, 🖳 thechequersmarlow.co.uk; **fb**; 7D/2D or T; 🛏; WI-FI; 🐾), in the heart of the action at 53 High St, offers B&B from £47.50pp (sgl occ room rate).

A short walk from town at 126 West St, is the plush *Hand & Flowers* (☎ 01628-482277, 🖳 thehandandflowers.co.uk; 15D; 🛏; WI-FI; 🐾). The accommodation is in

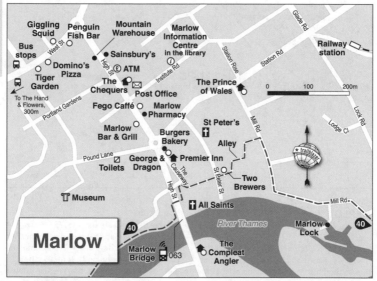

four elegantly furnished cottages all within a 5-minute walk of the pub. B&B costs £120-175pp (sgl occ room rate): not cheap, but the rooms do belong to a Michelin award-winning pub (see Where to eat). However, you will need to book a long way in advance – see the website for details.

Across the river there are some magnificent **hotel** rooms at *The Compleat Angler* (☎ 01628-484444, 🖳 macdonald hotels.co.uk; **fb**; 59D/5D or T; 🍺; WI-FI; 🐾), part of the Macdonald chain, but they also are not cheap: you can expect to pay from £140pp (sgl occ room rate) depending on demand and the season.

Where to eat and drink

Marlow has many options so finding somewhere to eat or drink won't be a problem.

On High St, a decent spot for **breakfast** is *Fego Caffé* (☎ 01628-475873, 🖳 hellofego.com/fego-marlow; **fb**; Mon-Sat 8am-4pm, Sun 9am-4pm; WI-FI; 🐾 outside only) where you'll get a Full English breakfast for £10.50 (they also do gourmet sandwiches, £5.50-7.50). Also on High St you'll find a top-notch spot for a brew and a pastry at *Burgers Bakery* (☎ 01628-483389, 🖳 burgersartisanbakery.com; **fb**; Mon-Sat 9am-4pm; WI-FI; 🐾 outside only; note Burgers is pronounced 'Burjers'). Afternoon tea costs £12.50pp and hungry canines are allowed but at the outside tables only.

For those staying at the Premier Inn (see opposite), the accompanying *George & Dragon* (☎ 01628-814312, 🖳 whitbread inns.co.uk; **fb**; WI-FI; food Mon-Sat 11.30am-10pm, Sun from noon) is ideal for those who want to set off on a full stomach; an all-you-can-eat breakfast (Mon-Fri 6.30-10.30am, Sat & Sun 7-11am) is available for £8.99.

Decent **pub meals** can be found at *The Chequers* (see Where to stay; food Mon-Thur noon-3pm & 5-9pm, Fri & Sat noon-9pm, Sun to 8pm; WI-FI; 🐾), a Brakspear pub where the menu includes not only Mount Grace Farm 35-day dry-aged 12oz sirloin steak (£26.95) but also pub standards such as fish & chips. Right on the trail, *Two Brewers* (☎ 01628-484140, 🖳 twobrewersmarlow.co.uk; **fb**; WI-FI; 🐾;

food daily 11am-9pm) is the oldest pub in Marlow. It is a smart and friendly place with a standard pub menu including garlic chicken (£14), as well as a good selection of burgers from £13.50.

Fish and meat dishes such as whole lobster thermidor (£48) can be reeled in at *Marlow Bar and Grill* (☎ 01628-488544, 🖳 therestaurantbarandgrill.com/ourrestau rants/marlow; **fb**; food Mon-Sat noon-11pm, Sun to 10.30pm; WI-FI; 92-94 High St). Cheaper meals such as burger and chips (£13.50) also appear on the menu.

The **restaurant** receiving the highest accolades in Marlow is *The Hand & Flowers* (see Where to stay; food Mon-Sat noon-2.30pm & 6.30-9.15pm, Sun noon-2.30pm). An establishment run by stellar chef Tom Kerridge and awarded two stars in the Michelin Guide. The menu changes regularly and is not cheap; Koffmann's new potato soup with pickled herring, tempura smoked eel and Oscietra caviar is priced at £27.50, yet one suspects that if you plan to treat yourself just once during your time by the river this may well be the place to do it. Booking is essential though (see the website).

If you fancy a pizza (£9-14) this can be found at *The Prince of Wales* (see Where to stay; food Mon-Fri 5-10pm, Sat & Sun noon-10pm; WI-FI; 🐾 bar area) and for Thai food try the town's branch of *Giggling Squid* (☎ 01628-483047, 🖳 gigglingsquid .com/restaurant/marlow; **fb**; Mon-Thur noon-10pm, Fri & Sat to 10.30pm, Sun to 9.30pm), where a chicken & cashew nut stir-fry will set you back £10.50.

A highly recommended **Indian** restaurant is *Tiger Garden* (☎ 01628-482211, 🖳 tigergarden.co.uk; daily noon-2pm & 6-11pm; WI-FI). The food, whether eaten in the restaurant or taken away, will not disappoint. Curries cost from £10.50.

Other **takeaway** options include *Domino's Pizza* (☎ 01628-477711, 🖳 dominos.co.uk; **fb**; daily 10am-11pm) and *Penguin Fish Bar* (☎ 01628-477271; **fb**; Mon-Sat 11am-10pm, Sun noon-9.30pm). Both are on West St and charge typical takeaway prices.

E → MARLOW TO WINDSOR   [MAPS 40-46]

This varied **14¼-mile (22.7km, 4½-5½hrs)** stage passes through a number of towns and villages each separated from the other by the serenity of some fine riverside tramping. With the magnificent and imposing view of Windsor Castle (see box on p182) dominating the final leg, this is one stage where you would be justified in setting off early.

The section begins with a quiet riparian stroll as far as **Bourne End** (see opposite; Map 41) where you cross to the southern side of the river to enter **Cock Marsh**, owned by the National Trust and an SSSI (see box on p71).

After a short but worthwhile diversion from the river to collude with the village of **Cookham** (see pp175-6; Map 42), an all-too-brief spell of woodland walking leads you to a hike through **Maidenhead** (see pp176-8; Map 43), a highlight of which is **Boulter's Lock** (see p177).

Having crossed the river and left Maidenhead in its wake the path gradually regains a sense of isolation, passing, on the opposite bank, **Bray** (see p179; Map 44). The tranquillity of this stretch is spoilt somewhat by the thunderous M4. With the sound of the motorway still resonant in your ears, glimpses of **Dorney Lake** (Map 45), home to Eton College's rowers, appear on your left and having navigated its length you arrive at the intriguing **Church of St Mary Magdalene** in Boveney. Finally, as **Windsor** (see pp183-5) looms into view you have only the town of **Eton** (see pp179-82; Map 46) – a worthwhile stop in its own right – to wander through before you arrive at Windsor Bridge... and at a castle fit for a queen.

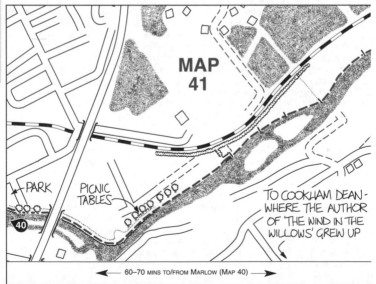

MAP 41

PARK

PICNIC TABLES

TO COOKHAM DEAN -
WHERE THE AUTHOR
OF 'THE WIND IN THE
WILLOWS' GREW UP

←—— 60–70 MINS TO/FROM MARLOW (MAP 40) ——→

BOURNE END   [Map 41]

Author Enid Blyton once lived in this large commuter village. That aside, and the fact that food is available by the river, unless you require a Tesco Express **supermarket** (daily 7am-11pm) or an **ATM** (BP petrol station; 24 hrs) – or a bus or train – there's really nothing at Bourne End to encourage you to leave the trail.

Bourne End is a stop on the branch **railway** line between Marlow and Maidenhead; services are operated by GWR (see box on pp56-7).

The 36 & 37/37A **bus** services (see pp58-61) call at the railway station.

On the southern side of the river, only a short distance from the railway bridge, is *The Bounty* (☎ 01628-520056; **fb**; WI-FI; 🐾; food Apr-Sep daily noon-8pm, Oct-Mar weekends only noon-5pm). One of the river's most colourful pubs, this popular free house welcomes walkers and all other folk who choose to follow the river. There's a vast range of burgers (£6.95-8.95) and their Rebellion (see box on p23) selection of ales is especially popular. Dogs are welcomed as if long-lost friends and they provide dog snacks (£2 for a bowl of sausage chunks). The **toilets** are also free for walkers.

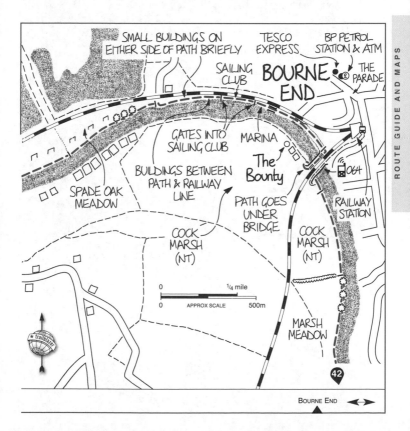

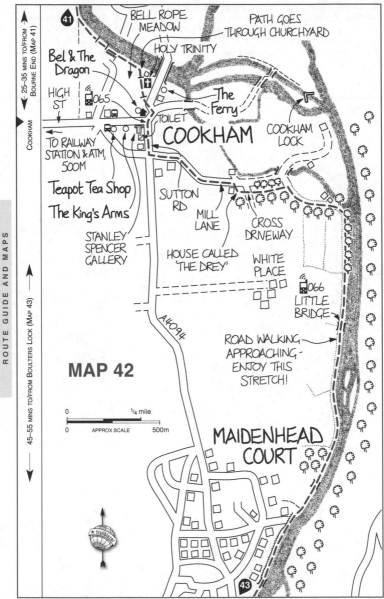

25-35 MINS TO/FROM BOURNE END (MAP 41)

COOKHAM

45-55 MINS TO/FROM BOULTERS LOCK (MAP 43)

41

BELL ROPE MEADOW

PATH GOES THROUGH CHURCHYARD

HOLY TRINITY

Bel & The Dragon

HIGH ST

065

TOILET

The Ferry

COOKHAM

COOKHAM LOCK

TO RAILWAY STATION & ATM, 500M

Teapot Tea Shop

The King's Arms

STANLEY SPENCER GALLERY

SUTTON RD

MILL LANE

HOUSE CALLED 'THE DREY'

CROSS DRIVEWAY

WHITE PLACE

066
LITTLE BRIDGE

ROAD WALKING APPROACHING - ENJOY THIS STRETCH!

A4094

MAP 42

0   1/4 mile
0   APPROX SCALE   500m

MAIDENHEAD COURT

trailblazer

43

COOKHAM [Map 42]

Famous as the home of the artist Stanley Spencer (see box on p176), Cookham has a long history. Bronze Age burial mounds exist nearby and abundant Roman and Saxon skeletons have been found, with the riverbed hiding relics from every period. Author of *The Wind in the Willows*, Kenneth Grahame (see box on p150) grew up in nearby Cookham Dean.

A branch of *Bel and The Dragon* (☎ 01628-521263, 🖳 belandthedragon-cook ham.co.uk; **fb**) is in a 600-year-old hostelry just a few steps from the path. Offering both **accommodation** (10D; 🛏; WI-FI; 🐾;

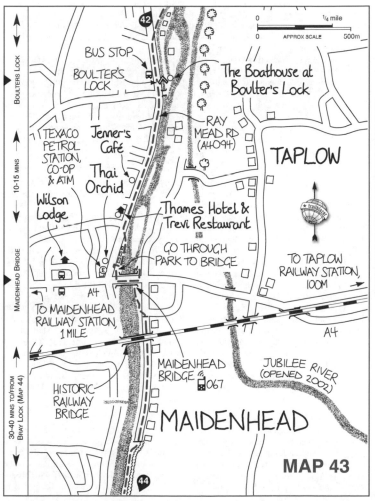

ROUTE GUIDE AND MAPS

MAP 43

❑ STANLEY SPENCER

The Thames has been a constant source of inspiration for artists (see box on pp46-7) and none more so than Stanley Spencer (1891-1959). Born in and spending much of his life in Cookham, his style was very distinctive, with Biblical scenes superimposed on to the village and its inhabitants. Indeed, such was his affection for the village that his contemporaries at the Slade School of Art in London – amongst them the famous war artist Paul Nash – nicknamed him 'Cookham'. Having seen action in WWI, in 1918 he was invalided from the army and returned to his parents' house in the village to continue to work on his art. Leaving in April 1920 he briefly moved to Bourne End before leading a somewhat nomadic existence, painting wherever he went.

In 1923, whilst residing in Hampstead, he began work on one of his most celebrated paintings, *The Resurrection, Cookham*. Set in the grounds of Cookham's Holy Trinity Church, it depicts his family and friends emerging from the graves, all watched over by God, Christ and the saints. Having exhibited the picture in 1927, Spencer sold the painting, its purchaser eventually donating it to Tate Britain (see p230). Spencer returned to Cookham in 1932 and the village would form the backdrop to numerous of his other works including *View from Cookham Bridge* (1936) and *Christ Preaching at Cookham Regatta* (1952-59). Sadly, this last he would not live to complete.

A wealth of information on the artist can be found at **Stanley Spencer Gallery** (☎ 01628-531092, 🖳 stanleyspencer.org.uk; **fb**; Apr-Oct daily 10.30am-5.30pm, Nov-Mar Thur-Sun 11am-4.30pm; £6; High St) in Cookham.

from £60pp, sgl occ room rate) and **food** (Mon-Fri noon-3pm & 6-10pm, Sat noon-10pm, Sun to 7pm; 🐾 bar area), the hostelry's menu changes according to the season but you may find marinated spring lamb rump (£22.50), or linguine of Devon crab (£18.50).

There are also two pubs with basically the same extensive menu (including a vegan one) as they are both part of the Mitchell & Butler group. Beside the river on Sutton Rd you'll find *The Ferry* (☎ 01628-525123, 🖳 theferry.co.uk; **fb**; WI-FI; 🐾 in bar; food Sun-Thur noon-9pm, Fri & Sat to 10pm); there's a patio on which you can enjoy your meal as you gaze over the river. The other is *The King's Arms* (☎ 01628-530667, 🖳 thekingsarmscookham.co.uk; **fb**; food daily noon-9pm; WI-FI; 🐾 bar area and garden

only) is on the High St. The lunch menu at both includes steak sandwiches (£10.95) and salad bowls from £9.75; the all-day menu includes spit-roast half chicken with skinny fries (£13.95) and rotisserie pork belly & scallops (£18.95).

Also on the High St, the friendly and bright *Teapot Tea Shop* (☎ 01628-529514; **fb**; WI-FI; 🐾; daily 10am-5pm) sells baked potatoes with salad (£8.50), baguettes (£8) and slices of home-made cake (£4).

There is a **convenience store** with an **ATM** very close to the railway station.

Cookham is on the Marlow to Maidenhead branch line; for details of GWR's **train services** see box on pp56-7. The railway station is a 15- to 20-minute walk from the path. The 37/37A **bus** service (see pp58-61) stops on Cookham High St.

MAIDENHEAD   [Map 43, p175]

Of note along the stretch of river which bypasses Maidenhead is the railway bridge you go beneath. Designed by Isambard Kingdom Brunel and opened in 1839, it features in JMW Turner's famous painting *Rain, Steam and Speed* (see box on pp46-7).

Along the path there are several amenities for walkers, including a Texaco petrol station with a **Co-op** (daily 6am-11pm) and **ATM** near the bridge. On the same road is *Jenner's Café* (☎ 01628-621721, 🖳 jennerscafe.com; **fb**; Apr-Aug daily 8am-5pm, Sep-Mar Mon-Fri to 3pm, Sat & Sun to 4pm; 🐾) which sells cakes and ice-cream as well as lunches such as gammon, egg & chips (£6.90).

On the island at **Boulter's Lock** is *The Boathouse at Boulters Lock* (☎ 01628-621291, 🖥 boathouseboulterslock.co.uk; **fb**; food Mon-Sat 9.30am-10pm, Sun to 9pm; WI-FI; 🐾 bar only), a brasserie and bar. On the bar menu expect to see beer-battered haddock & chips (£15) and warm Moroccan salad (£13). The No 8 bus service calls here, see pp58-61.

Accommodation is available at the 19th-century *Thames Hotel* (☎ 01628-

628721, 🖥 thameshotel.co.uk; **fb**; 6S/15D/5T/3D or T/2Qd; ☛; WI-FI), with a super-fast wi-fi connection and comfortable rooms that cost around £35pp (sgl from £60, sgl occ room rate) but the rate varies depending on demand. *Trevi Restaurant* (food Mon-Thur 6.30-9.30pm, Fri & Sat to 9.30pm, Sun noon-8.30pm), on the ground floor, serves good Italian food such as *guazzetto di pesci*, Italian-style fish and seafood medley (£16.95).

Also near the river, on Ray Drive, is *Wilson Lodge* (☎ 07444-873074, 🖥 wilson-lodge-maidenhead.hotelmix.co.uk; **fb**; 8D or T/3Qd, 1D private facilities; ☛; WI-FI;

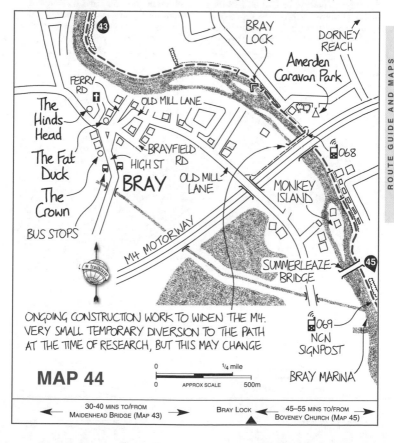

ONGOING CONSTRUCTION WORK TO WIDEN THE M4. VERY SMALL TEMPORARY DIVERSION TO THE PATH AT THE TIME OF RESEARCH, BUT THIS MAY CHANGE

MAP 44

0 — ¼ mile
0 — APPROX SCALE — 500m

ROUTE GUIDE AND MAPS

← 30-40 MINS TO/FROM MAIDENHEAD BRIDGE (MAP 43) → ▲ BRAY LOCK ← 45-55 MINS TO/FROM BOVENEY CHURCH (MAP 45) →

🐾 ; from £42.50pp, sgl occ room rate). One of the rooms can sleep up to five and another up to six people. The rate includes breakfast and guests can use the kitchen facilities to prepare what they want from the selection provided. Between the two hotels is *Thai Orchid* (☎ 01628-777555, 🖥 thaiorchidmaidenhead.com; **fb**; Wed-Fri & Sun noon-2pm, Sun-Fri 5.30-10pm, Sat to 10.30pm) with mains from £13.50.

Maidenhead is a stop on GWR's **railway** services between London Paddington and Didcot Parkway; the branch line to Marlow starts here (see box on pp56-7). Both Maidenhead and Taplow (off Map 43) are stops on TfL Rail's service from London Paddington.

Bus services 8, 15, 16/16A, 37, 127 & 239 also call here; see pp58-61.

DORNEY REACH [Map 44, p177]

For **campers**, near to the river and the M4 is *Amerden Caravan Park* (☎ 01628-627461, 🖥 amerdencaravanpark.com, **fb**; WI-FI at reception; 🐾 on lead; £14/18 for a tent and one/two walkers; Apr-Sep) though it was closed throughout 2021 due to the widening of the M4. Assuming it reopens note that there is no shop so you'll need either to carry any supplies required or head to Bray (crossing over the river on the footpath on the M4) for a meal; see opposite. Alternatively the caravan park has phone numbers for Indian, Chinese and pizza places that will deliver to the park.

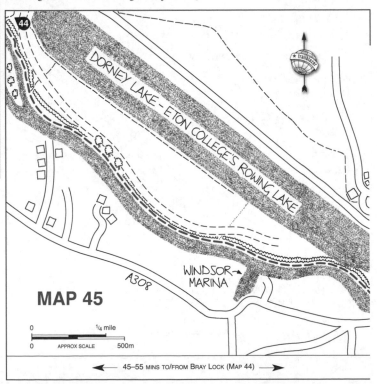

MAP 45

0 ———— ¼ mile
0 ———— APPROX SCALE ———— 500m

DORNEY LAKE - ETON COLLEGE'S ROWING LAKE

A308

WINDSOR→ MARINA

ROUTE GUIDE AND MAPS

←— 45–55 MINS TO/FROM BRAY LOCK (MAP 44) —→

BRAY [Map 44, p177]

Chef Heston Blumenthal owns two of **Bray**'s restaurants, the most famous of which is *The Fat Duck* (🖥 thefatduck .co.uk). Not a place you just stroll into in muddy boots; if you plan to visit you'll need to book months in advance. *The Hinds Head* (🖥 hindsheadbray.com) is not as well known but still requires booking.

The best opportunity for walkers to enjoy a taste of Blumenthal's gastronomy, though it is now independently owned, is at

The Crown (☎ 01628-621936, 🖥 thecrown atbray.com; **fb**; food Mon-Thur noon-2.30pm & 5.30-8.30pm, Fri & Sat noon-8.30pm, Sun to 5.30pm; WI-FI; 🐕 on lead). The menu still has the hamburgers (£19) and fish & chips (£18.95) with Heston's special twists added but also has other dishes. Booking remains advisable especially at the weekend.

The No 16/16A **bus** services (see pp58-61) call in Bray.

ETON [map p183]

Synonymous with its college (see box on p181), Eton is a good alternative if you don't wish to dally in Windsor. It is far less hectic and with great views of Windsor Castle – from the bridge which spans the river between the two – the town, despite being the smaller twin, still has everything a walker needs.

On High St is a **Visitor Information Centre** (☎ 01753-852588, 🖥 windsor.gov .uk; **fb**; Tue-Sun 11am-3.30pm, winter may be Thur-Sun only), a **shop** (Eton Premier Stores; Mon-Sat 7am-8pm, Sun 8am-7pm), Eton **pharmacy** (Mon-Fri 9am-6pm, Sat to 2pm) and a **post office/Budgens store** (Mon-Sat 7am-9pm, Sun 10am-8pm).

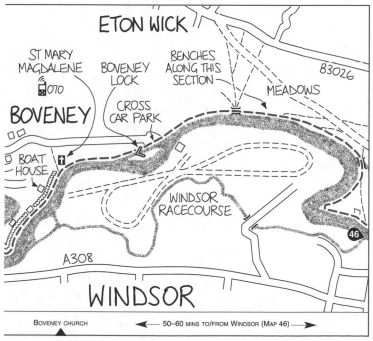

ROUTE GUIDE AND MAPS

BOVENEY CHURCH ◀━━ 50–60 MINS TO/FROM WINDSOR (MAP 46) ━━▶

The No 15 **bus** service (see pp58-61) stops near the river. See Windsor (p184) for rail services.

Relatively reasonably priced **accommodation** can be found on High St. *The Crown and Cushion* (☎ 01753-861531, 🖥 thecrownandcushioneton.co.uk; **fb**; 🐾 bar only; No 84) offers **B&B** (8D; WI-FI; £44.50-49.50pp, sgl occ room rate) and also dishes up pub classics (**food** Mon-Sat noon-7.45pm, Sun to 5.45pm) and has a large range of burgers on the menu including 'The Hot One', topped with Swiss cheese, jalapeno & chilli sauce (£11).

More expensive, *The George Inn* (☎ 01753-861797, 🖥 georgeinn-eton.co.uk; **fb**; 2S/4D/1T/1Tr; WI-FI; 🐾 bar area and garden only; No 77) provides breakfast in with the price of your 'boutique' room (from £60pp, sgl £90, sgl occ room rate). The menu (**food** Mon-Fri noon-3pm & 5-9pm, Sat noon-9pm, Sun to 6pm) includes cod loin wrapped with pancetta (£15.95) and sausages & mash (£14.95).

Rates at *The Christopher Hotel* (☎ 01753-852359, 🖥 thechristopher.co.uk; **fb**; 1S/17D/11D or T; 🍷; WI-FI; 🐾 in Courtyard rooms and bar; No 110) change throughout the year but in summer you can expect to pay about £65pp (sgl around £100, sgl occ room rate) for B&B; some rooms can sleep three people. Here the menu (**food** daily noon-9.30pm) includes modern European mains from £12.95.

High St has a number of **cafés**, including a branch of *Costa* (🖥 costa.co.uk; **fb**; daily 7am-5pm, Sun 8am-6.30pm; WI-FI) and, a little further from the water, *Eaten Café* (☎ 01753-864725, 🖥 eatencafe.co.uk; **fb**; Mon-Sat 8.30am-4pm, Sun 10am-4pm; WI-FI; 🐾). You'll find full English breakfasts (£8) here and water is provided for dogs though if the café is crowded you'll have to eat with yours at a table outside.

❑ ETON COLLEGE

Eton College (Map 46) was founded by Henry VI in 1440, originally as a charity to educate underprivileged boys, many of whom then went on to King's College, Cambridge, which he founded the following year. Eton College remains an all-boys school though in the 1980s there was an initiative to trial a few girl-pupils.

Eton – as it is commonly known – has educated much of the British aristocracy down the years as well as 20 prime ministers, amongst them Robert Walpole, William Pitt the Elder, Harold Macmillan, David Cameron and Boris Johnson. Other famous alumni, both real and imagined, include Justin Welby (the Archbishop of Canterbury), authors George Orwell and Aldous Huxley, PG Wodehouse's Bertie Wooster, Ian Fleming's James Bond and even Tarzan; one imagines he did well at PE.

As you enter Eton, the first **pub** you arrive at is *The Watermans Arms* (☎ 01753-861001, 🖥 watermans-eton.com; **fb**; **food** Mon-Fri noon-3pm & 6-9pm, Sat noon-9pm, Sun to 4pm; WI-FI; 🐾; Brocas St). Brimming with character, this place has up to eight locally brewed real ales to accompany your Cumberland sausage ciabatta (£6.50), or chilli con carne (£11.50). Next to the bridge and with great views of

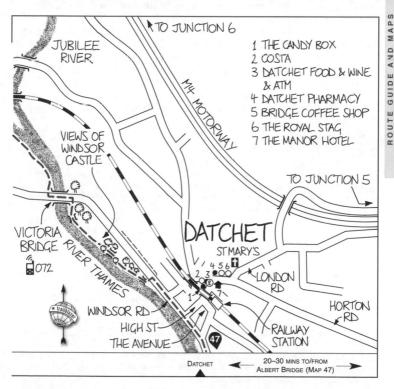

1 THE CANDY BOX
2 COSTA
3 DATCHET FOOD & WINE & ATM
4 DATCHET PHARMACY
5 BRIDGE COFFEE SHOP
6 THE ROYAL STAG
7 THE MANOR HOTEL

TO JUNCTION 6
JUBILEE RIVER
M4 MOTORWAY
VIEWS OF WINDSOR CASTLE
TO JUNCTION 5
VICTORIA BRIDGE
RIVER THAMES
072
DATCHET
ST MARY'S
LONDON RD
HORTON RD
WINDSOR RD
HIGH ST
THE AVENUE
47
RAILWAY STATION
DATCHET ← → 20–30 MINS TO/FROM ALBERT BRIDGE (MAP 47)

both river and castle is a branch of *Côte Brasserie* (☎ 01753-868344, 🖥 cote.co.uk; **fb**; Mon-Fri 11.30am-11pm, Sat & Sun 10am-10pm; WI-FI); the menu may include poulet Breton (£12.95). *Golden Curry* (☎ 01753-863961, 🖥 goldencurryeton.co.uk; **fb**; Mon-Sat noon-3pm & 6pm-midnight, Sun noon-midnight; WI-FI; 46 High St) is Eton's Indian restaurant. Mains start at £8.95 and are available also for **takeaway**.

W ← WINDSOR TO MARLOW   [MAPS 46-40]

[Route section begins on Map 46, pp180-1] This varied **14¼-mile (22.7km, 4½-5½hrs)** stage passes through a number of towns and villages, each separated from the other by the serenity of some fine riverside walking. Crossing **Windsor Bridge** you leave the crowds behind and begin a peaceful riparian stroll with views back to the Castle and soon after passing **Boveney Lock** you arrive at the intriguing **Church of St Mary Magdalene** in **Boveney** (Map 45). This delightful pastoral stretch continues, with occasional glimpses of **Dorney Lake** on your right, home to Eton College's rowers. As you near the end of the lake the tranquility of this stretch is spoilt somewhat by the thunderous M4. Passing under the motorway you will see the village of **Bray** (p179; Map 44) on the opposite bank. Soon you arrive in **Maidenhead** (pp176-8, Map 43) where a section of road walking takes you to **Boulter's Lock**.

After this you leave the road for another stretch of meadow and woodland walking with excellent river views until, near **Cookham** (see pp175-6; Map 42) you leave the river to pass through the centre of the village. Back beside the river the path goes through **Cock Marsh**, owned by the National Trust and an SSSI (see box p71), before reaching **Bourne End** (see p173; Map 41) where you cross to the northern bank. From here a peaceful stroll through riverside meadows takes you to **Marlow** (see pp169-71). *[Next route overview on p168]*

❑ WINDSOR CASTLE

An official residence of Elizabeth II, Her Majesty the Queen, Windsor Castle is the oldest and largest occupied castle in Europe. Similar to the castles that the Normans built upstream at Wallingford and Oxford in order to control the river's populace in its upper reaches, the castle at Windsor was built between 1070 and 1086 both to protect the Thames valley and also to guard the western approaches to London.

Windsor was originally designed as a motte-and-bailey castle and built with timber, the defences gradually being replaced with stone. Since the time of William the Conqueror's son, Henry I (1100-35), Windsor Castle has been used by 39 English and British monarchs, many of whom have added extra buildings and rooms to it. During the English Civil War (1642-51) it was controlled by the Parliamentarians who imprisoned Charles I within its walls and during the following Restoration (1660-88) much of it was rebuilt by Charles II. Huge expense was lavished on the castle by George III (1760-1820) and George IV (1820-30) and much of the current design – including the magnificent State Apartments, which are one of the sections of the castle which can be visited – dates back to this time.

Queen Victoria (1837-1901) used the castle to host bountiful royal events and the Second World War saw it used as a refuge for the two royal princesses, Elizabeth and Margaret, protecting them from the might of the German war machine just as it had protected King John eight centuries earlier during the First Barons' War (1215-17).

WINDSOR

Windsor is dominated by its castle, which over the years has had many inhabitants but can now also be visited by ordinary mortals: **Windsor Castle** (see box opposite; 🖥 rct .uk/visit/windsorcastle; Thur-Mon Mar-Oct 10am-5.15pm, Nov-Feb to 4.15pm) covers an area of approximately 13 acres and over 500 people live and work within its walls. The Queen's main residence now, it is also used as a venue for state visits and banquets. Many of the castle's apartments, collections and galleries can be visited (£23.50 inc multimedia tour, £12.90 when the state apartments are closed), items from the Royal Collection are often exhibited and you may also be able to see the Changing of the Guard (usually Tue, Thur & Sat at 11am). The town which has grown below the castle is a vibrant and hectic place. Expect the soundtrack to your day to be that of clicking cameras, their owners gawping in awe at one of England's most impressive buildings.

Windsor and Royal Borough Museum (☎ 01628-685686, 🖥 windsor museum.org.uk; Tue-Sat 10am-4pm, Sun & Bank Hols noon-4pm; £2; High St) tells the local area's tale but at the time of writing it was closed due to Covid and also because the information centre was scheduled to move into the museum in Feb 2022.

One place that's photographed almost as much as the castle is **The Crooked House of Windsor**; it stands out because of its wonky appearance which is due to it being restructured with unseasoned green oak.

Services

Staff at **Royal Windsor Information Centre** (☎ 01753-743900, 🖥 windsor.gov .uk; **fb**; Thur-Sun 10am-4pm) can book accommodation. At the time of writing they were due to move into Windsor and Royal Borough Museum (see above) in Feb 2022.

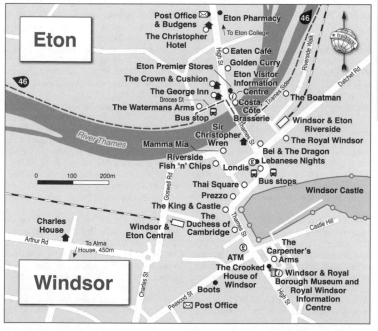

On Peascod St there is a **post office** (Mon-Fri 9am-5.30pm, Sat to 4pm) and a Boots **pharmacy** (Mon-Sat 8.30am-6.30pm, Sun 11am-5pm), while closer to the river on Thames St is a Londis **supermarket** (Mon-Fri 6am-midnight, Sat 7am-midnight, Sun to 11pm) with **ATM**. There are also ATMs along High St and scattered about the town.

Transport
Windsor is well-linked to the outside world as well as other Thames Path destinations by its **two railway stations** – GWR trains run from **Windsor and Eton Central** to London Paddington, while SWR serves **Windsor and Eton Riverside** from London Waterloo (see box on pp56-7).

Bus (8/8A & 16/16A; see pp58-61) services and Green Line Coaches 702 service (see box on p53) also call here.

Where to stay
A couple of **B&Bs** exist within walking distance of the river. *Charles House* (☎ 01753-831433, 💻 charleshousewindsor.co .uk; **fb**; 2D/2D or T; ✔; WI-FI; £40-57.50pp, sgl occ £70-105; 89 Arthur Rd). Breakfast is not provided but there is a fridge in each room and a Co-op shop opposite. *Alma House* (☎ 01753-862983, 💻 almahouse.co .uk; **fb**; 2D private facilities, 3Qd; ✔; WI-FI; from £37.50pp, sgl occ £60); the rate includes a self-service continental breakfast.

A **hotel** with some spectacular rooms overlooking the river is the *Sir Christopher Wren* (☎ 01753-442400, 💻 sirchristopher wren.co.uk; **fb**; 7S/102D/24D or T; ✔; WI-FI; Thames St). B&B normally costs from £67.50pp (sgl/sgl occ from about £100) although these prices can fluctuate dramatically depending on the time of year.

Where to eat and drink
Amongst the **pubs** serving **food** are *The Carpenter's Arms* (☎ 01753-863739, 💻 nicholsonspubs.co.uk; **fb**; WI-FI; 🐾 bar area; food daily noon-10pm; Market St) with hearty dishes such as steak & ale pie, or fish & chips (both £14); and *The Royal Windsor* (☎ 01753-980164, 💻 theroyal windsor.co.uk; **fb**; WI-FI; 🐾 in bar only;

food Mon-Fri noon-3pm & 5-10pm, Sat noon-10pm, Sun to 9pm; Datchet Rd). The main menu, available in both the bar and the restaurant, includes pie of the day (£14.95).

Nearby there's a branch of the *Bel and the Dragon* (☎ 01753-866056, 💻 beland thedragon-windsor.co.uk; **fb**; 🐾 in bar area; food Mon-Sat noon-5pm & 6-10pm, Sun noon-9pm) chain, conveniently situated on the corner of Thames St and Datchet Rd. In addition to their usual bar menu they also serve afternoon tea (from £26 for two people, up to £46 with champagne too) but this must be reserved in advance. However, at the time of research this was closed due to Covid-19.

On the climb up to the castle via Thames St, one of the finest establishments in which to enjoy a meal is *The Duchess of Cambridge* (☎ 01753-864405, 💻 the duchessofcambridgepub.co.uk; **fb**; food Mon-Sat noon-9.45pm, Sun to 8.45pm; WI-FI; Nos 3-4). They offer tapas-style sharing plates (£6.50 per dish, or £20 for four) including king prawns, and smoky Spanish chorizo, as well as burgers, steaks and a decent vegetarian selection.

Amongst the cheapest pubs to eat in is Windsor's Wetherspoon's: *The King and Castle* (☎ 01753-625120, 💻 jdwetherspoon .com; food daily 8am-9pm; WI-FI; 15-16 Thames St).

A short distance downstream from the bridge you'll come across *The Boatman* (☎ 01753-620010, 💻 boatmanwindsor.com; **fb**; WI-FI; 🐾 on lead & bar only; food Mon-Sat noon-9pm, Sun to 8pm). Serving what they describe as a Classic British menu, expect dishes such as sea bass fillet with new potatoes & spinach (£16.95), and lamb shoulder, mash & green beans (£18.95).

Prezzo (☎ 01753-840747, 💻 prezzo restaurants.co.uk; **fb**; Mon-Thur noon-10pm, Fri-Sun 11.30am-10.30pm; WI-FI; 🐾 outside only; 19 Thames St), and *Thai Square* (☎ 01753-868900, 💻 thaisq.com/ restaurants; **fb**; Mon-Fri noon-3pm & 5.30-10pm, Sat & Sun noon-10pm; WI-FI; No 29) represent their countries with pasta dishes (from £9.75) and tasty Thai meals (eg chicken green curry £9.75) respectively. For something completely different, *Lebanese Nights* (☎ 01753-832333, 🖳 lebanesenights.co.uk; **fb**; Mon-Sat 6-10pm, Sun 5-10pm; No 41) offers some delicious Middle Eastern fare, including *lahem meshwi* (char-grilled lamb cubes with shallots, tomatoes, peppers & flat bread; £14.95);

note they have belly dancing on Friday & Saturday nights from 8.30pm. They also offer a **takeaway**.

Fish & chips can be sourced from either *Riverside Fish 'n' Chips* (daily 10am-6/7pm), or nearby *Mamma Mia* (☎ 01753-620166, 🖳 mammamiacafe.weebly .com; daily 8.30am-9.30pm).

E → WINDSOR TO CHERTSEY BRIDGE [MAPS 46-50]

This **12-mile (19.5km, 4-5¼hrs)** stage begins with a riverside stroll through **Home Park** (Map 46), the tranquillity of which feels a far cry from the tourist-packed streets of Windsor. En route there are some majestic views of Windsor Castle over your shoulder.

Having switched banks to skirt the village of **Datchet** (see below) the path crosses to the southern bank again, toying with the outskirts of **Old Windsor** (see p186; Map 47) before entering Surrey to arrive at **Runnymede** (see p186 & p188; Map 48), the site of the signing of the Magna Carta in 1215 (see box on p186).

Soon after **Bell Weir Lock** (see p189) a more modern reminder of humanity's progress appears as you pass below the roaring **M25 motorway**. The trail continues to hug the Thames, crossing the water again between **Egham** (see p189) and **Staines** (see p189 & p192; Map 49) – this section actually offering some surprisingly attractive ambling – to arrive at **Penton Hook Lock**. The adjacent **Penton Hook Island** was created by the construction of the lock in 1815 and is home to heron and water vole amongst other wildlife.

Having passed **Laleham** (see p192; Map 50) and beneath the M3 motorway you arrive at **Chertsey Bridge**. Chertsey (see pp192-3) is on the opposite bank; there are some services by the bridge but the main part of town – and the railway station – is a 15- to 20-minute walk along the road.

DATCHET [Map 46, p181]
The Candy Box (daily 7am-9pm; High St), part of the Londis chain, sells basic goods. Just up the street on the corner is a second and larger general store, **Datchet Food & Wine** (Mon-Sat 9am-9pm, Sun 10am-9pm) which has an **ATM** (£1.60). On Horton Rd is Datchet **Pharmacy** (Mon-Fri 9am-6pm, Sat to 1pm).

Datchet is a stop on SWR's **train** services to Windsor & Eton Riverside (see pp58-61).

Hotel accommodation can be found at *The Manor* (☎ 01753-543442, 🖳 themanor windsor.com; **fb**; 10T/43D; ✐; WI-FI). Rates (£50-120pp, sgl occ room rate) exclude breakfast (£9.95pp). The hotel was being

refurbished in 2021 so these details may have changed by the time you are here.

Centrally, caffeine fixes can be had at *Bridge Coffee Shop* (Mon-Fri 9am-3pm; WI-FI), a very inexpensive place (a hot chocolate costs only £1, for example, and sandwiches are only £2.50) with friendly staff. There's also a branch of *Costa* (🖳 costa.co.uk; **fb**; Mon-Sat 7am-6pm, Sun 8am-5pm); whilst for something more substantial *The Royal Stag* (☎ 01753-584231, 🖳 royalstagdatchet.com; **fb**; food Mon-Sat noon-9.45pm, Sun to 7.45pm; WI-FI; 🐾) has plenty of dishes fit for walkers including burgers (from £11.50) and slow-cooked lamb shoulder (£16.95).

ROUTE GUIDE AND MAPS

OLD WINDSOR
[Map 47; Map 48, pp188-9]
There is evidence that Windsor was inhabited long before the first wood was cut for the Conqueror's timber castle (see box on p182). Recorded in the *Anglo-Saxon Chronicle*, the original Windsor was home to a Saxon palace owned by Edward the Confessor.

RUNNYMEDE   **[Map 48, pp188-9]**
The **site of the signing of Magna Carta** has several monuments worth viewing (see box below).

The Bells of Ouzeley (Map 48; ☎ 01753-861526, 🖳 harvester.co.uk/thebells ofouzeleyoldwindsor; **fb**; food Mon-Fri 11.30am-9pm, Sat & Sun 9am-9pm; WI-FI; 🐾 outside) offers a huge range of food and several special deals.

Bus route No 8/8A (see pp58-61) stops outside the pub.

A good old-fashioned brew can be had at *National Trust Magna Carta Tearoom* (🖳 nationaltrust.org.uk; **fb**; Feb-Nov daily

---

❏ RUNNYMEDE AND THE MAGNA CARTA
King Richard I (aka Richard the Lionheart; 1189-99) spent most of his reign abroad, crusading in Palestine and fighting in France. Following his death from a crossbow wound in 1199 the rule of England fell on the shoulders of his younger brother, King John (1199-1216). He would not be a popular monarch. In the early 13th century the country was run according to feudal law with the king relying on his barons for both money – which they gathered through taxation – and men to fight in his foreign wars. Tradition dictated that before new taxes were imposed on the populace they first had to have the consent of the barons. This relationship worked as long as the king's foreign escapades were successful. John, however, would not be a successful military campaigner and he began to lose his grip on the lands he owned in northern France.

Eager to win back these French territories, in 1214 John returned from France to oversee the imposition of even higher taxes on his subjects to fund his fighting. But on this occasion he did so without consulting his barons. As a result they rebelled and quickly captured London from the hapless monarch, though they failed to win a decisive victory. A stalemate ensued until by the spring of 1215 the two sides were ready to discuss terms. They would meet at Runnymede in June and the terms to which both parties agreed would become known as the **Magna Carta**. Latin for 'Great Charter', the document consisted of a number of guarantees given to the barons by the king. It was primarily concerned with the English legal system and amongst its clauses was one that gave everyone, irrespective of wealth, access to the courts of law.

Future adaptations would state that no one could be imprisoned without first having the proper rule of law applied in deciding their guilt. Today the charter is seen as one of the foundations of civil liberty – indeed, a first step towards democracy itself – and it has influenced the constitutions of many nations.

The meadows of **Runnymede** (☎ 01784-432891, 🖳 nationaltrust.org.uk/runny mede-and-ankerwycke) are now managed by the National Trust and there are several monuments which are worth a detour from the path. The **Magna Carta Monument** was erected by the American Bar Association in 1957 and is surrounded with informative boards. Commemorating a more willing supporter of civil liberty than King John, the **John F Kennedy Memorial**, along with the acre of land which surrounds it, was gifted to the people of the USA by Queen Elizabeth II in 1965.

A series of 12 intricately worked bronze chairs by the artist Hew Locke, called **The Jurors**, was unveiled for the 800th anniversary of the signing of the Magna Carta in 2015 and **Writ in Water**, an installation by Mark Wallinger, was unveiled in 2018.

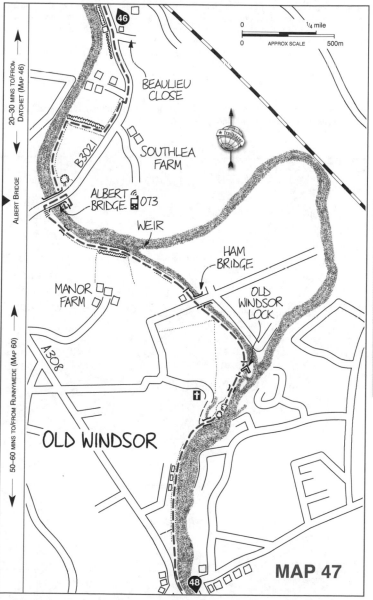

0   1/4 mile

0   500m
APPROX SCALE

46

20–30 MINS TO/FROM DATCHET (MAP 46)

BEAULIEU CLOSE

B3021

SOUTHLEA FARM

ALBERT BRIDGE

ALBERT BRIDGE 073

WEIR

HAM BRIDGE

MANOR FARM

OLD WINDSOR LOCK

A308

50–60 MINS TO/FROM RUNNYMEDE (MAP 60)

OLD WINDSOR

MAP 47

48

10am-4.30pm, Jan & Dec to 3.30pm; WI-FI; ⚐). However, it was open only at weekends in 2021 due to Covid-19 but hopefully will be open daily in 2022. There are plenty of picnic benches from which to gaze over the historic meadows and enjoy a hot drink or a cream tea; it's just a shame it's set by such a busy road.

On the other side of the road in Runnymede Pleasure Ground is *Runnymede Café* (☎ 01784-479661, 🖳 runnymedecafe.weebly.com; daily 8am-8pm; ⚐ outside) which offers a wide range of food from all-day breakfasts to toasted teacakes.

A more extensive menu is available at *Italian Concept Restaurant* (☎ 01784-432244, 🖳 italianconceptrestaurant.com; **fb**; Tue-Fri noon-2.30pm & 5.30-9.30pm, Sat noon-9.30pm, Sun to 3.30pm; WI-FI; Windsor Rd) with pasta dishes and pizzas (£8.50-15.50).

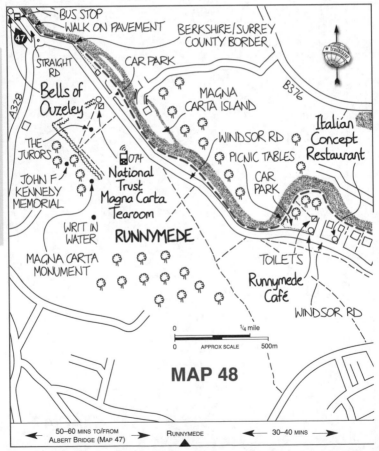

MAP 48

BELL WEIR LOCK [Map 48]

Splendidly located overlooking the lock is *The Runnymede-on-Thames* (☎ 01784-220600, 🖳 runnymedehotel.com; **fb**; 10S/168D or T; 🍴; WI-FI; 🐾 bedroom only), though the tariff (from £85pp, sgl/sgl occ £155) is probably high enough to give the average Thames walker an aneurysm.

The hotel has two **restaurants** for which booking is generally essential but you could always drop in and enquire about the possibility of afternoon tea (Wed-Sun 2-5pm; £32pp), though if you want to sit in the conservatory booking is recommended.

EGHAM [Map 48; Map 49, p190]

On Egham's riverbank is *The Swan Hotel* (Map 49; ☎ 01784-452494, 🖳 swanstaines.co.uk; **fb**; 15D; 🍴; WI-FI; 🐾); B&B costs around £63-70pp (sgl occ room rate) though can be much higher. One room here can sleep two adults and up to two children. As well as accommodation there is a somewhat eclectic menu (**food** Mon-Thur noon-3pm & 5-9.30pm, Fri & Sat noon-9.30pm, Sun

to 8.30pm); it changes regularly but always includes standard items such as burgers (£13.75) and fish & chips (£14.50).

Close by is a **supermarket** (Map 48), a large branch of Sainsbury's (Mon-Fri 7am-10pm, Sat to 9pm, Sun 10am-4pm) with an **ATM**.

Buses (8/8A; see pp58-61) stop near the Sainsbury's.

STAINES [Map 49, p190]

The site of a Roman, Saxon and Norman bridge, Staines's current crossing was opened in 1832. The Roman town Ad Pontes ('By the Bridges') which once lay here is predated by evidence of a Neolithic settlement nearby. Officially the town's name is Staines-upon-Thames but it is generally referred to as Staines. A copy of the **London Stone**, a pillar that once marked the limits of jurisdiction of the City of London, is by the

path. The site was chosen because it was here that the high tide could be perceived. Beyond this, therefore, the City had no rights over the land or the parishes upstream. (The original London Stone is in Spelthorne Museum in Staines.)

The High St has several **ATMs** and a **post office** in WH Smith (Mon-Fri 9am-5.30pm, Sat to 12.30pm). The shopping centre has a variety of shops. *(cont'd on p192)*

ROUTE GUIDE AND MAPS

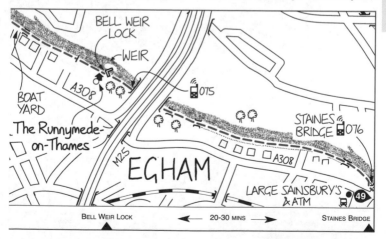

BELL WEIR LOCK ◄— 20-30 MINS —► STAINES BRIDGE

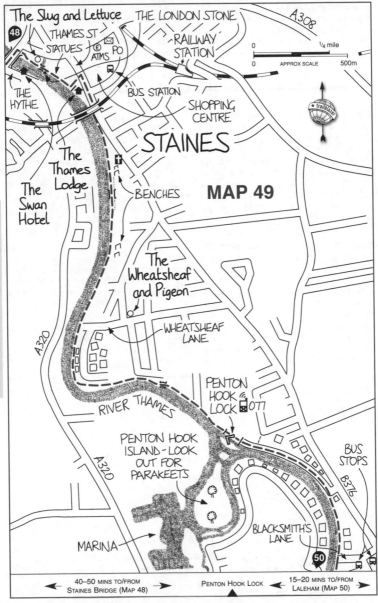

The Slug and Lettuce

48

THE LONDON STONE

A308

THAMES ST
STATUES

ATMS   PO

RAILWAY
STATION

0   ¼ mile
0   APPROX SCALE   500m

THE
HYTHE

BUS STATION

SHOPPING
CENTRE

STAINES

The
Thames
Lodge

BENCHES

MAP 49

The
Swan
Hotel

The
Wheatsheaf
and Pigeon

A320

WHEATSHEAF
LANE

PENTON
HOOK
LOCK   077

RIVER THAMES

PENTON HOOK
ISLAND - LOOK
OUT FOR
PARAKEETS

BUS
STOPS

B376

A320

BLACKSMITH'S
LANE

MARINA

50

ROUTE GUIDE AND MAPS

← 40–50 MINS TO/FROM
STAINES BRIDGE (MAP 48) →

PENTON HOOK LOCK

15–20 MINS TO/FROM ←
LALEHAM (MAP 50)

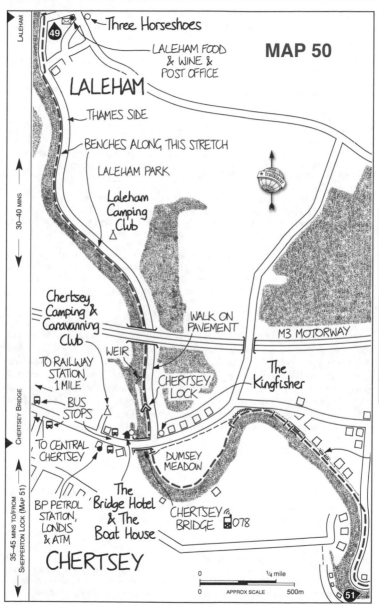

MAP 50

Three Horseshoes

LALEHAM FOOD & WINE & POST OFFICE

49

LALEHAM

THAMES SIDE

BENCHES ALONG THIS STRETCH

LALEHAM PARK

Laleham Camping Club

Chertsey Camping & Caravanning Club

WALK ON PAVEMENT

M3 MOTORWAY

WEIR

TO RAILWAY STATION, 1 MILE

BUS STOPS

CHERTSEY LOCK

The Kingfisher

TO CENTRAL CHERTSEY

DUMSEY MEADOW

BP PETROL STATION, LONDIS & ATM

The Bridge Hotel & The Boat House

CHERTSEY BRIDGE 078

CHERTSEY

51

LALEHAM

30–40 MINS

CHERTSEY BRIDGE

35–45 MINS TO/FROM SHEPPERTON LOCK (MAP 51)

ROUTE GUIDE AND MAPS

0   ¼ mile
0   APPROX SCALE   500m

(cont'd from p189) Staines is well connected by **train** (SWR; see box on pp56-7) to London and numerous other destinations along the Thames Path and also by **bus** (8/8A, 446, 456 & 458); see pp58-61.

Should you be tempted by a night by the river try *The Thames Lodge* (also known as *Mercure London Staines Hotel*; ☎ 01784-334800, ☐ mercure.accor.com; **fb**; 78D/10Qd; ☞; WI-FI; ✿; Thames St). Rates vary but for a room on a single night in summer expect to pay from £47.50pp (sgl occ room rate); allow £10pp for breakfast.

Very close to the bridge, right beside the path is a branch of *The Slug and*

Lettuce (☎ 01784-456914, ☐ slugandlettuce.co.uk/staines; **fb**; food daily noon-9pm; WI-FI; ✿ terrace area only). If you'd prefer a **pub** dealing in real ale and home-made food, fear not: a short diversion from the path is *The Wheatsheaf and Pigeon* (☎ 01784-452922, ☐ wheatsheafandpigeon.co.uk; **fb**; food Tue-Sat noon-2.30pm & 5-9pm, Sun noon-5pm; WI-FI; ✿). A bustling place with a great variety of house and guest ales and meals such as slow-roasted ribs (£11.90 for half a rack, £15.90 for a full rack), this is the type of place of which real-ale-powered ramblers dream.

LALEHAM [Map 50, p191]

On Shepperton Rd there is a **post office** and **convenience store**, Laleham Food & Wine (Mon-Sat 6am-7pm, Sun to 2pm) and a pub; *Three Horseshoes* (☎ 01784-455014, ☐ threehorseshoeslaleham.co.uk; **fb**; food daily noon-9pm; WI-FI; ✿ bar area). The lunch menu includes a steak sandwich (£9.25) and sausage & mash (£13.25).

Bus service No 458 (see pp58-61) stops by Blacksmith's Lane; see Map 49.

Laleham Camping Club (☎ 01932-564149, ☐ www.lalehamcampingclub.co.uk; ✿ on lead and not unattended; Apr-early Oct; Thames Side) is a large family orientated site (there is a quieter site at Chertsey). The rate (from £12pp) includes use of the shower and toilet facilities.

W ← CHERTSEY BRIDGE TO WINDSOR [MAPS 50-46]

[Route section begins on Map 50, p191] This **12-mile (19.5km, 4-5¼hrs)** stage offers some surprisingly attractive rambling in its early stages. Leaving **Chertsey** you pass beneath the M3 motorway and continue via **Laleham** (see above) to **Penton Hook Lock** (Map 49). The adjacent **Penton Hook Island** was created by the construction of the lock in 1815 and is home to heron and water vole amongst other wildlife. The path continues to **Staines** (see p189) where, after a slight detour into town, you cross the river to **Egham** (Map 48). Soon after this you pass below the roaring **M25 motorway** and on to **Bell Weir Lock** (see p189).

Leaving behind the noise of the M25 a peaceful stroll takes you to **Runnymede** (see p186 & p188), the site of the signing of the Magna Carta in 1215 (see box on p186). Then entering Berkshire the path skirts **Old Windsor** (see p186) before crossing to the northern bank and the village of **Datchet** (see p185; Map 46). Finally yet another river crossing brings you via **Home Park**, with stunning views of **Windsor Castle** (see box on p182), into the bustling atmosphere of **Windsor** (see pp183-5). *[Next route overview on p182]*

CHERTSEY [Map 50, p191]

Etymologically the 'island of Cerotus', Chertsey was originally a small parcel of land surrounded by marsh, the Thames and

its tributary streams. Who Cerotus was remains a mystery; what *is* known, however, is that despite being pillaged twice by the

Vikings – and rebuilt by Saxon King Edgar in AD964 – the Benedictine Abbey of St Peter, founded here in AD666, was once the wealthiest religious house in Surrey. The abbey's monks established the town here – one of England's oldest – in the 12th century. Keeping the story alive is **Chertsey Museum** (☎ 01932-565764, 🖥 chertsey museum.org; **fb**; Tue-Fri 12.30-4.30pm, Sat 11am-4pm; free), 33 Windsor St, about a 20-minute walk inland from the river.

Chertsey's **railway** station, about 1½ miles inland from the river, is a stop on SWR's services (see box pp56-7) to London Waterloo. **Bus** Nos 446, 456 & 557 (see pp58-61) stop by the river.

Staying near to the river, however, you will find a BP petrol station on Bridge Rd which has an **ATM** and Londis **convenience store** (24hrs). *Chertsey Camping & Caravanning Club* (☎ 01932-562405, 🖥 campingandcaravanningclub.co.uk; **fb**; WI-FI; 🐾) is perfectly located a short way from the bridge. The rate for a non-member walker is from £7.80pp. At weekends (Apr-Nov Fri & Sat evenings) there is often a takeaway van on site selling fish & chips and burgers; also breakfasts in peak season (July & Aug Sat & Sun mornings).

The most convenient **accommodation** for trail walkers is *The Bridge Hotel* (☎ 01932-565644, 🖥 bridgehotelchertsey .com; **fb**; 44D or T; ☎; WI-FI; 🐾). The price (from £30pp, sgl occ room rate) can vary drastically depending on the season so booking online in advance is advised. Breakfast costs £10pp. The hotel's restaurant, *The Boat House* (Mon-Thur noon-9.30pm, Fri & Sat to 10pm, Sun to 8.30pm), overlooks the Thames; the food is classic British fare with beer battered cod & chips priced at £15.

Pub food by the bridge is also available from *The Kingfisher* (☎ 01932-579811, 🖥 thekingfisherchertsey.co.uk; **fb**; food Mon-Sat noon-9.45pm, Sun to 8.45pm; WI-FI; 🐾 in bar area). There's a reasonable outside dining area from which you can consider both the river and the menu, which may include such delights as king prawn, crab & chorizo linguine (£13.50).

E → CHERTSEY BRIDGE TO KINGSTON UPON THAMES
[MAPS 50-53]

This, your final stage before you arrive in London, includes the Thames Path's solitary **ferry** crossing (see box on p195). For any arch-landlubbers who would prefer to boycott the boat there is the option of sticking to dry land and following an **alternative route**. Utilising the ferry will lead to your day being **11¼ miles (18.2km, 3¾-4¾hrs)**, while undertaking the whole section on foot makes for a slightly longer **12-mile (19.5km, 4-5hrs)** hike.

The day begins by passing through **Dumsey Meadow** (Map 50), an SSSI (see box on p71), before arriving at **Shepperton Lock** (see p194; Map 51) and the point at which you need to make a choice: foot or ferry? While the pedestrian option includes a visit to **Shepperton** (see p194 & p196), the route is convoluted and at times hard to follow; if you choose this option keep your eyes peeled for National Trail acorns and follow Map 51 carefully. Opting for the ferry (see box on p195) then involves a simple walk along the opposite riverbank before both routes eventually meet at **Walton Bridge**. Once at the bridge, **Walton-on-Thames** (see pp196-7) provides amenities a short stroll away.

From the bridge the path embarks on a straightforward journey along the riverbank via **Sunbury Lock** (Map 52), **East Molesey** (see pp197-8; Map 52 & Map 53) and **Molesey Lock** (Map 53) to the London Borough of Richmond and **Hampton Court** (see pp197-9) with its **Palace**. The path here skirts the palace's grounds and follows **Barge Walk**, an historic towpath, to arrive at **Kingston Bridge** – some 150 miles from the river's source and the gateway to London. However, if, after so long spent on the riverbank, the chaos of England's primary metropolis is too much to face, consider spending the night on the western bank in laidback **Hampton Wick** (see p199, p200 & p202), or in **Kingston** itself (see pp202-4).

SHEPPERTON LOCK [Map 51]

Just upstream from the lock is *Thames Court* (☎ 01932-221957, 🖥 vintageinn .co.uk; **fb**; food daily noon-10pm; WI-FI; 🐾 bar only). The lunch menu includes roast salmon with vine tomatoes & baby potatoes (£16.95) and sandwiches (from £7.75). Actually at the lock are two more options:

Riverside Refreshments (daily noon-5pm) where a mug of tea costs £2 and *The Ferry Coffee Shop* (☎ 01932-221094, 🖥 nauti calia.com/shepperton; **fb**; WI-FI; 🐾; Mon-Sat 9am-5pm, Sun from 10am) offering hot and cold drinks and tempting cakes (£3.50).

SHEPPERTON [Map 51]

The final resting place of poet Thomas Love Peacock and also long the home of writer J G Ballard (1930-2009), this small village has several establishments in which to eat and sleep. In the atmospheric Church Square is *Warren Lodge Hotel* (☎ 01932-242972, 🖥 warrenlodgehotel.co.uk; **fb**; 16S/32D/1T/2Qd; 🍺; WI-FI; from

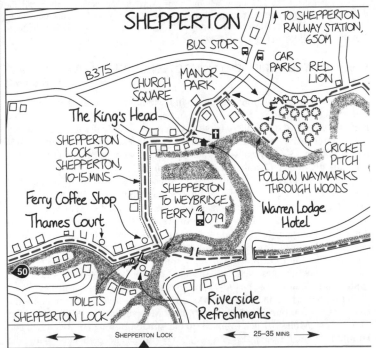

❏ THE SHEPPERTON TO WEYBRIDGE FERRY

When requested (by ringing the bell), the ferry (£3/5 single/return; 🐾; Apr-Sep weekdays 8am-6pm, Sat 9am-6pm, Sun 10am-6pm; Oct-Mar weekdays 8.30am-5.30pm, Sat 9am-5pm, Sun 10am-5pm) runs every 15 minutes and takes less than five minutes to cross the river. For further information call ☎ 01932-221094 (The Ferry Coffee Shop, see opposite).

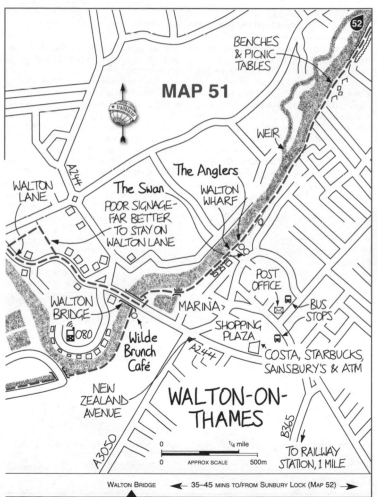

MAP 51

BENCHES & PICNIC TABLES

★ trailblazer

WEIR

The Anglers

WALTON LANE

A244

The Swan

POOR SIGNAGE – FAR BETTER TO STAY ON WALTON LANE

WALTON WHARF

POST OFFICE

BUS STOPS

WALTON BRIDGE

080

Wilde Brunch Café

MARINA

SHOPPING PLAZA

COSTA, STARBUCKS, SAINSBURY'S & ATM

A244

NEW ZEALAND AVENUE

WALTON-ON-THAMES

A3050

B365

TO RAILWAY STATION, 1 MILE

0 ¼ mile
0 APPROX SCALE 500m

WALTON BRIDGE ◄— 35–45 MINS TO/FROM SUNBURY LOCK (MAP 52) —►

£32.50pp, sgl £55, sgl occ room rate; breakfast £11.95pp). The restaurant normally serves dinner in the evenings and on Sundays a roast lunch is available but due to Covid this is not certain so call to check the situation.

Also in Church Square is *The King's Head* (☎ 01932-221910, 🖳 kingsheadshep perton.uk; **fb**; food Mon-Sat noon-4pm & 6-10pm, Sep-June Sun 12.30-2.30pm); the menu may include moules & frites (£12) and pizzas from (£10).

Shepperton is a stop on the Nos 458, 555 & 557 **bus** services (see pp58-61); it is also connected by **train** to London Waterloo (SWR; see box pp56-7).

WALTON-ON-THAMES
[Map 51, p195; Map 52]

Take a five-minute walk away from the river along New Zealand Avenue and you'll find a **shopping plaza** with a Sainsbury's **supermarket** (Mon-Sat 7am-9pm, Sun 11am-5pm), an **ATM** and branches of *Costa* (🖳 costa.co.uk; **fb**; Mon-Sat 8am-6pm, Sun to 5pm) and *Starbucks*. There are numerous other chain cafés and food outlets; however, if you want to stick by the river *Wilde Brunch* (🖳 wildebrunch.com; **fb**; daily 8.30am-5pm), just before the bridge, has full English breakfasts for £9.50 as well as a clear view to the river. On Church Rd is a **post office** (Mon-Fri 9am-5.30pm, Sat to 1pm).

For **accommodation**, just upriver from Sunbury Lock, **B&B** (and food; Mon-Sat noon to 9.30pm, Sun to 7.30pm) can be found at *Weir Hotel* (Map 52; ☎ 01932-784530, 🖳 weirhotel.co.uk; **fb**; 4D/2T; ☛; WI-FI; 🐾 restaurant only; £42.50-60pp, sgl occ room rate).

Keep to the river rather than heading along New Zealand Avenue and you'll find two pubs at **Walton Wharf**: *The Anglers* (☎ 01932-223996, 🖳 bestcitypubs.co.uk/anglers-waltononthames; **fb**; WI-FI; 🐾; food daily 11am-10pm) has standard pub food; whilst *The Swan* (☎ 01932-225964, 🖳 swanwalton.com; **fb**; food Sun-Thur noon-9.30pm, Fri & Sat to 10pm; WI-FI; 🐾 in bar) also has a plethora of dishes and even its own burger shack (May-Sep); try the classic burger & fries (£10.50) or ox cheek shortcrust pie, chard & new potatoes (£16).

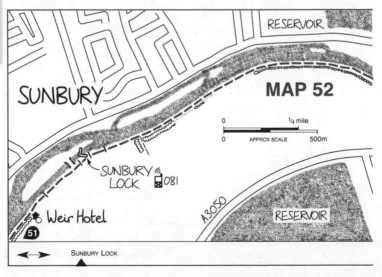

Bus services 458, 461 & 555 (see pp58-61) call here as do **trains** (SWR; see box pp56-7). Walton-on-Thames railway station is about 1½ miles south of the river.

EAST MOLESEY/HAMPTON COURT
[Maps 52 below; Map 53, pp201]

Amongst the **cafés** here are *Eight on the River Café* (Map 53; ☎ 020-8941 1777, 🖳 eightontheriver.com; **fb**; Mon-Fri 8am-4pm, Sat & Sun to 5pm; WI-FI; 🐾 on lead), in Molesey Boat Club; enjoy a bacon sandwich (£5.50) or the Big Breakfast (£9.95) whilst taking in the views from the roof terrace.

Right beside the lock is *H at Molesey Lock* (☎ 07912-221748; **fb**; daily 9.30am-5pm, possibly close earlier in winter; WI-FI; 🐾), with toasties from £5.25 and cakes from £3. Near the bridge, on Bridge Rd, are *Mada Deli* (🖳 madadeli.com; **fb**; daily 7am-6pm; WI-FI; 🐾), where there is a fine mixture of gourmet open sandwiches such

as spicy sausage with goat's cheese & roasted peppers (£7.50); and *Henry's Kitchen* (☎ 020-8783 1020, 🖳 henrykitchen.co.uk; **fb**; Mon 9am-6pm, Tue-Thur to 9pm, Fri to 10pm, Sat 8am-10pm, Sun to 9pm; WI-FI), at which you'll find more substantial meals such as lamb tagine (£14.95).

Real ale and classic **pub food** such as sausage & mash (£13) is to be found hidden a little further along Bridge Rd at *The Albion* (☎ 020-8783 9342, 🖳 thealbion eastmolesey.co.uk; **fb**; food daily noon-9pm; WI-FI; 🐾); booking essential at the weekend.

Also on Bridge Rd is a **convenience store**, Hampton Court Superstore (daily

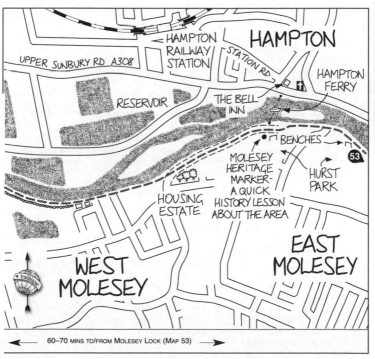

8am-8pm); an **ATM** can be found outside Hampton Court railway station.

Both Hampton (Map 52) and Hampton Court (Map 53) **railway stations** are stops on SWR's services to London Waterloo but they are on different lines (see box pp56-7). The 411 & 461 **bus** services (see pp58-61) stop at either end of Hampton Court Bridge.

Hampton Ferry (⌨ www.hampton ferryboathouse.co.uk/the-ferry; Apr to end Oct Mon-Fri 7.45am-6pm, Sat & Sun 11am-6pm, but Apr and Oct no service weekdays between 9am and 4pm; £2/3 single/return; 🐾 free) provides a convenient link from Hampton to Hurst Park (Map 52), though services are dependent on the weather and river conditions. This has operated since the 16th century and is the oldest ferry service on the Thames.

● **Hampton Court side** Hampton Court Bridge marks the boundary between Surrey and the London Borough of Richmond-upon-Thames. King Henry VIII's chief advisor Cardinal Wolsey began construction of the lavish **Hampton Court Palace** palace here in 1514 and both the buildings and grounds are steeped in royal history. Entry to the palace, maze and gardens (☎ 033 3320 6000, ⌨ hrp.org.uk/Hampton CourtPalace; **fb**; daily during school holidays, rest of year Wed-Sun Apr-Oct 10am-5.30pm, Nov-Mar to 4.30pm) costs £25.30; tickets should be pre-booked.

Opposite the gates of Hampton Court Palace is *Mitre Hotel* (☎ 020-8979 9988, ⌨ mitrehamptoncourt .com; **fb**; 33D or T/3Qd; 🍷; WI-FI; 🐾). The building was originally commissioned by Charles II in the 17th century to house the guests who couldn't be accommodated at the palace. **B&B**

ROUTE GUIDE AND MAPS

☐ A BRIEF HISTORY OF LONDON

The city of London owes its very existence to the Thames. When Julius Caesar and the **Romans** first arrived on the banks of what he referred to as Tamesis in 55BC (see box on pp44-5), they were not planning on settling in what was then the wild and sparsely populated Thames valley; his marching legions were merely searching for a place to ford the river. The location of this first Roman crossing point is open to much debate with Westminster and Brentford being two suggested sites. A century later, during the Roman Conquest of AD43, they again crossed the Thames, their traversal of the river a necessity in order to connect the Kent coast where they had landed with their garrison in Colchester. This time, however, it can be safely assumed, given the pattern of the surrounding Roman roads, that Westminster was where they crossed.

Having built a wooden bridge across the river in AD47 they then needed to establish defences to protect it, so a military encampment was placed on the northern bank to protect the crossing. With no defensive wall, this first encampment was vulnerable to attack and in AD61, the Iceni tribe of East Anglia – a force numbering around 100,000 and led by the inspirational Boudicea – destroyed the Roman settlement.

The Romans eventually regained control, of course, and rebuilt the town, adding stone defences in approximately AD100 to protect the encampment (on three sides) with the river demarcating its southern boundary. Incidentally, the area enclosed by the Romans' defensive wall measured approximately one 'square mile' – from which the city's financial district gets its nickname.

By the early 3rd century **Londinium**, as the Romans knew it, was a provincial capital and a lively port which traded with the rest of the Roman Empire. But in AD410 the Romans, with their empire in decline, left Britain and the city was abandoned. What they left behind, however, would not crumble so quickly.

The **Anglo-Saxons** from northern Europe and Scandinavia who followed in the Romans' wake initially chose not to repopulate the old Roman towns, opting instead to establish their own. **Lundenwic** – Anglo-Saxon London – was initially located approximately a mile up the river from the abandoned Roman walls (*wic* signifies a riverside

rates vary depending on availability but as a guide expect to pay a minimum of £75pp (sgl occ room rate) for B&B. Next door is *The Mute Swan* (☎ 020-8941 5959, ☐ brunningandprice.co.uk/muteswan; fb; food

Mon-Thur 11.30am-9pm, Fri & Sat to 10pm, Sun to 9pm; WI-FI; ✖). It is a classy joint; main courses may include grilled sea bass fillets with crab croquette, pea purée & sauce vierge (£16.95).

HAMPTON WICK   [Map 53, p201]

The site of a Roman ford, the first wooden bridge to cross the Thames here dates from 1219, though this is not the structure you see today, of course.

Once just a village, although now incorporated within the London Borough of Richmond-upon-Thames, Hampton Wick today remains a leafy and peaceful alternative to Kingston with a number of decent accommodation and dining options.

At 56-58 High St there is a **post office** and **general store** (Mon-Sat 7am-7pm, Sun 8am-2pm) with **ATM**.

SWR **trains** (see box pp56-7) call at Hampton Wick railway station; the 461 bus (see pp58-61) also stops in Hampton Wick.

Accommodation and excellent **food** are available at *The Foresters* (☎ 020-8943 5379, ☐ the-foresters.com; fb; 1S/2D/1T; WI-FI; ✖ bar area only; 45 High St). The rates (£50-60pp, sgl occ room rate) are for room only; they do not provide breakfast but guests have a 10% discount in the restaurant. There are some splendid meals (food Mon 5-10pm, Tue-Sat noon-10pm, Sun to 6pm), such as whole spatchcock

trading point). The Venerable Bede (AD673-735), author of *The Ecclesiastical History of the English People*, described it as a 'bustling trading town'; but due to its location on the river, the settlement was always vulnerable to attack and the Vikings continually harassed the town. Finally, having survived for 300 years, Lundenwic was abandoned by the Anglo-Saxon King Alfred (AD849-899) in AD886 and the settlement was moved back within the old Roman walls. From this point the city's development became one of almost continual growth until, by the early 11th century, it was by far the largest settlement in England. The Anglo-Saxons' seat of power had moved now from Winchester to London, though the Vikings, as was their wont, would continue to invade, pillage and burn down the town, on one occasion even pulling down one of the wooden Anglo-Saxon bridges (see pp232-3).

The **Viking Age** (AD793-1066) was, symbolically, at least, ended by King Harold (1022-66), whose men defeated the invading Norwegians in Yorkshire at the Battle of Stamford Bridge in 1066. But as the king's exhausted army celebrated a momentous victory, another threat was landing on England's southern shores...

Following the Battle of Hastings in 1066, the victorious Normans were refused entry to London via the city's bridge and instead had to cross upriver at Wallingford. The city, though, could not resist them for long and London inevitably fell, William the Conqueror being crowned King of England at Westminster Abbey. The arrival of the Normans would see stone used significantly for the first time since the departure of the Romans and they soon started work on the Tower of London and Old London Bridge (see box on pp232-3). Primarily a defensive line across the Thames rather than a crossing point, Old London Bridge prevented larger craft from continuing upriver, meaning that they had to moor – and so trade – east of the bridge. The expanse of water immediately east of London Bridge would become known as the Pool of London and develop into the greatest seaport in the world (see box on pp232-3).

Today, many of London's main historical sites are located on the river and can quite easily be incorporated into your walk along the Thames Path.

ROUTE GUIDE AND MAPS

poussin (£13); see the hungry stampede through the door.

At 1 High St is *The White Hart Hotel* (☎ 020-8977 1786, 🖥 whiteharthoteluk.co.uk; **fb**; 22D/10D or T/5Tr; 🍺; WI-FI; 🐕).**B&B** costs from £42pp (sgl occ room rate) but can easily climb to £100pp or more should you ramble into town during one of the many other major events in the area (see p15). The place is also renowned for its **food** (daily noon-9.45pm); the dinner menu changes regularly but may include Dorset Texel lamb neck fillet, burnt aubergine & fregola salad (£15.95).

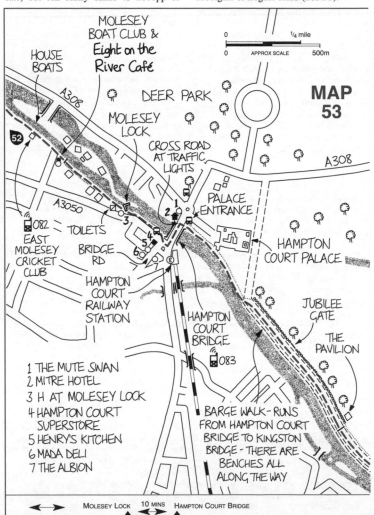

MOLESEY BOAT CLUB & *Eight on the River Café*

HOUSE BOATS

A308

DEER PARK

MOLESEY LOCK

CROSS ROAD AT TRAFFIC LIGHTS

52

A3050

082 EAST MOLESEY CRICKET CLUB

TOILETS

BRIDGE RD

HAMPTON COURT RAILWAY STATION

3

5
6

PALACE ENTRANCE

HAMPTON COURT PALACE

0   1/4 mile
0   APPROX SCALE   500m

MAP 53

A308

HAMPTON COURT BRIDGE
083

1 THE MUTE SWAN
2 MITRE HOTEL
3 H AT MOLESEY LOCK
4 HAMPTON COURT SUPERSTORE
5 HENRY'S KITCHEN
6 MADA DELI
7 THE ALBION

JUBILEE GATE

THE PAVILION

BARGE WALK - RUNS FROM HAMPTON COURT BRIDGE TO KINGSTON BRIDGE - THERE ARE BENCHES ALL ALONG THE WAY

←→ MOLESEY LOCK 10 MINS HAMPTON COURT BRIDGE

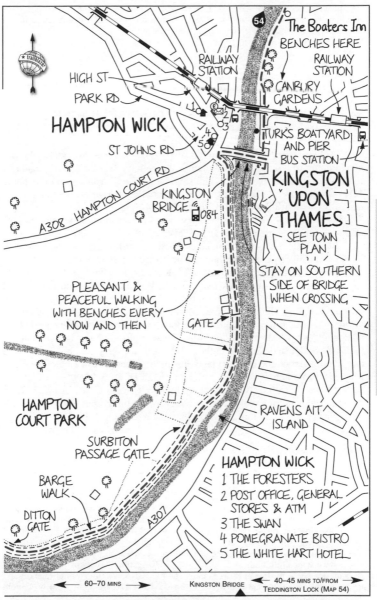

54

The Boaters Inn

BENCHES HERE

RAILWAY
STATION

RAILWAY
STATION

CANBURY
GARDENS

HIGH ST

PARK RD

HAMPTON WICK

ST JOHNS RD

TURK'S BOATYARD
AND PIER

BUS STATION

KINGSTON
UPON
THAMES

SEE TOWN
PLAN

KINGSTON
BRIDGE 084

A308 HAMPTON COURT RD

STAY ON SOUTHERN
SIDE OF BRIDGE
WHEN CROSSING

PLEASANT &
PEACEFUL WALKING
WITH BENCHES EVERY
NOW AND THEN

GATE

HAMPTON
COURT PARK

RAVENS AIT
ISLAND

SURBITON
PASSAGE GATE

BARGE
WALK

A307

DITTON
GATE

HAMPTON WICK
1 THE FORESTERS
2 POST OFFICE, GENERAL
  STORES & ATM
3 THE SWAN
4 POMEGRANATE BISTRO
5 THE WHITE HART HOTEL

ROUTE GUIDE AND MAPS

← 60–70 MINS →   KINGSTON BRIDGE   ← 40–45 MINS TO/FROM →
TEDDINGTON LOCK (MAP 54)

There are several **cafés** on High St, including *Pomegranate Bistro* (☎ 020-7998 8808, 💻 pomegranatebistro.co.uk; **fb**; Mon 8am-6pm, Tue-Sun to 10pm; WI-FI; 🐕 outside) where the menu offers an array of meals including the 'breakfast bomb' (two eggs, two rashers of bacon, two sausages, chips, tomatoes, beans & black

pudding) for £8.15, to lunches (create-your-own panini from £5.20) through to dinner (grilled salmon £11.35).

Classic **Thai food** (mains £10-15) is on offer at *The Swan* (☎ 020-8977 2644, 💻 hongthai.co.uk; **fb**; food Mon-Sat 5-9pm; WI-FI; 🐕; 22 High St).

W ← KINGSTON UPON THAMES TO CHERTSEY BRIDGE
[MAPS 53-50]

[Route section begins on Map 53, pp200-1] This stage includes the Thames Path's solitary **ferry** crossing (see box on p195). For any arch-landlubbers who would prefer to boycott the boat there is the option of sticking to dry land and following an **alternative route**. Utilising the ferry will lead to your day being **11¼ miles (18.2km, 3¾-4¼hrs)**, while undertaking the whole section on foot makes for a slightly longer **12-mile (19.5km, 4-5hrs** hike.

This is the day you leave London; begin by crossing **Kingston Bridge** (Map 53) and heading along **Barge Walk**, an historic towpath. A straightforward journey along the riverbank takes you to **Hampton Court** (pp198-9) with its Palace and then across Hampton Court Bridge where you leave London and enter Surrey. Your walk continues via **Molesey Lock** (Map 53), **East Molesey** (pp197-8) and **Sunbury Lock** (Map 52) to **Walton Bridge** and the point at which you need to make a choice: foot or ferry? While the pedestrian option includes a visit to **Shepperton** (see p194 & p196), the route is convoluted and at times hard to follow; if you choose this option keep your eyes peeled for National Trail acorns and follow Map 51 carefully. For the easier route go under the bridge and walk along the riverbank to the ferry (see box p195). The two routes meet on the northern bank just before **Shepperton Lock** (see p194; Map 51). From here it is an easy tramp through **Dumsey Meadow** (Map 50), an SSSI (see box on p71) to **Chertsey Bridge**. **Chertsey** (see pp192-3) is on the opposite bank; there are some services by the bridge but the main part of the town is a 15- to 20-minute walk along the road.

[Next route overview on p192]

KINGSTON UPON THAMES

With a name derived from either 'king's town' or 'king's stone' this place is undoubtedly of great historical significance. In AD838 Alfred the Great's grandfather, King Egbert, held a Great Council here and it remains the site of the first of England's thrones, the **king's stone**, on which at least seven of the Anglo-Saxon kings of Wessex were crowned. The actual king's stone can be seen outside the **Guildhall**.

Kingston lay on the border between the ancient kingdoms of Mercia and Wessex and following Athelstan's coronation here in AD925, and subsequent victory over the Northumbrians 12 years later, it was from this seat of power that he united and controlled the Kingdom of England – the first Saxon monarch to do so. Next to the 12th-century **All Saints Church**, the outline of the Church of St Mary – where the coronations occurred – is marked by a plaque.

Kingston Museum (☎ 020-8547 6440, 💻 www.kingstonheritage.org.uk/visit; **fb**; Fri 10am-5pm; free) hosts both permanent and guest exhibitions concerned with the history of the local area. At the time of research they were open only on Fridays but they hope to be open more in 2022.

Services

Kingston has branches of most high street **banks** and **ATM**s can be found in Market Place. The nearest **supermarket** to the bridge is Waitrose (Mon-Fri 8.30am-8pm, Sat to 7pm, Sun 11am-5pm), in the basement of the John Lewis store on Wood St,

while more centrally there is an Aldi (Mon-Sat 8am-10pm, Sun 11am-5pm) just off Wheatfield Way. A **pharmacy**, Superdrug (Mon-Sat 8.30am-7pm, Thur to 9pm, Sun 11am-5pm), is on Clarence St.

There is a **post office** (Mon-Wed & Fri-Sat 8am-7pm, Thur to 9pm, Sun 10am-5pm) next to WH Smith's on the lower ground floor in the Bentall Centre.

The town is well connected by **bus** (services include the 411, 458 & 461; see pp58-61) and **train** (SWR; see box on pp56-7) to places on the Thames Path.

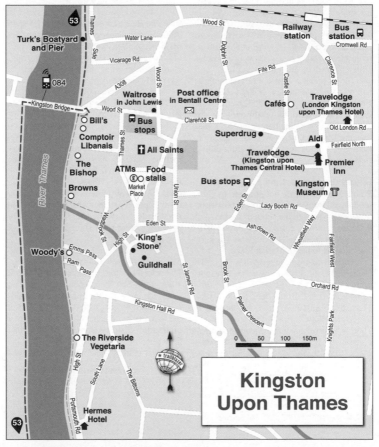

Kingston Upon Thames

ROUTE GUIDE AND MAPS

Where to stay

There are two branches of *Travelodge* (🖳 travelodge.co.uk) within easy walking distance of the river: London Kingston upon Thames Hotel (☎ 0871-984 6241; 21/23 Old London Rd) and Kingston upon Thames Central Hotel (☎ 0871-984 6428; Wheatfield Way). Next door to the latter is a *Premier Inn* (London Kingston upon Thames; ☎ 0333 003 3403, 🖳 premierinn.com; Wheatfield Way). See p21 for general information about these chain hotels.

B&B is available at *Hermes Hotel* (☎ 020-8546 5322, 🖳 hermes-hotel.co.uk; **fb**; 6S share facilities, 3D; 🐾; WI-FI; 🐕; 1 Portsmouth Rd) where the rate (£29.50-40.50pp, sgl/sgl occ from £49) depends on whether the room is en suite and/or has a river view. There is a separate bathroom with a bath which any guest can use.

If you prefer a hostel, and assuming it has reopened, the closest is *YHA London Earl's Court* (see p220 & p222); it is less than an hour from the path by train to Wimbledon (SWR; see box on pp56-7) and then the District Line to West Brompton or Earls Court – it is an easy walk from either station.

Where to eat and drink

Walkers will certainly not struggle to find food here. **Pubs** and (chain) **restaurants** line the riverbank to the south of the bridge, there are numerous **cafés** on Castle St and a selection of **food stalls** (Kingston Market) can often be found in Market Place.

Closest to the bridge, *Bill's* (☎ 020-4512 6634, 🖳 bills-website.co.uk/restaurants/kingston; **fb**; Mon & Tue 8am-9.30pm, Wed & Thur to 10pm, Sat 8.30am-11pm, Sun 9am-10pm; WI-FI; 🐕 outside; 2 Riverside Walk) is perfectly located. There's a varied breakfast menu including home-made blueberry & buttermilk pancakes (£7.50 for three). Options for the rest of the day include steak & eggs (£13.95) and Thai green chicken curry (£13.75).

Dogs are welcome to admire the river from the outside seating area.

Lebanese cuisine is available nearby at *Comptoir Libanais* (☎ 020-7657 1966, 🖳 comptoirlibanais.com; Mon-Sat 11am-10pm, Sun 11.30am-9pm; WI-FI); there's a fine variety of dishes from falafel (£5.45) to tagines including a lamb kofta one (£12.95). Also by the river is *Browns* (☎ 020-8974-5698, 🖳 browns-restaurants.co.uk; **fb**; Mon-Thur 9am-11pm, Fri & Sat to midnight, Sun to 11.30pm); their menu is extensive and they have daily fish specials. Mains cost from £12.95.

Hungry herbivores may be ecstatic to find *The Riverside Vegetaria* (☎ 020-8546 7992, 🖳 riversidevegetaria.co.uk; Mon-Sat noon-10pm, Sun to 9pm; 🐕 on terrace only; 64 High St). The award-winning vegetarian restaurant has outdoor tables by the river and generously priced meals including a Caribbean casserole (£10.50).

There are a few **pubs** near Kingston Bridge, amongst them is *The Bishop* (☎ 020-8546 4965, 🖳 thebishopkingston.co.uk; **fb**; food daily 11am-9pm; WI-FI; 🐕). The menu changes regularly but may include Scottish mussels, creamy white wine sauce, bacon & fries (£15.50). Also on the riverbank is *Woody's* (☎ 020-8541 4984, 🖳 woodyspubco.com; **fb**; food daily noon-10pm; WI-FI; 🐕) which specialises in homemade hot dogs: the Elwood, a dry aged beef brisket and smokey chipotle hot dog is £9.50.

A short way north of the bridge (Map 53) is *The Boaters Inn* (☎ 020-8541 4672, 🖳 boaterskingston.com; **fb**; food Mon-Sat 10am-9pm, Sun from noon; WI-FI; 🐕 on lead). Set in the perfect location for considering which side of the river to follow on the next stage, the menu varies but may offer other difficult choices such as that between the butternut squash & sage agnolotti (£14.50) and pan-fried sea bass (£17).

E → KINGSTON UPON THAMES TO PUTNEY BRIDGE
[MAPS 53-59]

Following an uncomplicated two-mile stretch to **Teddington Lock** (Map 54) – from where the Thames becomes tidal – this stage leaves you with a decision to make: whether to follow the **southern bank (13½ miles/21.7km, 4½-5¼hrs)**, or to cross just before the lock to the **northern bank (16¼ miles/26km, 5¾-7hrs)**. Our advice, simply put, is this: take the southern route (see below). The route along the northern bank (see pp216-22) is significantly longer and also involves a considerable amount of road walking, while the southern bank of the Thames is also – for much of the way at least – more 'rural' (a relative term of course) and thus feels more in tune with the river. However, it must be said that in many areas the view of the river is blocked by trees and bushes. The various bridges en route do, though, mean that you can swap banks easily – it only takes 5-10 minutes to cross over – and if you would like to walk on the northern bank for a bit we recommend the stretch between Kew Bridge and Hammersmith.

E → Kingston to Putney Bridge: southern bank

TEDDINGTON LOCK   [MAP 54]

There are actually three locks (see box on p44) – and a weir – here making this the largest lock system on the non-tidal Thames. Since Richmond's lock is operational at low tide only, Teddington's is generally referred to as being the last – or first.

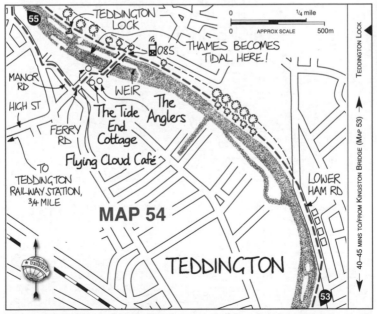

MAP 54

TEDDINGTON

TEDDINGTON LOCK

40-45 MINS TO/FROM KINGSTON BRIDGE (MAP 53)

ROUTE GUIDE AND MAPS

HAM [Map 55]

The path follows the shores of the 72-hectare **Ham Lands Local Nature Reserve** with its mixture of woodland, grassland and wetlands. **Ham House** (🖳 nationaltrust.org.uk; house Thur-Sun noon-4pm, garden daily 10am-5pm, café to 4.30pm; £13, garden only £6.50) is a 17th century Stuart house that has survived largely unscathed though a conservation project was completed in 2021. It is set in formal gardens that were designed to impress. For details of Hammerton's Ferry service to the northern bank, see p216.

RICHMOND [Map 55; map p208]

Richmond is also known as **Richmond upon Thames**, to distinguish it from its namesake in Yorkshire. Recorded in the *Domesday Book* as part of an area called Shene (now Sheen), the town gained its modern name from Henry VII's Richmond Palace, built in 1501. The palace was one of Elizabeth I's favourite residences and she died there in 1603. Following the execution, in 1649, of Charles I – who fled to Richmond to escape the plague – the palace fell into decay and little remains of it now.

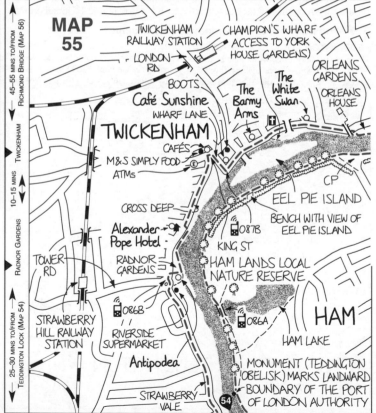

45-55 MINS TO/FROM RICHMOND BRIDGE (MAP 56)

TWICKENHAM

10-15 MINS

RADNOR GARDENS

25-30 MINS TO/FROM TEDDINGTON LOCK (MAP 54)

ROUTE GUIDE AND MAPS

MAP 55

TWICKENHAM RAILWAY STATION

CHAMPION'S WHARF (ACCESS TO YORK HOUSE GARDENS)

LONDON RD

ORLEANS GARDENS

BOOTS

Café Sunshine

The Barmy Arms

The White Swan

ORLEANS HOUSE

WHARF LANE

TWICKENHAM

CAFÉS

M&S SIMPLY FOOD

ATMs

CP

EEL PIE ISLAND

CROSS DEEP

087B

BENCH WITH VIEW OF EEL PIE ISLAND

Alexander Pope Hotel

KING ST

HAM LANDS LOCAL NATURE RESERVE

TOWER RD

RADNOR GARDENS

STRAWBERRY HILL RAILWAY STATION

086B

RIVERSIDE SUPERMARKET

Antipodea

086A

HAM

HAM LAKE

MONUMENT (TEDDINGTON OBELISK) MARKS LANDWARD BOUNDARY OF THE PORT OF LONDON AUTHORITY

STRAWBERRY VALE

54

> ❏ **WARNING**
>
> **Certain sections along this stage may flood at high tide** and since the tide can rise
> as fast as an inch a minute it is well worth checking 🖥 tidetimes.org.uk before setting
> off, or download the Port of London Authority app: 🖥 pla.co.uk/Media-Centre/PLA-
> Tidal-Thames-app. In some places alternative routes are signed, but sometimes the
> flooding is unexpected – so you will need to find another way out or retrace your steps.

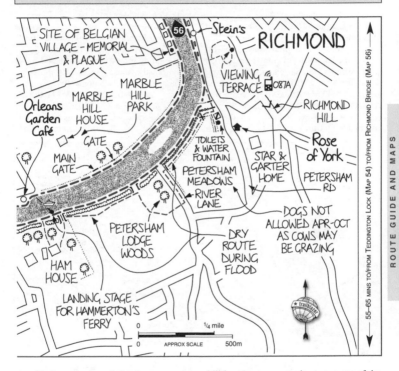

Between April and October you may see cattle grazing in **Petersham Meadows** (Map 55) and when they are you can't take dogs through the meadows. The map shows the dry route options for when the towpath by the river is flooded (see box above).

The gigantic **Star and Garter Home** (Map 55), originally for 'disabled sailors and soldiers', but now converted to upmarket flats, peers down at you from the top of **Richmond Hill**. Taking the time to climb to the viewing area on Richmond's famous

hill is a great opportunity to see one of the finest views of the river – and the only one protected by an Act of Parliament! The view has also been painted by both JMW Turner and Joshua Reynolds and even inspired the naming of Richmond, Virginia (USA), after the city founder thought the curve in James River there resembled the meander of the Thames as seen from the hill.

The **Museum of Richmond** (🖥 muse umofrichmond.com; Tue-Fri 11am-5pm, Sat Apr-Sep 11am-5pm, Oct-Mar to 4pm;

free) is in the old town hall and is worth a visit if you are interested in the history of the town. **Old Deer Park** (Map 56, p210) is part of a hunting park created by James 1 in 1604; the 'old' is because there are no longer any deer here.

Services

For general information about Richmond visit 🖳 visitrichmond.co.uk.

On George St there is: a Tesco Metro **supermarket** (Mon-Sat 6am-midnight, Sun 11am-5pm); a Boots **pharmacy** (Mon-Fri 8am-7pm, Sat to 6.30pm, Sun 11am-5pm); a **post office** (Mon-Sat 9am-5.30pm, Sun 11am-3pm) in a WH Smith's, and some banks with **ATMs**. At the riverside are free **toilets** in a mobile 'hut' (daily noon-8pm).

Richmond is well connected to the rest of London by **tube** (District line) and **train**

(SWR and London Overground; see box on pp56-7), as well as bus services.

Where to stay, eat and drink

Richmond has several **accommodation** options though mostly in the higher price-bracket and also not particularly near the river. *Rose of York* (Map 55; ☎ 020-8948 5867, 🖳 samuelsmithshotels.co.uk/rose-york-richmond-upon-thames; 7D/2Tw/3Tr, all en suite; ✉; WI-FI; 🐾), which describes itself as a 'country pub with rooms'. B&B costs from £45pp (sgl occ room rate).

Finding somewhere to **eat** and drink is easy. Neatly housed in one of the brick arches beneath Richmond Bridge, *Tide Tables Café* (☎ 020-8948 8285, 🖳 tidetab lescafe.co.uk; Mon-Fri 7.30am-6.30pm, Sat & Sun to 8pm, winter months hours variable; WI-FI; 🐾) has a spacious outdoor

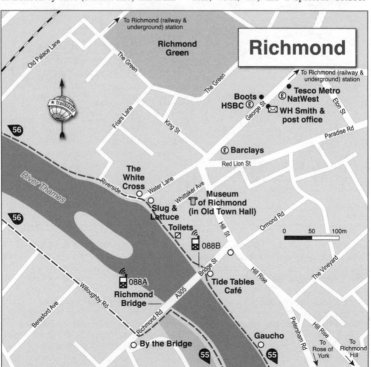

space backed by a large bank of wild flowers – it's really quite idyllic. The prices are not as wince-making as some places in Richmond and the food is good, with baked potatoes from £3.50 (extra for topping) and delicious cakes & pastries from £3.95! All food is vegetarian and they also have plenty of vegan and gluten-free options.

Gaucho (☎ 020-8948 4030, 🖳 gaucho restaurants.com/restaurants/richmond; food Sun-Thur noon-11pm, Fri & Sat from 11.30am; WI-FI; 🐾) focuses on Argentinian steak (from £18) but also offers a set lunch (daily noon-3pm) for £23/26 two/three courses. If you eat here you may spot a plaque about the **London Plane tree** between the tables around the tree; see also box on p67.

For German food and beer go to *Stein's* (Map 55; ☎ 020-3746 6240, 🖳 stein -s.com; Wed-Sun noon-9pm but if the weather is good they may also open on Tue; WI-FI; 🐾); the menu includes *Munchner bratwurst* (pork sausages, from Munich, served with pan-fried potatoes and salad (£13.60); vegan option available.

Pub food can be found either side of Water Lane. *The White Cross* (☎ 020-8940 6844, 🖳 thewhitecrossrichmond.com; food Mon-Sat noon-10pm, Sun to 9pm; WI-FI; 🐾) has a perfect location and serves real ale and has a decent and imaginative menu (mains from £14) and delicious roasts (from £15) on Sunday. If cocktails rather than real ale are your thing head to *Slug and Lettuce* (☎ 020-8743 7733, 🖳 slugand lettuce.co.uk/richmond; food daily 10am-10pm; WI-FI; 🐾).

If you prefer to get away from the river there are other options along both Old Palace Lane and Water Lane and of course in central Richmond.

KEW [Map 57, p212]

Kew's **Royal Botanical Gardens** (☎ 020-8332 5655, 🖳 kew.org/kew-gardens; daily late Mar-end Aug Mon-Thur 10am-7pm, Fri-Sun to 8pm, rest of year fewer hours; adult online £17.50, on the day £19.50, see website for further details), the world's most famous, are home to a plethora of flora and fauna. The Temperate House is the largest Victorian glasshouse in the world. Sadly from the path there are very few glimpses into the gardens.

Kew has a couple of pubs (both freehouses): *The Greyhound* (☎ 020-8332 9666, 🖳 thegreyhoundkew.co.uk; food Mon-Sat noon-10pm, Sun to 9pm; WI-FI; 🐾) and *Cricketers* (☎ 020-8940 6904, 🖳 thecrick eterskew.com; WI-FI; 🐾; food Tue-Fri noon-3pm & 4.30-8.30pm, Sat noon-8.30pm, Sun to 5pm) serving food and drink, but otherwise few useful services by the river for walkers. However, there are lots of *cafés* and a Tesco Metro **supermarket** (daily 7am-11pm) by Kew Gardens **tube** (District Line) and rail (London Overground; see box on pp56-7) stations.

MORTLAKE [Map 57, p213]

Mortlake was once one of the many sites where a ferry would cross the Thames. For most years since 1845 the bridge here (**Chiswick Bridge**) has overlooked the finishing line for The University Boat Race (see box on p211).

At *The Ship* (☎ 020-8876 1439, 🖳 greeneking-pubs.co.uk; food Mon-Sat noon-9pm, Sun noon-8pm; WI-FI; 🐾). There's a wide-ranging selection of traditional pub grub such as burgers (from £11.99) and sausages & mashed potatoes (£9.99) but they also have a vegan and vegetarian option and there is a beer garden.

In a courtyard set back from Mortlake High St is *Rick Stein* (🖳 rickstein.com/ restaurants; food daily noon-3pm & 6-9pm; WI-FI; 🐾 outside on terrace), another in the TV chef's chain, with smart fish dishes including a seafood gratin for £23.95. Should you wish to make a reservation call ☎ 020-4548 4855 – this is a central reservation system and it is likely the person you will talk to will be in Cornwall!

The local branch of **Sainsbury's** (daily 7am-10pm) is near Barnes railway bridge. Next door, *Orange Pekoe* (☎ 020-8876 6070, 🖳 orangepekoeteas.com; Mon-Fri

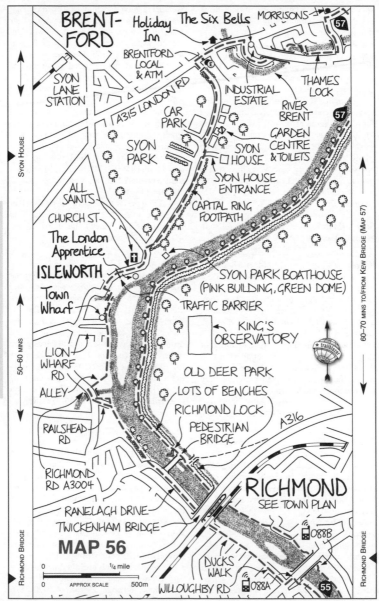

BRENT-FORD

Holiday Inn

The Six Bells

MORRISONS

SYON LANE STATION

BRENTFORD LOCAL & ATM

A315 LONDON RD

CAR PARK

INDUSTRIAL ESTATE

THAMES LOCK

RIVER BRENT

GARDEN CENTRE & TOILETS

SYON PARK

SYON HOUSE

SYON HOUSE ENTRANCE

ALL SAINTS

CHURCH ST

CAPITAL RING FOOTPATH

The London Apprentice

ISLEWORTH

Town Wharf

SYON PARK BOATHOUSE (PINK BUILDING, GREEN DOME)

TRAFFIC BARRIER

KING'S OBSERVATORY

LION WHARF RD

ALLEY

OLD DEER PARK

RAILSHEAD RD

LOTS OF BENCHES

RICHMOND LOCK

PEDESTRIAN BRIDGE

A316

RICHMOND RD A3004

RANELAGH DRIVE

TWICKENHAM BRIDGE

RICHMOND
SEE TOWN PLAN

MAP 56

0 ¼ mile
0 APPROX SCALE 500m

DUCKS WALK

WILLOUGHBY RD

088B

088A

SYON HOUSE

50-60 MINS

60-70 MINS TO/FROM KEW BRIDGE (MAP 57)

RICHMOND BRIDGE

RICHMOND BRIDGE

trailblazer

57

57

55

8am-5pm, Sat & Sun 9am-5pm; 🐾; WI-FI) specialises in brewing **tea** of a superior standard to your average mug of builders but also offers juices and smoothies (from £4.60). Lunches including salads and sandwiches are available as are cream teas (all day; £8.95) and an afternoon tea (from 2pm; £22.95).

The menus at *The White Hart* (☎ 020-8876 5177, 🖥 whitehartbarnes.co.uk; food

Mon-Sat noon-10pm, Sun to 9pm; WI-FI; 🐾 bar only) for both Canon Bar and the Terrace Kitchen change regularly but include imaginative dishes such as curried hake fillet, Jersey royals, tenderstem broccoli, garden pea & coconut broth (£18); the lunch menu includes sandwiches from £8.

SWR's services call at both Mortlake and Barnes Bridge **railway stations** (see box pp56-7).

BARNES
[Map 57, p213; Map 58, p214]
Leg o'Mutton Reservoir is a local nature reserve that is home to a range of flora and fauna including butterflies, birds such as herons, greater-spotted woodpecker and kestrels; the flora includes common reed. It is well worth a diversion from the official path.

Birdwatchers, in particular, are likely to want to visit **WWT London Wetland Centre** (Map 58; ☎ 020-8409 4400, 🖥 wwt .org.uk/wetland-centres/london; Mar-end Oct daily 9.30am-5pm; £13.40, free for WWT members); it has a *café* (same hours) serving snacks and hot food.

The Bull's Head (☎ 020-8876 5241, 🖥 thebullsheadbarnes.com; food Mon-Sat noon-10pm, Sun to 9pm; WI-FI; 🐾 in bar) is on Lonsdale Rd. The menu changes monthly but is generally standard British pub food (mains from £13).

Obviously the closest **railway station** is Barnes Bridge; SWR's services (see box pp56-7) call here. The pedestrian bridge on the eastern side of Barnes Railway bridge provides a convenient way to cross to the northern bank.

See p219 for information about **Hammersmith Bridge**.

ROUTE GUIDE AND MAPS

❑ THE UNIVERSITY BOAT RACE
In 1829 the first-ever Boat Race between Oxford and Cambridge universities was held between Hambleden Lock (Map 39) and Henley Bridge (Map 38), Henley-on-Thames. Organised by two school friends who were studying at the rival universities, this inaugural competition attracted a crowd of 20,000 who witnessed an easy Oxford win. The second race wasn't held until 1836 when the two universities raced between Westminster and Putney. Back then, however, the event was constantly interrupted by commercial traffic and a row broke out over where to hold the race – with Oxford wanting to race at Henley while Cambridge preferred London. In 1839 it was decided definitively that London would host the race, with the route moved to a 4-mile, 374-yard course between Putney Bridge (Map 59) and Mortlake (Map 57), just shy of Chiswick Bridge, in 1845. And there it remained, save for the odd exception such as the Second World War when it was moved from London and in 2021 when it was held on the River Great Ouse (Ely, Cambridgeshire). However, for 2022 it will be back on the River Thames in London.

The Boat Race is held on a Saturday near Easter and, as of 2021, Cambridge men had won 84 times and Oxford 80 (Cambridge women 44 and Oxford 30). For further information visit 🖥 theboatrace.org.

On the Fulham side of the river near Putney Bridge (see Map 59) look out for the mosaic on the ground saying 'Oxford & Cambridge Boat Race since 1829' along the bottom and round the top 'The world's longest surviving sporting challenge'.

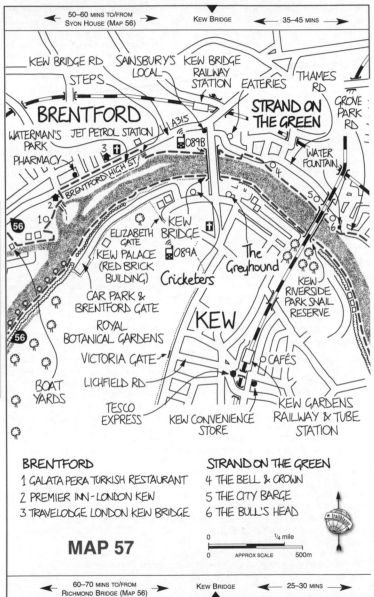

50–60 MINS TO/FROM SYON HOUSE (MAP 56)

KEW BRIDGE

35–45 MINS

KEW BRIDGE RD

SAINSBURY'S LOCAL

KEW BRIDGE RAILWAY STATION

EATERIES

THAMES RD

GROVE PARK RD

STEPS

BRENTFORD

WATERMAN'S PARK

JET PETROL STATION

PHARMACY

3

BRENTFORD HIGH ST

A315

089B

STRAND ON THE GREEN

WATER FOUNTAIN

4

2

10

56

ELIZABETH GATE

KEW PALACE (RED BRICK BUILDING)

CAR PARK & BRENTFORD GATE

ROYAL BOTANICAL GARDENS

VICTORIA GATE

LICHFIELD RD

TESCO EXPRESS

KEW BRIDGE

089A

Cricketers

The Greyhound

KEW

5

6

KEW RIVERSIDE PARK SNAIL RESERVE

CAFÉS

56

BOAT YARDS

KEW CONVENIENCE STORE

KEW GARDENS RAILWAY & TUBE STATION

BRENTFORD

1 GALATA PERA TURKISH RESTAURANT
2 PREMIER INN - LONDON KEW
3 TRAVELODGE LONDON KEW BRIDGE

STRAND ON THE GREEN

4 THE BELL & CROWN
5 THE CITY BARGE
6 THE BULL'S HEAD

MAP 57

0   ¼ mile
0   APPROX SCALE   500m

PUTNEY   [map p215]

Between Putney and Fulham (see p220 & p222) stands the only bridge along the river with a church at both ends: All Saints on the Fulham side and St Mary's on the Putney side.

In 1647 **St Mary's Church** hosted the Putney debates between members of Oliver Cromwell's New Model Army, during which the then radical idea of 'one man one vote' was first articulated. There is a small

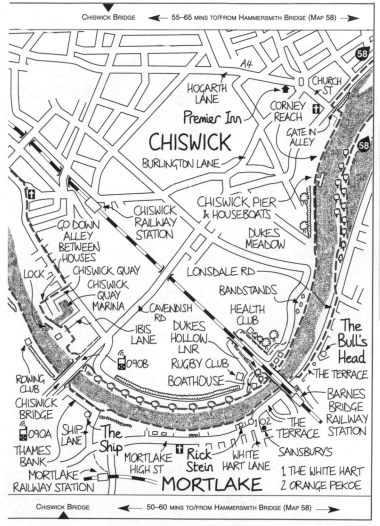

CHISWICK BRIDGE   ⬅— 55–65 MINS TO/FROM HAMMERSMITH BRIDGE (MAP 58) —➤

A4

HOGARTH LANE

CHURCH ST

CORNEY REACH

GATE IN ALLEY

Premier Inn

CHISWICK

BURLINGTON LANE

CHISWICK PIER & HOUSEBOATS

CHISWICK RAILWAY STATION

DUKES MEADOW

GO DOWN ALLEY BETWEEN HOUSES

LONSDALE RD

BANDSTANDS

CHISWICK QUAY

LOCK

CHISWICK QUAY MARINA

HEALTH CLUB

CAVENDISH RD

DUKES HOLLOW LNR

IBIS LANE

090B

RUGBY CLUB

BOATHOUSE

The Bull's Head

THE TERRACE

BARNES BRIDGE RAILWAY STATION

ROWING CLUB

CHISWICK BRIDGE

090A

SHIP LANE

The Ship

THE TERRACE

THAMES BANK

MORTLAKE RAILWAY STATION

MORTLAKE HIGH ST

Rick Stein

WHITE HART LANE

SAINSBURY'S

1 2

MORTLAKE

1 THE WHITE HART
2 ORANGE PEKOE

CHISWICK BRIDGE   ⬅— 50–60 MINS TO/FROM HAMMERSMITH BRIDGE (MAP 58) —➤

ROUTE GUIDE AND MAPS

58

exhibition about this in the church (generally open Mon-Sat 10am-4pm; free).

The numerous rowing **club boathouses** (Map 59) on the western side of Putney Bridge mean that at any time of the day you are likely to see teams going out to practise.

Services

Along Putney High St there is a Boots **pharmacy** (Mon-Fri 9am-7.30pm, Sat to 6.30pm, Sun 11am-5pm). For **supermarkets** there's a branch of Waitrose (Mon-Sat 8am-8pm, Sun 11am-5pm) in Putney

ROUTE GUIDE AND MAPS

HAMMERSMITH BRIDGE (NORTHERN BANK)

HAMMERSMITH BRIDGE (SOUTHERN BANK)

55-65 MINS TO/FROM CHISWICK BRIDGE (MAP 57)

50-60 MINS TO/FROM KEW BRIDGE (MAP 57)

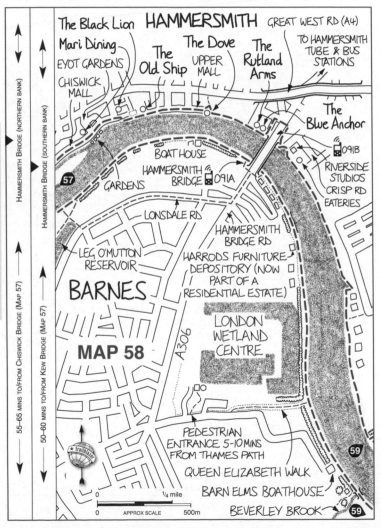

The Black Lion
Mari Dining
EYOT GARDENS
CHISWICK MALL
HAMMERSMITH
The Old Ship
The Dove
UPPER MALL
GREAT WEST RD (A4)
The Rutland Arms
TO HAMMERSMITH TUBE & BUS STATIONS
The Blue Anchor
091B
RIVERSIDE STUDIOS
CRISP RD EATERIES
BOAT HOUSE
HAMMERSMITH BRIDGE 091A
57
GARDENS
LONSDALE RD
HAMMERSMITH BRIDGE RD
LEG O'MUTTON RESERVOIR
HARRODS FURNITURE DEPOSITORY (NOW PART OF A RESIDENTIAL ESTATE)
BARNES
A306
LONDON WETLAND CENTRE
MAP 58
trailblazer
PEDESTRIAN ENTRANCE 5-10 MINS FROM THAMES PATH
QUEEN ELIZABETH WALK
BARN ELMS BOATHOUSE
BEVERLEY BROOK
59
0   1/4 mile
0   APPROX SCALE   500m

Exchange Shopping Centre and a Sainsbury's (Mon-Sat 7am-10pm, Sun noon-6pm) on Werter Rd. **ATMs** and **banks** are dotted along the High St.

Transport

Services to **Putney railway station**, on the High St, are operated by SWR (see box pp56-7). East Putney **tube station**, on Upper Richmond Rd, is on the District line.

The RB6 **river bus** (see p55) calls at the pier on the west side of the bridge.

Where to stay, eat and drink

The best option for **accommodation** is the Premier Inn on the Fulham side of the river; see p21. For hostel accommodation *YHA London Earl's Court* (see p220 & p222) is a short journey on the tube (District line) from either East Putney or Putney Bridge stations.

The riverbank, Putney High St and many of its tributary side streets are lined with high-street chain cafés, pubs and restaurants. If seeking breakfast or other sustenance, *Putney Pantry* (☎ 020-8789 1137, 🖳 putneypantry.com; Mon-Fri 10am-3pm, Sat to 5pm, Sun 11.30am-5pm; WI-FI; 🐾) is ideal. Part of St Mary's Church, here you'll find all-day breakfasts (from £6), as well as lunches (including sandwiches from £6.50) and delicious home-made cakes/tarts.

There are also several **pubs**. West of the bridge is *Duke's Head* (☎ 020-8788 2552, 🖳 dukesheadputney.com; food Mon-Sat noon-10pm, Sun to 9pm; WI-FI; 🐾 bar only). Owned by Young's Brewery, it's a classy establishment with decent food (smoked haddock & salmon fish cake £16.50). There's also an outdoor seating area, perfect to enjoy a pint at the end of a long day's walk with your goal for the day – Putney Bridge – in your sights.

Past St Mary's Church is *The Rocket* (☎ 020-8780 8970, 🖳 jdwetherspoon.com; food daily 8am-10pm; WI-FI). Wetherspoon's Putney branch offers a large

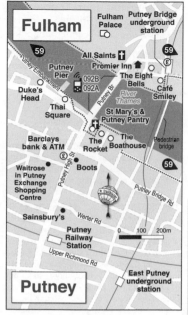

selection of ales and lagers and the usual lengthy, cheap no-frills menu, with mains for £8-11. Nearby, *The Boathouse* (☎ 020-8789 0476, 🖳 boathouseputney.co .uk; food summer Mon-Sat 10am-9.30pm, Sun noon-8.30pm; WI-FI; 🐾 in bar) is rightly proud of its seafood; the menu is seasonal but may include Scottish mussels & fries (£18) and battered cod & triple-cooked chips £16. Options also include at least one vegan dish.

Should English pub grub be giving you a bellyache there is a branch of *Thai Square* (☎ 020-8780 1811, 🖳 thaisq.com/ restaurants; Mon-Fri noon-3pm & 6-11pm, Sat noon-11.30pm, Sun to 10.30pm; WI-FI) overlooking the river from Putney Embankment. Jungle curry (from £12.95) and all things Thai are available.

W ← Putney Bridge to Kingston upon Thames: southern bank

Route shown on following maps – **Map 59** p220, **Map 58** p214, **Map 57** p212, **Map 56** p210, **Map 55** p206, **Map 54** p205, **Map 53** p201

ROUTE GUIDE AND MAPS

E → Kingston upon Thames to Putney Bridge: northern bank

Kingston For the first two miles the route is the same as for the southern bank, but at the bridge at Teddington Lock (see p205) cross over for Teddington itself.

TEDDINGTON   [Map 54, p205]

Flying Cloud Café (**fb**; Mar-end Oct daily 8.30am-5.30pm) serves hot drinks, ice-cream and cakes (from £2.75) from an Airstream but there is a covered area where you can sit and enjoy your refreshment.

Pub food is also available. The chefs at *The Anglers* (☎ 020-8977 7475, 🖳 ang lers-teddington.co.uk; food daily 9am-9pm; WI-FI; 🐾), a Fullers pub, offer some fine meals; the menu changes seasonally but may include roast salmon with watercress,

grilled lettuce, celery, green olive & raisin salsa £17.75. *The Tide End Cottage* (☎ 020-8977 7762, 🖳 greeneking-pubs.co.uk/pubs/middlesex/tide-end-cottage; food daily noon-9pm; WI-FI; 🐾) has an extensive menu and does a fine line in burgers and pies; mains around £10-12.

Teddington **railway** station (SWR; see box pp56-7) is a three-quarter mile walk from the path. See also pp54-5 for information about transport in London.

TWICKENHAM   [Map 55, p206]

Twickenham offers all the services a walker needs and, should you want a break from walking, two houses to visit. **Orleans House** (☎ 020-8831 6000, 🖳 orleanshouse gallery.org; Tue-Sun 10am-5pm; free but donations welcome) is now home to an **art gallery**, but in 1815 this 18th-century house was leased by the exiled King of France, Louis Philippe Duc d'Orleans. Though he actually resided here for only two years, it is his name that remains. **Marble Hill House** (☎ 020-8892 5115, 🖳 english-heritage.org.uk) is a Palladian Villa that was built for the mistress of King George II when he was the Prince of Wales. At the time of research the house was closed for refurbishment work but the grounds (daily 6.30am-7.30pm, winter 4.30pm, free) are open.

Eel Pie Island is a private island on which The Rolling Stones, Pink Floyd and The Who all once rocked. It is accessed by a footbridge but the public are only admitted twice a year.

Services

A number of **shops** dot the route through Twickenham, including Riverside Supermarket (Mon-Sat 7.30am-11pm, Sun 8am-11pm), an M&S Simply Food (Mon-Sat 8am-9pm, Sun 9am-8pm) and for a **chemist** a Boots (Mon-Sat 8.30am-6.30pm, Sun 11am-5pm). You'll see several **ATMs** just across the road on King St.

Twickenham has a **railway station** (SWR; see box pp56-7). **Hammerton's Ferry** (🖳 hammertonsferry.com; Mar-Oct daily 10am-1pm & 1.45-6pm, ferry on demand; £1 one-way) service has operated here since 1908. Card payment is accepted but there is a 2% charge.

Where to stay, eat and drink

Accommodation can be found at *Alexander Pope Hotel* (☎ 020-8892 3050, 🖳 alexanderpope.co.uk; 20D/12T, all en suite; ♥; WI-FI; 🐾). The tariff varies widely but on average B&B in a classic double room costs £54.50-84.50pp (sgl occ £89-159); book direct for the best rates. **Food** (daily noon-9pm) is also served.

As well as the **cafés** in central Twickenham there are three en route: *Antipodea* (☎ 020-8161 4449; WI-FI; 🐾; Tue-Sat 7.30am-5pm, Sun to 4pm), where the menu includes Turkish eggs (£9.50) as well as cakes, coffees and ice-creams; *Orleans Garden Café* (summer generally daily 8.30am-6pm, winter to 3.30pm) has sandwiches (from £3.40), ice-creams and hot drinks; and *Café Sunshine* (☎ 020-8538 9599; Apr-end Oct daily 10.30am-5pm, rest of year to 4pm, meals served 11am-3pm; WI-FI; 🐾), at the end of Wharf Lane, where there are sandwiches and also jacket potatoes (from £4.50).

The path passes two **pubs**. Rugby-fan favourite, *The Barmy Arms* (☎ 020-8892

0863, 🖳 greeneking-pubs.co.uk; food daily noon-9pm; WI-FI; 🐾 on lead), has an extensive menu of sandwiches, burgers and pub classics but it can be very busy, particularly if there's a game on at the nearby stadium, the home of English rugby.

In stark contrast is the tranquillity offered at *The White Swan* (☎ 020-8744

2951, 🖳 whiteswantwickenham.co.uk; food Mon-Sat noon-9pm, Sun noon-6pm; WI-FI; 🐾), a free house with a peaceful beer garden right next to the river. The menu changes regularly but should include a good selection of burgers, salads and main dishes such as a halloumi, beetroot & guacamole burger with chips (£12).

RICHMOND (western bank)
[map p208]
Richmond Bridge is London's oldest, having been built between 1774 and 1777, that is still in use. However, it is now wider than the original bridge.

By the Bridge (Bтb; ☎ 020-8892 7926; daily 9am-5pm; WI-FI; 🐾 outside) sells breakfasts (from £5) as well as sandwiches and wraps (from £4.50); eat in or take away.

ISLEWORTH   [Map 56, p210]
Syon Park (☎ 020-8560 0882, 🖳 syonpark .co.uk; mid Mar to end Oct: house Wed, Thur, Sun & Bank Hols 11am-5pm; gardens daily Wed-Sun 10.30am-4.30pm; house and gardens £13.50, gardens only £8) was originally the London home of the Duke of Northumberland; this is the last surviving ducal residence in London. The gardens were designed by Capability Brown.

The Thames Path passes by **two great pubs**. *Town Wharf* (☎ 020-8847 2287; food Tue-Fri noon-3pm & 6-9pm, Sat & Sun noon-6/5pm; 🐾 in downstairs bar) is your typical Samuel Smith Brewery establishment with no music but is also a place

for a digital detox. There is a varied menu which generally includes sandwiches (triple club from £8.70) and pies (from £10.50). The other is *The London Apprentice* (☎ 020-8560 1915, 🖳 greene king-pubs.co.uk; food daily noon-9pm; WI-FI; 🐾); they offer cashback to ensure you can afford to fill up on their woodland mushroom and ale pie (£12.99) and any other items from their extensive menu.

Syon Lane **railway station** is a stop on SWR's services (see box on pp56-7). It is a 20- to 25-minute walk from Isleworth. Isleworth station is a similar distance but not shown on the map.

BRENTFORD
[Map 56, p210; Map 57, p212]
Situated at the confluence of the rivers Brent and Thames, Brentford could once boast fords across both waterways and evidence of a Bronze Age trading centre suggests humans settled the area before London itself. It is also one of the sites where Julius Caesar and his army could have traversed the river in AD54; the area also witnessed a Civil War battle between the Royalists and Parliamentarians in 1642.

NB: If walking east to west note that the signpost by **Thames Lock** (Map 56) is angled incorrectly for Thames Path walkers; ensure you take the path nearest to you at the bottom of the steps by the lock.

Services
On London Rd (Map 56) there is a convenience store, *Brentford Local* (daily 6am-10pm), and on Brentford High St a **supermarket**, Morrisons (Mon-Sat 7am-11pm, Sun 10am-4pm) with an **ATM** and a **pharmacy** (Map 57; Mon-Fri 9am-5.30pm).

For a **train** the nearest station to the path is Kew Bridge (Map 57; SWR; see box pp56-7). See also pp54-5 for information about transport in London.

Where to stay, eat and drink
Accommodation is available at branches of three chain hotels: *Holiday Inn* (Map 56; London Brentford Lock; ☎ 020-8232 2000,

hibrentfordlock.co.uk); *Premier Inn* (Map 57; London Kew Bridge; ☎ 0333 321 1271, premierinn.com); and *Travelodge* (London Kew Bridge; ☎ 0871-984 6040, travelodge.co.uk). See pp21 for general information about these chains.

The Six Bells (Map 56; ☎ 020-8066 51188; food daily noon-9pm; WI-FI; 🐾 bar area and garden), on Brentford High St, was refurbished in 2021 and now has a pizza oven so for most of the week pizzas are the main thing to eat but on Sundays they serve a roast. It is a Fuller's pub and they serve London Pride.

On the path itself is *Galata Pera* (Map 56; ☎ 020-8560 1798, galatapera.co.uk; food Mon-Fri 4-11pm, Sat & Sun noon-11pm; WI-FI; 🐾 outside), which dishes up Turkish food such as kebabs, steak, seafood, and falafel (from £10.90). Takeaway also available.

STRAND ON THE GREEN
[Map 57, p212]

Strand on the Green was originally a fishing village and by the 19th century there were at least five malthouses here because barley grew well in the surrounding fields. This short stretch combines a scenic riverside walk (perhaps the best on the Thames in London) with a number of fine historic pubs (all dating from the 18th century if not before) and a Victorian water fountain (press hard to get water) at the eastern end.

On Thames Rd is Fuller's *The Bell & Crown* (☎ 020-8994 4164, bell-and-crown.co.uk; food Mon-Sat 9am-10pm, Sun 9am-9pm; WI-FI; 🐾), a very dog-friendly **pub** where the menu has standard pub options but also dishes such as blackened salmon with salad & new potatoes (£17). They serve breakfast but note that this finishes at 11.15am on Sunday and lunch service doesn't start till noon.

Two more pubs on either side of the railway bridge are The City Barge and The Bull's Head. *The City Barge* (☎ 020-8994 2148, citybargechiswick.com; food Mon-Sat noon-10pm, Sun to 9pm; WI-FI; 🐾 in bar area), an upmarket establishment that featured in The Beatles' *Help* film.

The menu is standard pub food but with an interesting twist such as short rib & flank burger with smoked Applewood cheddar, burnt onions, bone marrow crumb, gherkins & skin-on fries (£16) and there are also daily specials. At *The Bull's Head* (☎ 020-8994 1204, chefandbrewer.com; food daily noon-9.30pm; WI-FI; 🐾 bar area), as well as real ales there are also ciders and craft lagers on tap. From the lunch menu (Mon-Sat noon-4pm) you can purchase main meals such as mac 'n cheese or scampi, for as little as £6.29/6.99. They also serve brunch (Sat & Sun 9.30-11.30am).

Should you be tired of pub food there are some **eateries** near Kew Bridge: *The Strand* (☎ 020-8995 1012, strandcafew4.com; WI-FI; Mon-Sat 7am-5pm & 6.30-9.30pm, Sun 7.30am-3pm) is a café during the day and a restaurant specialising in Thai food in the evening; next to it is *La Vera Pizzeria* (☎ 020-8995 2452, la-vera-napoli.co.uk; Mon-Sat noon-11pm, Sun 1-11pm).

Kew Bridge **railway station** (SWR; see box pp56-7) is the closest for Strand on the Green.

CHISWICK   [Map 57, p213]

It's a pleasant riverside walk along the bank of **Dukes Meadows**, home to the 0.27-hectare **Dukes Hollow Local Nature Reserve (LNR)**. A new floating walkway under Chiswick bridge should be open by April 2022 to make this more accessible.

If you feel you've walked enough, consider *Premier Inn* (see p21; London Chiswick; ☎ 0333 234 6456, premierinn.com) for the night.

Chiswick railway station is a stop on SWR's **train** services (see box pp56-7).

Barnes Bridge has a pedestrian bridge on the eastern side providing access to both Barnes Bridge railway station (see p211) and the southern bank.

HAMMERSMITH [Map 58, p214]

The ornate green and gold **Hammersmith Bridge** (dating from 1887) was designed by Sir Joseph Bazalgette and is the only bridge of its kind in Britain. Like many old bridges it was designed to carry horses and carts so it is not surprising that the concerns (microfractures were found in the bridge in 2019) about its strength have returned. At the time of writing motor vehicles are banned but pedestrians and cyclists can go across the bridge and also under it. However, when repairs start Uber Boat by Thames Clippers (see p55) will provide a temporary ferry service (daily 6am-10pm) for pedestrians and cyclists. It is expected that fares will be similar to bus services. The embarkation points will be close to the bridge.

Services

There are two **tube stations** around Hammersmith Broadway, approximately a 10-minute walk from the Path. The entrance on Beadon Rd is for the Hammersmith & City and Circle lines; the other, in the centre of the Broadway, is for the District and Piccadilly lines. See pp54-5 for general information about transport in London.

Where to eat and drink

Pubs west of Hammersmith Bridge include *The Black Lion* (☎ 020-8748 2639, 🖥 blacklion.london; food Mon-Sat noon-10pm, Sun to 9pm; WI-FI; 🐾) and *The Old Ship* (☎ 020-8748 2593, 🖥 oldshiphammersmith.co.uk; food Mon-Thur noon-9.30pm, Fri & Sat to 10pm, Sun to 8.30pm; WI-FI; 🐾). Both have real ales to imbibe and particularly good food. For a break from a pub consider *Mari Deli & Dining* (☎ 020-7041 9251, 🖥 maridelidining.com;

daily 7.15am-9pm), Eyot Gardens; it's both a deli and a café. The deli part has breads and cakes (from £2/£2.40 eat out/in), pizza (slice from £3/3.70) and panini (from £5.60/6.70). Mains in the café may include meatball, tomato & nduja pasta (£9.80).

On the western side of the bridge there are **three pubs** brimming with history, character and fine ale. *The Dove* (☎ 020-8748 9474, 🖥 dovehammersmith.co.uk; food Mon-Sat noon-10pm, Sun to 9pm; WI-FI; 🐾 on lead) is one of London's most famous drinking haunts. It has the world's smallest bar-room and should you choose to stop for a libation you are in good company: Charles II, Ernest Hemingway and Dylan Thomas have all supped from the pub's taps. Owned by Fuller's Brewery, The Dove has a menu of tempting options such as Devonshire crab cake (£16) or Shepherd's pie (£15.50). *The Rutland Arms* (☎ 020-8748 5586, 🖥 greeneking-pubs.co.uk/pubs/greater-london/rutland-arms; food Mon-Fri 11am-9pm, Sat & Sun 10am-9pm; WI-FI; 🐾) is very dog-friendly, has several guest ales on the go at any one time and serves items such as steak & ale pie (£11.99), or sandwiches and toasties (from £6.49). An outside seating area affords views of the bridge. Next door is *The Blue Anchor* (☎ 020-3951 0580, 🖥 blueanchorlondon.com; food Mon-Sat noon-10pm, Sun to 9pm; WI-FI; 🐾). It was first licensed in 1722 and is now a popular place with film crews; the pub has featured in a number of television series as well as the film *Sliding Doors*. The varied menu includes salads (from £11.50) and they may also have monkfish corn tacos (£17.50).

There are also some **eateries** by and at Riverside studios.

❏ DIVERSION WARNING

We can think of no other section of any national trail that is as subject to so many **diversions**, so often, as the London section of the Thames Path, particularly at the moment due to the Thames Tideway project (see p71) but also due to flooding in some areas (see box on p207). This does, of course, reflect the ever-changing nature of the capital, which is part of its charm, but it does mean you have to keep your wits about you.

FULHAM [map p215]

Bishop's Park is a pleasant park but the main sight is **Fulham Palace** (Map 59; 🖥 fulhampalace.org; free), the 'country' residence of the bishops of London from the 11th century until 1973. Parts of the Palace can be visited including the museum (Wed-Sun 10.30am-5pm); the palace's historic gardens (daily dawn to dusk); and the walled garden (10.15am-4.15pm). The Palace also has a *café* (daily 9.30am-5pm).

At the time of writing it is necessary to divert from the river and walk round **Craven Cottage** (home to Fulham Football Club) along Stevenage Rd; the bonus is that you get to see the stadium's impressive facade. However, hopefully in 2022 you will be able to walk along the river itself.

Services

There are two free **ATMs** to the left of the entrance to Putney Bridge **tube station** (District line).

The best options for food supplies are to cross the bridge to Putney (see pp213-15) or walk to the Sainsbury's (see p230) on Townmead Rd.

Where to stay, eat and drink

A short walk from the station is *Premier Inn* (see p21; London Putney Bridge; ☎ 0333-321 1273, 🖥 premierinn.com).

● For **hostel accommodation** the best place is *YHA London Earl's Court* (☎ 0345-371 9114, 🖥 yha.org.uk/hostel/london-earls-court; 186 beds, 2-, 3-, 4- & 6-bed

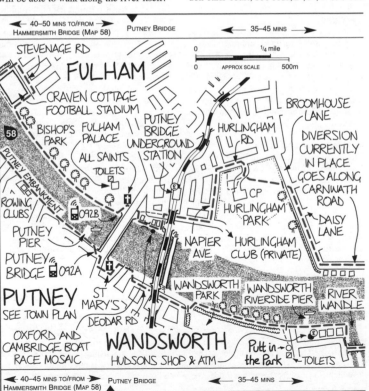

ROUTE GUIDE AND MAPS

← 40–50 MINS TO/FROM → HAMMERSMITH BRIDGE (MAP 58) PUTNEY BRIDGE ← 35–45 MINS →

STEVENAGE RD

FULHAM

0 ¼ mile
0 APPROX SCALE 500m

CRAVEN COTTAGE FOOTBALL STADIUM

BROOMHOUSE LANE

BISHOP'S PARK FULHAM PALACE

PUTNEY BRIDGE UNDERGROUND STATION

HURLINGHAM RD

DIVERSION CURRENTLY IN PLACE GOES ALONG CARNWATH ROAD

ALL SAINTS

TOILETS

58

PUTNEY EMBANKMENT

CP

DAISY LANE

ROWING CLUBS

092B

HURLINGHAM PARK

PUTNEY PIER

NAPIER AVE HURLINGHAM CLUB (PRIVATE)

PUTNEY BRIDGE 092A

PUTNEY SEE TOWN PLAN

ST MARY'S

DEODAR RD

WANDSWORTH PARK

WANDSWORTH RIVERSIDE PIER

RIVER WANDLE

OXFORD AND CAMBRIDGE BOAT RACE MOSAIC

WANDSWORTH HUDSONS SHOP & ATM

Putt in the Park

TOILETS

← 40–45 MINS TO/FROM → HAMMERSMITH BRIDGE (MAP 58) PUTNEY BRIDGE ← 35–45 MINS →

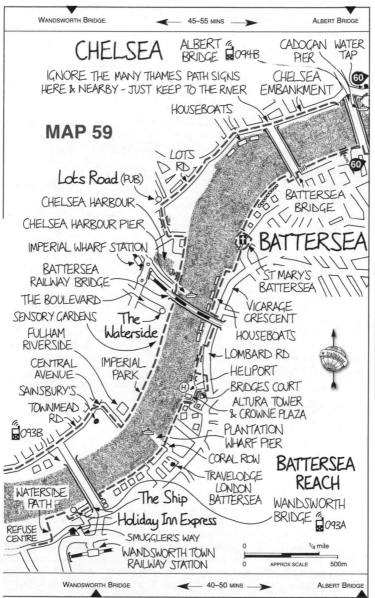

CHELSEA

ALBERT BRIDGE 094B

CADOGAN PIER

WATER TAP

IGNORE THE MANY THAMES PATH SIGNS HERE & NEARBY - JUST KEEP TO THE RIVER

CHELSEA EMBANKMENT

HOUSEBOATS

MAP 59

60

LOTS RD

Lots Road (PUB)

CHELSEA HARBOUR

CHELSEA HARBOUR PIER

IMPERIAL WHARF STATION

BATTERSEA RAILWAY BRIDGE

THE BOULEVARD

SENSORY GARDENS

FULHAM RIVERSIDE

CENTRAL AVENUE

SAINSBURY'S

TOWNMEAD RD

093B

WATERSIDE PATH

REFUSE CENTRE

The Waterside

IMPERIAL PARK

60

BATTERSEA BRIDGE

BATTERSEA

ST MARY'S BATTERSEA

VICARAGE CRESCENT

HOUSEBOATS

LOMBARD RD

HELIPORT

(H)

BRIDGES COURT

ALTURA TOWER & CROWNE PLAZA

PLANTATION WHARF PIER

CORAL ROW

TRAVELODGE LONDON BATTERSEA

The Ship

Holiday Inn Express

SMUGGLER'S WAY

WANDSWORTH TOWN RAILWAY STATION

BATTERSEA REACH

WANDSWORTH BRIDGE 093A

0 ¼ mile

0 APPROX SCALE 500m

ROUTE GUIDE AND MAPS

rooms; some with a double bed and a few en suite) at 38 Bolton Gardens. It is a short journey on the District Line from Putney Bridge tube station. See p19 and for up-to-date information see the YHA website.

For **food**, *Café Smiley* (*Nunu*; Mon-Fri 7.30am-5pm, Sat 8am-3.30pm) is right by the path and it serves sandwiches and paninis (from £3.50), salads (from £4.90)

and cakes/biscuits (from £2). If it is closed there are two more *cafés* opposite the station offering both eat in and takeaway.

Alternatively head to *The Eight Bells* (☎ 020-7736 6307, choose option 3; **fb**; food Mon-Fri noon-3pm & 5-9pm, Sat & Sun noon-9pm; WI-FI; 🐾) serves real ales alongside pub **food** such as steak & ale pie (£11.45).

W ← Putney Bridge to Kingston upon Thames: northern bank

Route shown on following maps – **Map 59** p220, **Map 58** p214, **Map 57** p212, **Map 56** p210, **Map 55** p206, **Map 54** p205, **Map 53** p201

W ← PUTNEY BRIDGE TO KINGSTON UPON THAMES
[MAPS 59-53]

[Route section begins on Map 59, pp220-1] As with previous stages you have a decision to make: whether to follow the southern bank (**13½ miles/21.7km, 4½-5¼hrs**), or the northern (**16¼ miles/26km, 5¾-7hrs**). Our advice, simply put, is this: take the southern route. The northern bank route is significantly longer and also involves a considerable amount of road walking, while the southern bank is – for much of the way at least – more 'rural' and thus feels more in tune with the river. However, in many areas the view of the river is blocked by trees and bushes.

The various bridges en route do though mean that you can swap banks easily – it only takes 5-10 minutes to cross over – and if you would like to walk on the northern bank for a bit we recommend the stretch between Hammersmith and Kew Bridge. The northern bank path ends just after **Teddington Lock** (Map 54) and from there you have to cross to the southern bank for an uncomplicated (two-mile) stretch to Kingston.

[Next route overview on p202]

E → PUTNEY BRIDGE TO TOWER BRIDGE   [MAPS 59-61]

As with the previous stage you need to make a decision over which bank to follow. Both sides have plenty to savour; the northern side is a **10-mile (16km, 3¼-4¼hrs)** walk and the southern is **9¼-miles (14.7km, 3½-4¾hrs)**, but note that even though the distance is less on the southern side it is likely to take longer owing to the number of tourists.

Overall, though, the **southern bank** probably edges it again, primarily due to it encompassing both the pleasant stroll through Battersea Park and also the excitement of London's Southbank area. The views of Westminster and the Tower of London (both on the north bank) are also splendid from the south side. The best part of the **northern bank** is the area around Westminster and the stretch between Millennium Bridge and Tower Bridge. And, of course, if you wish to visit them, all you need do is cross over any of the bridges. Indeed, with the stage being quite short, there's no reason not to cross the river as often as takes your fancy! But before starting off, see box on p219; see p230 for the northern bank route.

E ➔ Putney Bridge to Tower Bridge: southern bank

WANDSWORTH [Map 59, pp220-1]

Wandsworth grew around the mouth of the **River Wandle** – London's largest Thames tributary – and is the city's oldest industrial area. Wandsworth Park provides some green refreshment as well as a licensed café, *Putt in the Park* (☎ 020-8877 0713; daily 9am-6pm, winter to 4/5pm) serving hot & cold drinks and snacks. There is also a **toilet** block behind it. Hudson's **shop** (Mon-Fri 6.30am-11pm, Sat & Sun from 7am), near Wandsworth Park, has an **ATM**.

There is a *Holiday Inn Express* (see p21; London Wandsworth; ☎ 020-8877 5950, 🖳 expresswandsworth.co.uk) on Smuggler's Way.

For a place with a bit of history consider *The Ship* (☎ 020-8870 9667, 🖳 the ship.co.uk; food daily noon-9.30pm; WI-FI; 🐾 in bar). There are various menus featuring standard pub food, particularly burgers, as well as less common dishes such as pickled rhubarb, mango & falafel salad. Brunch menu options start from £5.50; mains start from £13. Note card/app payment only.

Wandsworth Town **railway station** is a short walk from the Holiday Inn; services are operated by SWR (see box pp56-7).

The RB6 **river bus** (see p55) calls at Wandsworth Riverside Quarter.

BATTERSEA REACH [Map 59, p221]

Battersea Reach is an apartment complex. There is a Tesco Express (daily 7am-11pm) **supermarket** with an **ATM** outside. On York Rd, a few minutes' walk inland is a branch of the *Travelodge* (see p21; London Battersea; ☎ 0871 984 6189, 🖳 travelodge .co.uk) chain. The RB6 **river bus** (see p55) calls at Plantation Wharf pier.

BATTERSEA
[Map 59, p221; Map 60, p224]

St Mary's Church (Map 59) is notable both as the place where William Blake (1757-1827), the poet, married in 1782 but also for having a 1611 Bible (on display) and some modern stained-glass windows including ones showing William Blake and Joseph Mallord William Turner (1775-1851). Assuming it is open do pop in.

Battersea Park (Map 60; daily 6am-10.30pm) hosts a peace pagoda and children's zoo and is a relaxing place to be.

The iconic **Battersea Power Station** (🖳 batterseapowerstation.co.uk) building was originally a coal-fired power station and the largest brick-building in the UK. But it and the surrounding area have been undergoing a transformation for several years. A major part of the office space within the original building will, in 2022, become Apple's UK campus. But the area also provides upmarket accommodation, shops and restaurants, entertainment venues and leisure spaces – some already open but plenty more still to come. A good place to sit and take it all in is on **Coaling Jetty**.

Whichever direction you are walking it is preferable to go through this complex rather than follow the official route.

Services

On Battersea Park Rd there is a Sainsbury's Local (daily 7am-11pm) **supermarket** with an **ATM**. There are (free) public **toilets** under Battersea railway bridge.

Southern operates services to **Battersea Park railway station** and SWR to the nearby **Queenstown Road** station; see box pp56-7. Battersea Power Station **tube** station is an extension of the Northern Line from Kennington/Waterloo and Battersea Power Station pier is a stop on the RB1 (eastbound only), RB2 & RB6 **river buses** (see p55).

Where to eat and drink

Battersea Park has several kiosks offering takeaway drinks and snacks (hot & cold).

The closest to the path is **Pier Point Café** (daily 8.30am-6pm, earlier in winter). For a sit-down meal with a view of a lake rather than the river, head to **Pear Tree Café** (☎ 020-7978 1655, 💻 peartreecafe.co.uk/pear-tree-cafe-battersea; daily 8am to dusk; lunch menu to 3pm). Get a table first and then go and place your order. The menu is varied and the sweet potato fries (£4.50) are well worth having whether or not you have a Pear Tree Burger (£10); sandwiches and cakes are also available. In the summer they sometimes serve burgers and pizzas to 9pm; see website for details.

Eateries abound in **Circus West Village (Battersea Power Station)**. For a sit-down hot drink (coffee!) go to **Black Sheep Coffee** (daily gen 7am-7pm); they also serve bagels and toasties. Facing the river are: **Fiume** (💻 fiume-restaurant.co .uk; food Tue-Sun noon-3pm & 6-9pm), serving *pinsa* (Roman-style pizza) from £10 and pasta from £14; **Wrights Brothers** (💻 thewrightbrothers.co.uk/restaurant/bat tersea; Mon-Fri noon-10pm, Sat 9am-11pm, Sun to 8pm), an upmarket seafood bar, and **Megan's** (💻 megans.co.uk/locations/me gans-battersea; Mon-Fri 8am-10.30pm, Sat to 11pm, Sun 9am-10pm) where the extensive menu includes brunch plates from £7.50 and kebabs from £12.50.

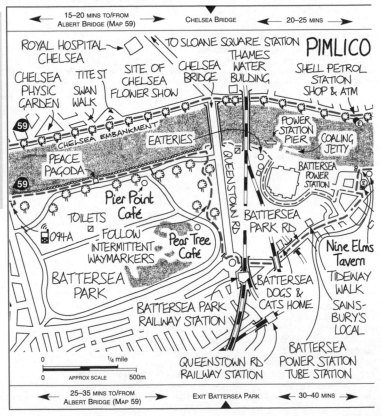

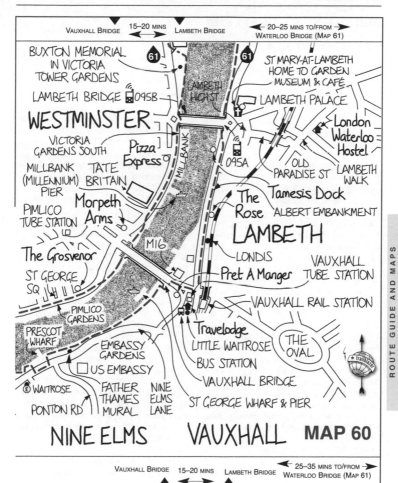

BUXTON MEMORIAL IN VICTORIA TOWER GARDENS

LAMBETH BRIDGE 095B

WESTMINSTER

VICTORIA GARDENS SOUTH

MILLBANK (MILLENNIUM) PIER

TATE BRITAIN

Pizza Express

Morpeth Arms

PIMLICO TUBE STATION

The Grosvenor

ST GEORGE SQ

MILLBANK

M16

PIMLICO GARDENS

PRESCOT WHARF

EMBASSY GARDENS

US EMBASSY

WAITROSE

PONTON RD

FATHER THAMES MURAL

NINE ELMS LANE

NINE ELMS

ST MARY-AT-LAMBETH HOME TO GARDEN MUSEUM & CAFÉ

LAMBETH PALACE

LAMBETH HIGH ST

095A

OLD PARADISE ST

London Waterloo Hostel

LAMBETH WALK

The Rose

Tamesis Dock

ALBERT EMBANKMENT

LAMBETH

LONDIS

Pret A Manger

VAUXHALL TUBE STATION

VAUXHALL RAIL STATION

THE OVAL

Travelodge

LITTLE WAITROSE

BUS STATION

VAUXHALL BRIDGE

ST GEORGE WHARF & PIER

VAUXHALL

MAP 60

★ trailblazer

NINE ELMS [Map 60]

The **US Embassy** provides an impressive backdrop to the **Father Thames mural**, by Stephen Duncan, on Riverside Walk. It is a terracotta relief set under water with the bearded Father Thames (river god) holding a dolphin over his head.

There is a large Waitrose (Mon-Sat 7.30am-10pm, Sun noon-6pm) **supermarket** with an **ATM**.

Nine Elms Tavern (☎ 020-3437 0004, 🖥 www.nineelmstavern.co.uk; food Mon-Sat noon-10pm, Sun to 9pm; WI-FI; 🐾) has a riverside terrace and the menu includes small plates (£5-12) such as Halloumi fries and harissa yoghurt and mains such as chicken katsu burger (£14). A roast is available on Sundays.

VAUXHALL [Map 60, p225]

Right by the bus station is a branch of *Travelodge* (see p21; London Vauxhall; ☎ 0871 559 1860, 🖳 travelodge.co.uk); it is also above a branch of *Little Waitrose* (daily 7am-11pm) if you want to stock up on food supplies.

Vauxhall has both **railway** (SWR; see box on pp56-7) and **tube** (Victoria line) stations as well as a large **bus** station with **toilets**. The RB1 (eastbound only), RB2 & RB6 **river bus** (see p55) services stop at St George Wharf (Vauxhall).

LAMBETH [Map 60, p225]

Lambeth Palace (Map 60; 🖳 www.arch bishopofcanterbury.org/about-lambeth-palace) is the London home of the Archbishop of Canterbury. It isn't generally open to the public other than on a guided tour; see the website for details. In St Mary-at-Lambeth Church (Map 60), near the Palace, there is a **Garden Museum** (☎ 020-7401 8865, 🖳 gardenmuseum.org.uk; Sun-Fri 10.30am-5pm; £12, church tower only £4) focusing on the art, history and design of gardens. Note that the museum is always closed on the first Monday of the month. Those without green fingers may be more interested in climbing the 131 steps in the **church tower** for views of London.

South of Westminster Bridge, and extending for about a third of a mile towards Lambeth Bridge, is the **National Covid Memorial Wall** (Maps 60 & 61); the wall was originally the memorial place for those who died of Human BSE (vCJD) but since March 2021 red and pink hearts have been painted on – the aim is to have a heart for everyone who has died from Covid.

There is a Londis **convenience store** (daily 24hrs) on Albert Embankment.

Where to stay, eat and drink

Budget **accommodation** is available at *London Waterloo Hostel* (☎ 020-7582 3088, 🖳 londonwaterloohostel.com; shared facilities; WI-FI). The hostel has private rooms (with a double and single bed) that sleep up to three people, and there are also 9- and 12-bed dorms though at the time of research, due to Covid, occupancy was reduced. The rate (£15-25pp) includes a simple continental breakfast.

One of the better-value eateries on the path in the capital is *The Rose* (☎ 020-7735 3723, 🖳 therosepublondon.co.uk; **fb**; food daily 11.30am-10.30pm; WI-FI; 🐾). The menu includes standard pub food (mains £11-20) and you can peruse Westminster on the northern bank.

Should the idea of a **floating restaurant** entice, hop aboard *Tamesis Dock* (☎ 020-7582 1066, 🖳 tdock.co.uk; food daily 11am-10pm; 🐾; WI-FI). It's moored off Albert Embankment, and the boat's menu focuses on pizzas (from £8.80) including vegan and gluten-free options.

The menu at the *café* (daily 10.30am-5pm, lunch noon-3pm) in the **Garden Museum** (see above) is limited but tempting and may include *salmorejo* (a creamy tomato soup; £8) for a starter at lunch; tea, cakes and the like are available the rest of the day. For something fast if you want to keep on the move there is a *Pret A Manger* (daily 5.30am-9pm) by the bridge.

SOUTHBANK AREA [Map 61, pp228-9]

The London Eye, originally called the Millennium Wheel, was designed as part of a competition to provide a landmark celebrating the millennium in London. It was due to be taken down after five years but its popularity brought about a change of plan. It goes without saying that this 443ft-/135m-high observation wheel (Map 61; 🖳 londoneye.com; daily 11am-6pm; approx 30 mins; standard/fast track entry from £24.50/34.50 if booked online, from £31/41 on the day; packages available, see the website) provides great 360° views of London.

County Hall was home to London's government between 1922 and 1986, but now hosts all manner of tourist attractions (such as Sea Life Aquarium, Shrek

Adventure & London Dungeon), several restaurants as well as a couple of hotels including a branch of *Premier Inn* (see p21; London County Hall; ☎ 0333 321 1246, ⌨ premierinn.com). The other major attractions in the Southbank area (⌨ southbanklondon.com) are the **National Theatre (NT)**, **BFI Southbank** and the **Southbank Centre** which includes the Royal Festival Hall and Hayward Gallery.

The service providers for both Waterloo and Waterloo East **railway stations** are SWR, Southern, Southeastern & Thameslink (see box on pp56-7). Waterloo **tube station** is on the Northern, Jubilee and Bakerloo lines; Southwark is also a stop on the Jubilee line.

The RD1 **river bus** (see p55) stops at London Eye (Waterloo).

BLACKFRIARS (southern bank)
[Map 61, pp228-9]

For those walking east to west *Doggett's* (⌨ nicholsonspubs.co.uk) claims to be the last riverside pub for 3.5km. Officially called 'Doggett's Coat and Badge' the pub is named after Thomas Doggett who, in 1715, started the London Bridge to Chelsea rowing race (⌨ doggettsrace.com) – the oldest rowing race in the world. It is usually held in June and the winner is awarded a coat and a badge! The menu includes burgers and fish & chips (from £13) as well as bar snacks. You can eat inside or by the river.

For **accommodation** consider either *ibis London Blackfriars* (☎ 020-7633 2720) or *Hotel Novotel London Blackfriars* (☎ 020-7660 0834); both are part of the Accor group (⌨ all.accor.com; see p21) and are next to each other on Blackfriars Rd, a short walk from the bridge.

See p232 for information about **Blackfriars Bridge**.

SOUTHWARK / BANKSIDE
[Map 61, pp228-9]

The many attractions in this area include: **Tate Modern** (☎ 020-7887 8888, ⌨ tate.org.uk/visit/tate-modern; daily 10am-6pm; free except for special exhibitions), a gallery focusing on contemporary art; Shakespeare's **Globe Theatre** (⌨ shakespearesglobe.com), a reconstruction of the theatre Shakespeare wrote for and part-owned; **Southwark Cathedral** (⌨ cathedral .southwark.anglican.org), the oldest Gothic church building in London; **The Shard** (⌨ the-shard.com) at 1016ft/310m high; *HMS Belfast* (⌨ www.iwm.org.uk/visits/hms-belfast), a cruiser from WW2; and *Golden Hinde* (⌨ goldenhinde.co.uk) a reconstruction of the first ship to sail round the world.

Situated by Southwark Bridge is a branch of *Premier Inn* (see p21; London Southwark Bankside; ☎ 0333 321 1274, ⌨ premierinn.com). **Hays Galleria** (⌨ www .hays-galleria.com) was originally a warehouse but it is now a mixed-use building with various shops and restaurants.

Southwark Cathedral (see above) has a *café* (daily 10am-5pm), which serves salads (main course £9.75), sandwiches (from £4.95), home-made cakes and pink Prosecco (£6).

Unsurprisingly there are several **pubs**. For bard-watchers there's *Swan at The Globe* (☎ 020-7928 9444, ⌨ swanlondon .co.uk; food Mon-Sat 10.30am-midnight, Sun to 8pm; WI-FI; 🐾 bar only), which as well as fine views of St Paul's Cathedral on the opposite bank also supplies temptingly tasty fare such as Herdwick lamb shepherds pie (£16). Booking for the restaurant and afternoon tea (Mon-Sat noon-6pm, Sun to 5pm; from £32.50) is recommended.

The Anchor Bankside (☎ 020-7407 1577, ⌨ greeneking-pubs.co.uk; food Mon-Sat noon-10pm, Sun to 9pm; WI-FI; 🐾) has a rather macabre past: occupying the site of a Roman grave, it is said to have been built on a bear-baiting venue and allegedly also on one of the pits where plague victims were buried in 1603. Luckily, there's a extensive, reasonably priced, menu (eg pies and burgers from £10.99) as well as views of the river to keep your mind away from such morbid thoughts.

ROUTE GUIDE AND MAPS

The Mudlark (☎ 020-7403 7364, 🖥 www.nicholsonspubs.co.uk; food Mon-Sat 10am-10pm, Sun noon-6pm; WI-FI) takes its name from the practice of making a living by collecting and selling items found in the mud when the tide is out; however, if you want to **mudlark** now you must have a Foreshore permit issued by the Port of London Authority. Mains (standard pub food) start from £11.50.

However, if you're looking for food in the region of London Bridge you should really head to **Borough Market** (🖥 boroughmarket.org.uk; Mon-Thur 10am-5pm, Fri to 6pm, Sat 8am-5pm, Sun 10am-2pm); it has been on this site since 1851 and has

been a film set for movies such as *Bridget Jones's Diary* and *Harry Potter and the Prisoner of Azkaban*. It is now where cuisines from all over the world are available. It's a bit of a tourist attraction but it's a characterful place and the food is, on the whole, great. Note that on Monday and Tuesday some shops/stalls may not be open.

London Bridge **railway station** is a stop for SWR, Southern, Southeastern & Thameslink services (see box on pp56-7) and London Bridge **tube station** is on the Northern and Jubilee lines. The RB1, RB2 & RB6 **river bus** services (see p55) stop at both Bankside and London Bridge City piers.

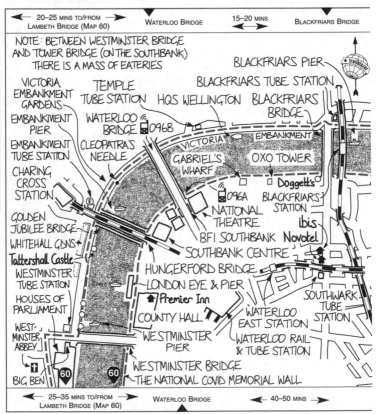

W ← Tower Bridge to Putney Bridge: southern bank
Route shown on following maps – **Map 61** p229, **Map 60** p225, **Map 59** p220

TOWER BRIDGE: southern bank
[Map 61]

Tower Bridge, the city's most impressive bridge and the only one that can open for shipping, is also one of the river's more recent crossing points. By the 1870s a million people lived east of London Bridge but with no way across the river and congestion rife it was conceded that a new crossing was needed, though one that still allowed large ships through to discharge their cargo at the Pool of London (see box on pp232-3). As a result, a part-suspension, part-fixed bridge design was agreed. Built in 1894, its medieval appearance is meant to complement the nearby Tower of London.

Tower Bridge Exhibition (☎ 020 7403 3761, 🖳 towerbridge.org.uk; Apr-Sep daily 9.30am-6pm, Oct-Mar to 5pm; £10.60), actually on the bridge, allows you up on to the bridge's walkways and also into its engine rooms.

There is a branch of *Premier Inn* (see p21; London Tower Bridge Hotel; ☎ 0333 321 1275, 🖳 premierinn.com) at 159

MAP 61

ST PAUL'S CATHEDRAL
YHA St Paul's
MILLENNIUM BRIDGE
The Samuel Pepys
SOUTHWARK BRIDGE
BANKSIDE PIER
TATE MODERN
Swan at the Globe
GLOBE THEATRE
GOLDEN HINDE
The Anchor Premier Inn
Bankside SOUTHWARK
BOROUGH MARKET
SOUTHWARK CATHEDRAL
The Mudlark
The London Banker
LONDON BRIDGE CITY PIER
LONDON BRIDGE TUBE
THE SHARD
LONDON BRIDGE STATION

TOWER GATEWAY DLR
TOWER HILL TUBE STATION
FENCHURCH STREET STATION
CANNON STREET STATION
LONDON BRIDGE
THE TOWER OF LONDON
TOWER PIER
UPPER REACHES OF HISTORIC POOL OF LONDON
HAY'S GALLERIA
CITY HALL
HMS BELFAST
TOWER BRIDGE EXHIBITION
SAINSBURY'S LOCAL
EATERIES
Travelodge
097B
62
LOCK STATUE
62
EATERIES
TOWER BRIDGE 097A
Premier Inn

LONDON BRIDGE ← 20-25 MINS → ← 15-20 MINS → TOWER BRIDGE

LONDON BRIDGE ← 15-20 MINS → TOWER BRIDGE

0   ¼ mile
0   APPROX SCALE   500m

ROUTE GUIDE AND MAPS

Tower Bridge Rd and a Sainsbury's Local (Mon-Sat 7am-11pm) **supermarket** on the western corner of Tower Bridge Rd and Queen Elizabeth St. The nearest **railway station** is London Bridge (see p228 and box pp56-7). London Bridge is also a stop on the Jubilee & Northern tube lines (see pp54-5).

[For details about services on the northern side of the river see pp234-5].

E ➜ Putney Bridge to Tower Bridge: northern bank

FULHAM   [Map 59, p220]
(See also p220) **Hurlingham Park** is an 8-hectare park which was originally part of Hurlingham Club (a prestigious private social and athletic club) and used as their polo grounds. In 1951 this land was bought by London County Council to be used as a park for everyone.

On Townmead Rd there is a large branch of Sainsbury's (daily 7am-11pm), the **supermarket** chain.

IMPERIAL WHARF   [Map 59, p221]
Chelsea Harbour is a large development with luxury flats, a marina and a hotel.

At *The Waterside* (☎ 020-7371 0802, 🖥 watersideimperialwharf.co.uk; food Mon-Sat 10am-10pm, Sun 11am-9pm; WI-FI; 🐾) the menu includes classic pub meals as well as more unusual dishes such as monkfish curry, saffron wild rice & crispy shallots (£21). On Lots Rd its namesake pub,

Lots Road (☎ 020-7352 6645, 🖥 lotsroad chelsea.co.uk; food Mon-Fri noon-3pm & 5-10pm, Sat & Sun noon-9pm; WI-FI; 🐾) offers a limited menu which may include ratatouille stuffed wellington (£13.50).

Both London Overground & Southern services (see pp56-7) stop at **Imperial Wharf** railway station. The RB6 **river bus** (see p55) calls at Chelsea Harbour pier.

CHELSEA
[Map 59, p221; Map 60, p224]
The Mercian king Offa called a synod (a council) here in the 8th century, though these days you're more likely to hear discussions about flowers than debates between Saxon monarchs.

Founded in 1673, **Chelsea Physic Garden** (Map 60; ☎ 020-7352 5646, 🖥 chelseaphysicgarden.co.uk; Apr-early Nov Mon-Fri, Sun & Bank Holidays 11am-5pm; £13.50) is the second oldest botanic garden in England and one of the most important botanical centres in the world. The entrance is on Swan Walk. The **Royal Hospital Chelsea**, home to veterans of the British Army, is the site of Chelsea Flower Show (see p15) every May.

For **Sloane Square tube station** (Circle/District lines) turn left at Chelsea Bridge and walk along Chelsea Bridge Rd; this becomes Lower Sloane St and it leads to Sloane Square.

The RB6 **river bus** service (see p55) stops at Cadogan Pier.

PIMLICO / MILLBANK
[Map 60, pp224-5]
Tate Britain (☎ 020-7887 8888, 🖥 tate.org .uk/visit/tate-britain; daily 10am-6pm; free except for special exhibitions) is an art gallery that focuses on British art from 1500 to the present day; it was first opened in 1897. See also box p46.

On Grosvenor Rd there is a Shell petrol station with a **convenience store** (24hrs) and an **ATM** (£1.85).

The menu at *The Grosvenor* (☎ 020-7821 8786; **fb**; WI-FI; 🐾; **food** daily 11am-9.30pm) includes burgers from £9.50 and the extensive menu at *Morpeth Arms* (☎ 020-7834 6442, 🖥 morpetharms.com; food daily 10am-9pm; WI-FI; 🐾 in bar) has sandwiches (from £7.50), small plates (from £4.50) and mains such as pork and chorizo sausages with Jersey royals, roast tomato & garlic salsa (£14). Also on Millbank is a branch of *Pizza Express* (☎ 020-7976 6214, 🖥 pizzaexpress.com; Thur-Sat noon-10pm, Sun-Wed to 9pm; WI-FI). Pizzas of all types are available (from £9.95).

Pimlico **tube station** (Victoria line), on Bessborough St, is a short way from Vauxhall Bridge. Victoria station, about 10 minutes' walk along Vauxhall Bridge Rd,

has both tube (District, Circle & Victoria lines) and railway services (operated by Southern, box pp56-7). Victoria Coach Station (see p53) is on Buckingham Palace Rd, about a 10-minute walk from the railway station. The RB2 & RB6 **river boat** services (see p55) stop at Millbank (Millennium) pier.

WESTMINSTER
[Map 60, p225; Map 61, p228]
Westminster is of course the area of London with the most iconic buildings.

Westminster Abbey was founded in AD960 as a Benedictine monastery, but rebuilt by King Edward and again (1245-69) by Henry III in the Gothic style. Since 1066 it has been the setting for virtually all coronations and is the burial site of many English and British monarchs. Note that the opening days and hours at the Abbey (Map 61; ☎ 020-7222 5152, 🖥 westminster-abbey.org; £18) vary and it can be closed at short notice so check in advance.

The Palace of Westminster is home to both the United Kingdom's **Houses of Parliament** (Map 61; ☎ 020-7219 4114, 🖥 www.parliament.uk) – and commonly referred to as such – and Big Ben. A medieval palace, built in 1097, used to occupy this site though a fire destroyed most of the original building in 1834. Today's replacement opened in 1867. The Houses of Parliament comprise the House of Commons and the House of Lords.

See the website for details about visiting the Houses of Parliament.

While **Big Ben** is the name often used to refer to Parliament's tower, its actual name is **Elizabeth Tower**, Big Ben being the nickname of the tower's bell – and its actual title is the Great Bell. Peering down at the river from the palace's northern end since 1858, the Elizabeth Tower is perhaps the most iconic London building. An £80 million five-year restoration of the clock and the tower will be completed in 2022. The familiar black clock face is now blue.

Victoria Tower Gardens (daily from 7am, generally in summer to 9pm and in winter to 4pm) is home to some memorials including **Buxton Memorial** which commemorates the emancipation of slaves following the 1833 Slavery Abolition Act; and, by the northern entrance, a statue of Suffragette leader Emmeline Pankhurst.

Westminster **tube station** (Circle/District/Jubilee lines) is by Westminster Bridge. The RB1, RB2 & RB6 **river boat** services (see p55) stop at Westminster Pier.

CHARING CROSS [Map 61, p228]
Since 2002 **Hungerford Bridge**, a railway bridge, has had pedestrian bridges (called **Golden Jubilee**) either side providing a convenient way to cross the river. **Cleopatra's Needle** is one of the many statues and monuments along the embankment but it is perhaps unusual because it stood by the banks of the River Nile for 3000 years; it was moved to its current location in 1878.

Anchored at Hungerford Bridge is *The Tattershall Castle* (☎ 020-7839 6548, 🖥 thetattershallcastle.co.uk; WI-FI; 🐾 deck

only; food daily 11am-10pm), a **floating restaurant**, aboard which the menu includes pie of the day (£15).

This area is a transport hub with **Embankment tube station** (Circle, District & Bakerloo) by the river and **Charing Cross railway** (Southeastern; see box on pp56-7) and **tube** (Northern & Bakerloo lines) stations a few minutes' walk inland. The RB1, RB2 & RB6 **river boat** services (see p55) stop at Embankment Pier. Further east, **Temple tube** station is a stop on the Circle & District lines.

ROUTE GUIDE AND MAPS

BLACKFRIARS (northern bank)
[Map 61, pp228-9]

Blackfriars Bridge marks the western boundary of the City of London; the railway bridge next to it is unusual in that the bridge itself acts as the station (Southeastern & Thameslink; see box on pp56-7). The platforms can be accessed from both the northern and southern banks.

Blackfriars is also a stop on the tube (Circle & District lines) and the RB1 and RB6 river bus services (see p55; peak hours only).

❑ LONDON'S BRIDGES

Until relatively recently it was believed that the **Romans** were the first to build a bridge across the Thames in London. However, in 2001 the study of a number of wooden stakes discovered in the riverbed close to Vauxhall Bridge led archaeologists to wonder if there had once been a walkway across the river that dated back to the **Bronze Age**. Caesar came and went in 55BC and again the following year, though he never mentioned a bridge, Bronze Age or otherwise, and he and his troops forded the river instead. But his Roman compatriots who followed a century later, in AD43, built a bridge across the Thames in approximately AD47. This wooden bridge traversed the river a little downstream from today's London Bridge and was built so that the Roman roads of Stane Street (from Chichester) and Watling Street (from Kent), which met at the Thames, could connect with the road continuing north-west across the Midlands. (The Romans built another bridge across the Thames at Staines, but these were the only two. Preferring to move troops and goods by fording the river or ferry, it would appear that they saw bridges as strategic weak links.)

Over the following half century this wooden Roman bridge was replaced with a more permanent stone edifice; however, following the Roman desertion of the British Isles, the bridge too disappeared and it is not known what happened to this crossing.

In 994 the **Vikings** ransacked London. This would lead to the Anglo-Saxons building *their* first bridge across the river: lying low across the water, it was a defensive barrier as much as a crossing point. Not that this deterred the Vikings. In 1014 King Olaf of Norway simply attached his boats to the bridge with cables, waited for the tide, and pulled it down.

The **Anglo-Saxons** would build a number of wooden bridges in the vicinity of London to try to protect both their capital and the populace upstream but they were forever falling foul of the tides and inadequate construction. Indeed, their London Bridge was such a frequent victim that the bridge's numerous disasters are believed to have been the inspiration behind the nursery rhyme '*London Bridge is falling down*.'

So it was left to the **Normans** to place the first lasting structure across the river. Built with stone, **Old London Bridge** was completed in 1209, having taken 30 years to construct. Miraculously, considering the lifespan of other London bridges, it lasted six centuries until 1831 when it was replaced with a new bridge – which in 1973 was replaced with today's structure. Boasting 19 small arches, Old London Bridge acted as a weir when the tide came in and the difference in the height of the waters on either side of the bridge could be several feet. The bridge was covered in houses and shops and in winter the water about the bridge – its flow slowed by the tiny arches – could freeze, leading to what would become known as 'Frost Fairs' where thousands of people would take to the ice to skate and frolic.

Blocking off the river to all but the smallest craft meant that traders approaching the city from the sea had to moor below the bridge, so creating the **Pool of London**

CITY OF LONDON [Map 61, p229]

St Paul's Cathedral (Map 61; general enquiries ☎ 020-7246 8350, 🖳 stpauls.co .uk; Mon-Sat noon-4.30pm; £20, £17 online in advance) was designed by Christopher Wren and its construction in the late 17th century was part of London's rebuilding programme following the Great Fire of London in September 1666. Its iconic dome is the subject of many a post-card and, famously, it somehow avoided the German bombs during the Blitz.

The **Millennium Bridge** is a pedestrian bridge (see box below) which provides great vistas particularly north to St Paul's Cathedral and south to the Tate Modern (see p227).

(see box pp198-9 and p239) – the stretch of the Thames immediately downstream of London Bridge. It also meant the area of land directly about the bridge – The City – accumulated massive wealth from this riverine trade.

It was to be five centuries after the construction of Old London Bridge before the London Thames would be traversed again in either wood or stone. The City had a vested interest in keeping their monopoly over the Old London Bridge and any plans for a second bridge were also opposed by the ferrymen and watermen who plied their trade carrying people across the river; another bridge, they predicted, would lead to the demise of their business. But in 1726 King George I finally gave the go-ahead for a new wooden bridge to be built at Fulham (Putney Bridge). A fair distance from London Bridge, its construction was begrudged by those whose livelihoods it threatened. Opposition was greater still for the next bridge though in 1736 the king once again accepted the case for a new crossing at Westminster and an Act of Parliament granted it the final go-ahead. Opening in 1750, the arrival of **Westminster Bridge** was to be a watershed moment.

With Old London Bridge's monopoly broken the City finally gave up its struggle and began to build more bridges, the first being **Blackfriars** in 1769. The City of London's crossings were free but the idea of building a bridge to the west of the Square Mile and charging a toll attracted much private enterprise. **Chelsea** (1776), **Vauxhall** (1816), **Waterloo** (1817) and **Southwark** (1819) were all originally **toll bridges**. Their charge, however, merely led to congestion at the City of London's bridges – people preferring not to pay a toll if it wasn't necessary. The City's response was to purchase Southwark Bridge in 1866 and remove the charge, so 'freeing' the bridge and relieving congestion at its own bridges. The 'freeing' of a further 11 bridges would occur in 1877 thanks to their purchase by the Metropolitan Board of Works, a body initially formed to construct the city's sewers and a precursor to London's County Council (1889-1965). **Albert Bridge** (1873) is the only one of London's bridges still to have its toll booths. For information about Tower Bridge see p229.

Most of the bridges that span the Thames today between Kingston and the Tower Bridge have been rebuilt; the oldest still standing is **Richmond** (1777). The newest is the **Millennium Bridge** (2002). There are three combined rail and pedestrian bridges: Barnes, Fulham and the Golden Jubilee footbridges at Hungerford Railway Bridge. Plans for new bridges, primarily pedestrian/cycle bridges, are often being proposed but are either stalled by objections from residents and/or a lack of funding.

If you still have energy after a day's walking consider going to see the art installation (**Illuminated River**; 🖳 illuminatedriver.london) that is transforming the appearance of nine bridges (London Bridge to Lambeth Bridge) till 2am every night; each bridge is lit differently and has an LED light display. The installation was completed in 2021 and is expected to last at least 10 years.

At 26 Carter Lane, near the iconic landmark of St Paul's Cathedral, is *YHA London St Paul's* (☎ 0345-371 9012, or ☎ 020-7236 4965, 💻 yha.org.uk/hostel/london-st-pauls; 213 beds: 5 x 1-, 6 x 2-, 8 x 3-, 9 x 4-, 8 x 5-, 6 x 6-, 1 x 7-, 4 x 8-, 1 x 10- & 1 x 11-bed rooms, shared facilities but one en suite). The hostel has male & female dorms and some rooms have double beds. See p19 for further details.

Finding somewhere to eat could not be easier. Diverting from the path will lead to innumerable pubs, cafés, takeaways and restaurants. On Stew Lane, off Upper Thames St, is *The Samuel Pepys* (☎ 020-7489 1871, 💻 samuelpepys.pub; food Wed-Fri noon-3pm & 5-9pm; WI-FI; small 🐾); it is a fairly sedate place and the menu includes sandwiches from £5.50, small plates such as vegetable gyoza (£6.50) and burgers (from £12.95).

Fuller's *The Banker* (☎ 020-7283 5206, 💻 banker-london.co.uk; food Mon noon-8pm, Tue-Fri to 10pm; WI-FI; small 🐾) is on Cousin Lane. Unlike the profession after which it is named, this place is quite popular, with a menu including sharer boards (£12.50-23.50). Note this pub is only open Monday to Friday.

Cannon Street **railway station** (Southeastern & Thameslink; see box on pp56-7) can be accessed from this stretch of the river. Cannon Street is also a stop on the Circle & District **tube** lines. See also pp54-5 for information about public transport in London.

W ← Tower Bridge to Putney Bridge: northern bank
Route shown on following maps – **Map 61** p229, **Map 60** p225, **Map 59** p220

W ← TOWER BRIDGE TO PUTNEY BRIDGE [MAPS 61-59]

[Route section begins on Map 61, pp228-9] Both sides of the river have plenty to savour; the northern side is a **10-mile (16km, 3¼-4¼hrs)** walk with highlights such as the Tower of London and Westminster. However, the **9¼-mile (14.7km, 3½-4¾hrs)** section on the southern bank probably edges it, primarily due to it encompassing both the excitement of London's Southbank area and the greenery of Battersea Park. The views of the Tower of London and Westminster are also splendid from the southern side. The best part of the northern bank is the area around Westminster and the stretch between Tower Bridge and Millennium Bridge. Indeed, with the stage being quite short and so many bridges en route, there's no reason not to cross the river as often as takes your fancy! Before starting off, see the box on p219.

[Next route overview on p222]

TOWER BRIDGE: northern bank
[Map 61, p229]
[For details about both the bridge and services on the southern bank see p229]
The Tower of London was once the city's most feared building and the home of many an infamous inmate. The Tower (Map 61; 💻 hrp.org.uk/TowerOfLondon; Mar-Oct daily 9am-5.30pm; Nov-Feb same but to 4.30pm; £29.90, offpeak £28.90) has served as many things – fortress, Royal palace, home to both the Crown Jewels and for 600 years a menagerie of exotic wild animals, prison (one of its most famous prisoners being Anne Boleyn), place of execution, arsenal and mint – during its 900-plus year history. Construction was begun by William the Conqueror in 1078 and has been guarded by the Yeoman Warders (nicknamed 'Beefeaters') since Tudor times.

On the eastern side of Tower Bridge is a Tesco Metro (daily 6am-midnight) **supermarket** with an ATM.

There are numerous transport options; the closest stations are **Tower Gateway** (DLR line; see box pp56-7) and **Tower Hill** (District/Circle lines) for the **tube**.

The RB1, RB2 & RB6 **river bus** services (see p55) stop at Tower pier.

Note that Tower Bridge is the last place you can cross to the southern side of the river on foot if you aren't happy at the thought of walking through Greenwich Foot Tunnel (see p239).

Where to stay and eat

There are branches of *Premier Inn* (Map 62; London City Tower Hill; ☎ 0333 321 1245, ▢ premierinn.com), at 22-24 Prescot St, and also *Travelodge* (Map 61; London

Central Tower Bridge; ☎ 0871-984 6388, ▢ travelodge.co.uk), at Goodmans Yard, here. See p21 for general information about both chains.

There are plentiful **chain cafés** plying their trade about the Tower of London and there is a selection of **eateries** on St Katherine's Way (north of St Katherine's Dock). Options include: *Côte Brasserie* (▢ cote.co.uk); *Slug & Lettuce* (▢ slugandlettuce.co.uk), *Café Rouge* (▢ caferouge .com) and many more. Many open for breakfast and serve food all day.

E ➜ TOWER BRIDGE TO GREENWICH   [MAPS 61-63]

With the goal in sight this stage is just **6¾ miles (11km, 2¼-3hrs)** in length on the northern bank (including the walk in the tunnel) and even shorter at **5¾-mile (9.2km, 2-2½hrs)** on the southern bank.

Both banks get you away from the tourists and famous historic sites: on the **northern bank** you see another side of the city at **London Docklands** (see box p239) but this route means you need to burrow under the river in the Greenwich Foot Tunnel (see p239) as the bifurcated trail becomes one once more. The **southern bank** offers the history of the Rotherhithe area and may be preferable if you don't want to go down into Greenwich Foot Tunnel.

See below for the northern bank route and p239 for the southern.

E ➜ Tower Bridge to Greenwich: northern bank

WAPPING   **[Map 62, pp236-7]**

Once pastures and fields, Wapping has changed a lot over the centuries. What was once a tenement slum that became depopulated by the rise of the city's 19th-century docks, the area was devastated by the blitz before blossoming, thanks to the post-war closure of the docks, into today's modern area, full of luxury apartment blocks and estate agents. The route through here is at times awkward as you walk along a mixture of cobbled road and embankment.

St Katherine's Docks were the last of London's docks to be built (see box on pp232-3 & p239) but now converted to a mixed-use development with apartment blocks, hotels, restaurants, shops and a marina.

On Wapping High St you'll find a **convenience store**, Docklands General Store (daily 7.30am-8pm), and two historic **pubs**. At *Town of Ramsgate* (☎ 020-7481 8000,

▢ townoframsgate.pub; food Mon-Sat noon-4pm, Mon-Thur 5-9pm, Fri & Sat 5-10pm, Sun noon-9pm; WI-FI; 🐾) there's a fine selection of pub classics on the menu (pies from £11.50) whilst at *Captain Kidd* (☎ 020-7480 5759; food Mon-Sat 12.30-2.30pm & 6.30-8.30pm, Sun noon-4pm; 🐾) there's your normal cheap Samuel Smith drinks and meals such as a decent Sunday roast from £11.95.

Along **Wapping Wall** and claiming to be London's oldest riverside inn is *The Prospect of Whitby* (☎ 020-7481 1095, ▢ greeneking-pubs.co.uk; food Mon-Sat noon-10pm, Sun to 9pm; WI-FI; 🐾); it has a large selection of food including their 'Big Fish & Chips' (£15.99). All three pubs have **beer gardens** overlooking the river.

Wapping **railway station** (London Overground line; see box pp56-7) is on Wapping High St.

LIMEHOUSE   **[Map 62]**

Meaning 'place of lime oasts', lime kilns operated here from the 14th century until 1935. Known for shipbuilding in the 18th century and for its opium dens in the 19th, the area long had a seedy reputation. Decimated by the closures of the nearby docks in the 1960s, Limehouse, like Wapping, is now an area dominated by expensive apartments. A convenient place to stay is *Holiday Inn Express* (London Limehouse; see p21; ☎ 020-7791 3850, 🖥 ihg.com/holidayinn express).

On Narrow St there is a **shop**, Riverside Store (daily 7am-9.30pm), which has an **ATM** (£1.65) and also a tremendous

ROUTE GUIDE AND MAPS

← 40–50 MINS TO/FROM TOWER BRIDGE (MAP 61) →   WAPPING STATION   ← 40–50 MINS →

PRESCOT ST
SHADWELL BASIN SHADWELL
The Prospect of Whitby
Premier Inn
DOCK ST VAUGHAN WAY
PARK
ST KATHERINE'S DOCKS
WAPPING HIGH ST
WAPPING
61 SMITH'S
WAPPING WALL
DOCKLANDS GENERAL STORE
Town of Ramsgate
WAPPING RAILWAY STATION
The Mayflower
WATERSIDE GARDENS
Captain Kidd
STEPS
STATUE
61 IGNORE SIGNPOST
ALLEY
LONDON DOCKLANDS
BRUNEL RD
RAILWAY AVE
SURREY WATER
THROUGH ARCHWAY
ALLEY
BRUNEL MUSEUM
The Salt Quay
EAST LANE
CHAMBERS ST
The Angel
ST MARY'S
JAMAICA RD
ST SAVIOURS & DOCK BRIDGE
THAMES TIDEWAY
ROTHERHITHE ST
ROTHERHITHE RAILWAY STATION
BERMONDSEY TUBE STATION
ROTHERHITHE
BERMONDSEY
YHA London Thameside
MAP 62

0   ¼ mile
0 APPROX SCALE 500m

← 30–40 MINS TO/FROM TOWER BRIDGE (MAP 61) →   BRIDGE (ROTHERHITHE ST)

pub: as brimming in character as they come, *The Grapes* (☎ 020-7987 4396, 🖥 thegrapes.co.uk; food Mon-Fri noon-3.30pm & 6.30-9.30pm, Sat & Sun noon-9.30pm; 🐕 downstairs) has a traditional Victorian long bar and a terrace hovering over the Thames. Who knows, maybe it was the 'Surf & Turf' (£11.95), or the taste of 'The Grapes Sliders' (£10.95) which

once compelled Charles Dickens to dance on the tables here? Note that they may close in the afternoon (4-6pm) during the week.

The Narrow (☎ 020-7592 7950, 🖥 gordonramsayrestaurants.com/the-narrow; food Mon-Sat noon-10.30pm, Sun to 9.30pm; WI-FI; 🐕) is foul-mouthed TV chef Gordon Ramsay's contribution to the local cuisine. The menu varies but may

include ricotta and basil ravioli, cherry tomatoes, black olives & pesto (£19). Booking is advisable, especially if you want a table on the terrace.

CANARY WHARF   [Map 62, p237]

Part of **West India Docks** – once the busiest in the world – Canary Wharf (⌨ canary wharf.com) takes its name from the cargoes of fruit which used to be disembarked here from the Canary Islands and Mediterranean. Since the dock's closure and subsequent regeneration the area has been transformed into London's second business district (after The City) with some of the tallest office buildings in Britain. It is also a huge shopping centre with plenty of options for eating and drinking.

By the river there are several **restaurants** around Westferry Circus though most are unlikely to appeal to the humble rambler: *Gaucho* (⌨ gauchorestaurants.com; Sun-Thur noon-11pm, Fri & Sat 11am-11pm) for Argentinian steaks; *Royal China* (⌨ royalchinagroup.co.uk); daily noon-9pm)

Limehouse DLR station (Map 62) is a short way from the path; adjacent to it is **Limehouse railway station** – c2c's services (see box pp56-7) call here.

for all things Chinese and *Mala Kitchen & Bar* (⌨ www.malarestaurant .com; Tue-Sun noon-3pm & 6-10.30pm) for North Indian food.

Up the colourful steps, *Café Brera* (⌨ www.cafebrera.com; Sun-Wed 10am-11pm, Thur-Sat to midnight) is an Italian café and bakery. Pasta and pizza dishes start from £9.50 and if you have a sweet tooth there are delicious desserts (from £5.80).

Canary Wharf, Heron Quays and South Quay are stops on the **DLR** (see box pp56-7) and Canary Wharf is also on the Jubilee (**tube**) line.

The RB1 & RB6 **river bus** (see p55) services call at the pier; the RB4 crosses the river between the pier and (Doubletree Docklands) Nelson Dock Pier (Map 62).

ISLE OF DOGS   [Map 63, pp240-1]

Originally Stepney Marshes, the name 'Isle of Dogs' (actually a peninsula, not an island) possibly derives from the fact that Tudor monarchs kept their hunting hounds here. Decimated by the Blitz and the closures of the docks, the area, as with Millwall, doesn't feel as if it's been rewarded with quite the same level of regeneration as its western neighbours which reside closer to the city.

Greenwich (see pp243-4) remains the best option for a range of food on this stage but for those who need a drink or lunch before they even contemplate walking beneath the river there is a pub and a restaurant, *Ferry House* (☎ 020-7537 7813, ⌨ ferrygood.co.uk; bar daily noon-11pm; WI-FI; 🐾); it dates from around 1722 and is the oldest pub on the island. At the time of research they weren't serving food though

---

❏ 'PRIVATE PROPERTY'

The purpose of walking the Thames Path is to be as close to the river as possible. But in London many residential developments are making this daunting – you will see signs saying 'Private property' and 'No right of way' and that there are CCTV cameras. Developers were often given permission to build as long as they agreed to provide pedestrian access to walkways along the river for Thames Path walkers – they were allowed to offer a permissive path (sometimes with time/day restrictions) rather than a right of way. This makes it hard for walkers to know where they can and can't legally walk. However, many of the boroughs in London are now trying to change this and hopefully soon walking by the river will feel more welcoming. In the interim if you see people walking there and/or a Thames Path sign you can feel reassured.

❏ LONDON DOCKLANDS

Between the start and end of the 18th century the number of ships mooring in the **Pool of London** (see the boxes on pp198-9 and pp232-3) trebled until, by the 19th century, it had become the world's greatest seaport. With the river becoming so heavily congested crime became rife, boats would have to wait for days to disembark their cargo and pollution increased. Something had to be done. The solution was to carve out huge swathes of land, beginning on the Isle of Dogs, to create what would become known as the London Docklands, the construction of which would irrevocably change the city's landscape once again. The first docks to be constructed were **West India Docks** (now Canary Wharf), which opened in 1802; when the last, **St Katherine's Docks**, opened in 1828, it meant that the Docklands had spread all the way back to the City and the Pool of London, where their story begun.

Badly damaged by the Blitz and deemed redundant by the advent of both 'containers' and ever larger ships, which the docks and river could not accommodate, the demise of the docks occurred swiftly in the late 1960s. In 1981 Margaret Thatcher created the **London Docklands Development Corporation**, which, offering investors the opportunity to develop free of planning controls and commercial rates, proved a remarkable success and led to foreign investment flooding in, so leading to the affluence of much of the old dockland areas which you walk through today.

they hope to in 2022. If you have had enough of pub food consider *Kinko Thai* (☎ 020-7987 7999, 🖳 www.kinkao.co.uk; food Mon-Fri noon-3pm & 5.30-11pm, Sat noon-midnight, Sun to 11pm); the menu is extensive and mains start from around £10.

There is a **DLR station** at Island Gardens (see box pp56-7) and the RB1 **river bus** (see p55) calls at Masthouse Terrace Pier. **Greenwich Foot Tunnel** (open 24hrs) was built to replace an unreliable ferry and enable workers to get to work on the other side of the river; it was opened in 1902 and can be accessed by both stairs and lifts. Not surprisingly this connects Island Gardens with Greenwich.

W ← Greenwich to Tower Bridge: northern bank
Route shown on following maps – **Map 63** p241, **Map 62** p236, **Map 61** p229

E → Tower Bridge to Greenwich: southern bank

BERMONDSEY   [Map 62, p236]

Appearing in *The Domesday Book* as 'Bermundesy', initially Bermondsey was developed by the monks of the local 11th-century Benedictine Abbey. The 18th century saw the area's growth as a manufacturing centre specialising in tanning and the production of glue; old trades which are still evident in some of the road names – such as Tanner St. By the 19th century the coming of industrialisation and the docks led to the area being one of the worst slums in London; Charles Dickens immortalised the notorious Jacob's Island rookery in *Oliver Twist*, with his character Bill Sikes meeting a true villain's end here. A 20th-century riverscape of warehouses and wharves was targeted during the Blitz and fell further into decline after the war. As a result, the Bermondsey of today certainly feels far more upmarket than one imagines its predecessors to have been.

The Angel (☎ 020-7394 3214; bar open all day, food daily 1-3pm & 5.30-9pm; 🐾 on ground floor only) is a Samuel Smith boozer and the menu includes sandwiches from £5.95 and mains from £8.95.

Bermondsey is a stop on the **tube** (Jubilee Line).

ROUTE GUIDE AND MAPS

ROTHERHITHE [Map 62, pp236-7]

Rotherhithe's main claims to fame are its (former) shipyards and tunnels.

It was from here in 1620 that *The Mayflower* set sail for Southampton, then Plymouth, en route to the New World; a **statue** (The Sunbeam Weekly and The Pilgrim's Pocket) on Cumberland Wharf marks the approximate spot where *The Mayflower* departed. The captain of the boat, Christopher Jones, returned to Britain in 1621 but died a year later; he is buried at **St Mary's Church**.

Rotherhithe also plays host to two tunnels under the Thames – Thames Tunnel was the first built under a river anywhere in the world; the other is Rotherhithe Tunnel. Thames Tunnel was designed by Sir Marc Brunel and his son, Isambard Kingdom Brunel, played a key role in its construction. Their work is celebrated at **The Brunel Museum** (☎ 020-7231 3840, 💻 thebrunel museum.com; Sat & Sun 11am-5pm; £6). If **Surrey Docks Farm** (☎ 020-7231 1010, 💻 surreydocksfarm.org.uk; gates open daily

summer 10am-5pm, winter to 4pm; free but donation requested), a working inner-city farm, is open simply pass through but if not follow the diversion signs or consult Map 62. *Barn Kiosk* (daily 9am-4.30pm) serves hot and cold drinks, biscuits and cakes from £1.85 and sandwiches (inc vegan) from £3.95. At the time of research the toilets here were closed but they hope to open them in 2022. A Co-op **convenience store** (daily 7am-10pm) is on Rotherhithe St near Globe Wharf.

YHA London Thameside (☎ 0345-371 9756, 💻 yha.org.uk/hostel/yha-london-thameside; 70 rooms; 2-, 3-, 4-, 5-, 6- & 10-bed rooms, all en suite) is at 20 Salter Rd. Some rooms have double beds and the rooms for 3/5 people have a pull-out bed. Rates vary but a dorm bed may cost from £15pp, and a private room for up to two people from £35. See p19 for more information.

The Mayflower (☎ 020-7237 4088, 💻 mayflowerpub.co.uk; food Mon-Sat noon-10pm, Sun to 9pm; 🐕 in bar only) was built in the 17th century and was originally

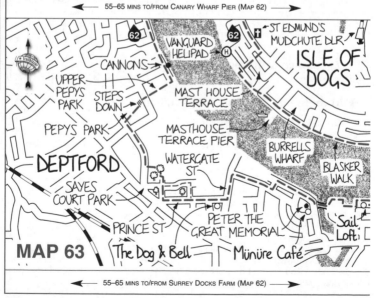

MAP 63

55–65 MINS TO/FROM CANARY WHARF PIER (MAP 62)

55–65 MINS TO/FROM SURREY DOCKS FARM (MAP 62)

called *The Spread Eagle*, but the name was changed in 1957 to commemorate Rotherhithe's role in *The Mayflower*'s voyage. The Mayflower has a visitors' book for descendants from the actual *Mayflower* and it is the only pub in Britain licensed to sell both US & UK postage stamps; ask at the bar for both. The pub has guest ales and the menu focuses on standard pub food with burgers (from £12.95) and a pie of the day (£13.95); baguettes (from £7.50) are available Mon-Fri noon-3pm.

The Salt Quay (☎ 020-7394 7108, 🖥 greeneking-pubs.co.uk; food Mon-Sat noon-9pm, Sun to 8pm; WI-FI; 🐾 downstairs only) has an extensive menu full of pub classics (from about £10) and sandwiches

(from £6.79); there are also several vegan options. Meanwhile, *The Blacksmith's Arms* (☎ 020-7231 8838, 🖥 theblack smithsse16.com; food Mon-Fri 4-9.45pm, Sat noon-9.45pm, Sun to 8.45pm; WI-FI; 🐾 in bar and garden) offers British and Thai fare including fish & chips (£13.95) and pad Thai (from £11.95).

Rotherhithe's **railway station** (London Overground line, see box pp56-7) is a short walk from the path.

The RB4 **river bus** service operates between Doubletree Docklands (Nelson Dock Pier) and Canary Wharf. Further south the RB1 **river bus** calls at Greenland Pier (Surrey Quays). See p55 for more details about both.

DEPTFORD [Map 63]
There now follows a stint pacing residential streets, fortunately split by the occasional pretty park. However, the area played an important part in Britain's naval history, being the site of the first royal dockyard due to Henry VIII; ships were built and

maintained here and the dockyard was in use for over 300 years, though sadly now derelict. Many famous names including Peter the Great studied shipbuilding there; the **Peter the Great Memorial** celebrates that he went on to found the Russian Navy.

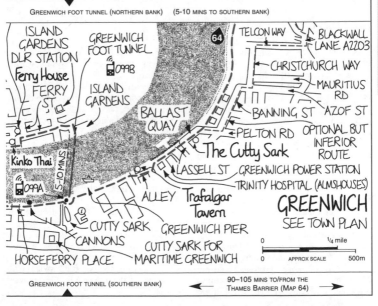

There has been a pub here since 1741 but you can't miss *The Dog and Bell* (**fb**; WI-FI; 🐾; food Mon-Sat noon-3pm & 6-9pm, Sun 12.30-3.30pm) with its bright red paint. They serve real ales and craft beers but expect standard pub food (burgers around £10) with roasts on a Sunday.

Münüre Café (Tue-Thur 8am-6pm, Fri & Sat to 8pm, Sun 9am-8pm; WI-FI; 🐾)

small dogs) serves hot and cold drinks, cakes and baguettes (from £4) and, at lunchtime, omelettes (£6). A bit away from the crowds of Greenwich, *Sail Loft* (☎ 020-8222 9310, 🖥 sailloftgreenwich.co.uk; food Mon-Sat noon-10pm, Sun to 8pm; WI-FI; 🐾) is a Fuller's pub and the menu includes standard fare but also dishes such as Norfolk chicken Kiev (£16).

W ← Greenwich to Tower Bridge: Southern bank
Route shown on following maps – **Map 63** p241, **Map 62** p236, **Map 61** p229

W ← GREENWICH TO TOWER BRIDGE   [MAPS 63-61]
[Route section begins on Map 63, pp240-1] Since the trail bifurcates at Greenwich Foot Tunnel, from here till Teddington you can walk on either the southern or northern bank of the river. Whichever you choose this is a relaxing day; just **6¾ miles (11km, 2¼-3hrs)** on the northern bank (including the walk in the tunnel) and even shorter at **5¾-mile (9.2km, 2-2½hrs)** on the southern bank. On the northern bank you see another side of the city at Canary Wharf and **London Docklands** (see box on p239) before you reach the tourists and famous historic sites. The **southern bank** offers the history of the Rotherhithe area and will be preferable if you don't want to go down into Greenwich Foot Tunnel.   *[Next route overview p234]*

GREENWICH
As a UNESCO World Heritage Site, Greenwich has plenty of history. The site of the 15th-century Palace of Placentia, where both Henry VIII and Elizabeth I were born, is now the **Old Royal Naval College** (☎ 020-8269 4747, 🖥 ornc.org; grounds 8am-11pm; free) with the current twin-domed Christopher Wren-designed master-piece built between 1696 and 1712. A high-light is the painted hall (daily 10am-5pm, £12.50, valid for a year), the UK's Sistine Chapel; tickets are sold in the visitor centre (see below).

Greenwich Tourist Information Centre (☎ 020-8305 5235, 🖥 visitgreenwich.org.uk; daily 10am-5pm) is in the **Discover Greenwich Visitor Centre** (same hours; free); this has a deluge of maps, pamphlets and guidebooks detailing the town's historic sites and museums, including the Naval College, **National Maritime Museum**, and **Royal Observatory**. Standing at the latter you are at the Prime

Meridian of the World: Longitude 0. For further information on Greenwich's royal museums or visiting the Cutty Sark, consult the website.

Greenwich Market (🖥 greenwichmarket.london; daily 10am-5.30pm) has food, antiques, fashion and jewellery stalls.

Unless planning to follow the northern bank to Tower Bridge you will probably just walk past the entrance to the **Greenwich Foot Tunnel** (see p239).

Supermarkets include an M&S Simply Food (Mon-Sat 8am-10pm, Sun 9am-9pm) and the **chemist** Boots (Mon-Sat 9am-6pm, Sun 10am-6pm) near the Cutty Sark. **ATMs** can be found outside Cutty Sark DLR station.

Greenwich has a **DLR station** (Cutty Sark for Maritime Greenwich) near the river and a **railway station** (Southeastern) and another DLR station (Greenwich) a little further inland. For details of services see box pp56-7.

The RB1 **river bus** (see p55) service stops at Greenwich pier.

Where to stay and eat

Right by Greenwich station is a branch of *Novotel* (London Greenwich; ☎ 020 7660 0682), part of the Accor chain (see p21; 💻 all.accor.com); also part of this chain is the *ibis* (London Greenwich; ☎ 020-8305 1177), on Greenwich High Rd.

Pub food can be found adjacent to the Visitor Centre at *The Old Brewery* (☎ 020-3437 2222, 💻 oldbrewerygreenwich.com; WI-FI; 🐾; food Mon-Sat 10am-9pm, Sun to 8.30pm), with lovely outside seating and a menu consisting of sandwiches (Mon-Fri noon-3pm; from £7.50) and mains such as pork sausages with carrot & potato mash, cumin spiced tomato salsa, crispy shallots & gravy (£13.50).

A short way back from the river is *The Gipsy Moth* (☎ 020-8858 0786, 💻 thegipsy mothgreenwich.co.uk; **fb**; food daily noon-10pm; WI-FI; 🐾). There's outdoor seating; the extensive menu includes a pale ale & steak pie with spring greens and chips or mash (£15) to chomp on as you watch Greenwich Mean Time go by.

There are also two decent pubs further along the path and away from the tourist masses. *Trafalgar Tavern* (Map 63; ☎ 020-3887 9886, 💻 trafalgartavern.co.uk; food Mon-Sat noon-10pm, Sun to 9pm; WI-FI; 🐾 in bar only) has a large menu including Trafalgar whitebait (£7.50), although the whitebait no longer come fresh from the river as they did in days gone by; while *The Cutty Sark* (Map 63; ☎ 020-8858 3146, 💻 cuttysarkse10.co.uk; food Mon-Sat 11am-10pm, Sun noon-9pm; WI-FI; 🐾 in bar) also

ROUTE GUIDE AND MAPS

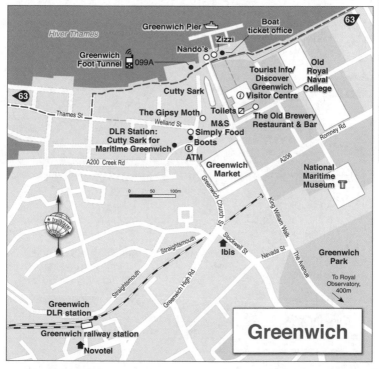

Greenwich

serves whitebait (£6.50) and has an interesting menu with options such as small plates (from £4.50), sharers and main dishes (both from £13). The pub has an outdoor area by the river. Chicken lovers will find a *Nando's*

(☎ 020-8269 1770, 🖳 nandos.co.uk; daily 11.30am-10pm; WI-FI) by the entrance to the foot tunnel; while nearby is a *Zizzi* (☎ 020-3581 9819, 🖳 zizzi.co.uk; daily 11.30am-10pm) serving Italian food.

E → GREENWICH TO WOOLWICH   [MAPS 63-65]

And so, via weir, lock and bridge, on footpath, bridleway and road, you've made it to this your final stage of the Thames Path. This stretch is **5½ miles (8.6km, 1¾-2¼hrs)** and the official path is only on the southern side of the river. The route goes round the North Greenwich peninsula and on to the Thames Barrier. Once at Woolwich Foot Tunnel your riverside odyssey will be at an end.

NORTH GREENWICH (PENINSULA)
                                          [Map 64]
Built in 1999 to house an exhibition celebrating the start of the third millennium

(and at that time called the Millennium Dome) **The O2** (🖳 theo2.co.uk) was opened as an indoor events arena in 2007.

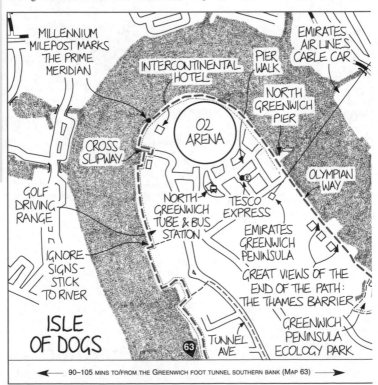

Should you want to feel you have had some elevation on your Thames Path walk consider climbing up and over the dome (from £32 – see the website for details.)

For an aerial perspective of this stretch of London consider a 'flight' on **Emirates Airlines Cable Car** (⌨ emiratesairline.co .uk, Apr-end Sep Mon Fri/Sat/Sun 7/8/9am-11pm, rest of year Mon-Thur/Fri/Sat/Sun 7/7/8/9am-10/11/11/10pm; one-way £5, £4 with Oyster card/contactless) to Emirates Royal Docks – and hopefully also back to continue on the path. **Greenwich Peninsula Ecology Park** (⌨ tcv.org.uk/

greenwichpeninsula; Wed-Sun 10am-5pm) is a freshwater habitat where wildlife – in what otherwise is a landscape of metal, concrete and stone – somehow thrives.

In the central area there is a **Tesco Express** (daily 6am-11pm) supermarket with an ATM, next door is Mangal Pharmacy (Mon-Fri 8.30am-7pm, Sat 10am-7pm, Sun 2-6pm) and all around is a range of **eateries** (such as branches of Wagamama and Subway).

North Greenwich is a stop on the Jubilee **tube** line; the RB1 **river bus** service (see p55) calls at North Greenwich pier.

CHARLTON [Map 64]

The *Anchor and Hope* (☎ 020-8858 0382, ⌨ anchorandhope.co.uk; food Mon-Fri 11am-5.45pm, Sat to 4pm, Sun 1-4pm; WI-

FI; 🐾 outside) is a friendly place where you can take advantage of the outdoor seating to stare out over the river but also of course sit

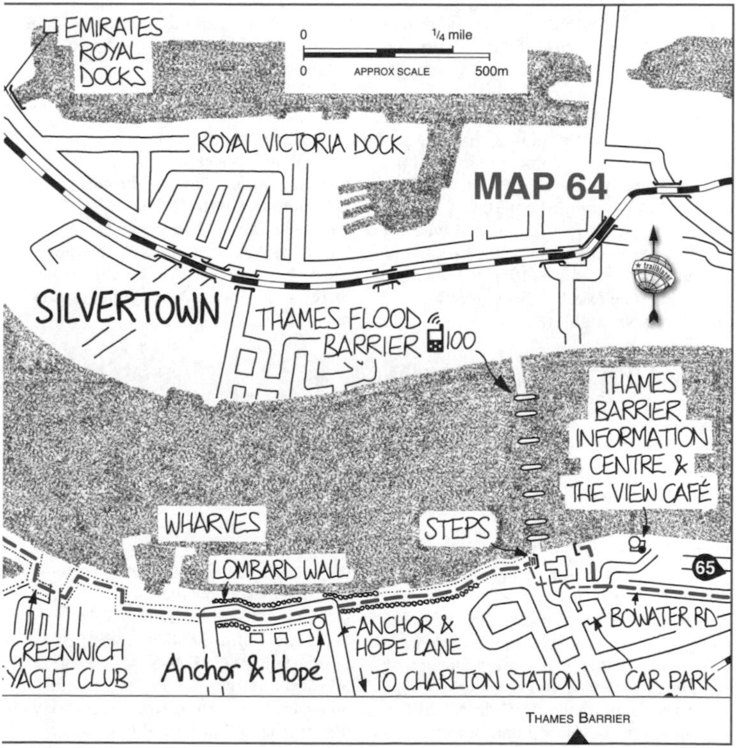

MAP 64

EMIRATES ROYAL DOCKS

ROYAL VICTORIA DOCK

0 ¼ mile
0 APPROX SCALE 500m

SILVERTOWN

THAMES FLOOD BARRIER 📷100

THAMES BARRIER INFORMATION CENTRE & THE VIEW CAFÉ

WHARVES

LOMBARD WALL

STEPS

65

GREENWICH YACHT CLUB

Anchor & Hope

ANCHOR & HOPE LANE

TO CHARLTON STATION

BOWATER RD

CAR PARK

THAMES BARRIER

ROUTE GUIDE AND MAPS

❑ **THE THAMES BARRIER**

Owing to the rather ominous fact that London – indeed the whole of the south-east of England – has been sinking, over the decades the city has grown ever more vulnerable to those very waters which gave it life: those of the River Thames. The embankments have to some effect held back the river's waters but in the 1950s it was estimated that in order to cope with the ever-rising tides the city's defences would have to be raised by another 6ft. And so plans for some form of barrier began. Work was started on the Thames Barrier in 1974 and completed in 1982, officially opening in 1984.

One of the largest moveable flood barriers in the world, it protects some 125 square kilometres of Central London. First used to fend off a dangerous tide in February 1983, between then and June 2021 it had been closed 199 times. Run by the Environment Agency since 1996, it stretches 520 metres across the river and comprises 10 steel gates which can be raised across the river whenever a tidal surge is predicted. When raised, the barrier's main gates are as high as a five-storey building and are as wide as the opening of Tower Bridge.

The barrier is tested once a month (see the website for the actual dates) and it is projected to remain effective against rising sea levels until 2030.

inside. The menu includes standard pub food but also Winkles seafood bar (Fri-Sun noon-5pm).

THAMES BARRIER   [Map 64,p245]
At the time of writing this is the (eastern) end of the Thames Path though by the time you are here it may have been officially extended to Woolwich Foot Tunnel.

Whichever direction you are walking you'll go through a tunnel with a profile of the Path – from Kemble (105m) to sea level (0m); this is an excellent way to reflect on/ anticipate your journey.

Charlton **railway station** (Southeastern; see box pp56-7) is about half a mile south from here.

The park on the eastern side of the barrier (see box above) has a good viewing spot for the barrier piers. **Thames Barrier Information Centre** (☎ 020-8305 4188, 🖳 gov.uk/the-thames-barrier) will be open only for pre-booked visits in 2022 but after that check their website for details. However, there are some interesting information boards outside the centre.

W ← WOOLWICH TO GREENWICH   [MAPS 65-63]

[Route section begins on Map 65, opposite] This first stretch of the trail is an easy **5½ miles (8.6km, 1¾-2¼hrs)** walk from Woolwich Foot Tunnel via the Thames Barrier and North Greenwich peninsula; the official path is only on the southern side of the river.   *[Next route overview on p242]*

WOOLWICH   [Map 65]
It is thought that the name 'Woolwich' derives from it being used as a port/trading settlement for sheep bred in the area. But Henry VIII is probably the person most responsible for the area's development as a naval and military base as he ordered a royal dockyard to be built here; later military weapons were developed and made here –

the Royal Arsenal was established in 1805, though it closed in 1994.

For a **supermarket** there is a M&S Food Hall (Mon-Fri 8.30am-10pm, Sat to 9pm, Sun 11.30am-5.30pm) next to Woolwich railway station (Elizabeth Line) and there's a **post office** (Mon-Fri 9am-5.30pm, Sat to 2pm) on Powis St.

Where to stay and eat

Convenient **accommodation** options for your first or last night are the branches of **Premier Inn** (London Woolwich Royal Arsenal; ☎ 0333 234 6542, 🖳 premierinn .com) and **Travelodge** (London Woolwich; ☎ 08719 846510, 🖳 travelodge.co.uk). See p21 for details of both chains. The historic arsenal site is the best place to eat and there

are two characterful pubs. **Dial Arch** (☎ 020-3130 0700, 🖳 dialarch.com; food Mon-Sat 10am-10pm, Sun to 9pm; WI-FI; 🐕) is in a restored armoury but also has a lot of seating outside including 'garden pods'. The extensive menu includes bar snacks, such as pork & chorizo scotch egg (£6.50), and mains such as steak & ale pie with salad & fries (£17.50). **The Guard**

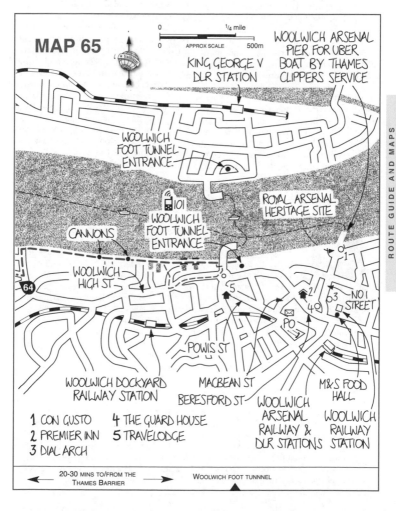

MAP 65

0   ¼ mile

0   APPROX SCALE   500m

KING GEORGE V DLR STATION

WOOLWICH ARSENAL PIER FOR UBER BOAT BY THAMES CLIPPERS SERVICE

WOOLWICH FOOT TUNNEL ENTRANCE

ROYAL ARSENAL HERITAGE SITE

101

WOOLWICH FOOT TUNNEL ENTRANCE

CANNONS

WOOLWICH HIGH ST

64

5

1

2

3

4

NO 1 STREET

PO

POWIS ST

WOOLWICH DOCKYARD RAILWAY STATION

MACBEAN ST

BERESFORD ST

WOOLWICH ARSENAL RAILWAY & DLR STATIONS

M&S FOOD HALL

WOOLWICH RAILWAY STATION

1 CON GUSTO   4 THE GUARD HOUSE
2 PREMIER INN   5 TRAVELODGE
3 DIAL ARCH

← 20-30 MINS TO/FROM THE THAMES BARRIER →

WOOLWICH FOOT TUNNEL

ROUTE GUIDE AND MAPS

House (☎ 020-3437 0900, 🖥 theguard
housewoolwich.co.uk; food Mon-Sat 10am-
10pm, Sun to 9pm; WI-FI; 🐕) is, as its name
suggests, the original guard house building
and even if you eat outside it is worth looking around inside. The menu may include
caramelised apricot and sage sausages with
crispy hispi cabbage & nduja potatoes
(£14.25).

Right by the Uber Thames Clipper
dock is *Con Gusto* (☎ 020-8465 7452, 🖥
congusto.co.uk; **fb**; Wed-Sat 6-9.30pm), an
Italian restaurant with a limited menu. The
pasta is home-made and the menu may
include tagliatelle with slow-cooked beef
ragû & peas (£13); takeaway available.

Transport

There is a myriad of transport options. By
train, Southeastern's (see box on pp56-7)
services call at both Woolwich Dockyard
and Woolwich Arsenal stations. Woolwich
Arsenal is also a stop on Thameslink's services and the DLR line to London City
Airport (or Bank/Tower Gateway). The
Elizabeth Line (Woolwich station; see box
on p52) may finally open in mid 2022.

To reach the northern bank walkers are
recommended to use **Woolwich Foot
Tunnel** (open 24hrs a day; lifts and steps)
as **Woolwich Ferry** (Mon-Sat 6.10am-8pm
4-8/hr; Sun 11.30am-7.30pm 3-4/hr; free)
is primarily for vehicles and anyhow services were suspended early in 2022 due to
engineering works.

East of the foot tunnel is **Woolwich
(Royal Arsenal) pier**. Unfortunately, during the week there are only **river bus** services (see p55) in the early morning and
then late afternoon and evening, though at
the weekend there is a shuttle service
(2/hr) to North Greenwich where you can
pick up the main services. Despite these
limitations this is the most enjoyable way
to arrive or leave – you will get a very different perspective on what you have just
walked or are about to walk.

❏ **THE THAMES PATH ENGLAND COAST PATH**

The Thames Path used to have a 10-mile (16km) extension path
(identified by a sailing barge icon rather than the acorn used for
national trails) to Crayford Ness, which linked up with the London
Loop. However, on 12th January 2022 this became Thames Path
England Coast Path (TPECP); the whole route is from Woolwich
Foot Tunnel east to Grain (Isle of Grain) on the Hoo Peninsula, in
all 47 miles (76km). Thus the approximate overall distance from the source (at Thames
Head) to the sea, via the southern bank in London, is 232 miles/374km. Some signs for
the TPECP have gone up but those for the extension path have not yet been removed.

The TPECP mostly goes along the coast though there are a few inland sections;
the route is obvious and it is flat, easy walking. However, flooding can be an issue. The
path passes near mudflats, saltmarshes and grazing marshes so there is a variety of
wildlife; highlights include Swanscombe Peninsula (an SSSI) and RSPB Cliffe Pools
(open all the time; free). Birds that may be spotted include: redshank, avocet, knot,
dunlin, sandpiper, oystercatcher, marsh harrier, egret, wheatear and little grebe.

Services are limited, unless you are happy to walk inland a bit, so taking a packed
lunch and plenty of water is recommended.

OS Explorer 162 (Greenwich & Gravesend) & 163 (Gravesend & Rochester)
maps and OS Landranger 177 (East London) & 178 (Thames Estuary) cover the area.

Convenient railway stations (apart from those in Woolwich) include Erith, Slade
Green, Greenhithe and Gravesend; services are operated by Southeastern. At the Isle of
Grain the only option is a bus; Arriva Kent & Surrey's No 191 (Mon-Sat 9/day, Sun
4/day) service operates between Grain and Chatham via Rochester railway station.
Rochester is a stop on both Southeastern and Thameslink services.

APPENDIX A: GPS WAYPOINTS

MAP	REF	GPS WAYPOINT	DESCRIPTION
1	001	N51 41.673 W2 01.783	Thames Head (source of the River Thames)
1	002	N51 40.806 W2 00.903	Cross A429
2	003	N51 40.587 W1 59.723	T-junction at Ewen
3	004	N51 39.099 W1 58.477	Join/leave road at Somerford Keynes
4	005	N51 38.817 W1 56.167	Ashton Keynes
4	006	N51 38.352 W1 54.844	Car park at Waterhay
5	007	N51 39.096 W1 52.525	Cross bridge by North Meadow NNR
5	008	N51 38.656 W1 51.291	Cricklade High St
7	009	N51 38.656 W1 49.345	Bridge crossing river
8	010	N51 39.657 W1 47.479	The Red Lion, Castle Eaton
8	011	N51 39.753 W1 44.921	Join/leave road by Hannington Bridge
10	012	N51 40.642 W1 42.594	Footbridge
10	013	N51 41.041 W1 42.269	Inglesham
10	014	N51 41.535 W1 41.571	Halfpenny Bridge
10	015	N51 40.895 W1 40.119	Buscot Lock
11	016	N51 41.261 W1 38.127	Turning to Kelmscott
12	017	N51 41.612 W1 35.324	Radcot Bridge
13	018	N51 41.910 W1 32.038	Bridge at Rushey Lock
13	019	N51 42.100 W1 31.040	Tadpole Bridge
13	020	N51 41.705 W1 29.342	Tenfoot Bridge
14	021	N51 42.414 W1 27.871	Shifford Lock
15	022	N51 42.613 W1 25.033	Bridge in Newbridge
15	023	N51 42.972 W1 22.633	Northmoor Lock
16	024	N51 44.103 W1 22.331	The Ferryman Inn
17	025	N51 45.619 W1 21.858	Pinkhill Lock
17	026	N51 46.459 W1 21.539	Swinford Toll Bridge
18	027	N51 47.346 W1 18.441	Kings Lock
18	028	N51 46.766 W1 17.996	Godstow Bridge
19	029	N51 46.010 W1 17.189	Turning to The Perch
19	030	N51 45.159 W1 16.334	Osney Bridge
20	031	N51 44.753 W1 15.384	Folly Bridge
20	032	N51 44.144 W1 14.543	Cross under B4495
21	033	N51 42.484 W1 13.982	Sandford Lock
22	034	N51 41.118 W1 13.324	Turning to Lower Radley and Radley
23	035	N51 40.294 W1 16.260	Abingdon Lock
23	036	N51 40.098 W1 16.726	Abingdon Bridge
24	037	N51 39.045 W1 15.961	Sutton Bridge (Culham)
25	038	N51 38.904 W1 12.663	Clifton Lock
25	039	N51 39.280 W1 12.659	Join road to cross bridge at Clifton Hampden
25	040	N51 38.304 W1 10.747	Day's Lock
26	041	N51 38.085 W1 09.988	Turning to Dorchester-on-Thames
26	042	N51 38.082 W1 08.901	Path joins/leaves A4074
26	043	N51 37.514 W1 08.360	Shillingford Bridge
27	044	N51 37.008 W1 06.969	Benson Lock
27	045	N51 36.058 W1 07.271	Cross Wallingford High St
28	046	N51 35.229 W1 07.464	A4130 (bridge over Thames)
29	047	N51 33.519 W1 08.588	Footbridge under two viaducts
29	048	N51 32.873 W1 08.888	Turning off/join A329
30	049	N51 31.381 W1 08.675	Bridge at Streatley

MAP	REF	GPS WAYPOINT	DESCRIPTION
31	050	N51 30.132 W1 06.369	Path leaves/joins river
32	051	N51 29.205 W1 05.129	Whitchurch Bridge (toll bridge)
33	052	N51 29.200 W1 02.412	Mapledurham Lock
33	053	N51 28.171 W0 59.766	Reading Thames-side Promenade starts/ends
34	054	N51 27.930 W0 58.653	Caversham Bridge
35	055	N51 28.030 W0 55.730	Footpath enters/leaves trees
35	056	N51 28.528 W0 54.810	Sonning Bridge
37	057	N51 30.702 W0 52.947	Path leaves/joins road
37	058	N51 31.646 W0 53.082	Southern end of long bridge
38	059	N51 32.253 W0 54.048	Henley Bridge
39	060	N51 33.607 W0 52.416	Hambleden Lock
39	061	N51 33.074 W0 52.214	The Flower Pot Inn
40	062	N51 33.043 W0 48.662	Hurley Lock
40	063	N51 34.052 W0 46.407	Marlow Bridge
41	064	N51 34.527 W0 42.823	Bourne End railway bridge
42	065	N51 33.602 W0 42.425	Cookham High St
42	066	N51 33.009 W0 41.530	Little bridge by fence
43	067	N51 31.449 W0 42.219	Maidenhead Bridge
44	068	N51 30.442 W0 41.158	M4 crosses river
44	069	N51 29.940 W0 40.830	National Cycle Network signpost
45	070	N51 29.391 W0 38.834	St Mary Magdalene church, Boveney
46	071	N51 29.151 W0 36.497	Windsor Bridge
46	072	N51 29.273 W0 35.493	Victoria Bridge
47	073	N51 28.278 W0 35.012	Albert Bridge
48	074	N51 26.942 W0 34.019	National Trust Tea Rooms, Runnymede
48	075	N51 26.240 W0 32.124	Path under M25
48	076	N51 26.012 W0 30.996	Staines Bridge
49	077	N51 24.880 W0 29.977	Penton Hook Lock
50	078	N51 23.337 W0 29.154	Chertsey Bridge
51	079	N51 22.964 W0 27.427	Shepperton to Weybridge Ferry
51	080	N51 23.024 W0 26.179	Walton Bridge
52	081	N51 24.297 W0 24.380	Sunbury Lock
53	082	N51 24.514 W0 21.192	East Molesey Cricket Club
53	083	N51 24.209 W0 20.567	Hampton Court Bridge
53	084	N51 24.668 W0 18.475	Kingston Bridge
54	085	N51 25.854 W0 19.292	Bridge by Teddington Lock

Southern bank

MAP	REF	GPS WAYPOINT	DESCRIPTION
55	086a	N51 26.288 W0 19.729	Bridge at Ham Lands Nature Reserve
55	087a	N51 27.085 W0 18.158	Buccleuch Gardens
56	088a	N51 27.456 W0 18.376	Richmond Bridge
57	089a	N51 29.187 W0 17.261	Kew Bridge
57	090a	N51 28.358 W0 16.241	Chiswick Bridge
58	091a	N51 29.268 W0 13.867	Hammersmith Bridge
59	092a	N51 27.964 W0 12.851	Putney Bridge
59	093a	N51 27.829 W0 11.231	Wandsworth Bridge
60	094a	N51 28.880 W0 09.995	Gate by Albert Bridge
60	095a	N51 29.643 W0 07.265	Lambeth Bridge
61	096a	N51 30.432 W0 06.969	Waterloo Bridge
61	097a	N51 30.260 W0 04.587	Tower Bridge
62	098a	N51 29.963 W0 01.954	Surrey Docks Farm
63	099a	N51 28.992 W0 00.607	Greenwich Foot Tunnel

MAP	REF	GPS WAYPOINT	DESCRIPTION
Northern bank			
55	086b	N51 26.374 W0 19.953	Radnor Gardens
55	087b	N51 26.735 W0 19.763	Wharf Lane meets river
56	088b	N51 27.395 W0 18.504	Richmond Bridge
57	089b	N51 29.264 W0 17.263	Kew Bridge
57	090b	N51 28.182 W0 16.041	Chiswick Bridge
58	091b	N51 29.364 W0 13.779	Hammersmith Bridge
59	092b	N51 28.088 W0 12.743	Putney Bridge
59	093b	N51 27.947 W0 11.325	Wandsworth Bridge
59	094b	N51 28.991 W0 10.040	Albert Bridge
60	095b	N51 29.680 W0 07.486	Lambeth Bridge
61	096b	N51 30.582 W0 07.092	Waterloo Bridge
61	097b	N51 30.397 W0 04.462	Tower Bridge
62	098b	N51 30.345 W0 01.703	Canary Wharf pier
63	099b	N51 29.207 W0 00.561	Greenwich Foot Tunnel
Southern bank			
64	100	N51 29.690 E0 02.221	Thames Barrier
65	101	N51 29.666 E0 03.778	Woolwich Foot Tunnel

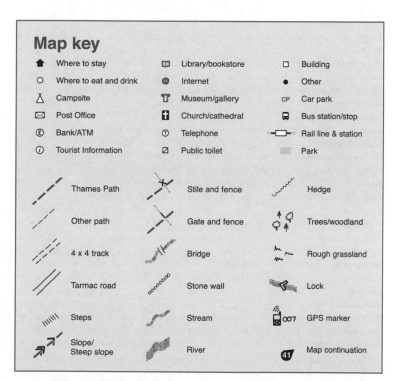

Map key

♠	Where to stay	📚	Library/bookstore	▫	Building
O	Where to eat and drink	@	Internet	●	Other
Λ	Campsite	🏛	Museum/gallery	CP	Car park
⊠	Post Office	✝	Church/cathedral	🚌	Bus station/stop
ⓔ	Bank/ATM	☎	Telephone	—▭—	Rail line & station
ⓘ	Tourist Information	☒	Public toilet		Park

	Thames Path		Stile and fence		Hedge
	Other path		Gate and fence		Trees/woodland
	4 x 4 track		Bridge		Rough grassland
	Tarmac road		Stone wall		Lock
	Steps		Stream	📱007	GPS marker
	Slope/ Steep slope		River	㊶	Map continuation

APPENDIX B: DISTANCE CHARTS

	Kemble	Ewen	Ashton Keynes	Cricklade	Lechlade	Radcot	Newbridge	Bablock Hythe	Eynsham Lock	Oxford	Sandford-on-Thames	Abingdon	Culham	Clifton Hampden	Shillingford	Benson	Wallingford
Kemble	0																
Ewen	2.7																
Ashton Keynes	7	4.2															
Cricklade	12.2	9.5	5.2														
Lechlade	23.2	20.5	16.2	11													
Radcot	30	27.2	23	17.7	6.7												
Newbridge	40	37.2	33	27.7	16.7	10											
Bablock Hythe	44	41.2	37	31.7	20.7	14	4										
Eynsham Lock	47.5	44.7	40.5	35.2	24.2	17.5	7.5	3.5									
Oxford	54	51.2	47	41.7	30.7	24	14	10	6.5								
Sandford-on-T	58.2	55.5	51.2	46	35	28.2	18.2	14.2	10.7	4.2							
Abingdon	63.7	61	56.7	51.5	40.5	33.7	23.7	19.7	16.2	9.7	5.5						
Culham	66	63.2	59	53.7	42.7	36	26	22	18.5	12	7.7	2.2					
Clifton Hampden	69	66.2	62	56.7	45.7	39	29	25	21.5	15	10.7	5.2	3				
Shillingford	74	71.2	67	61.7	50.7	44	34	30	26.5	20	15.7	10.2	8	5			
Benson	76	73.2	69	63.7	52.7	46	36	32	28.5	22	17.7	12.2	10	7	2		
Wallingford	77.2	74.5	70.2	65	54	47.2	37.2	33.2	29.7	23.2	19	13.5	11.2	8.2	3.2	1.2	
Moulsford	81.2	78.2	74.2	69	58	51.2	41.2	37.2	33.7	27.2	23	17.5	15.2	12.2	7.2	5.2	4
Goring & Streatley	84.2	81.5	77.2	72	61	54.2	44.2	40.2	36.7	30.2	26	20.5	18.2	15.2	10.2	8.2	7
Pangbourne	88.2	85.5	81.2	76	65	58.2	48.2	44.2	40.7	34.2	30	24.5	22.2	19.2	14.2	12.2	11
Caversham (Rdng)	95.2	92.5	88.2	83	72	65.2	55.2	51.2	47.7	41.2	37	31.5	29.2	26.2	21.2	19.2	18
Sonning	98.5	95.7	91.5	86.2	75.2	68.5	58.5	54.5	51	44.5	40.2	34.7	32.5	29.5	24.5	22.5	21.2
Lower Shiplake	102	99.2	95	89.7	78.7	72	62	58	54.5	48	43.7	38.2	36	33	28	26	24.7
Henley-on-Thames	105.4	102.7	98.4	93.2	82.2	75.4	65.4	61.4	57.9	51.4	47.2	41.7	39.4	36.4	31.4	29.4	28.2
Hurley	111.7	108.9	104.7	99.4	88.4	81.7	71.7	67.7	64.2	57.7	53.4	47.9	45.7	42.7	37.7	35.7	34.4
Marlow	113.9	111.2	106.9	101.7	90.7	83.9	73.9	69.9	66.4	59.9	55.7	50.2	47.9	44.9	39.9	37.9	36.7
Bourne End	117.2	114.4	110.2	104.9	93.9	87.2	77.2	73.2	69.7	63.2	58.9	53.4	51.2	48.2	43.2	41.2	39.9
Cookham	118.4	115.7	111.4	106.2	95.2	88.4	78.4	74.4	70.9	64.4	60.2	54.7	52.4	49.4	44.4	42.4	41.2
Maidenhead	121.7	119.9	114.7	109.4	98.4	91.7	81.7	77.7	74.2	67.7	63.4	57.9	55.7	52.7	47.7	45.7	44.4
Eton & Windsor	128.2	125.7	121.2	115.9	104.9	98.2	88.2	84.2	80.7	74.2	69.9	64.4	62.2	59.2	54.2	52.2	50.9
Datchet	130.2	127.4	123.2	117.9	106.9	100.2	90.2	86.2	82.7	76.2	71.9	66.4	64.2	61.2	56.2	54.2	52.9
Runnymede	133.7	130.9	126.7	121.4	110.4	103.7	93.7	89.7	86.2	79.7	75.4	69.9	67.7	64.7	59.7	57.7	56.4
Staines	136.7	133.9	129.7	124.4	113.4	106.7	96.7	92.7	89.2	82.7	78.4	72.9	70.7	67.7	62.7	60.7	59.4
Chertsey	140.2	137.4	133.2	127.9	116.9	110.2	100.2	96.2	92.7	86.2	81.9	74.2	71.2	66.2	64.2	62.9	58.9
Shepperton Lock	142.2	139.4	135.2	129.9	118.9	112.2	102.2	98.2	94.7	88.2	83.9	78.4	76.2	73.2	68.2	66.2	64.9
Walton-on-T*	144.2	141.4	137.2	131.9	120.9	114.2	104.2	100.2	96.7	90.2	85.9	80.4	78.2	75.2	70.2	68.2	66.9
Hampton Ct/E Mol	148.9	146.2	141.9	136.7	125.7	118.9	108.9	104.9	101.4	94.9	90.7	85.2	82.9	79.9	74.9	72.9	71.7
Hamptn W/Kingstn	152.2	149.4	145.2	139.9	128.9	122.2	112.2	108.2	104.7	98.2	93.9	88.4	86.2	83.2	78.2	76.2	74.9

* Reduce the distance walked from Shepperton Lock to Walton-on-Thames by 0.75 miles if you take the ferry

THAMES PATH
DISTANCE CHART 1

Kemble to Kingston-upon Thames

miles (approx) – 1 mile = 1.6km

	Moulsford	Goring & Streatley	Pangbourne	Caversham (Reading)	Sonning	Lower Shiplake	Henley-on-Thames	Hurley	Marlow	Bourne End	Cookham	Maidenhead	Eton & Windsor	Datchet	Runnymede	Staines	Chertsey	Shepperton Lock	Walton-on-Thames*	Hampton Court / East Molesey
Goring & Streatley	3																			
Pangbourne	7	4																		
Caversham (Reading)	14	11	7																	
Sonning	17.2	14.2	10.2	3.2																
Lower Shiplake	20.7	17.7	13.7	6.7	3.5															
Henley-on-Thames	24.2	21.2	17.2	10.2	6.9	3.4														
Hurley	30.4	27.4	23.4	16.4	13.2	9.7	6.2													
Marlow	32.7	29.7	25.7	18.7	15.4	11.9	8.5	2.2												
Bourne End	35.9	32.9	28.9	21.9	18.7	15.2	11.7	5.5	3.2											
Cookham	37.2	34.2	30.2	23.2	19.9	16.4	13	6.7	4.5	1.2										
Maidenhead	40.4	37.4	33.4	26.4	23.2	19.7	16.2	10	7.7	4.5	3.2									
Eton & Windsor	46.9	43.9	39.9	32.9	29.7	26.2	22.7	16.5	14.2	11	9.7	6.5								
Datchet	48.9	45.9	41.9	34.9	31.7	28.2	24.7	18.5	16.2	13	11.7	8.5	2							
Runnymede	52.4	49.4	45.4	38.4	35.2	31.7	28.2	22	19.7	16.5	15.2	12	5.5	3.5						
Staines	55.4	52.4	48.4	41.4	38.2	34.7	31.2	25	22.7	19.5	18.2	15	8.5	6.5	3					
Chertsey	55.9	51.9	44.9	43.9	41.7	38.2	34.7	28.5	26.2	23	21.7	18.5	12	10	6.5	3.5				
Shepperton Lock	60.9	57.9	53.9	45.9	43.7	40.2	36.7	30.5	28.2	25	23.7	20.5	14	12	8.5	5.5	2			
Walton-on-Thames*	62.9	59.9	55.9	47.9	45.7	42.2	38.7	32.5	30.2	27	25.7	22.5	16	14	10.5	7.5	4	2		
Hampton Court / East Molesey	67.7	64.7	60.7	53.7	50.4	46.9	43.5	37.2	35	31.7	30.5	27.2	20.7	18.7	15.2	12.2	8.7	6.7	4.7	
Hampton Wick / Kingston upon Thames	70.9	67.9	63.9	56.9	53.7	50.2	46.7	40.5	38.2	35	33.7	30.5	24	22	18.5	15.5	12	10	8	3.2

DISTANCE CHART 2
London – Northern Bank
miles (approx) – 1 mile = 1.6km

	H'ton / Ktn	Teddington Lock	Twickenham	Isleworth	Brentford	Strand on the Green	Hammersmith	Fulham	Chelsea	Pimlico	Westminster	City of London	Tower Bridge: northern bank	Wapping	Limehouse	Canary Wharf	Isle of Dogs	Charlton*
Hamptn W/K u T	0																	
Teddington Lock	2																	
Twickenham	3.5	1.5																
Isleworth	6.7	4.7	3.2															
Brentford	9	7	5.5	2.2														
Strand on the Gr	10.2	8.2	6.7	3.5	1.2													
Hammersmith	13.5	11.5	10	6.7	4.5	3.2												
Fulham	16.2	13.5	12.7	9.5	7.2	6	2.7											
Chelsea	19.7	17	16.2	13	10.7	9.5	6.2	3.5										
Pimlico	21	18.2	17.5	14.2	12	10.7	7.5	4.7	1.2									
Westminster	23.2	20.5	19.7	16.5	14.2	13	9.7	7	3.5	2.2								
City of London	25.2	22.5	21.7	18.5	16.2	15	11.7	9	5.5	4.2	2							
Tower Bridge	26.2	23.5	22.7	19.5	17.2	16	12.7	10	6.5	5.2	3	1						
Wapping	27.5	24.7	24	20.7	18.5	17.2	14	11.2	7.7	6.5	4.2	2.2	1.2					
Limehouse	28.7	26	25.2	22	19.7	18.5	15.2	12.5	9	7.7	5.5	3.5	2.5	1.2				
Canary Wharf	29.7	27	26.2	23	20.7	19.5	16.2	13.5	10	8.7	6.5	4.5	3.5	2.2	1			
Isle of Dogs	33	30.2	29.5	26.2	24	22.7	19.5	16.7	13.2	12	9.7	7.7	6.7	5.5	4.2	3.2		
Charlton*	37.5	34.7	34	30.7	28.5	27.2	24	21.2	17.7	16.5	14.2	12.2	11.2	10	8.7	7.7	4.5	

* Distance includes walking through the Greenwich Foot Tunnel

DISTANCE CHART 3
London – Southern Bank
miles (approx) – 1 mile = 1.6km

	H'ton / Kingston	Richmond	Mortlake	Barnes	Putney	Wandsworth	Battersea	Lambeth	Southwark	Tower Bridge: southern bank	Bermondsey	Rotherhithe	Greenwich	Charlton	Woolwich
Hamptn W/Kingstn	0														
Richmond	4.7														
Mortlake	9.5	4.7													
Barnes	10.2	5.5	0.7												
Putney	13.5	8.7	4	3.2											
Wandsworth	15	10.2	5.5	4.7	1.5										
Battersea	17.5	12.7	8	7.25	4	2.5									
Lambeth	19.5	16.7	12.5	9.2	6	4.5	2								
Southwark	21.5	18.7	14.5	11.2	8	6.5	4	2							
Tower Bridge	22.7	20	15.7	12.5	9.2	7.7	5.2	3.2	1.25						
Bermondsey	23.7	21	16.7	13.5	10.2	8.7	6.2	4.2	2.2	1					
Rotherhithe	24.7	22	17.7	14.5	11.2	9.7	7.2	5.2	3.2	2	1				
Greenwich	28.5	25.7	21.5	18.2	15	13.5	11	9	7	5.7	4.7	3.7			
Charlton	33	30.2	26	22.7	19.5	18	15.5	13.5	11.5	10.2	9.2	8.2	4.5		
Woolwich	34	31.2	27	23.7	20.5	19	16.5	14.5	12.5	11.2	10.2	9.2	5.5	1	

APPENDIX C: TAKING A DOG

TAKING DOGS ALONG THE PATH

Many are the rewards that await those prepared to make the extra effort required to bring their best friend along the trail. You shouldn't underestimate the amount of work involved, though. Indeed, just about every decision you make will be influenced by the fact that you've got a dog: how you plan to travel to the start of the trail, where you're going to stay, how far you're going to walk each day, where you're going to rest and where you're going to eat in the evening etc.

If you're also sure your dog can cope with (and will enjoy) walking 10 miles or more a day for several days in a row, you need to start preparing accordingly. Extra thought also needs to go into your itinerary. The best starting point is to study the village and town facilities tables on pp30-5 (and the advice below), and plan where to stop and where to buy food.

Looking after your dog

To begin with, you need to make sure that your own dog is fully **inoculated** against the usual doggy illnesses, and also up to date with regard to **worm pills** (eg Drontal) and **flea preventatives** such as Frontline – they are, after all, following in the pawprints of many a dog before them, some of whom may well have left fleas or other parasites on the trail that now lie in wait for their next meal to arrive. **Pet insurance** is also a very good idea; if you've already got insurance, do check that it will cover a trip such as this.

On the subject of looking after your dog's health, perhaps the most important implement you can take with you is the **plastic tick remover**, available from vets for a couple of quid. These removers, while fiddly, help you to remove the tick safely (ie without leaving its head behind buried under the dog's skin).

Being in unfamiliar territory also makes it more likely that you and your dog could become separated. For this reason, make sure your dog has a **tag with your contact details on** (a mobile phone number would be best if you are carrying one with you); the fact that all dogs now have to be **microchipped** provides further security.

When to keep your dog on a lead

● **When crossing farmland**, particularly in the lambing season (Mar-May) when your dog can scare the sheep, causing them to lose their young. Farmers are allowed by law to shoot at and kill any dogs that they consider are worrying their sheep. During lambing, most farmers would prefer it if you didn't bring your dog at all.

The exception is if your dog is being attacked by cows. Pretty much every year there are deaths in the UK caused by walkers being trampled as they tried to rescue their dogs from the attentions of cattle. The advice in this instance is to let go of the lead, head speedily to a position of safety (usually the other side of the field gate or stile) and, once there, call your dog to you.

● **In the presence of waterfowl** Ducks, swans and geese will not appreciate the approaches of your inquisitive hound.

● **Around ground-nesting birds** It's important to keep your dog under control when crossing an area where certain species of birds nest on the ground.

Most dogs love foraging around in the woods but make sure you have permission to do so; some woods are used as 'nurseries' for game birds and dogs are allowed through them only if they are on a lead.

● **At all locks** There's nearly always a sign at the start and end of every lock telling you to keep your dog on a lead; even if there isn't, assume you have to – it's only sensible.

What to pack

You've probably already got a good idea of what to bring to keep your dog alive and happy, but the following is a checklist:

● **Food/water bowl** Foldable cloth bowls are popular with walkers, being both light and taking up little room in a rucksack. You can also get a water-bottle-and-bowl combination, where the bottle folds into a 'trough' from which your dog can drink.

● **Lead and collar** An extendable one is probably preferable for this sort of trip. Make sure both lead and collar are in good condition – you don't want either to snap on the trail, or you may end up carrying your dog through sheep fields until a replacement can be found.

● **Medication** You'll know if you need to bring any lotions or potions.

● **Tick remover** See p255.

● **Bedding** A simple blanket may suffice, or you can opt for something more elaborate if you aren't carrying your own luggage.

● **Poo bags** Essential.

● **Hygiene wipes** For cleaning your dog after it's rolled in stuff.

● **A favourite toy** Helps prevent your dog from pining for the entire walk.

● **Food/water** Remember to bring treats as well as regular food to keep up your mutt's morale. That said, if your dog is anything like mine the chances are they'll spend most of the walk dining on rabbit droppings and sheep poo anyway.

● **Corkscrew stake** Available from camping or pet shops, this will help you to keep your dog secure in one place while you set up camp/doze.

● **Raingear** It can rain!

● **Old towels** For drying your dog.

How to pack

When it comes to packing, I always leave an exterior pocket of my rucksack empty so I can put used poo bags in there (for deposit at the first bin I come to). I always like to keep all the dog's kit together and separate from the other luggage (usually inside a plastic bag inside my rucksack). I have also seen several dogs sporting their own 'doggy rucksack', so they can carry their own food, water, poo etc – which certainly reduces the burden on their owner!

Cleaning up after your dog

It is extremely important that dog owners behave in a responsible way when walking the path. Dog excrement should be cleaned up. In towns, villages and fields where animals graze or which will be cut for silage, hay etc, you need to pick up and bag any excrement. If you're walking somewhere uncultivated and remote it's probably preferable for both you and the environment if you adopt the 'stick and flick' approach, grabbing hold of a nearby stick to flick the poo well away from the trail and the footwear of other walkers.

Staying and eating with your dog

In this guide the symbol 🐾 denotes where a hotel, pub or B&B welcomes dogs. However, this **always needs to be arranged in advance** and some places may charge extra (£2-20 per night or per stay). Also, many places have only one or two rooms suitable for people with dogs.

Hostels (both YHA and independent) do not permit them unless they are an assistance (guide) dog. Most campsites happily allow dogs through their gates but will have some restrictions in place, such as they must stay on a lead. When phoning to book a campsite, it's worth mentioning that you're walking with a dog as many will wish to check your pooch before allowing access.

When it comes to **eating**, most landlords allow dogs in at least a section of their pubs, though few restaurants do. Make sure you always ask first and ensure your dog doesn't run around the pub but is secured to your table or a radiator.

Henry Stedman

INDEX

Page references in red type refer to maps

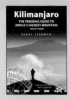

TRAILBLAZER TITLE LIST

Adventure Cycle-Touring Handbook
Adventure Motorcycling Handbook
Australia by Rail
Cleveland Way (British Walking Guide)
Coast to Coast (British Walking Guide)
Cornwall Coast Path (British Walking Guide)
Cotswold Way (British Walking Guide)
The Cyclist's Anthology
Dales Way (British Walking Guide)
Dorset & Sth Devon Coast Path (British Walking Gde)
Exmoor & Nth Devon Coast Path (British Walking Gde)
Great Glen Way (British Walking Guide)
Hadrian's Wall Path (British Walking Guide)
Himalaya by Bike – a route and planning guide
Iceland Hiking – with Reykjavik City Guide
Inca Trail, Cusco & Machu Picchu
Japan by Rail
Kilimanjaro – the trekking guide (includes Mt Meru)
London Loop (British Walking Guide)
London to Walsingham Camino
Madeira Walks – 37 selected day walks
Moroccan Atlas – The Trekking Guide
Morocco Overland (4x4/motorcycle/mountainbike)
Nepal Trekking & The Great Himalaya Trail
Norfolk Coast Path & Peddars Way (British Walking Gde)
North Downs Way (British Walking Guide)
Offa's Dyke Path (British Walking Guide)
Overlanders' Handbook – worldwide driving guide
Pembrokeshire Coast Path (British Walking Guide)
Pennine Way (British Walking Guide)
Peru's Cordilleras Blanca & Huayhuash – Hiking/Biking
Pilgrim Pathways: 1-2 day walks on Britain's sacred ways
The Railway Anthology
The Ridgeway (British Walking Guide)
Scottish Highlands – Hillwalking Guide
Siberian BAM Guide – rail, rivers & road
The Silk Roads – a route and planning guide
Sinai – the trekking guide
South Downs Way (British Walking Guide)
Thames Path (British Walking Guide)
Tour du Mont Blanc
Trans-Canada Rail Guide
Trans-Siberian Handbook
Trekking in the Everest Region
The Walker's Anthology
The Walker's Anthology – further tales
West Highland Way (British Walking Guide)

For more information about Trailblazer and our
expanding range of guides, for guidebook updates or
for credit card mail order sales visit our website:

www.trailblazer-guides.com

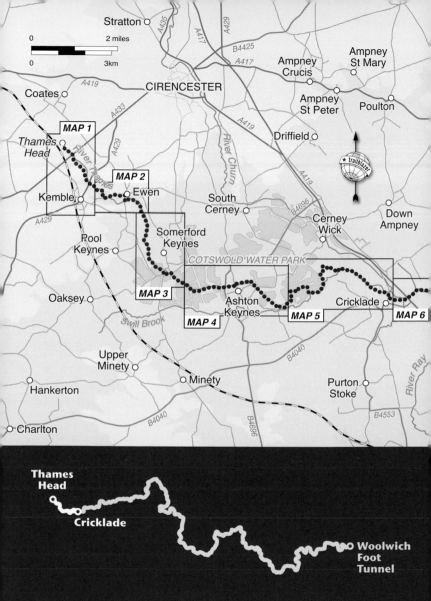

Maps 1 ↔ 5, Thames Head ↔ Cricklade

12¼ miles/19.7km – 4¼-5hrs

NOTE: Add 20-30% to these times to allow for stops

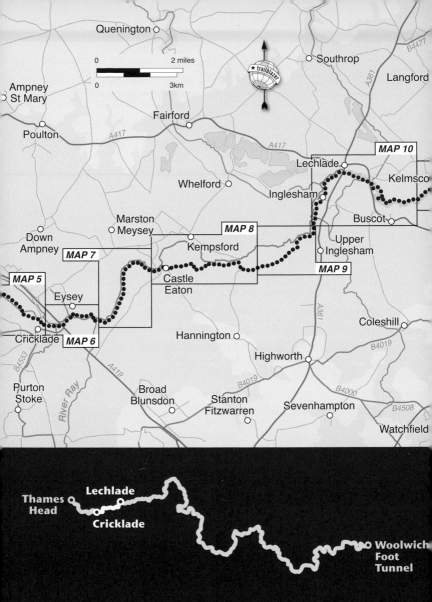

Maps 5 ↔ 10, Cricklade ↔ Lechlade
10¾ miles/17.3km – 3¾-4¾hrs

NOTE: Add 20-30% to these times to allow for stops

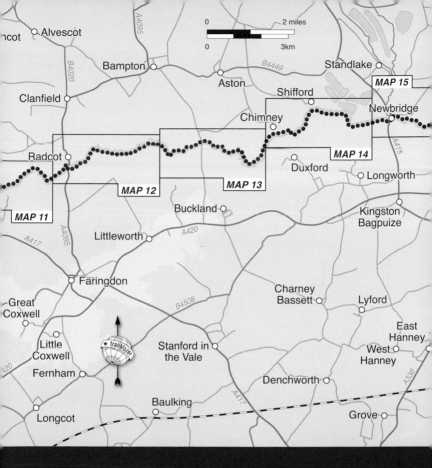

Maps 10 ↔ 15, Lechlade ↔ Newbridge
16¾ miles/26.7km – 5-6½hrs

NOTE: Add 20-30% to these times to allow for stops

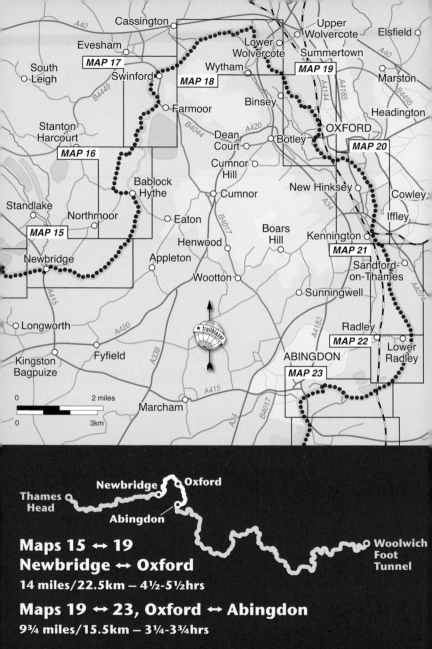

Maps 15 ↔ 19
Newbridge ↔ Oxford
14 miles/22.5km – 4½-5½hrs

Maps 19 ↔ 23, Oxford ↔ Abingdon
9¾ miles/15.5km – 3¼-3¾hrs

NOTE: Add 20-30% to these times to allow for stops

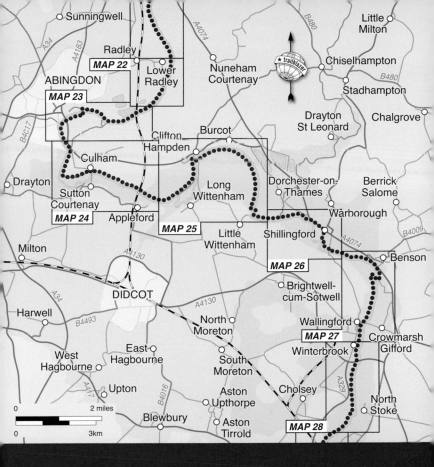

Maps 23 ↔ 27, Abingdon ↔ Wallingford

13½ miles/22km – 4½-5½hrs

NOTE: Add 20-30% to these times to allow for stops

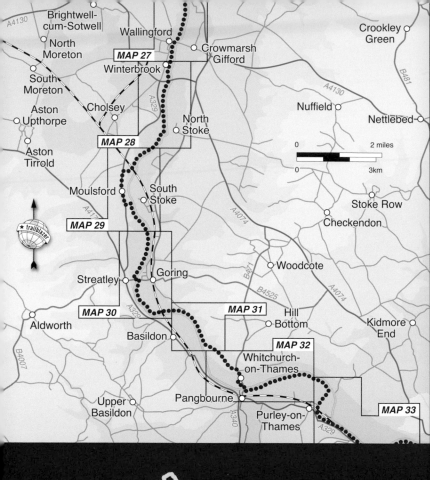

MAP 27

Brightwell-cum-Sotwell

Wallingford

Crowmarsh Gifford

Crookley Green

North Moreton

Winterbrook

South Moreton

Aston Upthorpe

Cholsey

Nuffield

Nettlebed

MAP 28

North Stoke

Aston Tirrold

Moulsford

South Stoke

Stoke Row

Checkendon

MAP 29

Streatley

Goring

Woodcote

Aldworth

MAP 30

MAP 31

Hill Bottom

Kidmore End

Basildon

MAP 32

Whitchurch-on-Thames

Upper Basildon

Pangbourne

Purley-on-Thames

MAP 33

trailblazer

0   2 miles
0   3km

Thames Head

Wallingford

Pangbourne

Woolwich Foot Tunnel

Maps 27 ↔ 32, Wallingford ↔ Pangbourne
11 miles/17.7km – 3¾-4¾hrs

NOTE: Add 20-30% to these times to allow for stops

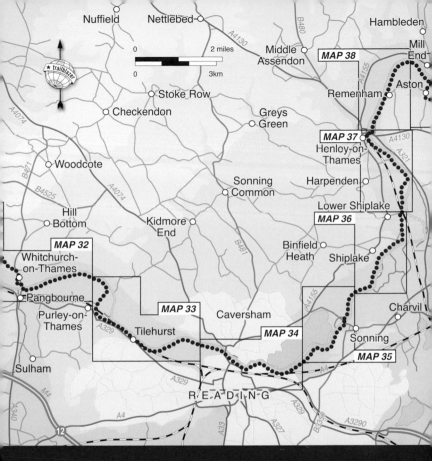

Maps 32 ↔ 37
Pangbourne ↔ Henley-on-Thames
17¼ miles/27.7km – 5½-6½hrs

NOTE: Add 20-30% to these times to allow for stops

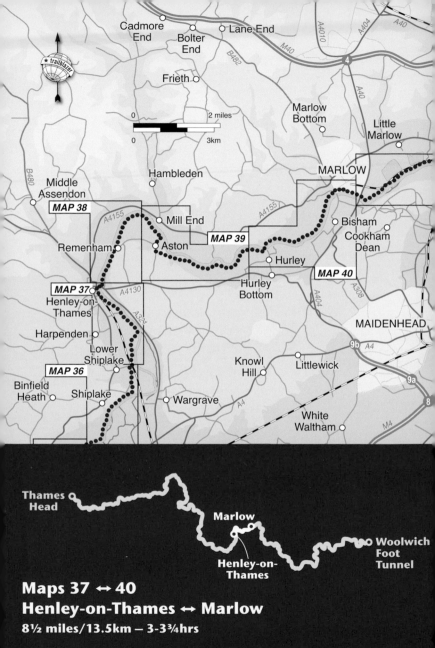

Maps 37 ↔ 40
Henley-on-Thames ↔ Marlow
8½ miles/13.5km — 3-3¾hrs

NOTE: Add 20-30% to these times to allow for stops

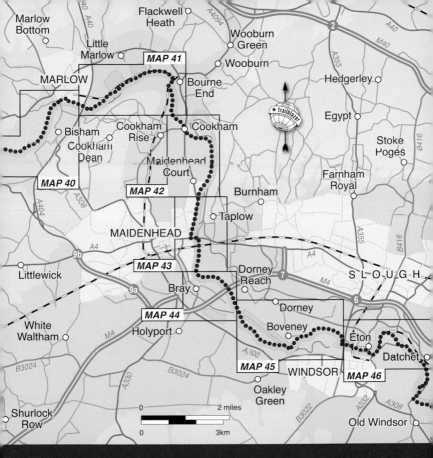

Maps 40 ↔ 46, Marlow ↔ Windsor
14¼ miles/22.7km – 4½-5½hrs

NOTE: Add 20-30% to these times to allow for stops

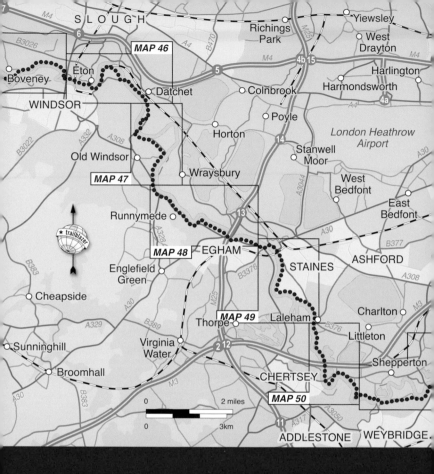

MAP 46

6 SLOUGH

Boveney

Eton

WINDSOR

Datchet

Old Windsor

MAP 47

Wraysbury

Runnymede

MAP 48

EGHAM

Englefield
Green

Cheapside

Thorpe

MAP 49

Laleham

STAINES

Virginia
Water

2 12

CHERTSEY

Sunninghill

Broomhall

MAP 50

ADDLESTONE

Richings
Park

Colnbrook

Poyle

Horton

Stanwell
Moor

West
Bedfont

East
Bedfont

London Heathrow
Airport

ASHFORD

Charlton

Littleton

Shepperton

WEYBRIDGE

Yiewsley

West
Drayton

Harlington

Harmondsworth

trailblazer

0   2 miles
0   3km

Thames
Head

Windsor

Chertsey Bridge

Woolwich
Foot
Tunnel

Maps 46 ↔ 50, Windsor ↔ Chertsey Bridge
12 miles/19.5km – 4-5¼hrs

NOTE: Add 20-30% to these times to allow for stops

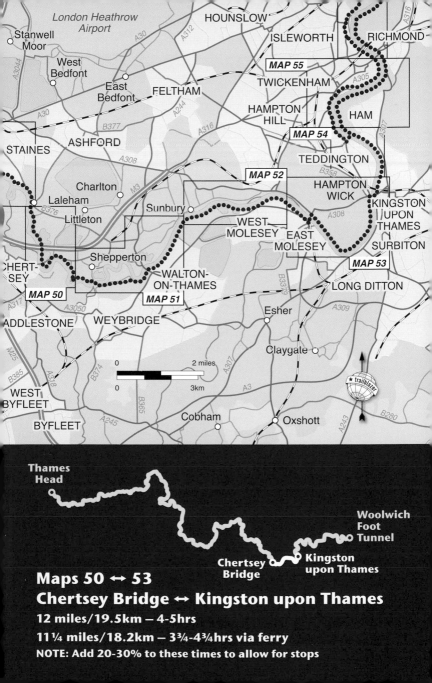

Maps 50 ↔ 53
Chertsey Bridge ↔ Kingston upon Thames
12 miles/19.5km – 4-5hrs
11¼ miles/18.2km – 3¾-4¾hrs via ferry
NOTE: Add 20-30% to these times to allow for stops

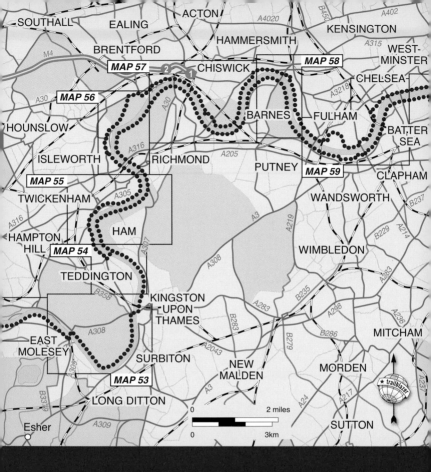

Maps 54 ↔ 59
Kingston upon Thames ↔ Putney Bridge
16¼ miles/26km – 5¾-7hrs via northern bank
13½ miles/21.7km – 4½-5¼hrs via southern bank
NOTE: Add 20-30% to these times to allow for stops

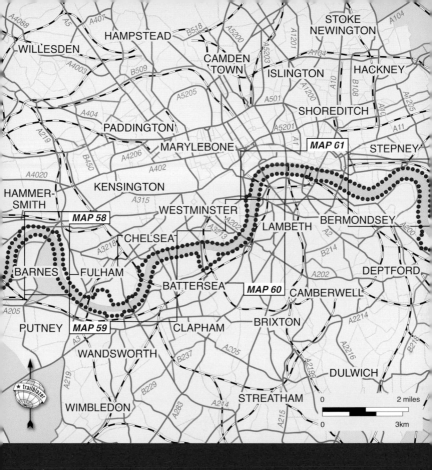

Maps 59 ↔ 61
Putney Bridge ↔ Tower Bridge

10 miles/16km — 3¼-4¼hrs via northern bank
9¼ miles/14.7km — 3½-4¾hrs via southern bank

NOTE: Add 20-30% to these times to allow for stops

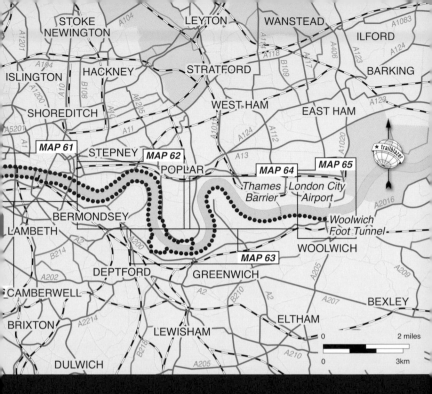

Maps 61 ↔ 65
Tower Bridge ↔ Greenwich
6¾ miles/11km – 2¼-3hrs via northern bank

5¾ miles/9.2km – 2-2½hrs via southern bank

Greenwich ↔ Woolwich Foot Tunnel
5½ miles/8.6km – 1¾-2¼hrs

NOTE: Add 20-30% to these times to allow for stops